Praise fo[r]

TRANSLATION OF

"A truly exciting guidebook to the Greek Bible—the one I have been waiting for! Simply and engagingly presented, it nonetheless brims with exacting research and real erudition. Gallagher urges renewed awareness and use of the Greek Bible, even as he patiently and judiciously deconstructs much of what has been written about it recently. In his telling, Jerome and Augustine agreed more than they differed, while Jerome's perspective was the one more in line with earlier Christian tradition. Indeed, Jerome's approach offers contemporary biblical interpreters a model worthy of emulation. Gallagher has produced an illuminating introduction for those who do not yet know the Greek Bible and a spirited rejoinder to many who think they already do."

—Stephen B. Chapman, associate professor
of Old Testament, Duke University

"It is frequently said that the Greek version of the Old Testament that we know as the Septuagint was the Bible of the early Christians. Undoubtedly, it was important to them. It remained the version in use among most Christians down to the fifth century. But what did they think about its relationship to the Hebrew text? Gallagher's careful investigation of the early Christian reception of the Septuagint offers a more nuanced view than is often presented. Much as they valued the Septuagint, they did not think it simply replaced the Hebrew as the Christian Old Testament. This book is an up-to-date introduction to the Septuagint that will also stimulate readers to think about its importance then and now."

—Richard Bauckham, senior scholar, Ridley Hall, Cambridge

"Gallagher provides readers with an accessible introduction to an enormously important, complex, and fluid set of translations from the ancient world—the earliest Greek version of the Old Testament, commonly called the Septuagint. This clearly written handbook moves readers sequentially through many of the major topics that have attracted scholarly attention over the past few decades. It is an ideal introduction for beginners, but it will also be useful for more advanced students and scholars, as Gallagher sets out to correct common misperceptions about the Septuagint that have crept into the literature. I highly recommend this book."

—Peter Martens, professor of early Christianity, Saint Louis University

"Apart from making a novel contribution on the contribution (or lack thereof) made by the Septuagint on the terrain of canon formation, the book serves as a valuable reference work on all aspects of the Greek versions of the Hebrew Bible. It is peppered with useful examples and tables. The reader will also be pleasantly surprised to find some popular perspectives neatly debunked. The true value of the book is its discussion of what form of the Scriptures counted for the Church Fathers as the correct Old Testament for Christians. This book can be called a truly wide view of a complex issue—the evidence supplied by the Septuagint (whatever that was) for our understanding of canon, authoritative Scripture, and divine inspiration."

—Dirk Büchner, professor of religious studies,
Trinity Western University

"Every student of the Greek Bible and of Greek and Latin Christianity from the first five centuries will benefit from this book. Gallagher manages to present in an accessible and comprehensible way the central information on the Septuagint while also including critical insights from the very latest English-language scholarship. His comprehensive analysis of both theory and practice in early Christian reception of the Septuagint is valuable to the novice and informed reader alike."

—Reinhart Ceulemans, associate professor of Greek and
Byzantine literature, Katholieke Universiteit Leuven

"Among the many books and introductions on the Septuagint on the market, Gallagher's approach is interesting and inspiring because it starts from a concise explanation of terms, moves on to a historical setting of the reception of the Septuagint in early Christianity, and mounts to an introduction into biblical scholarship in antiquity and modern times. For the obviously envisaged primary readership, students and the interested public, *The Translation of the Seventy* will find its place as a handy introduction—or rather *Hinführung*, as scholars used to call this in German—to the Septuagint and Septuagint studies beside the more scholarship-orientated books."

—Frank Feder, senior academic researcher,
Akademie der Wissenschaften zu Göttingen

TRANSLATION OF THE
SEVENTY

History, Reception, and
Contemporary Use
of the Septuagint

Edmon L. Gallagher

Abilene Christian University Press

Translation of the Seventy
History, Reception, and Contemporary Use of the Septuagint

Copyright © 2021 by Edmon L. Gallagher

ISBN 978-1-68426-171-0

Printed in the United States of America

ALL RIGHTS RESERVED

No part of this publication may be reproduced, stored in a retrieval system, or transmitted in any form by any means—electronic, mechanical, photocopying, recording, or otherwise—without prior written consent.

Scripture quotations marked NRSV are taken from the New Revised Standard Version Bible, copyright © 1989, the Division of Christian Education of the National Council of the Churches of Christ in the United States of America. Used by permission. All rights reserved.

Scripture quotations marked NETS are taken from A New English Translation of the Septuagint, ©2007 by the International Organization for Septuagint and Cognate Studies, Inc. Used by permission of Oxford University Press. All rights reserved.

Library of Congress Cataloging-in-Publication Data

Names: Gallagher, Edmon L., author.
Title: The translation of the seventy : history, reception, and contemporary use of the Septuagint / Edmon L. Gallagher.
Identifiers: LCCN 2021010638 (print) | LCCN 2021010639 (ebook) | ISBN 9781684261710 (trade paperback) | ISBN 9781684269198 (ebook)
Subjects: LCSH: Bible. Old Testament Greek—Versions—Septuagint. | BIble. Old Testament—Criticism, Textual.
Classification: LCC BS744 .G35 2021 (print) | LCC BS744 (ebook) | DDC 221.48—dc23
LC record available at https://lccn.loc.gov/2021010638
LC ebook record available at https://lccn.loc.gov/2021010639

Cover design by Bruce Gore | Gore Studio Inc.
Interior text design by Scribe Inc.

For information contact:
Abilene Christian University Press
ACU Box 29138
Abilene, Texas 79699
1-877-816-4455
www.acupressbooks.com

21 22 23 24 25 26 / 7 6 5 4 3 2 1

To Lee Martin McDonald,
for your friendship,
your encouragement,
and your books!

Contents

SECTION I:
Starting Points

SECTION II:
Canon and Text in Early Judaism and Earliest Christianity

SECTION III:
The Text of the Septuagint among the Fathers

List of Figures

Preface

The first Christian Bible was the Septuagint—or something like that. If I were really going to be comfortable with that statement, I would want to discuss what we mean by "Christian," what we mean by "Bible," and what we mean by "Septuagint," and maybe even what we mean by "first." Let me go ahead and briefly define one of those terms now and ask that you consult the fuller treatment of the term in Chapter One: the Septuagint is (more or less) the Greek Old Testament. (Even saying that makes me uncomfortable: I want to add more qualification.) The bare statement—the first Christian Bible was the Septuagint—is often enough made without any qualification that it has become in some quarters a truism, perhaps even a rallying cry for Christians to abandon or minimize the Hebrew Bible and take up the scriptural text quoted by the apostles and considered inspired and authoritative by the early church. In some ways, this book participates in that movement. I certainly encourage readers, particularly Christian readers, to pay attention to the Septuagint. On the other hand, I have no interest in abandoning or minimizing the Hebrew Bible, and I have a great deal of interest in probing whether the apostles really did quote the Septuagint and what the early church meant when it described the Septuagint as inspired and authoritative.

This book introduces the Septuagint and explores how early Christians made use of it. I confess that it is an odd book, designed both as an introduction for students who know nothing about the Septuagint and as a contribution to scholarship on the Septuagint. Section I, "Starting Points," is designed for students first approaching the subject who may need to know what the Septuagint is, why it's important for biblical studies, and how to get a copy for themselves, all of which is discussed in Chapter One. The story ancient Jews told about the origins of the Septuagint occupies Chapter Two, and the story modern scholars tell about the origins of the Septuagint is surveyed in Chapter Three. All of this material will be very familiar to Septuagint scholars, while biblical scholars without expertise in the Septuagint will hopefully find these chapters a helpful refresher.

The intensity of the discussion increases significantly in Sections II and III, sections that are more closely related to my primary areas of research, the text and canon of the Old Testament. It is in these sections that I believe I have made and am here making a contribution to scholarship on the reception of the Septuagint. In Chapter Four, I make the argument that the Septuagint did not materially affect the growth of the biblical canon, but rather the reverse is nearer the mark: the growth of the biblical canon affected the size of the Septuagint. While I have published several books and articles on the biblical canon, this particular argument on the relationship between the Septuagint and the canon has not appeared before, and scholars will have to judge its effectiveness. The remaining two chapters in Section II, on the place of the Septuagint within the textual plurality of ancient Jewish Scripture (Chapter Five) and on the Septuagint in the New Testament (Chapter Six), survey the scholarship in these areas as I understand it and stake out my position within these discussions.

Section III explores the role of the Septuagint within Greek- and Latin-speaking Christianity of the classical patristic period. Chapter Seven surveys the textual landscape for the Old Testament in these centuries, giving attention particularly to the groundbreaking textual work of the third-century Greek philologist Origen. Chapter Eight returns to a topic I have investigated in several other publications: the textual theory with which early Christians approached the Septuagint, that is, not so much how they used this Greek translation but more why they used it this way. The last two chapters give primary attention to the two great representatives of Latin-speaking biblical interpretation in the early fifth century and how the Septuagint featured in their works and imaginations. Chapter Nine argues that Jerome was not so hostile toward the Septuagint as scholars sometimes characterize him, and Chapter Ten argues that Augustine was not so thoughtless of the Hebrew Bible as he is sometimes represented.

While all of these chapters engage in historical research with little attention to theology, the Epilogue suggests some theological avenues worth pursuing in light of the historical role played by the Septuagint in early Christianity.

Acknowledgments

My wonderful wife, Jodi, contributes to my work in many ways, not least in filling my life with love and meaning beyond the narrow confines of the university office. Her dedication to our children, which she has decided to make the primary work of her life (at least for now), serves as an inspiration and a challenge. Thank you, Jodi, for loving me and letting me love you, and for the home we've made together for twenty-one years now. And to my kids (Miriam, Evelyn, Josiah, Jasmine, Marvin, and Elizabeth), thank you for your support, for your occasional interest in my work, and for throwing footballs and Frisbees and riding bikes with me.

It is a pleasure to thank the administration and my colleagues at Heritage Christian University for their support and encouragement of my scholarship. Our president, Kirk Brothers, and my academic dean, Michael Jackson, have forged a wonderful environment in which to study, teach, and research Scripture. Our librarian, Jamie Cox, has done amazing work in building a collection that can support work such as this.

The staff at ACU Press has been a joy to work with. Jason Fikes, the director of the press, has been very encouraging, and his help in formulating this book has been essential.

Several publishers have kindly granted me permission to adapt material from essays of mine originally published in various books and journals. I have indicated at the various points throughout the book where such reused material appears. I express my gratitude to the original publishers of the following works for allowing me to adapt them for representation here.

"1.1.2 The Greek Canon." In *Textual History of the Bible*, edited by Armin Lange. Vol. 2, *Deuterocanonical Scriptures*, edited by Frank Feder and Matthias Henze. Leiden: Brill, 2020.

"1.1.1.2 Hebrew and Greek Texts in Judaism and Christianity: Antiquity and Late Antiquity: Christian Scholarship." In *Textual History of the Bible*, edited by Armin Lange. Vol. 3, *History of Research*, edited by Russell Fuller and Armin Lange. Leiden: Brill, 2020. http://dx.doi. org/10.1163/2452-4107_thb_COm_000797.

"The Septuagint's Fidelity to Its *Vorlage* in Greek Patristic Thought." In *XIV Congress of the IOSCS, Helsinki, 2010*, edited by M. K. H. Peters, 663–76. Atlanta: SBL, 2013.

"The Septuagint in Patristic Sources." In *The T&T Clark Handbook of Septuagint Research*, edited by William A. Ross and W. Edward Glenny. London: Bloomsbury T&T Clark, 2021.

I also express my thanks to Oxford University Press for permission to reprint here (as Chapter Ten) in a slightly modified form my article "Augustine on the Hebrew Bible," *Journal of Theological Studies* 67 (2016): 97–114. Aside from these previously published pieces, two essays I originally wrote for other publications that have not yet appeared have been adapted here, for which I gratefully acknowledge the permission of the publishers.

"The *Hebraica Veritas*." In *Language and Culture in Early Christianity: A Companion*, edited by T. Denecker, M. Lamberigts, G. Partoens, P. Swiggers, and T. Van Hal. Leuven: Peeters, forthcoming.

"What Were the Scriptures in the Time of Jesus?" In *The Old Testament in the New: Israel's Scriptures in the New Testament and Other Early Christian Writings*, edited by Matthias Henze and David Lincicum. Grand Rapids: Eerdmans, forthcoming.

This book would likely not have been published without the friendship of Lee Martin McDonald. Several years ago, Jason Fikes emailed me with an invitation to begin talks about a book project after he had a conversation with Lee in which my name came up. This is just one of the many acts of kindness Lee has directed my way. Jodi and I, sometimes along with one of our children, have enjoyed meals with Lee during several SBL conferences. Our shared interest in the biblical canon has provided opportunities for many conversations, with some disagreements. He has supported my membership and participation in learned societies. I well remember our first encounter at an SBL meeting, perhaps in San Diego, when I was presenting in a session chaired by him. I sat down after making my presentation (in which Lee had to cut me off for long-windedness), and he handed me a note: "Can I get a copy of your paper?" That paper became one of my early publications, in a volume edited by Lee. And when Lee needed to downsize his personal library, he graciously shipped to me a very large number of books. Lee, thank you for your generosity and friendship.

SECTION I

Starting Points

1

Start

Introducing the LXX

But as I proceeded I thought it best to note down the result of my studies, especially as far as they related to the *Septuagint*, which about the year 1785 I began to read regularly, in order to acquaint myself more fully with the phraseology of the New Testament, as I found that this truly venerable version was that to which the evangelists and apostles appear to have had constant recourse, and from which they make their quotations. The study of this version served more to illuminate and expand my mind than all the theological works I had ever consulted. I had proceeded but a short way in it before I was convinced that the prejudices against it were utterly unfounded, and that it was of incalculable advantage toward a proper understanding of the literal sense of Scripture.

—Adam Clarke, "General Preface," in
*The Holy Bible . . . with a Commentary and Critical
Notes*, vol. 1 (New York: Ezra Sargeant, 1811), xv

Early Christians used a Greek translation of the Old Testament called the Septuagint. Later in this chapter, I will explain more fully what that sentence means, and I will lay bare some of the complexities hidden by it. Actually, this entire book is an exercise in unpacking that first sentence. Before getting to those details, I will try to justify this focus on the Septuagint, and then, after explaining that sentence, I will tell you how to get a Septuagint yourself.

Why Study the Septuagint?

A lot of people are doing it these days. Maybe that does not mean you should study the Septuagint too, but it means you might want to pay attention. Study of the Septuagint has become an enormous field in academic biblical studies. The Septuagint (abbreviated LXX—I'll explain later) is now recognized as an essential part of the study of the Old Testament and the New Testament. Ancient Jews and Christians fully acknowledged the importance of the Septuagint—after all, for many of them, it was their Bible—and the Greek Orthodox Church has always appreciated its significance (the Septuagint is still their Old Testament). But modern scholars have only really caught on to it in the past five or six decades (not coincidentally, paralleling the time that the Dead Sea Scrolls have been available).

I have not really answered the question, just put it off. Why are people so interested in the Septuagint? There are all kinds of reasons, so we should narrow down the question: Why should someone interested in the New Testament and early Christianity study the Septuagint? The answer is that the Septuagint had an enormous influence on the New Testament and early Christianity.

In the mid-nineteenth century, Edward Grinfield began his *Apology for the Septuagint* with the observation that "the entire phraseology of the New Testament is formed on the peculiar style of the LXX, as all our doctrinal terms are taken from its vocabulary, whilst by far the greater number of its quotations are transferred from its text."[1] More recently, in his book on the Septuagint and the New Testament, R. Timothy McLay highlights essentially the same three ways in which the Septuagint impacted the New Testament: vocabulary, theology, and text.[2] In the same chapter of his book, McLay also discusses the biblical canon, a topic of perennial interest and one in which the Septuagint plays a crucial role in the modern scholarly discussion, so we can add it as a fourth area in which the Septuagint is

---

[1] E. W. Grinfield, *An Apology for the Septuagint: In Which Its Claims to Biblical and Canonical Authority Are Briefly Stated and Vindicated* (London: William Pickering, 1850), 1.

[2] R. Timothy McLay, *The Use of the Septuagint in New Testament Research* (Grand Rapids: Eerdmans, 2003), 144. More or less the same trio appears in the chapter "The Septuagint and the New Testament" in Karen H. Jobes and Moisés Silva, *Invitation to the Septuagint*, 2nd ed. (Grand Rapids: Baker, 2015), 200–227.

important for the study of the New Testament and early Christianity. There are additional areas in which the Septuagint is important for biblical studies, but these four topics are enough to justify our concern in this book. Here we concentrate on the last three of those four topics: text, canon, and theology. Septuagint vocabulary is, of course, a very important topic as well and certainly important in a study of the New Testament, but it is not an area of my expertise.[3]

A little bit of reflection might generate more objections to the idea that the Septuagint deserves special treatment among biblical translations because of the influence it has had. In the English-speaking world, the King James Version (KJV) has had a similar impact—and, of course, William Tyndale also, since the KJV maintained much of the language from Tyndale's earlier translations. We could certainly say that the KJV has had an influence on English-speaking Christianity similar to the influence the Septuagint had on Greek-speaking Judaism and Christianity: the KJV clearly influenced the language of Christians, the text, the theology and, in some ways, the canon, even though that influence has begun to wane with the proliferation of English translations of the Bible over the past couple generations. Even so, the Septuagint was yet more influential, for one primary reason: it was quoted in the New Testament, and so its influence was "canonized," so to speak, in a way that the KJV's could not be. (I know you've heard the statement "If the KJV was good enough for Paul, it's good enough for me," but most people who repeat that line are joking—I think.) In Chapter Six, we will look at what exactly I mean by saying that the New Testament quoted the Septuagint and what sort of implications that fact has for Christian theology. In subsequent chapters, we will see how New Testament use of the Septuagint played a major role in the reception of the translation following the deaths of the apostles. Even if the Septuagint is just a translation, it happened to be the translation at the right time and place to be used by the apostles—just as Washington or Churchill were at the right time and place to become legendary figures.

---

[3] On Septuagint vocabulary, an authoritative discussion is John A. L. Lee, *The Greek of the Pentateuch: Grinfield Lectures on the Septuagint 2011–2012* (Oxford: Oxford University Press, 2018). On the influence of Septuagint vocabulary in the New Testament, see the introductory treatment by Jobes and Silva mentioned in the previous note.

What Is It?

We need to define some terms. Let us return now to the first sentence of this chapter: early Christians used a Greek translation of the Old Testament called the Septuagint. While most scholars would accept such a statement, almost every item in it is open to challenge. We are going to have to talk about what we mean by "the Septuagint" and what we mean by "the Old Testament" and what we mean by "early Christians," but first let's think about the significance of the word *used*. This book is all about that term. What does it mean that early Christians "used" the Septuagint? Used how? What implications did those early Christians think their use of the Septuagint entailed? How should modern Christians use the Septuagint in light of this ancient use by even the writers of the New Testament? Many people think that such early Christian use has very definite implications for discussions of the biblical canon and the biblical text. We will spend several chapters thinking through these ideas, examining early Christian use of the Septuagint and, in particular, early Christian thoughts on the significance of such use. For now, I will simply say that *used* in the first sentence above means that early Christians read Scripture in the Septuagint translation, and they quoted Scripture according to this translation.

Now for the other terms.

THE SEPTUAGINT

A basic definition of *the Septuagint* is "the Greek Old Testament." We will have to refine that basic definition in numerous ways, but it will give us a start. The title "Septuagint" is related to the traditional story about the origins of this translation. Our earliest account of the story of the translation is in a document usually called the Letter of Aristeas, in which the story goes like this: In the days of Ptolemy II Philadelphus (the Greek-speaking ruler of Egypt in the wake of the conquests of Alexander the Great), an official named Demetrius suggested to the king that his famous Library of Alexandria needed to acquire a copy of the Jewish Law (§§10–11). The problem was that it was written in a language called Hebrew and would therefore need to be translated into Greek. Ptolemy sponsored an expedition to Jerusalem to collect from the Jewish high priest copies of the Law written in Hebrew as well as Jewish experts who could translate the Law. The high priest supplied six translators from each of the twelve tribes of Israel (as requested by Demetrius; §32), for a total of seventy-two translators. The translators and the books arrived in Alexandria, and the translators completed their task in seventy-two days (§307). The word *septuaginta* is Latin for "seventy," and we call the Greek translation the Septuagint because of these seventy-two translators. We inherited this usage from ancient Latin Christians, who used the expression "the translation of the Seventy [septuaginta]," abbreviating for the more precise seventy-two. Often, we use the Roman numeral LXX (70) to refer to the translation. Greek speakers, of course, do not use the Latin term to refer to this translation; instead, they use the Greek word for "seventy," ἑβδομήκοντα (hebdomēkonta).

You probably noticed that this traditional story concerns only the translation of the Jewish Law, what we typically call the Pentateuch or the law of Moses, the first five books of the Old Testament or Hebrew Bible. In fact, all ancient Jewish tradition relates the "translation of the Seventy" exclusively to the Pentateuch, not to any other part of the Old Testament. (These other ancient Jewish accounts are found in Josephus and Philo and other writers; see Chapter Two.) Of course, there are ancient Greek translations of Isaiah, Joshua, Psalms, and every other part of the Old Testament, but according to the ancient Jewish accounts, such translations are not a part of the Septuagint, the "translation of the Seventy." So, one way in which we must tweak the definition of the Septuagint as "the Greek Old Testament" is by saying that, according to ancient Jews, the Septuagint is only the Greek Pentateuch.

It was in Christian circles that the term *Septuagint* (or *hebdomēkonta*, "translation of the Seventy") came to be applied to the Greek translation of the entire Old Testament. Our earliest Christian literature, the New Testament, uses the Septuagint quite often—that is to say, Paul and John and Peter and the other New Testament authors quoted the Old Testament all the time and always in Greek, given that they were writing in Greek. But the New Testament never talks about the Septuagint. Our earliest Christian mention of the Septuagint is in the second-century writer Justin Martyr, who wrote about the Septuagint as if it encompassed the entire Old Testament and not just the Pentateuch. Justin briefly narrates the story of the translation in terms not of the Jewish law but of the Jewish prophets (*1 Apology* 31) and critiques more recent translations that disagree with the "translation of the Seventy" on certain passages, such as Isaiah 7:14, the so-called prophecy of the virgin birth. These newer translations familiar to Justin originated among Jews close to his own time, and they do not have the word *virgin* (παρθένος, parthenos) in Isaiah 7:14, as the Septuagint does, but rather *young woman* (νεᾶνις, neanis). Justin did not know Hebrew at all, so he could not investigate the correct meaning of the Hebrew word underlying the Greek translations, but he felt no need for such knowledge. The fact is that the Seventy translators long before Justin's time rendered Isaiah 7:14 with the word *virgin*, which must then be correct, and these more recent translations simply result from anti-Christian bias (*Dialogue with Trypho* 68–73). The issue about whether the Seventy translators actually produced a translation of Isaiah never arises in Justin's writings; he simply assumes (or has received by tradition, perhaps) that the Greek translation of all of the books of the Old Testament in his possession originated with them. Perhaps Justin had never actually read the Letter of Aristeas and the other ancient Jewish accounts. Perhaps he did read them but did not discern how their story diverged from his own ideas about the extent of the translation of the Seventy. In any case, Justin's view became the common view in Christianity: the Septuagint is the Greek translation of the whole Old Testament.

But it was not the only ancient Greek translation of the Old Testament, as Justin shows us. We have just seen that Justin complained about some more recent translations that departed from the Septuagint in various ways. Ancient Christians often talked about three such translations in particular, known by the names of their (reputed) translators: Aquila, Symmachus, and Theodotion, all of whom worked in the first and second centuries CE. Modern research has revealed that, besides these three later translators, others were involved in various ways in producing Greek versions of the Scriptures that diverged more or less from the Septuagint. We must tweak our definition of the Septuagint somewhat further: the Septuagint is the earliest Greek translation of the Old Testament, as opposed to the later translations or revisions.[4] We have already seen that one might emphasize

---

[4] Kristin De Troyer speaks of "the Septuagint proper" in this sense; De Troyer, "The Septuagint," in *The New Cambridge History of the Bible*, vol. 1, ed. James Carleton Paget and

the story of the translation in Jewish sources and thereby limit the term *Septuagint* to the first translation of the Greek Pentateuch, in which case scholars have begun using the term *Old Greek* to refer to the first Greek translation of the other books of the Old Testament.[5] In this book, I will mostly use *Septuagint* (or *LXX*), but when I have reason to denote the form of the Greek text that scholars have judged to represent the earliest translation for a specific book, then I will use the term *Old Greek*.[6]

THE OLD TESTAMENT

What do we mean by "Old Testament"? There is more than one—the Roman Catholic Bible has forty-six books in the Old Testament, whereas Protestants have thirty-nine books in their Old Testament, and the Greek Orthodox Bible usually has forty-nine or so. A later chapter is focused on the biblical canon and how the Septuagint relates to it, but for now we can say that when modern people use *Septuagint*, usually they are quite inclusive in terms of the contents. The standard English translation of the Septuagint, NETS (*New English Translation of the Septuagint*) contains all the books of the Protestant Old Testament along with 1 Esdras, Judith, Tobit, 1–4 Maccabees, the Prayer of Manasseh, the Wisdom of Solomon, Sirach, the Psalms of Solomon, Baruch, the Letter of Jeremiah, Susanna, and Bel and the Dragon. That list is more inclusive than any Protestant group, more inclusive than the Roman Catholic Church (which excludes 1 Esdras, 3–4 Maccabees, the Prayer of Manasseh, and the Psalms of Solomon), and more inclusive than the Greek Orthodox Church (which generally excludes 4 Maccabees and the Psalms of Solomon). Nevertheless, most people these days would be comfortable using the term *Septuagint* to refer to the earliest Greek text of all of these books; for example, people might say things like "The Septuagint includes the Wisdom of Solomon" or "The Psalms of Solomon is in the Septuagint." On that definition, the Septuagint contains

---

Joachim Schaper (Cambridge: Cambridge University Press, 2013), 267–88.
    [5] See the discussion in Jobes and Silva, *Invitation to the Septuagint*, 14–17.
    [6] See again De Troyer, "Septuagint," 272.

certain books that are not translations at all but were composed in Greek, such as 2 Maccabees and the Wisdom of Solomon.

EARLY CHRISTIANS

To complete our interpretation of the first sentence of this chapter, we must think about the term *early Christians*. First of all, our focus on Christians should not lead the reader to infer that Jews did not use the Septuagint. The first readers of the Septuagint were Jews, and some Jews continued to use the Septuagint at least into the early centuries CE. Once other translations became available (such as Aquila, Symmachus, and Theodotion, mentioned earlier), Greek-speaking Jews often started using these newer translations, but the Septuagint continued to exert an influence within Jewish circles into the medieval period. Moreover, the earliest Christian writers were Jews, and they often used the Septuagint. But the use of the Septuagint has been much more long-lasting and pervasive within Christian circles—again, it is still the typical Old Testament version for the Greek Orthodox Church—and it is Christian use that will be the focus of our study.

We also need to think about what we mean by *early* Christians and exactly who are the Christians that will occupy our attention. My own field of study is in Greek and Latin Christian authors from the first four or five centuries, so that will be our concentration here. This period includes the New Testament and what is called patristic literature—that is, the literature produced by the Church Fathers. (The Greek word for "father" is *pater*—hence "patristic.") The Church Fathers were the influential Christian writers from after the time of the New Testament until about the seventh century. There are other early and important Christian writers (especially Syriac writers) besides the Greek and Latin Church Fathers, and we might mention these other language traditions along the way, but our focus will be on material in Greek and Latin.

Where Do I Get It?

We are in a boom time for Septuagint studies, meaning that there are all kinds of resources available for the study of the Septuagint. We will not cover all the resources or even all the major categories of resources. This brief discussion is for those students just starting out in this kind of study who need to get a handle on what we are talking about.

GREEK TEXT

The Septuagint is a Greek text—or a series of Greek translations. Modern editions of the Septuagint in Greek are based on ancient Greek manuscripts, and sometimes modern editors choose to follow different manuscripts so that modern editions will sometimes have different wording from each other. Today, scholars use two main editions of the Septuagint, and I will mention a third that might interest you:

- **Göttingen Septuaginta.** This is the major scholarly edition of the Septuagint, but it is not the one you will want to buy because it is too expensive (unless you buy it as a package with your biblical studies software, such as Accordance or Logos). Each book of the Bible is a separate volume of the Göttingen Septuaginta. Each volume contains a major introduction (written in German) to the text of that biblical book, along with a reconstruction of the original Greek translation with an extensive apparatus in which the editor provides evidence from manuscripts and ancient translations and quotations of the Septuagint. It is a major undertaking, and each volume takes years, decades, to produce. The series has been in progress for more than a century, and it is not yet complete. Its twenty-six volumes cover most of the Septuagint, but we still await volumes on most of the historical books and a few others.[7] For those books not yet available in the Göttingen series, scholars instead rely on the Rahlfs-Hanhart edition.

---

[7] For a recent survey of work on the Septuagint in Göttingen, see Felix Albrecht, "Report on the Göttingen Septuagint," *Textus* 29 (2020): 201–20.

- **Rahlfs-Hanhart.**[8] This is probably the one you will want to buy. Alfred Rahlfs published a small edition of the entire Septuagint in 1935, and it was updated by Robert Hanhart in 2006. This edition is available as a single volume, and often when people think of the Septuagint today, they think of this little (but fat!), blue book. The Rahlfs-Hanhart text is not a full critical edition in the way that the Göttingen series is. That means that the Rahlfs-Hanhart text is not based on a full evaluation of all of the available evidence. Rather, it is primarily based on three early and more or less complete manuscripts (manuscripts that we will encounter throughout this book): Codex Sinaiticus (from the fourth century CE), Codex Vaticanus (also fourth century), and Codex Alexandrinus (fifth century).

- **Reader's Edition.**[9] You might want to buy this one. It is a two-volume reader's edition, which means that instead of a critical apparatus at the bottom of the page detailing the readings of various manuscripts (as in the Göttingen series and in Rahlfs-Hanhart), it presents Greek-to-English vocabulary for that page of Greek text. Of course, you get sort of the same thing with your Bible software, but this reader's edition is for people who find pleasure in reading a print book and feel the need for help with vocabulary but do not want to be constantly looking up word definitions. The text used is the Rahlfs-Hanhart.

ENGLISH TRANSLATIONS

You can find English translations of the Septuagint available on many websites, but the one you should use is *The New English Translation of the Septuagint* (NETS).[10] You can also find this one available online,[11] but you will surely want to buy the print edition. (It is not expensive.) NETS

---

[8] Alfred Rahlfs and Robert Hanhart, eds., *Septuaginta*, 2nd ed. (Stuttgart: Deutsche Bibelgesellschaft, 2006).

[9] Gregory R. Lanier and William A. Ross, eds., *Septuaginta: A Reader's Edition*, 2 vols. (Peabody, MA: Hendrickson, 2018).

[10] Albert Pietersma and Benjamin G. Wright, eds., *A New English Translation of the Septuagint* (Oxford: Oxford University Press, 2007).

[11] "Electronic Edition of NETS," New English Translation of the Septuagint, last accessed April 26, 2021, http://ccat.sas.upenn.edu/nets/edition/.

is translated from the Göttingen edition when that edition is available; otherwise, it is translated from Rahlfs-Hanhart.

There are also a couple other recent English translations of the Septuagint. People associated with the Greek Orthodox Church have produced *The Orthodox Study Bible*, with an English translation of the Septuagint for the Old Testament (the New Testament is NKJV).[12] The translation is made from the Rahlfs text (1935, not the revised text from 2006). And there is *The Lexham English Septuagint* (*LES*),[13] translated from an older Greek text edited by Henry Barclay Swete and based primarily on Codex Vaticanus.[14] The main attraction of *LES* is that it is based on a translation strategy different from NETS: whereas NETS tried to represent in English what the translator was thinking, *LES* tries to represent what a Greek reader would have understood.

INTRODUCTIONS

There are two kinds of introductions to the Septuagint: ones designed for general students and ones designed for Septuagint students, which assume a lot more knowledge on the part of the reader:

- **General Student Introductions.** The one to get here is *Invitation to the Septuagint* by Karen Jobes and Moisés Silva.[15] They cover a lot of ground, and it is really an excellent, balanced book. At the beginning, the book assumes no knowledge of Greek or Hebrew; as you go through the text, you can probably still understand what is going on even if you do not read Greek or Hebrew, but you will have to pay more attention. In other words, the book gets harder as you go along. (They do that on purpose.) If you think you would rather have a briefer, simpler introduction to the Septuagint that covers all the

---

[12] *The Orthodox Study Bible* (Nashville: Thomas Nelson, 2008).

[13] Ken Penner, ed., *The Lexham English Septuagint*, 2nd ed. (Bellingham, WA: Lexham, 2019).

[14] H. B. Swete, ed., *The Old Testament in Greek according to the Septuagint*, 3 vols. (Cambridge: Cambridge University Press, 1887–94).

[15] Jobes and Silva, *Invitation to the Septuagint*.

bases, try Dines.[16] If you want less of a textbook and more of a story that still covers a lot of the modern study of the Septuagint, try Law.[17]

• **Septuagint Student Introductions.** By "student," I really mean graduate student or scholar—people devoting themselves to biblical studies and the Septuagint in particular. There are three main books, and they are all essential, each written by a different scholar in a different generation: Swete, Jellicoe, and Fernández Marcos.[18] They are all very demanding, wonderful surveys of the scholarship of their time. More recently, multiauthored books have updated such surveys of Septuagint scholarship. Just this year, two books surveying the entire field of Septuagint scholarship have appeared, one edited by Ross and Glenny and another edited by Salvesen and Law.[19] These books, like those by Swete, Jellicoe, and Fernández Marcos, are organized by topic, but each chapter is written by a different specialist. Another kind of introduction goes through the Septuagint book by book to discuss what can be known about the translation of each particular biblical book. Here, again, each chapter was written by a specialist, and again there are two recent books in this category: the first was edited by Aitken, and the second—originally in German and now translated into English—was edited by Kreuzer.[20] The one by Kreuzer is the first volume of an eight-volume series called *Handbuch zur Septuaginta*, which includes volumes on the language of the Septuagint and its theology and forthcoming volumes on other aspects of Septuagint study.

---

[16] Jennifer M. Dines, *The Septuagint* (London: T&T Clark, 2004).

[17] Timothy Michael Law, *When God Spoke Greek: The Septuagint and the Making of the Christian Bible* (Oxford: Oxford University Press, 2013).

[18] Henry Barclay Swete, *An Introduction to the Old Testament in Greek*, rev. R. R. Ottley (Cambridge: Cambridge University Press, 1914); Sidney Jellicoe, *The Septuagint and Modern Study* (Oxford: Oxford University Press, 1968); Natalio Fernández Marcos, *The Septuagint in Context: Introduction to the Greek Version of the Bible* (Leiden: Brill, 2000).

[19] William A. Ross and W. Edward Glenny, eds., *The T&T Clark Handbook of Septuagint Research* (London: Bloomsbury T&T Clark, 2021); Alison G. Salvesen and Timothy Michael Law, *The Oxford Handbook of the Septuagint* (Oxford: Oxford University Press, 2021).

[20] J. K. Aitken, ed., *The T&T Clark Companion to the Septuagint* (London: Continuum, 2015); Siegfried Kreuzer, ed., *Introduction to the Septuagint* (Waco, TX: Baylor University Press, 2019).

COMMENTARIES

Most commentaries on the books of the Old Testament give some attention to the Septuagint, but usually their primary focus is the Hebrew text. There are some commentary series aimed at interpreting the Septuagint itself. There are two major series of such commentaries in English:

- **SBL Commentary on the Septuagint.** This commentary series is sponsored by the International Organization for Septuagint and Cognate Studies (IOSCS), the premier scholarly society for Septuagint studies and the same group behind NETS, and it is published by the Society of Biblical Literature (SBL). So far only an introductory volume has been published.[21]
- **Septuagint Commentary Series.** This series, published by Brill, has been around longer and has advanced much further than the SBL series. Currently, sixteen volumes are available, covering a spectrum of books of the Septuagint. One of the distinctive features of the series is that each commentary is based on a single manuscript, such as Codex Vaticanus or Codex Alexandrinus (it varies book by book) rather than on a critical edition such as the Göttingen series.

A valuable series that covers only the Pentateuch is the *Notes* produced by John William Wevers,[22] who also edited the Pentateuch volumes of the Göttingen edition of the Septuagint. You might also want to know about another series, this one in French, called La Bible d'Alexandrie, which began publication in 1986 and now includes volumes on all the books of the Pentateuch, most of the Minor Prophets (not yet Amos or Micah), and an assortment of other books. This series is often the most helpful, at least

---

[21] Dirk Büchner, ed., *The SBL Commentary on the Septuagint: An Introduction* (Atlanta: SBL, 2017).

[22] John William Wevers, *Notes on the Greek Text of Genesis* (Atlanta: Scholars Press, 1993); Wevers, *Notes on the Greek Text of Exodus* (Atlanta: Scholars Press, 1990); Wevers, *Notes on the Greek Text of Leviticus* (Atlanta: Scholars Press, 1997); Wevers, *Notes on the Greek Text of Numbers* (Atlanta: Scholars Press, 1998); Wevers, *Notes on the Greek Text of Deuteronomy* (Atlanta: Scholars Press, 1995).

for the questions I have, such as "Why did the translator use that word?" and "Why is the Septuagint different from the Hebrew here?" and "How would an ancient reader have understood this Greek phrase?" But it is not in English.

Conclusion

Early Christians used a Greek translation of the Old Testament called the Septuagint. Here we have explored what that sentence means, why we should care, and how to get a hold of a Septuagint if we want one. Future chapters will continue to investigate the ways that early Christians used the Septuagint and what implications their use of this version might have for our understanding of the New Testament and Christian theology. First, we need to understand better what the Septuagint is and how the ancients thought about it, topics treated in reverse order in the next two chapters.

2

Story

What Ancient Jews Thought about LXX Origins

And so it came about that the work of transcription was completed in seventy-two days, as if this coincidence had been the result of some design.

—Letter of Aristeas §307[1]

A pagan king, hearing of the remarkable Jewish Law, commissioned a translation project that would change the world. He brought to his kingdom seventy-two Jewish scholars, who accomplished the first translation of the Hebrew Torah into Greek, such an accurate and pleasing translation that the Jewish community of Alexandria, Egypt, pronounced a curse on anyone who would change a syllable. These translators went down in history as the Seventy, and their work would become world famous, named for them: the translation of "the Seventy," or, in Greek, the *hebdomēkonta* and, in Latin, the *Septuaginta*. People often just use the Roman numeral for seventy, LXX. Some said the translators were inspired by God. Many said they translated not just the Jewish Law but the entire Hebrew Bible. Others thought the translation was not as accurate as it could be. Some said it had

---

[1] Translation by Moses Hadas, ed. and trans., *Aristeas to Philocrates (Letter of Aristeas)* (New York: Harper, 1951), 221.

been corrupted through the process of transmission. And scholars today believe none of it. (Well, they believe the corruption part.)

It might not be true, but it is a good story, a story worth knowing. It was enormously influential in ancient Judaism and Christianity, powerfully shaping the way Greek speakers thought about their Bible. These ancient believers understood that the writings of Moses and Isaiah and David existed in Hebrew, but the story of the Seventy translators told them how God had provided a Bible for people who could not read Hebrew. In the next chapter, we will look at where the Greek translations of the Old Testament actually came from; here, we will survey the stories ancient readers of the Septuagint told about its origins.[2] We will concentrate on the Jewish stories, with just a nod at the Christian stories, which will occupy our attention in Chapter Eight.

The Letter of Aristeas

The Letter of Aristeas is perhaps the earliest story we have about the translation, although it is possible that Aristobulus's account is earlier (see the next section). Certainly, it is the longest and the one that became most authoritative for ancient Jews. Though it is the longest version, it is not terribly long; I have an edition that prints it in English on about seventy pages.[3] It is an enjoyable story, and I encourage you to read it. You can easily find an older translation online.

The Letter of Aristeas is not really a letter (a description it first received in the 1300s; Josephus just called it a book),[4] and it might not have been written by a person named Aristeas. Nor is it really about the translation of

---

[2] For a much fuller account covering also later time periods, see Abraham Wasserstein and David J. Wasserstein, *The Legend of the Septuagint: From Classical Antiquity to Today* (Cambridge: Cambridge University Press, 2006).

[3] Hadas, *Aristeas to Philocrates*. This edition prints a Greek text on pages facing the translation. There is also an excellent full commentary with fresh translation by Benjamin G. Wright III, *The Letter of Aristeas: "Aristeas to Philocrates" or "On the Translation of the Law of the Jews"* (Berlin: de Gruyter, 2015).

[4] Josephus calls it "the book of Aristeas" (τὸ Ἀρισταίου βιβλίον; *A.J.* 12.100). See the discussion of genre in Wright, *Letter of Aristeas*, 43–51. I will continue to use the by-now traditional title Letter of Aristeas.

Scripture, or at least not much of it is. Instead, it covers all kinds of topics, including a long description of Jerusalem, a speech from the Jewish high priest Eleazar explaining the purpose behind some of the Jewish laws (like the prohibition on eating pork; cf. Lev. 11), and a seven-day banquet at which the Egyptian king peppers the Jewish translators with questions about life and government, and the translators always respond with brilliant answers. The actual business of translating occupies just a few paragraphs near the end of the work (§§301–307).

Outline of the Letter of Aristeas

Preface (§§1–8)

The Library Project (§§9–11). Demetrius mentions to the king the laws of the Jews and the need for translation.

The Liberation of the Jewish slaves (§§12–27)

Demetrius's Report (§§28–34a)

Ptolemy II's Letter to Eleazar (§§34b–40)

Eleazar's Reply to Ptolemy (§§41–51a)

The Construction of the King's Gifts (§§51b–82)

Jerusalem and Its Environs (§§83–120). Description of Jerusalem temple, water system, priests, the city, countryside, and so on.

Eleazar's Farewell to the Translators (§§121–27)

Eleazar's *Apologia* for the Law (§§128–71). Allegorical interpretation of Jewish Law, especially laws of clean and unclean animals.

The Reception of the Translators at Alexandria (§§172–86)

The Symposia (§§187–300)

The Execution of the Translation (§§301–307)

The Proclamation of the Translation (§§308–16)

The Departure of the Translators (§§317–321)

Epilogue (§322)

Adapted from Wright, Letter of Aristeas, 53–55.

The narrator of the Letter presents himself as a Gentile working in the court of Ptolemy II Philadelphus in the first half of the third century BCE. Ptolemy II was the son of the founder of the Ptolemaic dynasty in Egypt. Ptolemy I had been one of the generals of Alexander the Great; when Alexander died in 323, General Ptolemy quickly claimed control of Egypt and eventually became King Ptolemy I, ruling from Alexandria on the coast of the Mediterranean Sea. His son, Ptolemy II (reigned 285–246 BCE), who earned his moniker "Philadelphus" by marrying his full-blood sister, Arisonoe II,[5] was a known bibliophile, or at least a known book collector and supporter of textual scholarship, especially as produced out of the famous Mouseion and library in Alexandria. The narrator of the Letter calls himself "Aristeas" (§§19, 40, 43) and describes how the chief librarian, one Demetrius of Phalerum, suggested to the king that his library would benefit from acquiring the Law of the Jews, but that this Law would require translation before it could be added to the collection. Demetrius suggested that the king request from Eleazar, the high priest in Jerusalem, a copy of the Law and men who could translate it, six translators from each tribe (§32). Aristeas goes on the mission to Jerusalem to collect the Law and translators, and this becomes the basis for the long passages describing Jerusalem and explaining the Jewish food laws. On their arrival in Alexandria, the translators enjoy the banquet arranged by the king and answer all his questions before getting down to business. Demetrius took them to a quiet island—Pharos, of Lighthouse fame, but unnamed in the Letter:[6]

---

[5] Sheila L. Ager, "Familiarity Breeds: Incest and the Ptolemaic Dynasty," *Journal of Hellenic Studies* 125 (2005): 1–34, at 4.

[6] The following translations are taken from Wright, *Letter of Aristeas*, 433–34.

And they accomplished it, making each detail agree by comparisons with each other. And that which came out of the agreement Demetrius thus suitably set in writing. (§302)

So just as we have said previously, in this way each day they gathered together at this spot, which was delightful due to its quietness and brightness, in order to complete their appointed task. And thus it happened that the work of transcription was completed in seventy-two days, appearing as if this circumstance happened according to some plan. (§307)

It is important to note here that the Letter describes the translators making comparisons among themselves and thus producing an agreed-upon translation (§302). Moreover, there is a hint—but only a hint!—that the translators enjoyed supernatural supervision, or at least that God approved of their work. How else to explain that seventy-two translators accomplished their task in exactly seventy-two days?

It is a good story, but scholars do not believe it and generally have not believed it for more than three centuries.[7] One oft-cited objection to the historicity of the Letter of Aristeas is the role of Demetrius of Phalerum, a known historical person who was employed by Ptolemy I but was driven into exile by Ptolemy II. Demetrius does not belong in the position that the Letter of Aristeas assigns him, serving Ptolemy II.[8] This mistake, along with others, shows that the author of the Letter lived long after the events he describes; he was not actually a courtier to Ptolemy II, and he confused certain details of the distant past. Note further the Letter's reference to the habits of the Ptolemies: "For these kings used to administer everything through edicts and with great caution, and nothing was done negligently

---

[7] On the history of scholarship, see Wright, *Letter of Aristeas*, 6–15. Especially influential was Humphrey Hody's critique published in 1684. See Wasserstein and Wasserstein, *Legend*, 254–58.

[8] See the discussion of this point in Wright, *Letter of Aristeas*, 112–17. Our knowledge of Demetrius is based on the account in Diogenes Laertius (third century CE), *Lives of the Eminent Philosophers* 5.5.75–85. Tessa Rajak, *Translation and Survival: The Greek Bible of the Ancient Jewish Diaspora* (Oxford: Oxford University Press, 2009), 42, seeks to overturn this objection to the historicity of *Aristeas*.

or without purpose" (§28).[9] How could someone living under the second Ptolemaic king make this statement? It rather seems like our author is looking back at the time of Ptolemy II as one in the distant past. Scholars universally conclude that our author was, in fact, Jewish, not pagan. He praises the Jewish religion so much and is so disparaging of paganism that one might well wonder why Aristeas would not convert to Judaism if he were the person he represents himself to be.[10] He does not accurately describe the process of translation, and there were not really seventy-two translators but probably only five, one for each book of the Pentateuch (as we will see in the next chapter).[11]

Who is our author really? We do not know his name, though it may have been Aristeas, for all we know. Scholars do not know why our author chose the name *Aristeas* for his narrator; there was no famous Aristeas that our author was impersonating, but he is often now called "Pseudo-Aristeas" (or Ps-Aristeas).[12] Scholars generally place him in Alexandria, sometime in the second century BCE, often in the second half of the second century, and so more than a century after the events he describes.[13] Ps-Aristeas had a Jewish readership in view, and he had a variety of purposes (after all, he addressed a variety of topics, as we have seen), among which was the desire to promote the Greek translation of the Jewish Law, perhaps against the desire to revise the translation, perhaps in place of the Hebrew Torah itself.[14] All these points are debated by scholars, but everyone would agree that the views presented in this paragraph are reasonable, even if they would disagree.

---

[9] Translation from Wright, *Letter of Aristeas*, 141; see also his comment at 145.

[10] See the discussion of this point in Hadas, *Aristeas to Philocrates*, 5–6.

[11] Whence does Ps-Aristeas get the idea of seventy-two translators? See Hadas, *Aristeas to Philocrates*, 71–72; and A. C. McDonald, "The Seventy-Two Elders of Aristeas: An Evaluation of Speculation," *Journal for the Study of the Pseudepigrapha* 29 (2019): 36–53.

[12] This issue is discussed at Wright, *Letter of Aristeas*, 20.

[13] Wright, *Letter of Aristeas*, 21–30, discusses the date and opts for the second half of the second century BCE (28).

[14] For the first position, see Sebastian P. Brock, "To Revise or Not to Revise: Attitudes to Jewish Biblical Translation," in *Septuagint, Scrolls, and Cognate Writings: Papers Presented to the International Symposium on the Septuagint and Its Relation to the Dead Sea Scrolls and Other Writings*, ed. George J. Brooke and Barnabas Lindars (Atlanta: Scholars Press, 1992), 301–38, at 334. Wright, *Letter of Aristeas*, 71–72, takes the second position.

Near the end of the Letter of Aristeas, we read what happened after the work of translation:

> (§308) When the work was concluded Demetrius assembled the community of the Jews at the place where the translation was executed, and read it out to the entire gathering, the translators too being present; these received a great ovation from the community also, in recognition of the great service for which they were responsible. (§309) And they accorded Demetrius a similar reception, and requested him to have a transcription of the entire Law made and to present it to their rulers. (§310) When the rolls had been read the priests and the elders of the translators and some of the corporate body and the leaders of the people rose up and said, "Inasmuch as the translation has been well and piously made and is in every respect accurate, it is right that it should remain in its present form and that no revision of any sort take place." (§311) When all had assented to what had been said, they bade that an imprecation be pronounced, according to their custom, upon any who should revise the text by adding or transposing anything whatever in what had been written down, or by making any excision; and in this they did well, so that the work might be preserved imperishable and unchanged always.[15]

This curse, reminiscent of Deuteronomy 4:2, indicates that the translation—in the view of Ps-Aristeas—is perfect as is, so that any revision would necessarily make the translation worse. Perhaps also, as I have already said, this whole narrative aims to put the translation of the Law on the same level as the original text.[16] One might even think after reading the Letter of Aristeas that the Greek Pentateuch is an inspired translation, though such an interpretation would be reading into the document just a bit. The inspiration of the translation is not actually stated by Ps-Aristeas.

---

[15] Translation by Hadas, *Aristeas to Philocrates*, 221–23.
[16] Harry M. Orlinsky, "The Septuagint as Holy Writ and the Philosophy of the Translators," *Hebrew Union College Annual* 46 (1975): 94–95.

Aside from the Letter of Aristeas, there are four other main Jewish sources on the translation legend. We will take them one by one.

Aristobulus[17]

We know little about Aristobulus. He was a Jewish philosopher living in Alexandria in the mid-second century BCE. He wrote a philosophical dialogue addressed to King Ptolemy VI Philometor (180–145 BCE) in regard to certain exegetical issues in the Torah. His writings survive only in fragments—not literal fragments, but quotations in later writers. In other words, we have no manuscripts of the works of Aristobulus, just quotations of him. He mentions the Septuagint in one quoted passage:[18]

> It is clear that Plato followed the tradition of the law that we use and he is conspicuous for having worked through each of the details contained in it. For before Demetrius of Phalerum, before the dominion of Alexander and the Persians, others had translated accounts of the events surrounding the exodus from Egypt of the Hebrews, our countrymen, and the disclosure to them of all the things that had happened as well as their domination of the land, and the detailed account of the entire law, so that it is very clear that the aforementioned philosopher had taken over many ideas; for he was very learned, just as Pythagoras, having borrowed many of the things in our traditions, found room for them in his own doctrinal system.

---

[17] The fragments of Aristobulus are collected (in Greek with English translation) in Carl R. Holladay, *Fragments from Hellenistic Jewish Authors*, vol. 3, *Aristobulus* (Atlanta: Scholars Press, 1995). For a review of Aristobulus's testimony to the Septuagint, see Jennifer M. Dines, *The Septuagint* (New York: T&T Clark, 2004), 33–38, who believes that Aristobulus was dependent on the Letter of Aristeas. For a summary of the fragments of Aristobulus, see Folker Siegert, "Early Jewish Interpretation in a Hellenistic Style," in *Hebrew Bible/Old Testament: The History of Its Interpretation*, vol. 1, *From the Beginnings to the Middle Ages*, ed. Magne Sæbø (Göttingen: Vandenhoeck & Ruprecht, 1996), 130–98, at 156–58. There have been major and ongoing debates as to the authenticity of Aristobulus; see Holladay, *Aristobulus*, 49–72.

[18] Fragment 3 in the edition by Holladay. This quotation is preserved in Clement of Alexandria, *Stromata* 1.22.150.1–3; and Eusebius, *Praeparatio evangelica* 13.11.3b–12.2.

But the complete translation of everything in the law occurred at the time of the king surnamed Philadelphus, your ancestor, who brought great zeal to this undertaking, while Demetrius of Phalerum attended to matters relating to these things.[19]

The most interesting thing Aristobulus says is that there had been Greek translations of the Torah before the Septuagint,[20] translations that influenced earlier Greek philosophers, such as Plato. Modern scholars do not trust this report; probably Aristobulus just wanted to have some way of declaring that Plato's wisdom was derivative of Moses—a common enough assertion among ancient Jews (and some pagans).[21] As for the Septuagint, Aristobulus affirms in concert with the Letter of Aristeas that it was produced during the time of Ptolemy II Philadelphus and that it was a translation of the Law (i.e., the Pentateuch).

Philo[22]

Philo (ca. 15 BCE–ca. 45 CE) was a Jewish philosopher living in Alexandria. He wrote many works, mostly dealing with the interpretation of the Greek Pentateuch. He deals with the story of the translation in his work *On the Life of Moses* 2.25–44. I would like to quote the entire passage, but it is a little long. (You should find it online and read it.) Philo dates the translation to the reign of Ptolemy II Philadelphus, and he specifies that it was the Pentateuch that was translated, thus in agreement with the Letter

---

[19] Translation by Holladay, *Aristobulus*, 153–57.

[20] Some scholars have found the same idea at *Epist. Arist.* 30.

[21] See also *Epist. Arist.* 312–16. The theme of the dependence of pagan philosophers on Jews is found in some of the other fragments of Aristobulus as well, but without the statements about previous Greek translations of the law (see Frgs. 2.4; 4.4; 4.4b–6; 5.13–16). For other references to Jews and pagans (including Theophrastus and Clearchus of Soli) promoting this idea, see Holladay, *Aristobulus*, 212n64; see also his note 36.

[22] For a full account of Philo's life and works, see Adam Kamesar, ed., *The Cambridge Companion to Philo* (Cambridge: Cambridge University Press, 2009). On Philo's description of the Septuagint, see Adam Kamesar, "Biblical Interpretation in Philo," in Kamesar, *Cambridge Companion to Philo*, 65–91, at 65–72.

of Aristeas, which he had probably read.[23] Unlike the Letter, Philo does not mention the number of translators, but he does specify that it was the island of Pharos where the work was done (2.35) and where an annual festival still in Philo's day celebrates the translation (2.41; cf. *Epist. Arist.* 180). But Philo's most important and influential contribution to the story is his explicit and repeated affirmation that the translators were inspired. (In these excerpts and elsewhere, Philo uses the word *Chaldean* to refer to the Hebrew language. No one knows why he does this.)[24]

> The translators, sitting in seclusion and with no one present . . . as if possessed [ἐνθουσιῶντες], prophesied [προεφήτευον], in the course of translating, not each one something different, but all of them the same nouns and verbs, as if a prompter [ὑποβολέως] were invisibly giving them instructions. (2.37)

> If Chaldeans learn the Greek language and Greeks Chaldean, and they read both texts, that is, the Chaldean and the translation, they are filled with wonder and revere them as sisters, or rather as one and the same, both in matters and in words, calling the authors not translators but hierophants and prophets. To them it was granted to be in communion, through sheer thought, with the most pure spirit of Moses. (2.40)[25]

Remember that Ps-Aristeas said that the translators compared notes and produced a translation through a process of collaboration (§302). Philo represents the work of translation differently. When he emphasizes that the translators produced identical results (2.37), he seems to imagine that they did not work together; there was no process of collaboration. This idea—that the translators worked separately and each produced identical translations—will become a common trope in Christian retellings of this story. Here Philo already seems

---

[23] Wright, *Letter of Aristeas*, 6.

[24] See the discussion in Edmon L. Gallagher, *Hebrew Scripture in Patristic Biblical Theory: Canon, Language, Text* (Leiden: Brill, 2012), 123–24.

[25] I have slightly adapted the translation from Kamesar, "Biblical Interpretation in Philo," 66–67.

to assume it. He also asserts, what is perhaps more astonishing, that the translation corresponded perfectly to the Hebrew, word for word and sense for sense. To compare it to English Bibles, it is as if all the best features of the KJV and *The Message* were to meet together in one version. Of course, Philo knows that such a translation is impossible, but with God all things are possible, and these translators were inspired by God.

Does Philo know what he is talking about? Is the Septuagint really a perfect word-for-word and sense-for-sense translation of the Hebrew? No. The Greek Pentateuch diverges from the Hebrew Torah in many ways. Philo does not read Hebrew, and his readers probably do not read Hebrew, so who can check the accuracy of the claim? For Philo, the view that the Septuagint itself is inspired and a perfect representation of the Hebrew Torah means that there is no need to learn Hebrew, no need to go behind the Greek Pentateuch to the original text. The Greek Pentateuch is the Word of God just as much as the Hebrew Torah is.

Josephus

Josephus was a Jewish historian who was prominent in the second half of the first century CE. In his magnum opus, the *Antiquities of the Jews*, he narrates Jewish history from creation until his own day. As a part of this long story, he summarizes the account of the translation of the Pentateuch as told by Ps-Aristeas (*A.J.* 12.11–118). He greatly compresses Ps-Aristeas's account of the seven-day banquet welcoming the translators to Alexandria, but he tells his readers that they can read "the book of Aristeas" for a fuller version (12.100). Josephus knows that there are six translators from each tribe (12.39, 49, 56), but he never actually says there are seventy-two translators (and he never specifies how many tribes there are, at least not within the story of the translation). Instead, he talks about the "seventy" translators (12.57, 86). This is the first time in the developing story that the number "seventy" is used, which became the normal way of referring to the translators: the translation of the Seventy, the *Septuaginta*. Like Ps-Aristeas, Josephus also says the work was completed in seventy-two days (12.107). Josephus does not follow Philo in claiming inspiration for the translation, and he does not even follow Ps-Aristeas in reporting that a curse was pronounced on anyone who would alter the translation. Instead, in Josephus's reckoning, this is what happened after the translators finished their work:

> And all of them, including the priest and the eldest of the translators and the chief officers of the community, requested that, since the translation had been so successfully completed [ἐπεὶ καλῶς τὰ τῆς ἑρμηνείας ἀπήρτισται], it should remain as it was and not be altered [καὶ διαμεῖναι ταῦθ', ὡς ἔχει, καὶ μὴ μετακινεῖν αὐτά]. (§109) Accordingly, when all had approved this idea, they ordered that, if anyone saw any further addition made to the text of the Law or anything omitted from it [εἴ τις ἢ περισσόν τι προσγεγραμμένον ὁρᾷ τῷ νόμῳ ἢ λεῖπον], he should examine it [πάλιν ἐπισκοποῦντα τοῦτο] and make it known and correct it [καὶ ποιοῦντα φανερὸν διορθοῦν]; in this they acted wisely, that what had once been judged good might remain for ever. (A.J. 12.108–9)[26]

According to Josephus, while the original translation may have been perfect or close to it, the manuscripts do not necessarily attest this original perfection. Revision might be necessary to restore the translation to its pristine state.

The Talmud

The Babylonian Talmud is an enormous compendium of Jewish tradition, written in Hebrew and Aramaic, put together perhaps in the sixth century CE but full of older material.[27] The structure of the Talmud is sort of like the Bible, except that the individual pieces of the Talmud are not called

---

[26] Translation by Ralph Marcus in Josephus, *Jewish Antiquities, Books XII–XIII*, Loeb Classical Library (Cambridge, MA: Harvard University Press, 1943), 53–55.

[27] For a helpful guide, see H. L. Strack and Günter Stemberger, *Introduction to the Talmud and Midrash* (Edinburgh: T&T Clark, 1991).

"books" but "tractates." In tractate *Megillah*, the Greek translation of the Pentateuch is mentioned:

> R. Judah said: When our teachers permitted Greek, they permitted it only for a scroll of the Torah. This was on account of the incident related in connection with King Ptolemy, as it has been taught: It is related of King Ptolemy that he brought together seventy-two elders and placed them in seventy-two [separate] rooms, without telling them why he had brought them together, and he went in to each one of them and said to him, Translate for me the Torah of Moses your master. God then prompted each one of them and they all conceived the same idea. (*Megillah* 9a)[28]

The Talmud goes on to specify that the translators actually provided renderings of certain verses that diverged from the Hebrew text, in an apparent attempt to present to Ptolemy a version of the Jewish Law that he would not so easily misconstrue, or that would not anger him. The story is confusing, and it has provoked numerous interpretations.[29] I would rather not wade into that debate, so I will just point out some things that are on the surface of the text. The story presents God as involved in the translation; more than that, here for the first time we see explicitly the assertion that the translators did not work together but were separated and still produced identical translations, a sure sign of the inspiration they enjoyed. I think this idea was assumed by Philo, but the Talmud states it. Second, the translation involved the Torah and no other book of the Jewish Bible. In fact, that is the context of the discussion in the Talmud about which books are permitted to be read in Greek and not exclusively Hebrew. The story of the Seventy-two translators is a point in favor of reading the Torah in Greek. The Talmudic story also asserts that some passages in the Greek translation

---

[28] Translation in I. Epstein, ed., *The Babylonian Talmud: Translated into English with Notes, Glossary and Indices*, 35 vols. (London: Soncino, 1935–52).

[29] Philip Alexander, "The Rabbis, the Greek Bible and Hellenism," in *The Jewish-Greek Tradition in Antiquity and the Byzantine Empire*, ed. James K. Aitken and James Carleton Paget (Cambridge: Cambridge University Press, 2014), 229–46; Wasserstein and Wasserstein, *Legend*, 51–94.

diverge from the Hebrew Torah. Though Philo and the Talmud both say that God was involved in the translation, they disagree on the result: for Philo, the result is a perfect representation of the Hebrew Torah in Greek; for the Talmud, the result is a translation deviating from its source text. Whatever the Talmudic storytellers might mean by their assertion of deviations between Hebrew and Greek, a similar idea was voiced in Christian circles on occasion, especially by Jerome, who even seems to know something like the rabbinic tradition preserved for us here in the Talmud.[30]

Summary of the Story in Ancient Judaism

There are plenty of distinctive features among our ancient Jewish sources, but one of the consistent elements concerns the object of translation: it was the Jewish Law, the Pentateuch. The Letter of Aristeas, Aristobulus, Philo, Josephus, and the Talmud all describe the translation in terms of the law of Moses. None of them relays a story about the translation of any other book, and none of them suggests that the Seventy(-two) translators worked on Isaiah or Psalms or any book outside the Pentateuch. For ancient Jews, as far as our evidence takes us, the Septuagint was the Greek Pentateuch.

Was the Septuagint a good translation? How does it compare with the Hebrew Torah? It is difficult to understand what the Talmud is trying to relate on this matter, since God apparently inspires the translators to produce a translation divergent from the original text. Aristobulus is not very explicit on this subject. Josephus is somewhat more explicit than Aristobulus, but he is still noncommittal. His statement at 12.108–9 (quoted earlier) suggests that someone might find something inadequate about the transmission of the translation, which requires correction. But Josephus certainly supports the idea that the translation is very good. I emphasize this point because Josephus was certainly read by early Christians, and his views would have been influential. The two most influential reports on the Septuagint among early Christians were those of Philo and the Letter

---

[30] See Adam Kamesar, *Jerome, Greek Scholarship, and the Hebrew Bible: A Study of the Quaestiones Hebraicae in Genesim* (Oxford: Clarendon, 1993), 66–67.

of Aristeas, and for both of them the translation was so well done that it could not possibly be improved. Ps-Aristeas implied that God oversaw the process of translation, and he reported the curse pronounced on any who would dare alter the text. Philo went further, declaring in no uncertain terms that the translators were, in fact, prophets, inspired of God, communing with the spirit of Moses, and they therefore produced a perfect translation that completely reproduces the Hebrew (or Chaldean) text in Greek in every conceivable way. The Greek Pentateuch is the exact match of the Hebrew Torah.

The Translation Story among Ancient Christians

In Chapter Eight, we will explore more fully the development of the translation story in early Christianity (the first four centuries or so). Here we can just cover the broad developments. The first Christian writer to mention the Septuagint was Justin Martyr in the mid-second century CE, and his comment immediately reveals a momentous change that has happened in the transfer of the story from Jewish circles to Christian circles. The translation for Christians encompasses the entire Old Testament, or, at least, more than the Greek Pentateuch. Justin, for instance, refers to the Septuagint translation of Isaiah (*Dial.* 70–73). This view of the Septuagint becomes immediately universal for Christians. Irenaeus, later in the second century, relates the translation story, affirming the inspiration of the translators (in line with Philo) but also describing the translation of Isaiah as a part of the Septuagint (*Haer.* 3.21.1–3). The expansion of the Septuagint to include the Prophets and Psalms was an essential element in Christian apologetics, for they used the story of the separated translators—which we have seen in the Talmud and perhaps assumed in Philo—to prove the inspiration of the translation, which now can include the Prophets and the distinctive LXX wording of certain messianic prophecies. It was Jerome, in the late fourth and early fifth centuries, who read the Letter of Aristeas closely enough to realize that only the Pentateuch was translated,[31] and the earliest accounts say nothing about the translators being separated (*Praef. Pent.*). But even Jerome took it for granted that the Letter was an accurate historical account (e.g., *Comm. Dan.* 11:5). It was not until the early modern period, when doubts about the historicity of the Letter of Aristeas started to be proposed by scholars (especially Humphry Hody in 1684), that the way was opened for imagining an entirely new approach to the origins of the Septuagint.

---

[31] *Quaest. heb. Gen.* preface; *Comm. Ezech.* 5:12; *Comm. Mich.* 2:9.

3

Origins

What Modern Scholars Think about LXX Origins

> On the whole, though the direct evidence is fragmentary, it is prob-
> able that before the Christian era Alexandria possessed the whole,
> or nearly the whole, of the Hebrew Scriptures in a Greek translation.
>
> —Henry Barclay Swete, *An Introduction
> to the Old Testament in Greek*, 2nd ed.
> (Cambridge: Cambridge University Press, 1914), 25

The Letter of Aristeas says that the translation project for the Pentateuch originated in the court of King Ptolemy in Alexandria, Egypt. Should we trust that account? No. No one for the past few centuries has thought that the Letter of Aristeas is an authentic account of the translation of the Greek Pentateuch. We use the term *Septuagint* because of this translation story, but no one these days thinks that seventy or seventy-two translators actually participated in the work. Some scholars think that parts of the story in the Letter might be genuine reflections of how the translation actually happened: maybe King Ptolemy was involved in some way, for instance.[1] At least, the timing is right. Ptolemy II Philadelphus reigned during the first half of the

---

[1] Hadas considers royal involvement possible; Moses Hadas, ed. and trans., *Aristeas to Philocrates (Letter of Aristeas)* (New York: Harper, 1951), 72–73. A more recent argument for this view is in Tessa Rajak, *Translation and Survival: The Greek Bible of the Ancient Jewish Diaspora* (Oxford: Oxford University Press, 2009), ch. 2.

third century BCE, and other evidence suggests that the Greek Pentateuch originated in the first half of the third century BCE.[2] No one has ever really doubted that the translation took place in Alexandria, which the Letter also affirms. Certainly, ancient people seem to have thought that the Letter of Aristeas was a genuine account of the translation by an eyewitness, but since the early 1700s it has been commonly recognized as, basically, a made-up story from long after the translation by someone who wanted to glorify the translation. We really cannot take any part of the story at face value.

Where did the translation come from? As I just noted, evidence outside of the Letter of Aristeas suggests that the Greek Pentateuch originated in Alexandria in the first half of the third century BCE. Most scholars think that the large Jewish community of Alexandria must have been involved in some way in the translation project, beyond what the Letter says—that is, that the Jewish community gave their hearty approval of the translation after the work was already done. Many scholars think that the translation project was carried out entirely within the Jewish community of Alexandria—that is, that the Alexandrian king was not involved at all.[3] But other scholars have thought that the project would have been such a large-scale endeavor, on the one hand, and so desirable for a king like Ptolemy Philadelphus and his royal library, on the other hand, that perhaps royal patronage makes sense.[4] Who knows? At any rate, early-third-century Alexandria is the right time and place for the translation of the Pentateuch. Moreover, there seems to have been just one initial translation, not multiple translations carried out by different groups in different places.[5] And as I mentioned earlier, there were probably not seventy(-two) translators but only five, one for each book of the Pentateuch.[6]

---

[2] This evidence is the citations of the Greek Pentateuch in Jewish Hellenistic authors, such as Demetrius the Chronographer. See the discussion on citations later in this chapter.

[3] This view is especially associated with Henry St. John Thackeray, *The Septuagint and Jewish Worship: A Study in Origins* (London: British Academy, 1921).

[4] See the discussion of these ideas in Siegfried Kreuzer, "The Origins and Transmission of the Septuagint," in *Introduction to the Septuagint*, ed. Siegfried Kreuzer (Waco, TX: Baylor University Press, 2019), 3–56, at 11–20. Kreuzer says that some sort of royal involvement "cannot be ruled out" (19).

[5] Emanuel Tov, *The Text-Critical Use of the Septuagint in Biblical Research*, 3rd ed. (Winona Lake, IN: Eisenbrauns, 2015), 10–15.

[6] This is the general assumption in scholarship, but how early it became the assumption I do not know. Already in the early nineteenth century Adam Clarke surmised five translators;

There is no story about the translations of the other books of the Old Testament, but since we have found that scholars generally do not trust the Letter of Aristeas anyway, lack of a story is perhaps no great impediment to determining the circumstances of the translation of these books (no greater than what we face with the Pentateuch). Broadly, what we should imagine is that, at some point during the two or three centuries before the birth of Jesus, Jewish scholars—perhaps scattered about the Mediterranean world, but probably mostly in Egypt or Palestine—translated the various books not as a part of some unified project but merely piecemeal, working independently. Nevertheless, analysis of the preserved texts suggests that most of these books (like the Pentateuch) were translated once, not multiple times by different translators in different locations at different times. Possibly a single translator may have produced the Septuagint form of multiple books; such an idea has been proposed, for example, for Job and Proverbs, as well as for Jeremiah, Ezekiel, and the Twelve Minor Prophets, and also 1 Esdras and Daniel.[7] Possibly, some books may have been divided up among different translators so that each translator worked on a portion of a book; such an idea has been proposed but not demonstrated.[8] Most of the books were available in Greek by the late second century BCE. The

---

Adam Clarke, "General Preface," in *The Holy Bible . . . with a Commentary and Critical Notes*, vol. 1 (New York: Ezra Sargeant, 1811), xxvii. One of the preserved rabbinic accounts of the translation mentions five translators (*Massekhet Sopherim* 1.7–8; see Abraham Wasserstein and David J. Wasserstein, *The Legend of the Septuagint: From Classical Antiquity to Today* [Cambridge: Cambridge University Press, 2006], 71–73), but this number is best explained as a mere scribal error; see Harry M. Orlinsky, "The Septuagint and Its Hebrew Text," in *The Cambridge History of Judaism*, vol. 2, *The Hellenistic Age*, ed. W. D. Davies and Louis Finkelstein (Cambridge: Cambridge University Press, 1990), 534–62, at 538n2. For arguments that there were five translators for the Greek Pentateuch, see John A. L. Lee, *The Greek of the Pentateuch: Grinfield Lectures on the Septuagint 2011–2012* (Oxford: Oxford University Press, 2018), 174–75; and Hayeon Kim, *Multiple Authorship of the Septuagint Pentateuch: The Original Translators of the Pentateuch* (Leiden: Brill, 2019).

[7] On Job and Proverbs, see Bénédicte Lemmelijn, "The Greek Rendering of Hebrew Hapax Legomena in LXX Proverbs and Job: A Clue to the Question of a Single Translator?," in *In the Footsteps of Sherlock Holmes: Studies in the Biblical Text in Honour of Anneli Aejmelaeus*, ed. K. De Troyer, T. M. Law, and M. Liljeström (Leuven: Peeters, 2014), 133–50; on the prophetic books, see Pierre-Maurice Bogaert, "Jeremias/Ieremias/Jeremiah," in *Introduction to the Septuagint*, ed. Siegfried Kreuzer (Waco, TX: Baylor University Press, 2019), 531–47, at 538. For brief comments and bibliography, see Tov, *Text-Critical Use*, 16.

[8] On this idea, see Tov, *Text-Critical Use*, 17n21.

evidence for this statement consists in the Greek language employed in the translations, historical allusions within the translations, manuscripts, citations of the books in Greek, and theories regarding the history of the Greek translations and their revisions.

There are also a couple of explicit statements within the works themselves about the circumstances of the translation. These statements concern the book of Esther and the deuterocanonical book of Sirach (Ecclesiasticus). The very end of the Greek Esther transmits a colophon, a note left by a scribe:

> In the fourth year of the reign of Ptolemy and Cleopatra, Dositheus, who said he was a priest and a Leuite, and Ptolemy his son brought the above letter about Phrourai, which they said existed, and Lysimachus son of Ptolemy, one of those in Ierousalem, translated it. (LXX Esther F 11; NETS)

According to this colophon, Esther was translated in Jerusalem (Greek form: Ierousalem) during or before the reign of Ptolemy and Cleopatra—that is, probably Ptolemy XII Auletos and Cleopatra V, the fourth year of whose reign was 78 BCE.[9]

The Greek book of Sirach is a translation of a Hebrew work originally written in the early second century BCE, perhaps about the year 180, by a sage named Jesus ben Sira. When it was translated into Greek, the translator attached the following prologue, which has implications not only for the Greek Sirach but also for the Greek translations of the Bible in general:

> Many great teachings have been given to us through the Law and the Prophets and the others that followed them, and for these we should praise Israel for instruction and wisdom. Now, those who read the scriptures must not only themselves understand them, but must also as lovers of learning be able through the spoken and written word to help the outsiders. So my grandfather Jesus, who had devoted himself especially to the reading of the Law and the Prophets and the

---

[9] Elias J. Bickerman, "The Colophon of the Greek Book of Esther," *Journal of Biblical Literature* 63 (1944): 339–62.

other books of our ancestors, and had acquired considerable proficiency in them, was himself also led to write something pertaining to instruction and wisdom, so that by becoming familiar also with his book those who love learning might make even greater progress in living according to the law. You are invited therefore to read it with goodwill and attention, and to be indulgent in cases where, despite our diligent labor in translating, we may seem to have rendered some phrases imperfectly. For what was originally expressed in Hebrew does not have exactly the same sense when translated into another language. Not only this book, but even the Law itself, the Prophecies, and the rest of the books differ not a little when read in the original. When I came to Egypt in the thirty-eighth year of the reign of Euergetes and stayed for some time, I found opportunity for no little instruction. It seemed highly necessary that I should myself devote some diligence and labor to the translation of this book. During that time I have applied my skill day and night to complete and publish the book for those living abroad who wished to gain learning and are disposed to live according to the law. (New Revised Standard Version [NRSV])

According to this prologue, it was the grandson of Jesus ben Sira who made the translation in Egypt (presumably Alexandria) after having arrived there in the thirty-eighth year of Euergetes. That would be Ptolemy VIII Physcon Euergetes II, whose thirty-eighth year was 132 BCE. The translation was made sometime thereafter, perhaps after Euergetes died in 117 BCE. The translator also indicates that a good portion of the Old Testament had already been translated by this time, for it is their Greek translation that he references when he says that "even the Law itself, the Prophecies, and the rest of the books differ not a little when read in the original" (lines 24–25). While this statement does not specify exactly which books had already been translated, presumably the majority of the books of the Old Testament were available in Greek.

Citations[10]

Citations of Greek Scripture become especially numerous and extensive in the first century CE, with the New Testament and Philo and Josephus. The New Testament quotes from every book of the Jewish Bible (always, of course, in Greek)[11] except for Joshua, Judges, Ruth, 1–2 Chronicles, 2 Kings, Ezra, Nehemiah, Esther, Ecclesiastes, Song of Songs, Lamentations, Obadiah, Nahum, and Zephaniah.[12] The historical books (Judges–Esther) were all used extensively by Josephus and, in some cases, the earlier Jewish historians writing in Greek (Demetrius the Chronographer; Eupolemus).[13] The Minor Prophets were translated and circulated as a unit.[14] That leaves Ecclesiastes, Song of Songs, and Lamentations as translations unattested by the first century CE by these quotations, and scholars have accordingly posited rather late dates for these translations, especially for Ecclesiastes, though somewhat earlier dates are also defended.[15] Earlier authors cite the Greek Pentateuch and sometimes other books, authors such as Demetrius the Chronographer in the late third century BCE, Artapanus in the first half

---

[10] See Marguerite Harl, Gilles Dorival, and Olivier Munnich, *La Bible grecque des Septante: Du judaïsme hellénistique au christianisme ancien*, 2nd ed. (Paris: Cerf, 1994), 90–93.

[11] The one partial exception is Mark 15:34 // Matthew 27:46, which quote Psalm 22:1 in Aramaic before providing a Greek translation. The New Testament quotations of the Old Testament are discussed in Chapter Six.

[12] According to the "Index of Quotations," in *The Greek New Testament*, ed. B. Aland et al., 5th ed. (Stuttgart: Deutsche Bibelgesellschaft, 2014), 857–60. Admittedly, some of the proposed quotations are dubious: it is doubtful whether the New Testament contains any genuine quotation of Ezekiel (the cited index proposes 2 Cor. 6:16–17 as reliant on Ezek. 37:27 and 20:34, 41), but with respect to our present question, no one seriously doubts that a Greek version of Ezekiel existed by the time of the New Testament.

[13] For an index of such scriptural citations in general (not specific to Greek), but not including Philo, Josephus, or the New Testament, see Armin Lange and Matthias Weigold, *Biblical Quotations and Allusions in Second Temple Jewish Literature* (Göttingen: Vandenhoeck & Ruprecht, 2011).

[14] Cécile Dogniez, "Dodekapropheton/The Twelve Prophets," in Kreuzer, *Introduction*, 419–30, at 425.

[15] See the relevant articles in J. K. Aitken, ed., *The T&T Clark Companion to the Septuagint* (London: Continuum, 2015); Kreuzer, *Introduction*.

of the second century BCE, Eupolemus in the mid-second century BCE, and Aristeas the Exegete perhaps in the second century BCE.[16]

Manuscripts[17]

We have access to basically complete manuscripts of the Greek Old Testament dating from the fourth century CE: Codices Sinaiticus and Vaticanus, both of which are available for viewing online.[18] I say "basically complete" because Codex Sinaiticus is only fragmentarily preserved in the Old Testament; not much of the Pentateuch is preserved, for example, nor the historical books. Presumably Sinaiticus originally contained all the books of the Jewish Bible, as is still the case for Vaticanus. Aside from the books of the Jewish Bible, both of these two manuscripts also include Tobit, Judith, the Wisdom of Solomon, and Sirach. Vaticanus also has 1 Esdras, Baruch, and the Epistle of Jeremiah, and almost certainly Sinaiticus also originally contained these writings, though the fragmentary manuscript now lacks them. Moreover, Sinaiticus (but not Vaticanus) includes 1 Maccabees and 4 Maccabees. Most of the books now thought of as belonging to the Septuagint, then, are preserved in these manuscripts. In fact, for most of the books of the Septuagint, our earliest manuscripts are Sinaiticus and Vaticanus, and for almost all the books, our earliest complete Greek copies are these two manuscripts.

The extent of Vaticanus and Sinaiticus (containing basically the whole Old Testament) is unusual among Greek biblical manuscripts. It never became customary for Greek manuscripts to include the entire Bible, or even an entire Testament (Old or New); rather, Greek biblical manuscripts

---

[16] For a collection of the surviving writings of these authors, see Carl R. Holladay, *Fragments from Hellenistic Jewish Authors*, vol. 1, *Historians* (Chico, CA: Scholars Press, 1983). For an index of their quotations or allusions to the Greek Pentateuch, see Lange and Weigold, *Biblical Quotations*, 226 (Aristeas the Exegete), 227 (Artapanus), 229–30 (Demetrius the Chronographer), and 231–32 (Eupolemus).

[17] Adapted from Siegfried Kreuzer and Marcus Sigismund, "Overview of Textual Witnesses to the Septuagint," in Kreuzer, *Introduction*, 57–62.

[18] Codex Vaticanus: "Manuscript—Vat.gr. 1209," DigiVatLib, last accessed April 26, 2021, https://digi.vatlib.it/view/MSS_Vat.gr.1209. Codex Sinaiticus: "Home," Codex Sinaiticus, last accessed April 26, 2021, www.codexsinaiticus.org.

typically contain a section of text, such as the Pentateuch, or the Prophets, or books of poetry, or the Gospels, or Paul's letters. Our earliest manuscripts of the Septuagint usually contain only one biblical book, at least in their preserved form. The earliest manuscripts date to the second century BCE, and most of them derive from the Dead Sea Scrolls, and almost all are manuscripts of the Pentateuch: one manuscript of Exodus (7QLXX-Exod [Ra 805]);[19] one manuscript of Leviticus (4QLXXLev[a] [Ra 801]); two manuscripts of Deuteronomy (P. Ryl. Gr. 458 [Ra 957]; 4QLXXDeut [Ra 819]);[20] and a tiny fragment of the deuterocanonical Epistle of Jeremiah (7QLXXEpJer [Ra 804]). In the first century BCE or CE, we have a manuscript of Genesis (P. Fouad 266a [Ra 942]); one of Leviticus (4QpapLXXLev[b] [Ra 802]); one of Numbers (4QLXXNum [Ra 803]); two of Deuteronomy (P. Fouad 266b [Ra 848]; P. Fouad 266c [Ra 847]); one of Job (P.Oxy 3522 [Ra 857]); one of Psalms (P.Oxy 5101 [Ra 2227]); and one of the Minor Prophets (8HevXIIGr [Ra 943]). There is also a Qumran manuscript that is a paraphrase of Exodus in Greek (4QpapParaExodgr, 4Q127).

In manuscripts from the following centuries, the Pentateuch continues to be well represented.[21] There are also manuscripts of Joshua (second century: P.Schøyen 2648 [Ra 816]); 1 Samuel (fourth century: P.Feinberg 1 [Ra 842]); Esther (second century: P.Oxy 4443 [Ra 996]); the Psalter;[22] Isaiah;[23] Jeremiah (third century: P.Chester Beatty VIII [Ra 966]); and Sirach (Ra 828). And there are a few manuscripts that have multiple books: Ezekiel, Daniel, and Esther

---

[19] The "Ra" number is the Rahlfs number used by Septuagint scholars to identify Septuagint manuscripts.

[20] And maybe a third; see Émile Puech, "Lex fragments de papyrus 7Q6 1–2, 7Q9 et 7Q7 = pap7QLXXDt," *Revue de Qumran* 29 (2017): 119–28.

[21] Second century CE: P.Yale 1 (Ra 814, Genesis); P.Chester Beatty VI (Ra 963, Numbers and Deuteronomy); Heidelberg, Pap.Gr. 8 (Ra 970, Exodus and Deuteronomy); P.Schøyen 2649 (Ra 830, Leviticus). Third century CE: P.Oxy 656 (Ra 905, Genesis); P.Oxy 1007 (Ra 907, Genesis); P.Oxy 4442 (Ra 993, Exodus); P.Oxy 1075 (Ra 909, Exodus); P.Berlin, DSB cod. graec. fol. 66 I/II (Ra 911, Genesis); P.Chester Beatty V (Ra 962, Genesis). Fourth century CE: P.Amherst 1.3 (Ra 912, Genesis); P.Rylands Gk. 460 (Ra 958, Genesis and Deuteronomy, with Isaiah and 2 Chronicles).

[22] Greek Psalter manuscripts: second century CE: P.Barc. inv. 2 = Ra 2160; P.Bodl 5 = Ra 2082. Third century CE: P.Leipzig 170 = Ra 2014; P.Vindob/Wien 26035B = Ra 2094; P.Bodmer XXIV = Ra 2110. Fourth century CE: P.Vindob/Wien Rainer G 2312 = Ra 2031.

[23] Greek Isaiah manuscripts: third century CE: P.Berlin 6772 = Ra 902; P.Vindob/Wien Rainer 8024 = Ra 948; P.Chester Beatty VII = Ra 965. Fourth century CE: Ra 850.

together in a third-century manuscript (P.Chester Beatty IX and P.Köln. Theol. [Ra 967]); a third-century manuscript of Proverbs, the Wisdom of Solomon, and Sirach (P.Ant 8 [Ra 928]); a third-century manuscript of the Minor Prophets (Washington MS V [W]); and a fourth-century manuscript with Genesis, Deuteronomy, 2 Chronicles, and Isaiah (P.Rylands Gk. 460 [Ra 958]).

Revisions

The Greek Old Testament was constantly subject to revision. That is an easy concept for readers of the English Bible, because we are accustomed to a plethora—do you know what a plethora is?—of English Bible translations. We tend to think of translations existing on a continuum of literal to loose: the KJV is a literal translation, the *Message* is pretty loose, and then there are all kinds of translations at various points between these two poles. The various translations that make up the Septuagint show similar features: some were rather literal, some rather loose.[24] In Chapter Five, we will examine the state of the text of the Old Testament in ancient times in more detail, but here we can offer a brief introduction to the subject.

The Greek translations of the Old Testament books often diverge from the standard Hebrew text we now possess, which is called the Masoretic Text (MT). The reasons for these divergences are basically two: either the Greek translator decided to translate the book in a rather loose way, or he translated rather literally a Hebrew text that is different from the MT. The Dead Sea Scrolls have shown conclusively that for some books of the Hebrew Bible, there were multiple Hebrew editions. The situation is especially stark in respect to the book of Jeremiah (but also Samuel and Exodus and other books); both a longer and a shorter version of the book existed in Hebrew, and the Dead Sea Scrolls apparently include (fragmentary) copies of both versions. The longer version is preserved in the Masoretic Text and therefore has become the standard version of Jeremiah in the English Bible, while the shorter version served as the basis for the Greek translation of Jeremiah. So there are all kinds of differences between the LXX Jeremiah and the MT Jeremiah.

---

[24] For a more nuanced discussion of these issues, see Tov, *Text-Critical Use*, 18–31.

The point is that the Septuagint diverges from the MT either because of a loose translation style or because the translator used a Hebrew text different from the MT. As the texts that became the MT came to dominate the biblical landscape—that is, as the proto-MT became more popular and influential—some readers of Greek Scripture wanted their Bibles to match these prominent Hebrew texts more closely. And so we have evidence of revisions of the Septuagint, almost always revisions toward the proto-MT, to make the Greek text a more literal representation of the proto-MT. These revisions began at least in the second century BC and continued in various forms over the next several centuries. Early revisions are often anonymous, and one extensively studied revision is named after not a translator but a translation choice: the choice to use the Greek word *kaige* in certain instances (and thus "the *kaige* revision"). Sometimes the revisions are associated with particular people: Theodotion, Aquila, Symmachus, Origen, Lucian, and Hesychius are the most prominent, and we will discuss them all in later chapters.

I bring up these revisions here because they can provide additional evidence for dating the original translation of a book. If we have a *kaige* revision of the Minor Prophets, and if we can date the *kaige* revisional activity to the first century BCE, then the original translation of the Minor Prophets must have preceded this revision. On the other hand, sometimes a book in the Septuagint might have been translated for the first time within the *kaige* tradition (or, at least, our surviving evidence suggests as much), and so we might date the original translation to the first century BCE.

The Septuagint Book by Book (aside from the Pentateuch)

The following book-by-book survey does not, of course, provide the definitive answers for any of the books below—the frequency of question marks should sufficiently signal the uncertainty in these discussions. This chart is intended as a quick reference for what scholars generally say about the time and place of origin for the books of the Septuagint. Hopefully it will drive home the point that these translations did not all originate together as a single project. Since we discussed the origins of the Greek Pentateuch earlier, we leave it out of the account here. As mentioned near the end of the first chapter, there are a couple of works that survey the Septuagint book by book: the *T&T Clark Companion to the Septuagint*, edited by James Aitken, and the *Introduction to the Septuagint*, edited by Siegfried Kreuzer. The interested student should turn to these works for more information. In most cases, I have tried to provide a brief reference to the reasoning that has led scholars to suggest a certain location or time period for the translations. Dates are given as Roman numerals denoting centuries (i.e., II means second century):

Joshua: outside Palestine (geographical ignorance), probably Egypt (language); III or early II BCE (historical allusions; perhaps cited by Aristobulus)

Judges: Alexandria; II BCE (historical allusions)

Ruth: Place? I BCE? I CE?[25]

Samuel (1–2 Kingdoms): Alexandria (likelihood); early II BC (language; citations)

Kings (3–4 Kingdoms): Egypt? Alexandria? (language); early II BCE (citation by Demetrius and Eupolemus)

Chronicles (1–2 Paraleipomena): Egypt (language); early II BCE (citation by Eupolemus)

1 Esdras: Alexandria? Palestine? (language); II BCE (language; textual development)

2 Esdras: Egypt (geographical ignorance) or Palestine (language); I BCE? I CE? II CE? (language; earliest use is Eusebius, *Comm. Isa.*)

Esther: Jerusalem (colophon); 78 BCE (colophon)

---

[25] The extant form of LXX Ruth is considered a part of the *kaige* tradition, so the provenance and date of LXX Ruth depend on discussions regarding this wider tradition. But there is a question as to whether our extant *kaige* version of Ruth is the earliest version; perhaps a first translation was lost?

Judith: Palestine; I BCE (historical allusions)

Tobit: Egypt (language); II BCE (language)

1 Maccabees: Palestine; I BCE

2 Maccabees: Palestine; late II BCE

3 Maccabees: Alexandria; I BCE (historical allusions)

4 Maccabees: Alexandria? Antioch? Asia Minor?; late I CE

Psalms: Egypt? (language), Palestine? (language, literary history); early II BCE (literary allusions)

Psalms of Solomon: Jerusalem (historical allusions) or Alexandria (language); turn of era

Proverbs: Alexandria (likelihood); II BCE

Ecclesiastes: Palestine?; I CE or II CE (translation technique)

Song of Songs: Egypt? (language) Palestine?; I CE

Job: Alexandria (literary allusions); II BCE (citations)

Wisdom of Solomon: Alexandria (language); late I BCE

Sirach: Egypt; Alexandria? (prologue); 130–117 BCE (prologue)

Twelve Prophets (translated as a unit): Egypt (language); early II BCE (language)

Isaiah: Alexandria? Heliopolis? (historical allusions); II BCE (historical allusions)

Jeremiah: Alexandria (language); II BCE (citations, language)

Baruch: Palestine?; I CE

Lamentations: Palestine (*kaige*); I BCE (*kaige*)

Epistle of Jeremiah: Palestine; II BCE (manuscript; citation)

Ezekiel: Alexandria? (likelihood); II BCE (citations)

Daniel: Palestine? Alexandria?; II BCE (citations)

SECTION II

Canon and Text in Early Judaism and Earliest Christianity

In this section, we move beyond introductory matters into some of the areas in which the LXX has played a large role in defining the Bible, or at least in scholarly discussions about the definition of the Bible. First up is the canon of Scripture, the issue of which books belong to the Bible. Scholars have often insisted that the use of the LXX by early Christians led them to accept the deuterocanonical books (also known as the "Apocrypha") as Scripture, given that these books were in the LXX and not in the Hebrew Bible. In Chapter Four, we explore the problems with this view. While this long chapter treats the relationship between the LXX and the deuterocanonical books in "early Judaism" and "earliest Christianity," it also moves outside these confines—despite the title of the section—in order to pursue questions of canon into even the early modern period.

The next two chapters turn from the canon of Scripture to its text. In Chapter Five, we survey the variety of textual traditions available in early Judaism in order to arrive at a better understanding of the LXX as a witness to the text of the Bible. In this chapter, we discuss the Masoretic Text, the Samaritan Pentateuch, the Dead Sea Scrolls, and the LXX, all preserving distinctive textual streams of the Bible. We are also concerned here with gaining an appreciation for how ancient Jews perceived the LXX's place within this variety of texts. In Chapter Six, we look at how these various texts show up in the quotations in the New Testament. It is often said that the New Testament quotes the LXX; we will find that, while this assessment is true as a generalization, it is also somewhat simplistic.

4

Canon

The Influence of the LXX on the Size of the Bible

Read the Divine Scriptures, the twenty-two books of the Old Testament, these that have been translated by the Seventy-two translators.

—Cyril of Jerusalem, *Catechetical Lecture* 4.33[1]

The Septuagint had no bearing on the development of the canon of Scripture.

Let that sink in for a second. The Septuagint had no bearing on the development of the canon of Scripture.

All my readers will recognize, at least by its repetition, that this statement is significant, but you might not understand why it is significant. I need to explain what the canon of Scripture is, how it developed, and what scholars have tended to say about the relationship between the Septuagint and the canon of Scripture, all of which are fascinating topics independent of trying to explain the significance of the first sentence of this chapter. The first topic can be answered briefly: the term *canon of Scripture* refers to the collection of books in the Bible, and we often speak about the "canon" when we are talking

---

[1] The translation is slightly adapted from Edmon L. Gallagher and John D. Meade, *The Biblical Canon Lists from Early Christianity: Texts and Analysis* (Oxford: Oxford University Press, 2017), 112.

about which books belong in the Bible. The word *canon* entails authority, and this discussion has to do with identifying the books that carry God's authority. Scholars often claim that the Septuagint exerted significant influence on the development of the canon, arguing that, because the deuterocanonical books were in the Septuagint, these books were easily accepted as part of the Christian Bible. For instance, "reliance on the Septuagint also helped determine which books were regarded as canonical. That translation included a number of books that were not found in the Hebrew, and which Jews increasingly marginalized and excluded from their canon."[2] Such statements are common in the scholarly literature, but this chapter will show that such characterizations of the development of the canon are utterly misleading.

The Deuterocanonical Books

But first, what are the deuterocanonical books? These are more or less the same books Protestants often call "Apocrypha"—that is, the books in the Roman Catholic Bible that are not in the Protestant Bible. The Catholic Bible has seventy-three books, the Protestant Bible sixty-six, so there are seven books that are deuterocanonical, all in the Old Testament. They received this label in the sixteenth century as a way to indicate that they were recognized as canonical after the other books had already been accepted as part of the Bible. In other words, they are *deutero*canonical, recognized as canonical in a "second" phase, as opposed to books like Genesis and Isaiah and Matthew (etc.), which are called "protocanonical" because they were from the very beginning recognized as canonical (i.e., no one ever doubted the canonicity of the protocanonical books). Notice that the word *deuterocanonical*, as it was originally used, did not imply that these books enjoy less authority than the protocanonical books; the label referred only to the chronological development of the canon.[3]

---

[2] Philip Jenkins, *The Many Faces of Christ: The Thousand-Year Story of the Survival and Influence of the Lost Gospels* (New York: Basic, 2015), 41.

[3] See Edmon L. Gallagher, "The Latin Canon," in *Textual History of the Bible*, vol. 2A, *The Deuterocanonical Books: Overview Articles*, ed. Matthias Henze and Frank Feder (Leiden: Brill, 2020), §1.1.4.7.6.

The seven books are

1. Tobit,
2. Judith,
3. Wisdom of Solomon,
4. Sirach (a.k.a. Ben Sira, a.k.a. Ecclesiasticus),
5. Baruch,
6. 1 Maccabees, and
7. 2 Maccabees.

In addition to these seven books, there are also a couple of books that Catholic Bibles and Protestant Bibles share, but the version in the Catholic Bibles is bigger (longer) than the version in Protestant Bibles.

- Daniel, with Deuterocanonical Additions
- Esther, with Deuterocanonical Additions

We could also talk about the Bible among the Greek Orthodox Christians as containing deuterocanonical writings, and here there are a few more to consider. (Although some Greek Orthodox scholars have adopted the term *deuterocanonical* for these books, their own traditional term is *anaginoskomena*, or books "to be read," which has a meaning somewhat different from "deuterocanonical." The term *anaginoskomena* goes back to Athanasius of Alexandria in the fourth century; more on him later in the chapter.) The Greek Orthodox Bible has all the material of the Catholic Bible, plus 1 Esdras and 3 Maccabees, along with an extra psalm at the end of the book of Psalms (Ps. 151). That makes nine deuterocanonical books and three books with deuterocanonical parts. Actually, one of the deuterocanonical books in the Catholic Bible, Baruch, is a combination of two separate books that originated independently and somehow got joined together in Latin: Baruch and the Epistle of Jeremiah. The Greek Orthodox Bible keeps these two writings separate, so there are not nine but ten deuterocanonical books in the Greek Orthodox Bible as they usually count them.

And there are still more deuterocanonical books, if we take account of all the books appearing in the standard small edition of the Septuagint, published originally in 1935 in Germany.[4] Aside from the writings already mentioned, this edition contains also 4 Maccabees, the Odes, and the Psalms of Solomon. That makes thirteen books and three books with additions.

All these books originated in the Second Temple period, or in some cases a little bit later. Some of them might have been written before the Pentateuch was translated into Greek in the third century BCE, but most of them were written after that event. Often we are not sure about the date of composition. Most of them were written in Greek, a few in Hebrew (e.g., Sirach, 1 Maccabees) or Aramaic (e.g., Tobit), and in some cases we are not really sure about the original language (e.g., Judith). Some of them are important historical works of the Second Temple period (e.g., 1–2 Maccabees), some are novellas designed to encourage faithfulness (e.g., Tobit, Judith), some are Wisdom books similar to the book of Proverbs (e.g., the Wisdom of Solomon, Sirach), some are philosophical tracts (e.g., 4 Maccabees), some are liturgical compilations (e.g., Odes).[5] They were written at different times by different authors in different places. While they do not form a part of the Hebrew Bible and consequently have mostly (not entirely) been ignored by Jews for the past two millennia, they found a place in biblical manuscripts in Greek and Latin and other languages because Christians considered them useful and, at times, canonical.

---

[4] Updated now as Alfred Rahlfs and Robert Hanhart, eds., *Septuaginta*, 2nd ed. (Stuttgart: Deutsche Bibelgesellschaft, 2006).

[5] You can find a very brief introduction to each of these books in the appendix to Gallagher and Meade, *Biblical Canon Lists*, 261–84. For a more extensive introduction, see, e.g., David A. deSilva, *Introducing the Apocrypha: Message, Context, and Significance*, 2nd ed. (Grand Rapids: Baker, 2018). Better yet, read the deuterocanonical books for yourself.

The Deuterocanonical Books

These are the books beyond the modern Jewish Bible that are included in the Rahlfs-Hanhart *Septuaginta*.

	Date of Composition	Original Language	Roman Catholic Bible	Greek Orthodox Bible
1 Esdras	second century BCE?	Hebrew? Greek?		•
Tobit	200 BCE?	Aramaic	•	•
Judith	100 BCE?	Hebrew? Greek?	•	•
Wisdom of Solomon	first century BCE	Greek	•	•
Sirach	180 BCE	Hebrew	•	•
1 Maccabees	100 BCE	Hebrew	•	•
2 Maccabees	125 BCE	Greek	•	•
3 Maccabees	first century BCE	Greek		•
4 Maccabees	100 CE	Greek		
Baruch	second century BCE	Hebrew?	•	•
Epistle of Jeremiah	second century BCE	Hebrew?	•	•
Odes	N/A	Greek		
Psalms of Solomon	first century BCE	Hebrew		
Esther: Additions	first century BCE?	Hebrew? Greek?	•	•
Daniel: Additions	100 BCE?	Hebrew?	•	•
Psalm 151	100 BCE?	Hebrew		•

The Deuterocanonical Books and the Septuagint[6]

Are the deuterocanonical books "in the Septuagint"? The answer to this question could be as easy as picking up that standard hand-edition of the Septuagint I mentioned a moment ago, the one titled *Septuaginta*. A quick check of the table of contents will verify that, yes, these books are in the *Septuaginta*.[7] Then again, this edition dates only to 1935. What assurance do we have that such a collection represents anything extant in antiquity? None at all—for Rahlfs's edition of the Septuagint is intentionally a full collection, containing all the writings that appeared in (or even were mentioned by, in the case of the Psalms of Solomon) any one of the three great codices of the fourth and fifth centuries (Vaticanus, Sinaiticus, Alexandrinus). It does not represent a standard collection that existed in antiquity, though scholars generally assume that it does: "The Septuagint contains a number of additional books that are not in the Hebrew canon that rabbinic authorities and later the Reformers recognized as Scripture."[8]

The collection in the modern *Septuaginta* does not even represent the scope of books in the early printed editions of the Septuagint. The first printed edition of the Septuagint that was published (in 1518) is the Aldine,[9] which contained the ten deuterocanonical books commonly accepted among Greek Orthodox Christians, and the three expanded books (Esther, Daniel, Psalms), along with the Odes. The Roman Catholic edition of

---

[6] Much of what follows in the rest of this chapter is taken over (and sometimes significantly reworked) from my essays "The Greek Canon," in Henze and Feder, *Textual History of the Bible*; and "What Were the Scriptures in the Time of Jesus?," in *The Old Testament in the New: Israel's Scriptures in the New Testament and Other Early Christian Writings*, ed. Matthias Henze and David Lincicum (Grand Rapids: Eerdmans, forthcoming).

[7] Siegfried Kreuzer, "The Origins and Transmission of the Septuagint," in *Introduction to the Septuagint*, ed. Siegfried Kreuzer (Waco, TX: Baylor University Press, 2019), 3–56, at 21: "What is deemed to be part of the Septuagint is nowadays actually 'canonized' by the so-called 'concise edition' (*Handausgabe*) of Alfred Rahlfs, published in 1935."

[8] Henning Graf Reventlow, *History of Biblical Interpretation*, vol. 1, *From the Old Testament to Origen* (Atlanta: SBL, 2009), 20. There is a similar misunderstanding with Reventlow's statement in the same paragraph: "In the Roman Catholic Church, these were translated into the Vulgate, the standard translation of Saint Jerome."

[9] *Sacrae scripturae veteris novaeque omnia* (Venice: Aldus, 1518).

the Septuagint called the Sixtine,[10] from 1587, featured mostly the same books, without the Odes. The Complutensian Polyglot,[11] published in 1522, omits 1 Esdras, the Odes, and Psalm 151. Moreover, the editors of the Complutensian Polyglot systematically distinguished the Greek text of the deuterocanonical books from that of the protocanonical books by means of the running head at the top of the page: while the Greek translation of the protocanonical books is labeled "LXX.," the Greek translation of the deuterocanonical books is labeled "Greek translation."[12] Apparently, the editors of the Complutensian Polyglot, who did not accept the canonicity of the deuterocanonical books,[13] did not consider the Greek translation of these books to belong to the Septuagint.

The ancients also made a distinction. We should remember that the Septuagint did not originate all at once. As we have seen in previous chapters (especially Chapter Three), what we call the Septuagint is a collection of Greek translations from a variety of translators over several centuries. We call the collection "the Septuagint" out of convenience and tradition. But the ancients used the term *Septuaginta* (or ἑβδομήκοντα) in reference to a specific event, the translation of the Scriptures by the seventy-two Jewish sages under the patronage of Ptolemy II Philadelphus of Egypt. If something "belongs to the Septuagint," then it was translated by those sages for Ptolemy. While all our Jewish sources attribute to those translators only the Pentateuch, most of our Christian sources assume that the translators worked on more than the Pentateuch, but how much more? Opinions differed, as we are about to see. The main point right now is that the Septuagint is not a thing; it is an idea. (So also the biblical canon.) The deuterocanonicals were in the Septuagint only in so much as someone thought they were.

---

[10] *Vetus Testamentum iuxta Septuaginta ex auctoritate Sixti V. Pont. Max. editum* (Rome: Ex Typographia Francisci Zanetti, 1587).

[11] *Biblia Sacra Polyglotta, complectentia Vetus Testamentum*, 6 vols., ed. A. de Lebrixa et al. (Madrid: Complutenti Universitate, 1514–1517).

[12] I owe this point to John D. Meade, who attributes the initial insight to Peter J. Williams. Dr. Meade also pointed out to me that this observation does not apply to the Additions to Daniel, which are classified as "LXX." in the Complutensian Polyglot.

[13] See Gallagher, "Latin Canon," §1.1.4.7.1.

The Septuagint Collection in Early Printed Editions of the Septuagint

	Complutensian Polyglot (1522)	Aldine (1518)	Sixtine (1587)	Holmes-Parsons (1798–1827)[14]
1 Esdras		•	•	•
Tobit	•	•	•	•
Judith	•	•	•	•
Wisdom of Solomon	•	•	•	•
Sirach	•	•	•	•
1 Maccabees	•	•	•	•
2 Maccabees	•	•	•	•
3 Maccabees	•	•	•	•
4 Maccabees				
Baruch	•	•	•	•
Epistle of Jeremiah	•	•	•	•
Odes		•		
Psalms of Solomon				
Esther: Additions	•	•	•	•
Daniel: Additions	•	•	•	•
Psalm 151		•	•	•

Perhaps someone will say that the Septuagint did exist as a thing, as a book, as a codex. To be sure, there are biblical manuscripts of the Greek Old Testament. Complete Greek Bibles date to the fourth century CE, the three most well known being called the Codex Vaticanus, the Codex Sinaiticus (both from the fourth century), and the Codex Alexandrinus

---

[14] *Vetus Testamentum Graecum cum variis lectionibus*, 5 vols., ed. Robert Holmes and James Parsons (Oxford: Clarendon, 1798–1827).

(fifth century).[15] Actually, Codex Sinaiticus is no longer complete in the Old Testament, but it is complete enough that we can usually determine its original scope. These manuscripts do contain the Septuagint, and they do have deuterocanonical books, but there are several problems with considering these manuscripts as representing some monolithic entity called "the Septuagint." First, and most obviously, these codices do not share the same books. Of the three early complete Greek Bibles, all of them included 1 Esdras, Tobit, Judith, the Wisdom of Solomon, Sirach, Baruch, the Epistle of Jeremiah, and the expanded editions of Esther, Daniel, and the Psalter. Only one of them (Alexandrinus) contained the Odes. One of them (Vaticanus) contained no books of Maccabees, while Alexandrinus contained all four, and Sinaiticus contained only 1 Maccabees and 4 Maccabees.

---

[15] All three of these codices can be consulted online. Codex Sinaiticus: http://codexsinaiticus.org/. Codex Vaticanus: http://digi.vatlib.it/view/MSS_Vat.gr.1209. Codex Alexandrinus: "GA 02," Center for the Study of New Testament Manuscripts, last accessed April 26, 2021, http://www.csntm.org/Manuscript/View/GA_02. The images of Alexandrinus are not directly of the codex; the holding institution (the British Library) has made available only the New Testament (http://www.bl.uk/manuscripts/FullDisplay.aspx?ref=Royal_MS_1_D_VIII). The images of the Old Testament of Alexandrinus that are available online are actually images of the facsimile prepared by E. M. Thompson, *Facsimile of the Codex Alexandrinus*, 4 vols. (London: British Museum, 1879–80).

Deuterocanonical Books in Four Important Greek Codices

This chart shows the deuterocanonical literature contained in the three great Greek full-Bible manuscripts from the fourth and fifth centuries, along with Codex Venetus, a complete copy of the Greek Old Testament from the eighth century.[16]

	Vaticanus	Sainiticus	Alexandrinus	Venetus[17]
1 Esdras	●	●[18]	●	●
Tobit	●	●	●	●
Judith	●	●	●	●
Wisdom of Solomon	●	●	●	●
Sirach	●	●	●	●
1 Maccabees		●	●	●
2 Maccabees			●	●
3 Maccabees			●	●
4 Maccabees		●	●	●
Baruch	●	●[19]	●	●

---

[16] This chart does not preserve the order of the books in each manuscript; for this, see Gallagher and Meade, *Biblical Canon Lists*, 245–50. On the content of these manuscripts, see also Hengel, *Septuagint as Christian Scripture*, 57–60. Vaticanus and Sinaiticus, from the same century, may even derive from the same scriptorium, as argued by Pierre-Maurice Bogaert, "Aux origines de la fixation du canon: Scriptoria, listes et titres. Le Vaticanus et la stichométrie de Mommsen," in *The Biblical Canons*, ed. J.-M. Auwers and H. J. de Jonge (Leuven: Leuven University Press, 2003), 153–76, at 155–56. Bogaert relates the differences between the two manuscripts to the exiles of Athanasius (at 158).

[17] This manuscript in two parts is currently held in Rome and Venice. For a description, see Alfred Rahlfs and Detlef Fraenkel, *Verzeichnis der griechischen Handschriften des Alten Testaments: Die Überlieferung bis zum VIII. Jahrhundert* (Göttingen: Vandenhoeck & Ruprecht, 2004), 344–46 (Rome) and 372–74 (Venice).

[18] None of 1 Esdras is currently extant in the lacunose Codex Sinaiticus, but Ezra-Nehemiah is given the label "Esdras B," making it certain that Esdras A (1 Esdras) originally appeared in the manuscript.

[19] Lamentations immediately follows Jeremiah, but a lacuna in the manuscript stretches from Lamentations ch. 2 to the book of Joel. Despite this lacuna, it is virtually certain that Baruch and the Epistle of Jeremiah followed Lamentations.

	Vaticanus	Sainiticus	Alexandrinus	Venetus
Epistle of Jeremiah	●	● [20]	●	●
Odes			●	
Psalms of Solomon[21]				
Esther: Additions	●	●	●	●
Daniel: Additions	●	● [22]	●	●
Psalm 151	●	●	●	[23]

Perhaps we could say that, in the fourth century, the books shared by Codex Vaticanus and Codex Sinaiticus were considered a part of the Septuagint. We can test that idea by looking at the comments of ancient Christians on the extent of the Septuagint. Unfortunately, they are often frustratingly imprecise in their descriptions of the scope of the work of the Seventy translators. Eusebius of Caesarea, for instance, says merely that the translators worked on the sacred scriptures or the prophecies.[24] Some fourth-century Christians provide more detail and do include the deuterocanonical (or apocryphal, to use their own term) books within the scope of the translation. Epiphanius of Salamis advocates the Jewish canon as the correct Christian Old Testament—and he says that there are twenty-two books of the Jewish canon just as there are twenty-two letters

---

[20] See previous note.

[21] The Psalms of Solomon is contained in none of these codices, but it is listed in the table of contents of Alexandrinus as the final writing of the codex, after the New Testament.

[22] Despite the lacuna in the manuscript covering all of Daniel, it is virtually certain that Sinaiticus originally contained the expanded edition of this book.

[23] Codex Venetus presently contains no portion of the Psalter. For discussion, see Rahlfs-Fraenkel, *Verzeichnis*, 345–46.

[24] See Abraham Wasserstein and David J. Wasserstein, *The Legend of the Septuagint: From Classical Antiquity to Today* (Cambridge: Cambridge University Press, 2006), 109–12, where they quote from Eusebius, *Chronicon*; and *Praeparatio evangelica* 8.

in the Hebrew alphabet[25]—but he asserts that the translators produced versions of the twenty-two books of the Old Testament along with versions of seventy-two books of the apocrypha.[26] Epiphanius does not name the apocryphal books that the Seventy translated. In another context, Epiphanius similarly lists the twenty-two books of the Old Testament and then comments, "Now they [the Jews] also have two other books in dispute [ἐν ἀμφιλέκτῳ], the Wisdom of Sirach and the one of Solomon, separate from some other apocryphal books [χωρὶς ἄλλων τινῶν βιβλίων ἐναπο-κρύφων]."[27] Here Epiphanius is not talking about the Seventy translators, but perhaps he would say that Sirach and the Wisdom of Solomon were among the seventy-two apocryphal books that the Seventy translated and that Epiphanius mentions in his other work. On the other hand, Cyril of Jerusalem also brings up apocrypha in the context of his discussion of the translation, but he seems to distinguish the twenty-two books translated by the Seventy-two translators from the apocryphal writings, which he warns his readers to avoid: "Read the twenty-two books of these [translators], but have nothing to do with the apocryphal writings" (4.35).[28] A later Christian work, the *Dialogue of Timothy and Aquila* from the fifth or sixth century, specifies Tobit, the Wisdom of Solomon, and Sirach as books that the seventy-two translators "gave us in the apocrypha."[29]

So, yes, some fourth-century (and later) Christians thought that the Seventy translators produced versions of more than just the books of the Jewish canon, but it is not clear to me what relationship such conceptions of "the Septuagint" have to the Christian biblical canon or to the great codices of the fourth and

---

[25] Epiphanius's numbering scheme is actually a little more complex; see his *On Weights and Measures* 4–5 (Greek text and English translation) in Gallagher and Meade, *Biblical Canon Lists*, 163–65.

[26] This is the last sentence in *On Weights and Measures* 5; Gallagher and Meade, *Biblical Canon Lists*, 165.

[27] Epiphanius, *Panarion* 86.4; Greek text and English translation in Gallagher and Meade, *Biblical Canon Lists*, 160–62.

[28] Translation slightly adapted from Gallagher and Meade, *Biblical Canon Lists*, 113–14. I thank John D. Meade for help with the interpretation of Cyril.

[29] For Greek text and English translation, see William Varner, *Ancient Jewish-Christian Dialogues: Athanasius and Zacchaeus, Simon and Theophilus, Timothy and Aquila: Introductions, Texts, and Translations* (Lewiston, NY: Edwin Mellen, 2003), 144–45, where the relevant portion appears as §3.17b.

fifth centuries. It is dubious that the fourth- and fifth-century codices represent what their creators or users equated with the Septuagint.

It is even more dubious to imagine that these fourth- and fifth-century codices reveal what first-century Jews considered to be the Septuagint. I have stressed that Jewish sources—first century or otherwise—attribute to the Seventy translators only the Greek Pentateuch. Philo of Alexandria, for instance, an older contemporary of Jesus and Paul, used (sparingly, to be sure) Greek translations of other books of the Hebrew Bible, but he did not consider these books as belonging to the Septuagint, apparently, based on the way he tells the story of the translation, which includes only the books of Moses.[30] The New Testament quotes the Greek translation of many books of Jewish Scripture; we moderns commonly say that the New Testament quotes the Septuagint, or even specifically the Septuagint form of Isaiah or the Psalms. Would the apostle Paul have thought about his quotation of Isaiah in Greek as a quotation of the Septuagint? I cannot think of any reason to answer in the affirmative except that Christians from about a century later (Justin Martyr being the first) asserted that the Septuagint included Isaiah. On the contrary, I assume that a Jew such as Paul in the first century—if he knew anything about the origins of the Greek translations he used—would have accepted the only account of the Greek translations attested by his time: the Greek Pentateuch was produced for King Ptolemy by seventy-two Jewish sages, and other translators produced the Greek versions of the other books. What evidence would support the idea that Paul encountered a collection of Greek Scripture inclusive of the deuterocanonicals, a collection so well defined that citing the Greek text of one of its books implied the acceptance of the entire collection? Exactly this line of argument is pursued by Timothy McLay in the following paragraph:

> The use of the Greek Jewish Scriptures by the NT writers is itself a lethal argument against the view that there was any type of fixed "canon" of Jewish Scriptures in the first century C.E. Even if we were to grant that such a canon existed, NT writers clearly would not have regarded it as the only scriptural authority. The fact that the

---

[30] Philo's account of the translation is summarized in Chapter Two.

OG/LXX text was cited in the NT, in contrast to the Hebrew Scriptures, demonstrates that the Greek Jewish Scriptures as witnessed to
by the LXX were deemed to be Scripture for the Early Church;
therefore, these texts were regarded as normative for life, belief,
and practice. The Early Church's use of the Greek texts as Scripture
mirrors the same authority that the Greek Scriptures received from
the Hellenistic Jewish community. The *Letter of Aristeas*, which
was written to defend the authority of the LXX translation for the
Alexandrian Jewish community, clearly establishes that the Greek
translation of the Pentateuch was Scripture for the Greek-speaking
Jews. The external evidence of our Greek codices, which contain
the apocryphal/deutero-canonical writings, is a simple testimony
to the authority of the Greek Scriptures exercised in the life of the
Early Church.[31]

That is, because the apostles quoted the Septuagint, they must have accepted
the Septuagint as Scripture, the entire Septuagint—not the Septuagint as
defined by ancient Jews but as contained in codices from centuries later.
Obviously, I think this argument is hopelessly flawed. To rephrase the
faulty assertion: because Paul quoted Greek Isaiah, he must have accepted
Greek Tobit as Scripture. How can that argument stand? Is that not like
saying that if one of the Dead Sea Scrolls quotes the proto-MT form of Isaiah, then the author of that scroll must have accepted as Scripture the MT
collection? McLay confuses the issues of text and canon. He assumes that
a New Testament quotation of the Greek version of Isaiah confers on the
translation "scriptural status." And if the Septuagint text is Scripture, then
the Septuagint canon must be Scripture too. Despite the blatant logical flaws
in the argument, this line of reasoning is not at all uncommon, as we will
see at the conclusion of this chapter.

To understand more about why such an approach will not work, we
need to examine the evidence for the development of the biblical canon in
ancient Judaism and early Christianity.

---

[31] R. Timothy McLay, *The Use of the Septuagint in New Testament Research* (Grand
Rapids: Eerdmans, 2003), 144.

The Development of the Jewish Bible

Scholars disagree on the timing of the fixation of the Jewish Bible. Was there a recognized Jewish canon equivalent to the modern Jewish canon already in the second century BCE, or did it develop later, perhaps by the end of the first century CE, or not until the second century CE, or even sometime after that? Each of these positions has been taken by some scholars, and the debate is not close to resolution.

The modern Jewish Bible has twenty-four books—the same books as in the Protestant Old Testament, counted somewhat differently. The Jewish Bible includes the following as single books: Samuel, Kings, Chronicles, Ezra-Nehemiah, and the Twelve Minor Prophets. The Protestant Bible divides these books (two books of Samuel, two books of Kings, etc., and twelve books of the Minor Prophets) so that the total for the Old Testament comes to thirty-nine books (a counting scheme first attested in Augustine).[32] The Jewish Bible is arranged somewhat differently from the Christian Old Testament. It has three sections, as follows:

- Law, or Torah (five books): Genesis, Exodus, Leviticus, Numbers, Deuteronomy
- Prophets, or *Neviim* (eight books): Joshua, Judges, Samuel, Kings, Isaiah, Jeremiah, Ezekiel, Twelve Minor Prophets
- Writings, or *Ketuvim* (eleven books): Ruth, Psalms, Job, Proverbs, Ecclesiastes, Song of Songs, Lamentations, Daniel, Esther, Ezra-Nehemiah, Chronicles

The names of these three sections in Hebrew (Torah, Neviim, Ketuvim: T-N-K) gave rise to the word *Tanak*, which basically means the Jewish Bible. The contents of each of the three sections of the Tanak are standard, but the sequence of books within the third section, the Writings, is not uniform. Sometimes Ruth appears at the beginning of the Writings; other

---

[32] See *On Christian Teaching* 2.8.13, in Gallagher and Meade, *Biblical Canon Lists*, 226–29. Augustine included the deuterocanonical books, so his number for the Old Testament was actually forty-four, with Lamentations (and Baruch?) implicitly counted as part of Jeremiah.

times it appears later in the section, with Psalms or even Chronicles appearing at the beginning. The earliest clear attestation of the threefold arrangement with precisely the contents (not the sequence) listed above is in the Talmud, in a tradition probably going back to around the year 200 CE or a little earlier.[33]

But the Talmud does not contain the earliest claim of a universally accepted Jewish biblical canon. That honor belongs to Josephus, at the end of the first century CE. Unfortunately, Josephus does not spell out the contents of the canon in quite as much detail as we would wish (nor does he use the term *canon*, as we will see). The relevant statement comes in his work called *Against Apion*, in which Josephus argues against a Greek writer named Apion who had disparaged the Jewish way of life. Josephus wants to represent Judaism as noble and ancient. His statement on the ancient Jewish sacred books fits into this context:

> Naturally, then, or rather necessarily—seeing that it is not open to anyone to write of their own accord, nor is there any disagreement present in what is written, but the prophets alone learned, by inspiration of God [κατὰ τὴν ἐπίπνοιαν τὴν ἀπὸ τοῦ θεοῦ], what had happened in the distant and most ancient past and recorded plainly events in their own time just as they occurred—among us there are not thousands of books in disagreement and conflict with each other, but only twenty-two books, containing the record of all time, which are rightly trusted. Five of these are the books of Moses, which contain both the laws and the tradition from the birth of humanity up to his death; this is a period of a little less than 3,000 years. From the death of Moses until Artaxerxes, king of the Persians after Xerxes, the prophets after Moses wrote the history of what took place in their own times in thirteen books; the remaining four books contain hymns to God and instructions for people on life. From Artaxerxes up to our own time every event has been recorded, but this is not judged worthy of the same trust, since the exact line of succession of the prophets did not continue [διὰ τὸ μὴ γενέσθαι τὴν τῶν προφητῶν ἀκριβῆ διαδοχήν]. It is clear in practice how we

---

[33] b. B. Bathra 14b; see Gallagher and Meade, *Biblical Canon Lists*, 65–69.

approach our own writings. Although such a long time has now
passed, no-one has dared to add, to take away, or to alter anything;
and it is innate in every Judean, right from birth, to regard them
as decrees of God [θεοῦ δόγματα], to remain faithful to them and,
if necessary, gladly to die on their behalf. Thus, to date many have
been seen, on many occasions, as prisoners of war suffering torture
and all kinds of deaths in theaters for not letting slip a single word
in contravention of the laws and the records associated with them
[παρὰ τοὺς νόμους καὶ τὰς μετὰ τούτων ἀναγραφάς].[34]

According to Josephus, there are Jewish historical works chronicling world
history from the Creation all the way to his own day (§41), but only the
books written at the time of the Persian king Artaxerxes (Esther's husband,
in Josephus's telling)[35] or before his time deserved full confidence because
they were written under the inspiration of God (§37), whereas after the
time of Artaxerxes, the line of prophets did not continue in exact succession
as before. The books worthy of perfect faith, then, number no more than
twenty-two, but Josephus does not record the names of these books. The five
books of Moses (§39) are obvious, the thirteen prophetic-historical works
less so, as is also true for the four works containing hymns and precepts. We
have already seen that some later Christians also counted, like Josephus, the
Old Testament books as twenty-two, and they often did name the books.
The first writer to do this was Origen, whose list mirrors in content (not
arrangement) the twenty-four-book canon of the Talmud, with Ruth and
Judges counting as a single book, as also Jeremiah and Lamentations, to
bring the number down to twenty-two.[36] Does such an arrangement reflect

---

[34] *Against Apion* 1.37–43; translation by John M. G. Barclay, *Flavius Josephus, Translation and Commentary*, vol. 10, *Against Apion* (Leiden: Brill, 2007), 28–32. See also Barclay's excellent commentary on the same pages. The Greek text of Josephus and further commentary are available in Gallagher and Meade, *Biblical Canon Lists*, 57–65.

[35] See *Antiquities of the Jews* 11.184–296.

[36] Origen supplies this list, which he identifies as "the twenty-two encovenanted books, according to the Hebrew tradition," in his commentary on Psalm 1, and this section was later quoted by Eusebius, *Ecclesiastical History* 6.25.1–2. For Greek text and English translation, see Gallagher and Meade, *Biblical Canon Lists*, 84–87, where there are also comments on the problems presented by Origen's list, such as whether the list represents Origen's own opinion

the intentions of Josephus? Scholars have often thought so. If that is the case, then perhaps the four books of hymns and precepts would include Psalms, Proverbs, Ecclesiastes, and Song of Songs, and perhaps the thirteen prophetic-historical books would include Joshua, Judges with Ruth (cf. *Ant.* 5.318–37), Samuel, Kings, Chronicles, Ezra-Nehemiah (or 1 Esdras),[37] Esther,[38] Isaiah, Jeremiah with Lamentations (cf. *Ant.* 10.78), Ezekiel, the Twelve Minor Prophets (counted as one book), Daniel, and Job. Other scholars have guessed that, in numbering the sacred books as twenty-two, Josephus intended to omit one or two books now in the Jewish Bible, such as Song of Songs or Ecclesiastes (or both). In any case, the twenty-two books allow hardly any room for deuterocanonical literature, although Josephus does include the deuterocanonical additions to Esther in his retelling of the Esther narrative in his other work *Antiquities of the Jews*, in which he similarly included material from 1 Esdras. And Josephus relied extensively on 1 Maccabees in his narration of the events of the second century BCE,[39] although 1 Maccabees clearly falls outside the scope of Josephus's twenty-two books with their chronological limit at the time of Artaxerxes.

Prior to Josephus, there are no explicit statements of this kind, so we must rely on other types of evidence, including quotations and the contents of manuscripts. Without exploring these points in any detail here, we can say that the Dead Sea Scrolls—both in the manuscripts present among the scrolls and in the use made of Scripture by later writings—and the quotations of Scripture in the New Testament indicate that nearly all the books in the modern Jewish Bible were widely considered authoritative Scripture in the first century, with the possible exception of Esther and, perhaps, one or two others (Ecclesiastes? Song of Songs?). There is, furthermore,

---

as to the proper Old Testament canon, and his naming "the Letter" (of Jeremiah) alongside Lamentations as a part of Jeremiah.

[37] Josephus used 1 Esdras at *Ant.* 11.1–158, and Nehemiah at *Ant.* 11.159–83; see Juan Carlos Ossandón Widow, *The Origins of the Canon of the Hebrew Bible: An Analysis of Josephus and 4 Ezra* (Leiden: Brill, 2018), ch. 6.

[38] Josephus knew a version of Esther with more material than in the Hebrew text (cf. *Ant.* 11.184–296); see Ossandón Widow, *Origins of the Canon*, ch. 6.

[39] On Josephus's use of 1 Esdras, the additions to Esther, and 1 Maccabees, see Henry Barclay Swete, *An Introduction to the Old Testament in Greek*, 2nd ed. (Cambridge: Cambridge University Press, 1914), 378–79.

some evidence that a few books not in the Tanak were also considered authoritative, perhaps on par with (some of?) the scriptures in the modern Jewish Bible. In later sections, we will look at some of the evidence of manuscripts and quotations, but for now, we can say that more than a dozen manuscripts of Jubilees and of the various Enochic booklets were found at Qumran, and the only Jewish work outside the modern Jewish Bible to be explicitly quoted in the New Testament is the *Book of Watchers* (the first part of what is now called 1 Enoch; cf. Jude 14–15). Jubilees and 1 Enoch are usually not considered a part of the Septuagint, but some of the deuterocanonical writings were also discovered among the Dead Sea Scrolls: Tobit (four Aramaic scrolls and one in Hebrew), Sirach (two Hebrew scrolls), the Epistle of Jeremiah (one Greek scroll), and Psalm 151 (one Hebrew scroll).

Since Qumran does not offer us an explicit comment on the biblical canon, as Josephus does, we cannot really say for sure what the Qumran community thought about all these writings. Perhaps they regarded all these writings as divine Scripture, perhaps not. None of these deuterocanonical writings were explicitly quoted in the New Testament, and Josephus excluded them from his list of inspired scriptures, as we have seen (with the necessary caveats made a few paragraphs above). As Josephus is the earliest writer to comment so straightforwardly on the biblical canon, we cannot say for sure how widespread his views were. At nearly the same time as Josephus, another Jewish work, known as 4 Ezra, written in Hebrew, seems to imply a firmly established collection of Scripture when it mentions the twenty-four inspired books intended for public use (4 Ezra 14:45). Several decades after Josephus, a Christian writer, Melito of Sardis, offers a list of Old Testament books that very closely resembles (in content, not arrangement) what must have been Josephus's own collection of scriptures, without (most of) the deuterocanonical books. But we also begin to see, at the same time, Christian writers quoting and referring to deuterocanonical literature.

An Alexandrian Canon?

One idea that was popular in the early twentieth century and has made something of a comeback is the Alexandrian Canon theory. The theory was designed to explain how Christians ended up with more books (i.e., the deuterocanon) in their Old Testament than there are in the Tanak. Since Christians used the Greek translation of Scripture, the Septuagint, and since the Septuagint is most strongly associated with Alexandria, Egypt, the home of a vibrant Jewish population in antiquity, some scholars suggested that Christians inherited the canon of Alexandrian Jews, which was broader and more inclusive than the canon of Palestinian Jews. Before this idea became popular in the first half of the twentieth century, scholars had generally accepted the older idea formulated by Elias Levita in 1538 that the Jewish canon had been established by the Men of the Great Synagogue at the time of the scribe Ezra in the fifth century BC.[40] When this theory fell, so that scholars no longer assumed that there was, by the first century, a single and long-established biblical canon on which all Jews agreed, the way was open for the idea that Alexandrian Jews adhered to a canon different from that of Palestinian Jews, an idea first proposed in the eighteenth century.[41] But a lack of evidence for this Alexandrian Jewish canon also led

---

[40] See Elias Levita, *The Massoreth Ha-Massoreth*, ed. and trans. Christian D. Ginsburg (London: Longman, Green, Reader, & Dyer, 1867), 120. On the reception of this idea of Levita's, see Herbert Edward Ryle, *The Canon of the Old Testament* (London: Macmillan, 1892), 239–72, who shows that it was Johannes Buxtorf's (the elder) influence that led to the widespread acceptance of Levita's idea. The theory associating the biblical canon with the Men of the Great Synagogue was fatally critiqued by A. Kuenen, *Over de mannen der Groote Synagoge* (Amsterdam: C. G. van der Post, 1876). The rise and fall of the theory is also narrated by Albert C. Sundberg, *The Old Testament of the Early Church* (Cambridge, MA: Harvard University Press, 1964), 25–40.

[41] For a brief account of the history of the Alexandrian Canon theory, see Gilles Dorival, Marguerite Harl, and Olivier Munnich, *La Bible grecque des Septante*, 2nd ed. (Paris: Cerf, 1994), 112–19. However, despite their telling, and that of Sundberg, *Old Testament*, 18–19, the idea was not first proposed by John Ernest Grabe, either in the translation of his edition of the *Epistle of Aristeas* (*The History of the Seventy-Two Interpreters* [London: Hooke and Caldecott, 1715]), the English translation of which and the preface being, in any case, produced by Thomas Lewis and not Grabe (see https://sanctushieronymus.blogspot.com/2017/12/grabe-history-of-seventy-two.html), or anywhere else. The idea was first proposed, apparently, by Francis Lee in the Prolegomena to the second volume of Grabe's edition of the Septuagint based on Codex Alexandrinus: *Hē palaia diathēkē kata tous Hebdomēkonta*, vol. 2 (Oxford: E Theatro Sheldoniano, 1719), Chapter 1, Proposition 24, §§75–77. But the idea was more forcefully and influentially argued by Johann Salomo Semler, *Abhandlung von freier Untersuchung des Canon* (Halle: C. H. Hemmerde, 1771). For a brief account, see Harl, Dorival, and Munnich, *Bible grecque des Septante*, 112–13. On the early history of the idea, see Stephen B. Chapman, "Modernity's Canonical Crisis: Historiography and Theology

to the demise of the theory, especially after the forceful critique by Albert Sunderg in his Harvard dissertation, published in 1964.[42] Martin Hengel has more recently asserted, "We cannot prove the existence of a genuine Jewish, pre-Christian collection of canonical value, unambiguously and clearly delimited, distinguishable through its greater scope from the canon of the Hebrew Bible in the realm of the historical books and wisdom writings and written in Greek."[43]

Several prominent scholars have rehabilitated some version of the theory,[44] but difficulties remain. One problem with the Alexandrian Canon idea is that our major representative of Alexandrian Judaism, Philo—a contemporary of Jesus—cites the Pentateuch constantly, occasionally cites several other books now in the Tanak, but never quotes Jewish Scripture that did not find a place in the Tanak. This heightened prominence of the Pentateuch in Alexandrian Judaism has led some scholars to propose that the books of Moses alone served in Alexandria as canonical Scripture, the very opposite of the usual Alexandrian Canon idea.[45] Whether the literary coherence of the Greek writings provides evidence for a Greek canon larger than the Tanak is debatable, as is the extent of the perceived literary coherence. Hengel again: "It is fundamental that the documents in their Greek form comprise no unity whatsoever; rather, each must be investigated individually, although they all naturally draw on the great linguistic reservoir of the Greek Pentateuch and are, to a significant degree, linguistically

---

in Collision," in *Hebrew Bible/Old Testament: The History of Its Interpretation*, vol. 3, *From Modernism to Post-Modernism (The Nineteenth and Twentieth Centuries)*, ed. Magne Sæbø (Göttingen: Vandenhoeck & Ruprecht, 2013), 651–87.

[42] Sundberg, *Old Testament*.

[43] Martin Hengel, *The Septuagint as Christian Scripture: Its Prehistory and the Problem of Its Canon* (Edinburgh: T&T Clark, 2002), 19; see the similar comment at 22.

[44] See the discussion and references in Armin Lange, "Canonical History of the Hebrew Bible," in *Textual History of the Bible*, vol. 1A, *The Hebrew Bible: Overview Articles*, ed. Armin Lange and Emanuel Tov (Leiden: Brill, 2016), 35–48, at 39–40 (§1.1.2.1.2).

[45] David M. Carr, "Canonization in the Context of Community: An Outline of the Formation of the Tanakh and the Christian Bible," in *A Gift of God in Due Season: Essays on Scripture and Community in Honor of James A. Sanders* ed. Richard D. Weis and David M. Carr (Sheffield: Sheffield Academic, 1996), 22–64, at 35; Anneli Aejmelaeus, "Die Septuaginta als Kanon," in *Kanon in Konstruktion und Dekonstruktion*, ed. Eve-Marie Beker and Stefan Scholz (Berlin: de Gruyter, 2012), 315–28.

shaped by it."[46] Patristic authors who explicitly reflect on the relationship of their canon to that of the Jews did not think that they received a canon from Jews inclusive of the deuterocanonical books; often the biblical canon promoted by patristic authors excluded these books, and those authors who included the deuterocanonical books within the canon did so in full knowledge that they were expanding the canon beyond what Jews accepted.[47] If we can believe later Christian witnesses, who at times attribute their lists of Old Testament books to Jewish sources,[48] the biblical canon of at least some Greek-speaking Jews resembled closely that of the rabbis, in terms of scope if not in terms of sequence.[49] The deuterocanonical literature was important and influential within Hellenistic Judaism, but it is hard to be more specific regarding its status in relation to the books of the Tanak.[50]

The Christian Old Testament: Citations

We have briefly reviewed some of the data available on the development of the Jewish Bible. Now we turn our attention to the Christian Old Testament, keeping an eye on the relationship between the Septuagint and the Old Testament canon as ancient Christians understood that relationship. The data on hand on the development of the Christian biblical canon include

---

[46] Hengel, *Septuagint as Christian Scripture*, 84.

[47] For the biblical canons promoted by patristic authors, see Gallagher and Meade, *Biblical Canon Lists*. For a discussion of Christians promoting a canon explicitly wider than the Jewish canon, see Edmon L. Gallagher, *Hebrew Scripture in Patristic Biblical Theory: Canon, Language, Text* (Leiden: Brill, 2012), 53–60. Of course, we may doubt whether these patristic authors understood the historical process leading to their own biblical canon.

[48] Cf. esp. Origen, in Eusebius, *Ecclesiastical History* 6.25.1–2.

[49] Gilles Dorival, "L'apport des Pères de l'Église à la question de la clôture du canon de l'Ancien Testament," in *The Biblical Canons*, ed. J.-M. Auwers and H. J. de Jonge (Leuven: Leuven University Press, 2003), 81–110; Dorival, "La formation du canon biblique de l'Ancien Testament: Position actuelle et problems," in *Recueils normatifs et canons dans l'Antiquité: Perspectives Nouvelles sur la formation des canons juif et chrétien dans leur context culturel*, ed. Enrico Norelli (Prahins: Zèbre, 2004), 83–112.

[50] See Hengel, *Septuagint as Christian Scripture*, ch. 4, where he explores the "Diaspora Jewish canon" by examining the prologue to Sirach; Philo, *On the Contemplative Life* 25; and Josephus, *Against Apion* 1.37–43. Hengel's main point seems to be that we do not know much about the Diaspora Jewish canon.

patristic citations of Jewish writings, lists of canonical books, and Greek biblical manuscripts.[51] We will examine each of these categories sequentially, starting with citations.

We have just seen that Philo never quotes the deuterocanonical literature; there are, perhaps, a few allusions to Wisdom and Sirach.[52] Earlier we also noticed the limited use of the deuterocanonical literature in Josephus. The reception of apocrypha in the New Testament has received attention since ancient times and demands somewhat lengthier treatment. The New Testament contains one explicit quotation of a Jewish book not included in the Tanak—the quotation of the *Book of Watchers* (1 Enoch 1:9) in Jude 14–15.[53] This quotation in Jude has influenced the way both Jude and the Enochic writings were subsequently received, with some (e.g., Tertullian) thinking that Jude conferred scriptural authority on Enoch and others thinking that the quotation of Enoch cast doubt on the scriptural status of Jude. Other New Testament passages that have been cited as containing quotations of extracanonical books include Matthew 27:9, Luke 11:49, John 7:38–39, 1 Corinthians 2:9, and Ephesians 5:14, but none of the quotations in these passages mirror text found in any extant work, though some patristic authors claimed to have had access to apocryphal works containing such text.[54] As for the books traditionally considered deuterocanonical, the New

---

[51] See Harl, Dorival, and Munnich, *Bible grecque des Septante*, 321–22, who also mention patristic comments as a possible avenue of research on the canon.

[52] See J. Allenbach, ed., *Biblia Patristica: Supplément* (Paris: Éditions du centre national de la recherché scientifique, 1982). For discussion, see Hengel, *Septuagint as Christian Scripture*, 78–79.

[53] See Bruk Ayele Asale, *1 Enoch as Christian Scripture: A Study of the Reception and Appropriation of 1 Enoch in Jude and the Ethiopian Orthodox Tewahǝdo Canon* (Eugene, OR: Pickwick, 2020). See also J. Hultin, "Jude's Citation of 1 Enoch," in *Jewish and Christian Scriptures: The Function of "Canonical" and "Non-canonical" Religious Texts*, ed. L. M. McDonald and J. H. Charlesworth (London: T&T Clark, 2010), 113–28; N. J. Moore, "Is Enoch Also among the Prophets? The Impact of Jude's Citation of *1 Enoch* on the Reception of Both Texts in the Early Church," *Journal of Theological Studies* 64 (2013): 498–515.

[54] The list of NT passages is reproduced from G. Wildeboer, *The Origin of the Canon of the Old Testament: An Historico-Critical Inquiry* (London: Luzac, 1895), 52; see also Hengel, *Septuagint as Christian Scripture*, 109–10. As Wildeboer notes, Jerome claimed to have seen a Jeremiah apocryphon with the words of Matthew 27:9 (*Comm. Matt.* 27:9), but Jerome himself rejected this explanation for Matthew's quotation and instead insisted that the Evangelist was quoting the prophet Zechariah without concern for precise wording; see Edmon L. Gallagher, "Writings Labeled 'Apocrypha' in Latin Patristic Sources," in *Sacra Scriptura: How*

Testament contains no explicit quotations but some strong allusions, as we will see. The second century saw more Christian use of the deuterocanonicals, but Hengel also points out that evidence for such use is particularly prominent in the West, whereas these books "are scarcely transmitted in the East until Clement of Alexandria."[55] These writings became increasingly important for Christians, though even Origen still interacts with them relatively infrequently.[56]

NEW TESTAMENT

There is a remarkable similarity between the books popular at Qumran (judging by number of scrolls) and those most frequently quoted in the New Testament. In both cases, the three most popular books are Deuteronomy, Isaiah, and the Psalter. The New Testament quotes the Old Testament hundreds of times, and there are quotations of, or strong allusions to, all the books of the Tanak, except for Esther, Ecclesiastes, and Song of Songs.[57] Some books outside the Tanak also exerted an influence on the New Testament writers. The connections between the New Testament, particularly

---

"Non-Canonical" Texts Functioned in Early Judaism and Early Christianity, ed. James H. Charlesworth and Lee Martin McDonald (London: Bloomsbury, 2014), 1–14, at 12. Origen (*Comm. Matt.* ser. 117) said that the Apocalypse of Elijah was the source of 1 Corinthians 2:9, but Athanasius (*Epist.* 39.26–32) identified Paul's source as Isaiah 29:18–19, while Jerome (*Epist.* 57.9) pointed instead to Isaiah 64:4. Epiphanius (*Pan.* 42.12.3.37) said that the words quoted in Ephesians 5:14 circulate "in Elijah" (the Apocalypse of Elijah?), but his editor Holl suggested we emend the text to say "in Isaiah" so that Epiphanius would mean that Paul quoted loosely from Isaiah 26:19; see K. Holl, ed., *Epiphanius II: Panarion (Haer. 34–64)*, rev. J. Dummer, GCS 31 (Berlin: Akademie Verlag, 1980), 180; Frank Williams, trans., *The Panarion of Epiphanius of Salamis, Book 1 (Sects 1–46)* 2nd ed. (Leiden: Brill, 2009), 359.

[55] Hengel, *Septuagint as Christian Scripture*, 116; see the wider discussion at 112–22. On Clement of Alexandria, see J. L. Kovacs, "Introduction. Clement as Scriptural Exegete: Overview and History of Research," in *Clement's Biblical Exegesis: Proceedings of the Second Colloquium on Clement of Alexandria*, ed. V. Černušková, J. L. Kovacs, and J. Plátová (Leiden: Brill, 2017), 1–37, esp. 4–9.

[56] See the comments of Hengel, *Septuagint as Christian Scripture*, 67; but see also Gallagher, *Hebrew Scripture in Patristic Biblical Theory*, 30–49.

[57] But on Esther, compare Mark 6:23 with Esther 5:3, 6; 7:2. On Ecclesiastes, compare Romans 8:20 with Ecclesiastes 1:2. I am assuming that the Minor Prophets constitute a single book; there are no quotations of, or very strong allusions to, Obadiah, Nahum, and Zephaniah, but presumably they were included within the Book of the Twelve.

Paul, and the Wisdom of Solomon have long intrigued scholars.[58] The New Testament neither quotes nor mentions any literature commonly considered deuterocanonical, though there are several passages in the New Testament that probably have been influenced by the deuterocanonical literature in various ways. Christian writings after the New Testament, up to the end of the second century, incorporate some more explicit interaction with the deuterocanonical literature. At the end of the second century and the beginning of the third, beginning especially with Clement of Alexandria and then Origen, Christian writings feature many quotations of the deuterocanonical literature. Here we will survey the use of deuterocanonical literature in the New Testament and in second-century Christian literature.

The use of the deuterocanonical literature in the New Testament is well-trod territory for scholarly inquiry.[59] Since the New Testament does not actually quote deuterocanonical literature, scholars must compare New Testament passages to deuterocanonical literature and evaluate possible points of contact. Standard hand-editions of the New Testament contain lists of possible allusions. Based on an examination of such a list,[60] the following represents the parallels that I consider most likely to demonstrate literary dependence.

Probably the most obvious case is Hebrews 11:35: "Women received their dead by resurrection. Others were tortured, refusing to accept release, in order to obtain a better resurrection." Who are those who were tortured so

---

[58] Folker Blischke, "Die *Sapientia Salomonis* und Paulus," in *Sapientia Salomonis (Weisheit Salomos)*, ed. Karl-Wilhelm Niebuhr (Tübingen: Mohr Siebeck, 2015), 273–91; Lim, *Formation of the Jewish Canon*, 169–72.

[59] Wildeboer, *Origin of the Canon*, 52; A. E. Breen, *A General and Critical Introduction to the Study of Holy Scripture* (Rochester, NY: Smith, 1897), 61–62; Sundberg, *Old Testament*, 26, 54–55, who cites 152 NT passages that might rely in some way on a deuterocanonical book. He pulls this list from the margins of the twenty-second edition of Nestle-Aland's *Novum Testamentum Graece*. See further discussion in Lee Martin McDonald, *The Formation of the Biblical Canon*, 2 vols. (London: Bloomsbury, 2017), 1.299–314 (positively inclined toward NT use of deuterocanonical books); Timothy H. Lim, *The Formation of the Jewish Canon* (New Haven, CT: Yale University Press, 2013), ch. 9 and Appendix 4 (negatively inclined to NT use of deuterocanonical books as Scripture). Also: Christoph Markschies, "Die Septuaginta als Bibel der Kirche? Beobachtungen aus Vergangenheit und Gegenwart," in *Die Göttinger Septuaginta: Ein editorisches Jahrhundertprojekt*, ed. R. G. Kratz and B. Neuschäfer (Berlin: de Gruyter, 2013), 135–54, at 150.

[60] I have used the third appendix in the Nestle-Aland *Novum Testamentum Graece*, 28th ed. (Stuttgart: Deutsche Bibelgesellschaft, 2012), 869–74.

that they might obtain a better resurrection? It is hard not to see a reference here to the stories of the Maccabean martyrs, especially as narrated
in 2 Maccabees 6–7, which includes the story of old Eleazar (6:18–31) and
the seven brothers and their mother (chapter 7), all of whom refused to eat
pork despite the king's command. Some of the brothers explicitly mentioned
the resurrection for which they were hoping (7:9, 11, 13; and the mother,
7:23, 29). In the first century, these martyrs for the Jewish faith inspired
the author of 4 Maccabees, whose entire book constituted a philosophical/
theological reflection on their courage. And the stories of these Maccabean
martyrs became very influential later in the Christian tradition.[61]

Another example that is very suggestive involves the common themes
between Romans 1:19–32 and the Wisdom of Solomon 13–15. Here
again (as in Hebrews above), the parallels are not so much in common
language as in common thoughts, and in this case there are several common thoughts in each passage, increasing the likelihood that Paul had
read the Wisdom of Solomon and that the exposition of paganism in
Wisdom 13–15 influenced the apostle's own expressions in Romans 1.
Here are just a few of the most intriguing passages from the beginning
of the section in Wisdom:

Wisdom 13:1
For all people who were ignorant of God were foolish by nature; and they were
unable from the good things that are seen to know the one who exists, nor did
they recognize the artisan while paying heed to his works.

Wisdom 13:4–5
And if people were amazed at their power and working, let them perceive from
them how much more powerful is the one who formed them. For from the
greatness and beauty of created things comes a corresponding perception of
their Creator.

Wisdom 13:8
Yet again, not even they are to be excused.

---

[61] See, e.g., Jan Willem van Henten, "The Maccabean Martyrs as Models in Early Christian Writings," in *The Jew as Legitimation: Jewish-Gentile Relations beyond Antisemitism and
Philosemitism*, ed. David J. Wertheim (London: Palgrave Macmillan, 2017), 16–32.

Look at Romans 1:19–32 with these passages of Wisdom in mind and see for yourself if you think Paul had read the Wisdom of Solomon.

The passages below are further examples in which there is some affinity between the New Testament and the deuterocanonical literature. Again, these are the most obvious cases, in my opinion.[62] That is not to say that I believe in each case that the New Testament author was drawing on the cited deuterocanonical passage, but I consider each of the following suggested parallels to be plausible and worthy of reflection:

Hebrews 1:3

He is the reflection of God's glory and the exact imprint of God's very being.	ὃς ὢν ἀπαύγασμα τῆς δόξης καὶ χαρακτὴρ τῆς ὑποστάσεως αὐτοῦ.

Wisdom 7:26

For she is a reflection of eternal light, a spotless mirror of the working of God, and an image of his goodness.	ἀπαύγασμα γάρ ἐστιν φωτὸς ἀϊδίου καὶ ἔσοπτρον ἀκηλίδωτον τῆς τοῦ θεοῦ ἐνεργείας καὶ εἰκὼν τῆς ἀγαθότητος αὐτοῦ.

1 Peter 1:6–7

In this you rejoice, even if now for a little while [ὀλίγον ἄρτι] you have had to suffer various trials [λυπηθέντας ἐν ποικίλοις πειρασμοῖς], so that the genuineness of your faith [τὸ δοκίμιον ὑμῶν τῆς πίστεως]—being more precious than gold [πολυτιμότερον χρυσίου] that, though perishable [τοῦ ἀπολλυμένου], is tested by fire [διὰ πυρὸς δὲ δοκιμαζομένου]—may be found to result in praise and glory and honor when Jesus Christ is revealed [ἐν ἀποκαλύψει Ἰησοῦ Χριστοῦ].

Wisdom 3:3–7

And their going from us to be their destruction;
    but they are at peace.
For though in the sight of others they were punished,
    their hope is full of immortality.

---

[62] I have not cited every suggestive parallel between the New Testament and Sirach, since there are so many; see further Sirach 7:14 / Matthew 6:7; Sirach 7:34 / Romans 12:15; Sirach 11:19 / Luke 12:19–20; Sirach 14:1 / James 3:2; Sirach 15:11–20 / James 1:13; Sirach 28:2 / Matthew 6:14–15; Sirach 28:12 / James 3:10; Sirach 29:11–13 / Matthew 6:2–4. On these parallels, see David A. deSilva, *The Jewish Teachers of Jesus, James, and Jude: What Earliest Christianity Learned from the Apocrypha and Pseudepigrapha* (Oxford: Oxford University Press, 2012), 58–85.

Having been disciplined a little [ὀλίγα παιδευθέντες], they will receive great
   good,
   because God tested them [ὁ θεὸς ἐπείρασεν αὐτοὺς] and found them
      worthy of himself [εὗρεν αὐτοὺς ἀξίους ἑαυτοῦ];
like gold [ὡς χρυσὸν] in the furnace he tried them [ἐδοκίμασεν αὐτοὺς],
   and like a sacrificial burnt offering he accepted them.
In the time of their visitation they will shine forth,
   and will run like sparks through the stubble.

Sirach 2:5
For gold is tested in the fire [ἐν πυρὶ δοκιμάζεται χρυσὸς], and those found
acceptable, in the furnace of humiliation.

James 1:19
You must understand this, my beloved: let everyone be [ἔστω δὲ πᾶς ἄνθρωπος]
quick to listen [ταχὺς εἰς τὸ ἀκοῦσαι], slow to speak [βραδὺς εἰς τὸ λαλῆσαι],
slow to anger [βραδὺς εἰς ὀργήν].

Sirach 4:29
Do not be reckless in your speech [μὴ γίνου θρασὺς ἐν γλώσσῃ σου], or sluggish
[νωθρὸς] and remiss [παρειμένος] in your deeds.

Sirach 5:11
Be quick to hear [Γίνου ταχὺς ἐν ἀκροάσει σου], but deliberate [ἐν μακροθυμίᾳ]
in answering.

1 Corinthians 6:13
"Food [τὰ βρώματα] is meant for the stomach [τῇ κοιλίᾳ] and the stomach
for food," and God will destroy both one and the other. The body is meant not for
fornication but for the Lord, and the Lord for the body.

Sirach 36:23
The stomach [κοιλία] will take any food [πᾶν βρῶμα], yet one food is better
[κάλλιον] than another.

Matthew 11:28–30
Come to me, all you that are weary and are carrying heavy burdens, and I will
give you rest. Take my yoke upon you, and learn from me; for I am gentle and
humble in heart, and you will find rest for your souls. For my yoke is easy, and my
burden is light.[63]

---

[63] See Richard B. Hays, *Echoes of Scripture in the Gospels* (Waco, TX: Baylor University
Press, 2016), 153–59.

Sirach 51:23–27

Draw near to me, you who are uneducated,
    and lodge in the house of instruction.
Why do you say you are lacking in these things,
    and why do you endure such great thirst?
I opened my mouth and said,
    Acquire wisdom for yourselves without money.
Put your neck under her yoke,
    and let your souls receive instruction;
    it is to be found close by.
See with your own eyes that I have labored but little
    and found for myself much serenity.

APOSTOLIC FATHERS

The Apostolic Fathers is a collection of fifteen or so early Christian writings, usually from the late first century through the second century, sometimes a bit later. This collection contains our earliest Christian documents outside the New Testament.[64] Much like in the case of the New Testament, the Apostolic Fathers may at times be relying on the deuterocanonical literature without actually saying so; it may just be an allusion, a parallel in thought influenced by the earlier Jewish writing. There are not many suggested allusions.[65] But unlike in the New Testament, the Apostolic Fathers contains one explicit reflection on a deuterocanonical book (1 Clement 55). The following are the parallels that I find most plausibly indicating literary dependence:

---

[64] See the edition and translation of Michael W. Holmes, ed., *The Apostolic Fathers: Greek Texts and English Translations*, 3rd ed. (Grand Rapids: Baker, 2007). I have used this edition for all original language quotations and English translations.

[65] Hengel, *Septuagint as Christian Scripture*, 66–70, says that the Apostolic Fathers "ignored these documents almost entirely," with the exception of 1 Clement. For the use of deuterocanonical literature in early Christianity, see Hengel, 114–27. See also Oskar Skarsaune, "The Question of Old Testament Canon and Text in the Early Greek Church," in *Hebrew Bible/Old Testament: The History of Its Interpretation*, vol. 1, *From the Beginnings to the Middle Ages (Until 1300)*, ed. Magne Sæbø (Göttingen: Vandenhoeck & Ruprecht, 1996), 443–50. For a survey of suggested parallels, aside from Hengel see also Breen, *General and Critical Introduction*, 62–67.

1 Clement 3.4

Instead, all follow the lusts of their
evil heart, inasmuch as they have
assumed that attitude of unrighteous
and ungodly jealousy through which,
in fact, death entered into the world.

ζῆλον ... δι᾽οὗ καὶ θάνατος εἰσῆλθεν
εἰς τὸν κόσμον.

Wisdom 2:24

But through the devil's envy death
entered the world.

φθόνῳ δὲ διαβόλου θάνατος εἰσῆλθεν
εἰς τὸν κόσμον.

1 Clement 27.5

Who will say to him,
"What have you done?"
Or who will resist the might of his
strength?

τίς ἐρεῖ αὐτῷ
τί ἐποίησας;
ἢ τίς ἀντιστήσεται τῷ κράτει τῆς
ἰσχύος αὐτοῦ;

Wisdom 12:12

For who will say,
"What have you done?"
or will resist your judgment?

τίς γὰρ ἐρεῖ
τί ἐποίησας;
ἢ τίς ἀντιστήσεται τῷ κρίματί σου;

1 Clement 55.3–6

Many women, being strengthened by the grace of God, have performed many manly
deeds. The blessed Judith, when the city was under siege, asked the elders to permit
her to go to the enemy's camp. So she exposed herself to peril and went out for love
of her country and of her besieged people, and the Lord delivered Holophernes
into the hand of a woman. To no less danger did Esther, who was perfect in faith,
expose herself.

The continuation of the passage incorporates elements from the deuterocanonical additions to Esther.

Epistle of Barnabas 19:9 (cf. Didache 4.5)

Do not be someone who stretches out
the hands to receive, but withdraws
them when it comes to giving.

μὴ γίνου πρὸς μὲν τὸ λαβεῖν ἐκτείνων
τὰς χεῖρας, πρὸς δὲ τὸ δοῦναι
συσπῶν.

Sirach 4:36

Do not let your hand be stretched
out to receive and closed when it is
time to give.

μὴ ἔστω ἡ χείρ σου ἐκτεταμένη εἰς
τὸ λαβεῖν καὶ ἐν τῷ ἀποδιδόναι
συνεσταλμένη.

Epistle of Barnabas 6.7

For the prophet says concerning Israel: "Woe to their soul, for they have plotted an evil plot against themselves by saying, 'Let us bind the righteous one, because he is troublesome to us.'"

οὐαὶ τῇ ψυχῇ αὐτῶν, ὅτι βεβούλευνται βουλὴν πονηρὰν καθ᾽ ἑαυτῶν, εἰπόντες· Δήσωμεν τὸν δίκαιον, ὅτι δύσχρηστος ἡμῖν ἐστίν.

Isaiah 3:9–10

Woe to their soul! Because they have given evil counsel against themselves, saying, "Let us bind the just, for he is a nuisance to us." Therefore they shall eat the fruit of their works.

οὐαὶ τῇ ψυχῇ αὐτῶν, διότι βεβούλευνται βουλὴν πονηρὰν καθ᾽ ἑαυτῶν εἰπόντες Δήσωμεν τὸν δίκαιον, ὅτι δύσχρηστος ἡμῖν ἐστιν· τοίνυν τὰ γενήματα τῶν ἔργων αὐτῶν φάγονται.

Wisdom 2:12

Let us lie in wait for the righteous man, because he is inconvenient to us and opposes our actions.

ἐνεδρεύσωμεν τὸν δίκαιον, ὅτι δύσχρηστος ἡμῖν ἐστιν καὶ ἐναντιοῦται τοῖς ἔργοις ἡμῶν.

Polycarp, *Epistle to the Philippians* 10.2

When you are able to do good, do not put it off, because charity delivers one from death (*quia eleemosyna de morte liberat*).

Tobit 4:10

For almsgiving delivers from death and keeps you from going into the Darkness.

διότι ἐλεημοσύνη ἐκ θανάτου ῥύεται καὶ οὐκ ἐᾷ εἰσελθεῖν εἰς τὸ σκότος.

Tobit 12:9

For almsgiving saves from death and purges away every sin.

ἐλεημοσύνη γὰρ ἐκ θανάτου ῥύεται, καὶ αὐτὴ ἀποκαθαριεῖ πᾶσαν ἁμαρτίαν.

Hengel does not regard this parallel as strong enough to suggest actual literary dependence because the comment is "a basic moral injunction," though he points to 2 Clement 16.4 as offering a better possible allusion to Tobit.[66]

---

[66] Hengel, *Septuagint as Christian Scripture*, 116.

CITATIONS AND SEPTUAGINT

In the later second century and into the third century, Christian inter-action with the deuterocanonical literature became more common.[67] At the same time, Christians started to compose lists of authoritative biblical books (i.e., canon lists), usually excluding the deuterocanoni-cal literature, sometimes including some of it. For our purposes, how should we interpret these citations? Do they indicate that these books formed a part of the biblical canon of the authors that cite them? More pertinently for our discussion, do they indicate that these books were a part of the Septuagint? Some early Christian writers clearly did regard the deuterocanonical books as fully canonical, because they drew up a canon list that included these books (e.g., Augustine). Other writers drew up a canon list without these books but still cited them. Athanasius himself cites the Wisdom of Solomon three times under the label γραφή (*graphē*, "writing" or "scripture"),[68] though in his canon list, this book appears among the *anaginoskomena* (books for reading but not in the canon) intended for catechumens. He also freely cites other writings in his *anaginoskomena*, including Sirach and the Shepherd of Hermas.[69] According to Johan Lemans, "There is no difference between 'canonical books' and books to be read to the catechumens,"[70] judging by Athanasius's citations. Cyril of Jerusalem—another proponent of the twenty-two-book

---

[67] For a list of parallels and explicit citations, see Breen, *General and Critical Introduction*, 67 (Athenagoras), 68–70 (Hippolytus), 70–73 (Irenaeus), 73–84 (Clement of Alexandria), 85–116 (Origen), 126–28 (Tertullian), and 129–39 (Cyprian).

[68] See J. Lemans, "Athanasius and the Book of Wisdom," *ETL* 73 (1997): 349–68. The three citations with γραφή include *Contra Gentes* 11 (Wis. 14:12); 17 (Wis. 14:21); *Contra Arianos* 2.79 (Wis. 6:24).

[69] On Sirach, see J. Lemans, "Canon and Quotation: The Case of Athanasius' Use of Jesus Sirach," in Auwers and de Jonge, *Biblical Canons*, 265–77. On the Shepherd, see Athanasius, *Incarnatione Verbi Dei* 3 ("most edifying"), 18; *Ep. Fest.* 11.4 ("if any man is not offended at his testimony"); *De Decretis* 18 (350/1, citing Mand. 9.8); *Ep. Fest.* 39.7; *Ad Afros Ep.* 5.

[70] Lemans, "Athanasius and the Book of Wisdom," 368. See further Sundberg, *Old Testament*, 140–41; D. Brakke, "Canon Formation and Social Conflict in Fourth-Century Egypt: Athanasius of Alexandria's Thirty-Ninth Festal Letter," *Harvard Theological Review* 87 (1994): 395–419, at 397.

Old Testament—occasionally cites Wisdom and Sirach.[71] Those early Christians who do not transmit a canon list also make use of the *anaginoskomena*, such as Didymus the Blind.[72] It is doubtful that we should interpret these citations as an indication that the canon lists do not accurately represent the views of their authors,[73] but these citations rather suggest that the biblical canon of these authors did not contain all the scriptures they found helpful or edifying. As for whether these authors thought that all these writings were included in a collection of translations of the Seventy, I see no reason based on the citations to reach that sort of conclusion. It was not that the "Septuagint canon" exerted pressure on these early Christians and led them to cite a variety of scriptures in that canon; I do not believe that there was such a canon. After all, the earliest explicit citations by Christians of Jewish books outside the Tanak involve the Enochic literature (not only Jude 14–15 but also Barnabas 4.3), which is never transmitted within Greek manuscripts alongside biblical books, which never appears in the canon lists of early Christians, and which no one today (I believe) claims was a part of the Septuagint. These citations do not exhibit how the Septuagint influenced the biblical canon; rather, they show that early Christians (like all Christians throughout time and culture) read a variety of books, some not in the Tanak, and considered many works to be helpful in articulating their understanding of religion.

The Christian Old Testament: Canon Lists

Earlier we looked at the list of sacred books Josephus enumerated in his late-first-century work *Against Apion*. Around a century after Josephus, Christians started developing lists of sacred books.[74] Eusebius of Caesarea

---

[71] See *Catechetical Lectures*. 9.2, 16 (Wis. 13:5); *Catech.* 11.19 (Sir. 1:30; 3:22); *Catech.* 6.4 (Sir. 3:21–22).

[72] Bart D. Ehrman, "The New Testament Canon of Didymus the Blind," *Vigiliae Christianae* 37 (1983): 1–21.

[73] On such a suggestion in relation to Athanasius, see Ehrman, "New Testament Canon of Didymus the Blind," 18–19; Sundberg, *Old Testament*, 140–42.

[74] All the early lists are printed in original text and translation with notes in Gallagher and Meade, *Biblical Canon Lists*.

preserves our two earliest datable lists of the Old Testament books from Christian sources. Melito of Sardis traveled to Palestine in about 170 CE for research on the Bible. The list he submitted to his "brother" Onesimus closely matches the Tanak (in content, not arrangement) except, possibly, at two significant points: the list as preserved omits the book of Esther,[75] and it possibly includes the Wisdom of Solomon. Regarding the latter point, Melito mentions the books "of Solomon," beginning with Παροιμίαι ἡ καὶ Σοφία, a phrase probably to be translated "Proverbs, which is also Wisdom." If this translation is correct, Melito would be explaining that "Wisdom" is another title for the book of Proverbs, a point mentioned also by Eusebius (*Ecclesiastical History* 4.22.9). It seems that Rufinus of Aquileia, Eusebius's early fifth-century Latin translator, already interpreted the phrase in this way (*Proverbia quae et Sapientia*). Alternatively, Melito may intend to say, "Proverbs, as well as his Wisdom," thus indicating two distinct books, the latter being the Wisdom of Solomon.[76]

Origen's list of Old Testament books names "the Hebrews" as its source, and it does indeed stick closely to the rabbinic canon (the Tanak).[77] Origen names the Epistle of Jeremiah as included within the title Jeremiah (as common at the time), and after his list of twenty-two books (with the accidentally omitted Twelve Prophets), he notes that Maccabees stands "outside of these" (ἔξω τούτων). It is not clear whether Origen is advocating this canonical list for the Christian Old Testament or whether he is merely reporting the Jewish canon, though Eusebius, the preserver of the list, apparently assumes the former interpretation.[78]

---

[75] Possibly this omission results from scribal error (cf. the omission of the Twelve Prophets from Origen's list preserved at Eusebius, *Ecclesiastical History* 6.25.1–2). But a few other Christian lists also omit Esther, apparently reflecting in part the Jewish hesitation regarding the book; see Gallagher and Meade, *Biblical Canon Lists*, 270–71.

[76] If Melito refers to the Wisdom of Solomon, we might find a possibly contemporary parallel in the Muratorian Fragment, which also mentions Wisdom (lines 69–70). The date and provenance of the Muratorian Fragment are disputed, but traditionally it was ascribed to late-second-century Rome. Most scholars agree it was originally Greek. See discussion at Gallagher and Meade, *Biblical Canon Lists*, 175–83.

[77] Origen's list is preserved in Eusebius, *Ecclesiastical History* 6.25.1–2.

[78] On this debate, see Gallagher, *Hebrew Scripture in Patristic Biblical Theory*, 37–38.

One other list possibly from this period is that discovered by Bryennios in his famous manuscript containing the Didache. The Bryennios List also limits itself to the books of the rabbinic canon. The deuterocanonical books are hardly represented in these earliest Christian lists.

From the second half of the fourth century, we have canon lists from seven different Greek sources. This count does not include Eusebius of Caesarea, who did not compose his own Old Testament canon list, though he did include in his *Ecclesiastical History* three different Old Testament lists, all more or less agreeing in mirroring the Jewish canon.[79] The seven sources from the later fourth century include Cyril of Jerusalem, Athanasius of Alexandria, the Synod of Laodicea,[80] the Apostolic Canons, Gregory of Nazianzus, Amphilochius of Iconium, and Epiphanius of Salamis.[81] All but one of these sources present an Old Testament canon that essentially corresponds to the Jewish canon, with a few slight differences. For instance, several of these lists mention two books of Esdras, by which they almost certainly refer to the works known in the fourth-century LXX manuscripts as Esdras A (1 Esdras, or 3 Ezra) and Esdras B (Ezra-Nehemiah).[82] Some of these sources may have assumed a Psalter with the additional Psalm 151, though a few sources explicitly state that the Psalter contains 150 psalms.[83] Several lists clarify that the title "Jeremiah" includes some additional works,

---

[79] See *Ecclesiastical History* 3.10.1–5 (Josephus); 4.26.12–14 (Melito); 6.25.1–2 (Origen).

[80] The authenticity of the biblical canon list associated with this council is under dispute. Whether the list is authentic to the council or not, it seems to be a fourth-century list that early became associated with the council. It will be cited here as the list of the Synod of Laodicea, with due acknowledgment of the legitimate questions surrounding this attribution.

[81] For the full context and brief discussion of each of these lists, I point the reader again to Gallagher and Meade, *Biblical Canon Lists*, ch. 3.

[82] Fourth-century lists mentioning two books of Esdras include Cyril, Athanasius, the Greek Apostolic Canons, Amphilochius, all three of the lists by Epiphanius (*Panarion* 8.6; *Weights and Measures* 4–5; 22–23), and the Synod of Laodicea. On the reception of the books of Ezra, see Pierre-Maurice Bogaert, "Les livres d'Esdras et leur numérotation dans l'histoire du canon de la Bible latine," *Revue Bénédictine* 110 (2000): 5–26.

[83] So the canon list of the Council of Laodicea. As for the Apostolic Canons, see the edition of M. Metzger, *Les Constitutions Apostoliques*, 3 vols., SC 320, 329, 336 (Paris: Cerf, 1985–1987), which refers to 151 psalms, supported by a Latin fragment (designated FV, sixth century) and ms. Vaticanus gr. 1506 (designated "d," dated 1024); Metzger, *Constitutions Apostoliques*, 3.308. But an important Greek manuscript (Vaticanus gr. 839, tenth century, designated "a") mentions 150 psalms.

usually Lamentations, sometimes also Baruch and the Epistle of Jeremiah.[84] Of course, each of these Greek Christian authors also assumed the expanded versions of Daniel and Esther.

The one source that goes beyond these minor disagreements with the Jewish canon and includes more books is the Apostolic Canons, which has a very complicated textual history. The current standard text, edited by Marcel Metzger, includes Judith, four books of Maccabees, and five books of Solomon, presumably the protocanonical three along with the Wisdom of Solomon and Sirach, even though Sirach is labeled "outside" (ἔξωθεν) in the next line.[85] Tobit is also included in other language traditions (Syriac, Ethiopic, Coptic) of this work.[86] The Apostolic Canons contain, then, the earliest Greek canon list certainly to include some of the deuterocanonical books as distinct items within the list, not as parts of other books. Such a move apparently responds to the growing importance of the deuterocanonical literature in the fourth century.

Athanasius responded to this importance in a different way. His famous canon list in his *Festal Letter* 39 issued in the year 367 acknowledged the value—and promoted the reading of—certain books to which the bishop denied canonical status. He describes this group of books as "not canonized but prescribed by the fathers to be read to those who newly join us and want to be instructed in the word of piety" (οὐ κανονιζόμενα μέν, τετυπωμένα δὲ παρὰ τῶν πατέρων ἀναγινώσκεσθαι τοῖς ἄρτι προσερχομένοις καὶ βουλομένοις κατηχεῖσθαι τὸν τῆς εὐσεβείας λόγον). Presumably these books are especially appropriate for catechumens because they exhibit in a clear manner basic Christian doctrines and morality. The books inhabiting this category include the Wisdom of Solomon, Sirach, Esther—located here instead of among the canonized books, in contrast to the rabbinic biblical canon and most other fourth-century Greek Christian lists—Judith, and

---

[84] See the lists by Cyril, Athanasius, Epiphanius (*Panarion* 8.6; *Weights and Measures* 4–5), and the Synod of Laodicea.

[85] Metzger, *Constitutions Apostoliques*, 3.308. Whereas ms. Vaticanus gr. 839 mentions only three books of Solomon, Metzger prints the number "five" (πέντε) based on the authority of the Latin fragment FV and ms. Vaticanus gr. 1506. On ἔξωθεν here, compare other lists using similar terminology in reference to books outside the canon: Origen, Athanasius (*Festal Letter* 39.20, τούτων ἔξωθεν), and the *Hypomnestikon*.

[86] See the discussion in Gallagher and Meade, *Biblical Canon Lists*, 134–41.

Tobit, along with two Christian compositions, the Didache and the Shepherd of Hermas. Athanasius does not mention the books of the Maccabees in this context. Codex Vaticanus, roughly contemporary with the canon list from Athanasius, includes within its Old Testament section the very same Old Testament books labeled by Athanasius as canonized, on the one hand, and prescribed for reading, on the other. Athanasius's description of this category, τετυπωμένα . . . ἀναγινώσκεσθαι ("prescribed . . . to be read"), bequeathed to these books the label *anaginoskomena*. The only other fourth-century Greek canon lists that include something like this *anaginoskomena* category are two by Epiphanius (*Panarion* 8.6; *Weights and Measures* 4–5), which mention Sirach and the Wisdom of Solomon as outside the canon but valuable.[87]

Latin authors who drew up canon lists were often more accepting of the deuterocanonical books as full-fledged members of the canon.[88] Two of our earliest Latin canon lists—the list in the Codex Claromontanus (third or fourth century) and the Mommsen (or Cheltenham) List (mid-fourth century)—both contain the full complement of deuterocanonical books later accepted as canonical in the Roman Catholic Bible. (The list in Codex Claromontanus also includes 4 Maccabees.) Some Latin authors in the fourth century (and later) explicitly exclude the deuterocanonical books from the canon, sometimes grouping these books in a separate category similar to Athanasius's *anaginoskomena*, without that name. Rufinus of Aquileia, for instance, has a category that he calls "ecclesiastical books" that are not canonical but good for reading, and includes the Wisdom of Solomon, Sirach, 1–2 Maccabees, Tobit, Judith, and some Christian writings. Jerome, the Vulgate translator, includes these same Jewish works in a similar category without the name *ecclesiastical*; Jerome actually calls these deuterocanonical books "apocrypha"

---

[87] See also Cyril of Jerusalem, *Catech.* 4.36; Amphilochius of Iconium, *Iambi ad Sel.* 288. Contemporary Latin lists: Hilary of Poitiers, *Instr. Psal.* 15; Rufinus of Aquileia, *Symb.* 36; Jerome, *Praef. lib. Sal.*

[88] For the lists, see again Gallagher and Meade, *Biblical Canon Lists*, ch. 4. And on the reception of the deuterocanonical books in the Latin tradition through the sixteenth century, see Gallagher, "Latin Canon."

on one occasion,[89] though usually he regards them as noncanonical but edifying. The difference between the canonical books and the edifying noncanonical books is that the latter should not be used as prooftexts to establish Christian doctrine.[90]

The question we are pursuing is what kind of influence the Septuagint exerted on the Christian biblical canon, especially by broadening the canon beyond the Tanak, as scholars often assert. The canon lists give little reason to think that early Christians assumed that there was a Septuagint translation that included the deuterocanonical literature. Most of our Christian biblical canon lists from the first four centuries, especially the ones in Greek, exclude the deuterocanonical books. Some early lists, especially in Latin, do include the deuterocanonical books, but it is not apparent that these books were included because the authors of these canon lists thought the books were a part of the Septuagint.

The Christian Old Testament: Greek Manuscripts

The contents of Greek biblical manuscripts sometimes appear in accounts of the ancient Jewish canon in Greek. Unfortunately, we have for the deuterocanonical books only a single Greek manuscript that is certainly Jewish.[91] This is a scrap of the Epistle of Jeremiah found in Cave 7 at Qumran

---

[89] Jerome, *Preface to Samuel and Kings* (the *Prologus Galeatus*), at Gallagher and Meade, *Biblical Canon Lists*, 202; see also Edmon L. Gallagher, "The Old Testament 'Apocrypha' in Jerome's Canonical Theory," *Journal of Early Christian Studies* 20 (2012): 213–33.

[90] This distinction is articulated by Jerome (*Preface to the Books of Solomon*, quoted in Gallagher and Meade, *Biblical Canon Lists*, 212) and Rufinus (in his canon list; Gallagher and Meade, *Biblical Canon Lists*, 219).

[91] On Jewish manuscripts of the Greek Bible, see Pierre-Maurice Bogaert, "Septante et versions grecques," *Dictionnaire de la Bible, Supplément* 12 (1993):536–692, at col. 664–66; Nicholas de Lange, *Japheth in the Tents of Shem: Greek Bible Translations in Byzantine Judaism* (Tübingen: Mohr Siebeck, 2015), 70–75, who mentions as possibly Jewish an ostracon (Ra[999], late third century) containing a quotation of Judith and a papyrus codex (Ra[928], third century) containing Proverbs, the Wisdom of Solomon, and Sirach. De Lange acknowledges that we cannot be sure whether these manuscripts are Jewish or Christian. I have mentioned these manuscripts below as Christian manuscripts.

(pap7QLXXEpJer [Ra 804]), dating to the first century BCE and containing twenty-two letters from verses 43–44.[92] (The "Ra" number is the Rahlfs number used by Septuagint scholars to identify Septuagint manuscripts.)[93] For the rest of the deuterocanonical literature, our earliest Greek manuscripts date from the third century CE and derive from Christian circles.[94] For the most part, the earliest Greek manuscripts that contain the deuterocanonical books alongside other books are the great codices from the fourth and fifth centuries, particularly Vaticanus, Sinaiticus, and Alexandrinus.[95] All three of these codices contain, together with the books of the Jewish canon, most of the main deuterocanonical literature still considered a part of the Greek Bible, with still additional books besides (see the figure "Deuterocanonical Books in Four Important Greek Codices").

These great full-Bible codices began to be produced in the fourth century. In the period before the fourth century, we do have Christian biblical manuscripts, but they do not contain the full Bible, or anything close to it, and so they do not really throw much light on the reception of the deuterocanonical literature, at least not in terms of whether these books were viewed as Scripture. Second- and third-century biblical manuscripts usually contain only a single biblical book or, at most, a small section of the canon. For some of the deuterocanonical books (as for some of the protocanonical books), no manuscript evidence at all survives from earlier centuries: the books of the Maccabees, 1 Esdras, Baruch, and the Epistle of Jeremiah (not counting the Qumran scroll for this last work, mentioned in the previous paragraph). For the most part, second- and third-century manuscripts feature only individual books:[96]

---

[92] M. Baillet, "Lettre de Jérémie," in *Les "Petites grottes" de Qumran*, ed. M. Baillet, J. T. Milik, and R. de Vaux, Discoveries in the Judaean Desert III.1 (Oxford: Clarendon, 1962), 143.

[93] The LXX manuscripts numbers are given according to the scheme of Rahlfs-Fraenkel, *Verzeichnis*.

[94] See Rahlfs-Fraenkel, *Verzeichnis*, 472–97.

[95] The main exception is Ra 928, now in Oxford and deriving from the third century, containing material from Proverbs, the Wisdom of Solomon, and Sirach. See the information provided later in this section on this manuscript, as well as on Ra 967.

[96] The following discussion omits the abbreviation "Ra" (for Rahlfs) but still cites manuscripts according to the assigned Rahlfs number (Rahlfs-Fraenkel, *Verzeichnis*).

- 878 and 990, both early third century CE, each preserve a few verses from Tobit chapter 12.[97]
- 999, third century CE, ostracon, preserves a few verses from Judith chapter 15.[98]
- 828, third or fourth century CE, preserves a few verses from Sirach chapter 29.[99]
- 861, third or fourth century CE, preserves small portions of Theodotion-Daniel, including parts of Susanna.[100]

But two early manuscripts include portions of the deuterocanonical literature together with protocanonical books:

- 967, ca. 200 CE, preserves portions of Ezekiel, Daniel, and Esther, the latter two books inclusive of their deuterocanonical parts.[101]
- 928, third century CE, preserves portions of Proverbs, the Wisdom of Solomon, and Sirach.[102]

These manuscripts show, better than the canonical lists of Melito and Origen, that Christians were reading the deuterocanonical literature, but they usually do not reveal what status their readers attributed to these books. Kreuzer has argued that the blessing following Daniel in papyrus 967 suggests that the manuscript presents Esther as having a status inferior to that enjoyed by the other books in the manuscript.[103] The poor state of preservation of 928 prevents similar analysis regarding possible distinctions among the books.

---

[97] For 878, see Rahlfs-Fraenkel, *Verzeichnis*, 124–25; for 990, see Rahlfs-Fraenkel, 299–300.

[98] Rahlfs-Fraenkel, 165.

[99] Rahlfs-Fraenkel, 125.

[100] Rahlfs-Fraenkel, 61.

[101] Rahlfs-Fraenkel, 98–103.

[102] Rahlfs-Fraenkel, 284–87.

[103] S. Kreuzer, "Papyrus 967," in *Die Septuaginta—Texte, Kontexte, Lebenswelten*, ed. Martin Karrer and Wolfgang Kraus (Tübingen: Mohr Siebeck, 2008), 64–82.

Manuscripts of a Single Deuterocanonical Book (First Eight Centuries)

In addition to those manuscripts previously mentioned, manuscripts of the first eight centuries CE that attest a single deuterocanonical book include the following:

Rahlfs Number	Content	Date (Approx.)	Rahlfs-Fraenkel Page Number
841	1 Esdras (ostracon)	before 650	257
910	Tobit	fourth century	295–96
823	Judith	fifth/sixth century	64
859	Wisdom	fourth century	181–82
856	Wisdom	fourth century	306
950	Wisdom	fourth/fifth century	423–24
826	Wisdom	fourth/fifth century	66
oS-59	Wisdom	sixth century	402
888	Wisdom	ca. 700	195
964	Sirach	fourth century	103–4
864	Sirach	fourth/fifth century	114
863	Sirach	fourth/fifth century	444–45
938	Sirach	fifth century	411–12
882	Sirach	fifth century?	446–47
991	Sirach	sixth century	300
oS-55	Sirach	sixth/seventh century	335
929	Sirach (underwriting of a palimpsest)	sixth/seventh century	162
892	Sirach	seventh century	361
893	Sirach	eighth century	361
921	Bel & Dragon	fourth/fifth century	278
930	4 Maccabees	seventh century	329–30

In the first eight centuries CE,[104] most of the deuterocanonical books feature in only a very few manuscripts, and still most frequently there is no evidence that the manuscript in question contained more than one book (see the figure "Manuscripts of a Single Deuterocanonical Book"). Earlier we surveyed the important full Bible codices from the first eight centuries (Vaticanus, Sainiticus, Alexandrinus, Venetus; see the figure "Deutero-canonical Books in Four Important Greek Codices"). Here we will note those manuscripts from the fourth through eighth centuries that attest a deuterocanonical book with at least one other book:

- 889 (fourth century), attesting portions of Wisdom, Sirach, and Psalms.[105]
- 870 (fourth/fifth century), attesting portions of Ecclesiastes, Song of Songs, and the last few chapters of Sirach.[106]
- C (Codex Ephraemi Rescriptus, fifth century), containing the Wisdom books of the Old Testament—Job, Proverbs, Ecclesiastes, Song of Songs, Wisdom, Sirach—and most of the New Testament.[107]
- oS-50 (fifth/sixth century), attesting Sirach 39:14 with several verses from Psalms.[108]
- Q (Codex Marchalianus, sixth/seventh century), containing the sixteen prophets in the same sequence as Codex Vaticanus, thus transmitting Baruch, Epistle of Jeremiah, Susanna, and Bel and the Dragon.[109]
- 600 (eighth/ninth century), a Palimpsest of Euclid's *Elements*, the underwriting containing material from Proverbs, Song of Songs, and Sirach.[110]

---

[104] This time limit corresponds to that of vol. 1 of the updated edition of Rahlfs-Fraenkel, *Verzeichnis*.

[105] Rahlfs-Fraenkel, 303.

[106] Rahlfs-Fraenkel, 15–16.

[107] Rahlfs-Fraenkel, 313–15; see also D. C. Parker, *An Introduction to the New Testament Manuscripts and Their Texts* (Cambridge: Cambridge University Press, 2008), 73. The manuscript is missing 2 Thessalonians and 2 John from the New Testament.

[108] Rahlfs-Fraenkel, *Verzeichnis*, 301.

[109] Rahlfs-Fraenkel, 346–50.

[110] Rahlfs-Fraenkel, 317.

Later Greek biblical manuscripts very rarely contain the entire Bible,[111] but when they do, they include several of the deuterocanonical books.[112] Most often, biblical manuscripts contained a section of the Bible, such as the Octateuch (the Pentateuch plus Joshua, Judges, and Ruth), or the Wisdom books, or the Prophets, or historical books, or the Psalter, or two or three of these sections together. Frequently, a single codex would contain the Psalter with the Odes, but the Psalter also appeared by itself quite often.[113] A codex of wisdom books often contained Wisdom and Sirach, but not always.[114] A codex of the historical books would often contain Tobit and Judith,[115] but these two books might also appear in another type of codex, such as a wisdom codex.[116] The books of Maccabees appear in a variety of combinations. A few codices contain only 1–2 Maccabees, along with other biblical books.[117] Other codices contain 1–3 Maccabees alongside other

---

[111] James Miller considers it a "generous estimate" that as many as "seventeen manuscripts either now contain, or stand a chance of at one time having contained, the full Old Testament—this out of a total of some fifteen hundred manuscripts catalogued"; J. Miller, "The Prophetologion: The Old Testament of Byzantine Christianity," in *The Old Testament in Byzantium*, ed. P. Magdalino and R. S. Nelson (Washington, DC: Dumbarton Oaks, 2010), 55–76, at 58n3.

[112] For later Greek manuscripts, see A. Rahlfs and D. Fraenkel, *Verzeichnis der griechischen Handschriften des Alten Testaments* (Berlin: Weidmann, 1914), which catalogs manuscripts according to content, as follows: Octateuch (374–82), Kingdoms, Chronicles, Esdras (382–85), Esther, Judith, Tobit (385–87), Maccabees (387–90), Psalms and Odes (390–410), Wisdom books (410–24), Prophets (424–38).

[113] On the contents of manuscripts of the Psalter, see G. R. Parpulov, "Psalters and Personal Piety in Byzantium," in Magdalino and Nelson, *Old Testament in Byzantium*, 77–105, esp. 100–5. On the Odes and their reception, see M. Harl, *Voix de louange. Les cantiques bibliques dans la liturgie chrétienne* (Paris: Les belles lettres, 2014).

[114] For examples with Wisdom and Sirach, see the following manuscripts: 157, twelfth century; 296, eleventh century; 336, fourteenth century; 339, eleventh century; 471, thirteenth/fourteenth century; 613, thirteenth century, with the Prophets and the Psalter with Odes. For examples without Wisdom and Sirach, see 139, tenth/eleventh century; 161, fourteenth century; 295, fifteenth/sixteenth century; 425, fourteenth century; 766, twelfth century.

[115] E.g., manuscripts 243, tenth century; 236, eleventh century; 314, thirteenth century; 318, tenth/eleventh century; 319, dated 1021; 379, sixteenth century; 381, eleventh century; 392, tenth century.

[116] E.g., manuscripts 248, thirteenth century; 249, twelfth century; 311, twelfth century; 542, eleventh century.

[117] Manuscripts 106, fourteenth century; 98, thirteenth century; 243, tenth century; 379, sixteenth century. Manuscript 340 (eleventh century) has 1 and 4 Maccabees, like Sinaiticus.

books.[118] Many manuscripts contain 1–4 Maccabees with other books.[119] Sometimes a single Maccabean book appears alongside other books, such as in 134 (eleventh century), containing the Octateuch, Kingdoms, Chronicles, Esdras, and 1 Maccabees; or 768 (sixteenth? century), featuring Proverbs, Wisdom, Sirach, Susanna, Bel and the Dragon, Judith, and 4 Maccabees (cf. 380, twelfth century; 452, fourteenth century). Often 4 Maccabees constitutes the sole contents of a codex.[120]

The groupings were not rigidly defined, as we can easily see when surveying the contents of a few manuscripts featuring the first section of the Bible. We have manuscripts that contain the Octateuch with Kingdoms and Chronicles (127, tenth century) and others that add to this grouping Esdras (121, tenth century). To this latter grouping (Octateuch, Kingdoms, Chronicles, Esdras), some manuscripts add Esther, Judith, and Tobit (108, thirteenth century), some add these books along with 1–4 Maccabees (107, dated 1334), some add only 1–4 Maccabees and Esther (120, eleventh century), and some add all these books alongside the wisdom books (125, fourteenth century). Some have only Kingdoms, Chronicles, and Esdras (119, tenth century), and some have the Heptateuch with Judith and Tobit (126, dated 1475).

Such diversity in the manuscript groupings problematizes the common scholarly equation of codex with canon. Usually such a claim concentrates on only the major codices from the fourth and fifth centuries, though such full-Bible pandects never became the normal way of transmitting the biblical books in Greek. A wider view of the Greek manuscript tradition shows that the deuterocanonical books often appeared in manuscripts of single books

---

[118] Manuscripts 130, twelfth/thirteenth century; 68, fifteenth century; 19, twelfth century; 29, fourteenth century; 64, tenth century; 93, thirteenth century; 311, twelfth century; 381, eleventh century; 442, fifteenth/sixteenth century. Manuscript 671 (fifteenth century) contains 1–3 Maccabees alone.

[119] Manuscripts 44, fourteenth century; 46, thirteenth/fourteenth century; 52, fourteenth century; 55, tenth century; 58, eleventh century; 62, eleventh century; 71, thirteenth century; 74, thirteenth century; 107, dated 1334; 120, eleventh century; 125, fourteenth century; 236, eleventh century; 332, fifteenth century; 534, eleventh century; 542, ninth century; 610, fourteenth century; 631, fourteenth century; 728, fourteenth/fifteenth century; 731, fourteenth century.

[120] I counted seventy-seven instances; a few examples: 316, eleventh century; 322, twelfth century; 326, fourteenth century; 335, fifteenth century.

alone or in various combinations with other books, but certainly nothing resembling a biblical canon. Included in these combinations are works, such as 4 Maccabees, that have never really been considered as even possibly forming a part of the biblical canon for the Greek Orthodox Church. Greek Orthodox Christians continued to copy literature that they considered non-canonical presumably because they found this literature helpful, enlightening, and edifying. Some modern Greek Orthodox writers even insist that their church still does not officially receive the deuterocanonical books as fully canonical. Eugen J. Pentiuc writes, "That the Eastern Orthodox Church has always used the Greek text of the Septuagint does not mean necessarily that she adopted the whole list of books (forty-nine or so) contained in the Septuagint as her official canon."[121] (I would simply object to saying that these writings are "contained in the Septuagint." If we are talking about the Rahlfs-Hanhart *Septuaginta*, there are more than forty-nine. If we are talking about the manuscripts, the number varies considerably.) The canonicity of these documents for the Orthodox Church is under dispute, but Pentiuc is correct that no council considered ecumenical by the Orthodox Church has ever officially settled the question.[122] Since there is—and has been for centuries, at least—dispute among Orthodox Christians about the status of the deuterocanonical books, it would be strange to argue that the presence of these books in Greek manuscripts demonstrates their canonicity among those who produced the manuscripts. D. C. Parker seems to have the right idea: "Even when Greek-speaking Christianity came to agree a canon (*sic*), it did not really occur to anyone that such a canon should be the basis for the contents of a manuscript."[123]

---

[121] Eugen J. Pentiuc, *The Old Testament in Eastern Orthodox Tradition* (Oxford: Oxford University Press, 2014), 133.

[122] The oft-cited Council of Jerusalem in 1672 was a local council, as noted by Pentiuc, *Old Testament*, 213; and Eugenia Scarvelis Constantinou, *Guiding to a Blessed End: Andrew of Caesarea and His Apocalypse Commentary in the Ancient Church* (Washington, DC: Catholic University of America Press, 2014), 43–44. For a view of the reception of the deuterocanonicals contrary to that of Pentiuc, see D. J. Constantelos, "The Apocryphal / Deuterocanonical Books: An Orthodox View," in *The Parallel Apocrypha*, ed. J. R. Kohlenberger III (Oxford: Oxford University Press, 1997), xxvii–xxx.

[123] D. C. Parker, *Textual Scholarship and the Making of the New Testament* (Oxford: Oxford University Press 2012), 61.

Yet scholars routinely make just such an argument.[124] For instance, if we may veer into the field of the New Testament for a moment, J. K. Elliott insists that "we must assume that the authorities behind Codex Sinaiticus and Codex Alexandrinus"—manuscripts that include at the end some books not in the modern New Testament, such as the Epistle of Barnabas, the Shepherd of Hermas, and 1–2 Clement—"considered these works canonical and wished to promote them as such. Certainly the user of these codices would have accepted all the texts in their Bible codex as having equal status."[125] The statement by Loren Stuckenbruck is more modest: "Though warnings are heard against taking the evidence of the codices too seriously in relation to the problem of 'canon,' it remains that these manuscripts presuppose a process of *selection* which may not simply be attributed to the idiosyncratic decisions by copyists and local churches wishing to collect material potentially useful for liturgical purposes."[126] And Iain Provan: "This blurring [between canon and Apocrypha] was facilitated by the fact that already in the late second century AD a largely Greek-speaking Church had begun to find various of the Apocrypha included in their LXX codices—in

---

[124] See the sources cited by Harry Gamble, "Codex Sinaiticus in Its Fourth Century Setting," in *Codex Sinaiticus: New Perspectives on the Ancient Biblical Manuscript*, ed. Scot McKendrick et al. (Peabody, MA: Hendrickson, 2015), 15n10. Pierre-Maurice Bogaert, "Les frontiers du canon de l'Ancien Testament dans l'Occident latin," in *La Bible juive dans l'Antiquité*, ed. Rémi Gounelle and Jan Joosten (Lausanne: Éditions du Zèbre, 2014), 41–95, at 45: "Tout exemplaire de la Bible suppose une decision, plus ou moins explicite, sur le canon." Elsewhere Bogaert recognizes the difficulties of saying that only "canonical" books are transmitted in "biblical" manuscripts; "Aux origines de la fixation du canon," 153–54. Even here, though, Bogaert claims, "lorsqu'il deviant possible de regrouper tous les livres bibliques, la presence de tel livre dans cet ensemble est une indication en faveur de sa canonicité."

[125] J. K. Elliott, "Manuscripts, the Codex and the Canon," *Journal for the Study of the New Testament* 63 (1996): 105–23, at 111. I am not sure which "user" Elliott is thinking about when he refers to the user who would consider a magisterial codex like Sinaiticus or Vaticanus to be "their Bible codex."

[126] Loren T. Stuckenbruck, "Apocrypha and the Septuagint: Exploring the Christian Canon," in *Die Septuaginta und das frühe Christentum*, ed. Thomas Schott Caulley and Hermann Lichtenberger, WUNT 277 (Tübingen: Mohr Siebeck, 2011), 177–201, at 190. See also the similar statement by James Carleton Paget, *The Epistle of Barnabas: Outlook and Background*, WUNT 2/64 (Tübingen: Mohr Siebeck, 1994), 253.

their Bibles."[127] The evidence we have seen shows how misleading such statements are.

We have also seen that some early Christians had a revered position for the deuterocanonical books outside the canon. For instance, Athanasius of Alexandria in the mid-fourth century reported a canon list that included a category of books called *anaginoskomena*, books to be read but not canonical Scripture. These books were mostly the deuterocanonical literature. If Athanasius would say that Tobit is a good book to read but it is not a canonical book (which he did), would he have objected to a full-Bible codex containing Tobit? Would Athanasius have interpreted the presence of Judith in Codex Vaticanus as a testament to Judith's canonicity—or as a testament to Judith's being good to read? I have a pretty good idea that Athanasius would have been perfectly comfortable with the contents of Codex Sinaiticus and Codex Vaticanus even if he would not have considered all of the books therein to be canonical. After all, Athanasius provided us with an explicit statement on how he viewed these books. Other potential users of ancient Greek manuscripts have not always provided us with the same information, so we cannot be sure how all the users or producers of these manuscripts thought about their individual contents. And that is the point. Manuscripts are useful within the discussion of the biblical canon, but they are not self-interpreting. A manuscript is not a canon.

What does this have to do with the Septuagint? What do the manuscripts tell us about the claim that the contents of the Septuagint influenced the Christian biblical canon? The contents of the Greek manuscripts are so variable that it is difficult—impossible—to relate these to some standard "Septuagint collection" that helped determine the Old Testament canon of Christians. Not a single Greek manuscript of the first thousand years of Christianity corresponds to the Old Testament of any Christian group: not the Protestants, not the Roman Catholics, not the Eastern Orthodox, not any other group known to me. Very few, if any, Greek manuscripts of the

---

[127] Iain Provan, *The Reformation and the Right Reading of Scripture* (Waco, TX: Baylor University Press, 2017), 75. Provan says in the note that the evidence for his statement is the later codices (e.g., Sinaiticus, Vaticanus).

second millennium would pass this test. The manuscripts were not thought of as comprehensive deposits of either the Septuagint translation or the biblical canon.

Conclusion

The Septuagint had no bearing on the development of the canon of Scripture. It has been the burden of this chapter to justify this statement. Scholars have claimed that the Septuagint had a significant influence on the Christian biblical canon due to their anachronistic conceptions of some sort of fixed collection associated with the Septuagint, as if ancient people felt free or even compelled to use any book that was "in the Septuagint." There is today something like a fixed collection of the Septuagint, thanks to Alfred Rahlfs and his publication of the standard hand-edition of the *Septuaginta* in 1935. But there was nothing similar in antiquity. The only sort of fixed Septuagint collection from antiquity, as far as I can tell, was the Greek Pentateuch, on which all our Jewish sources agree. Almost all of our Christian sources broadened the scope of the translation beyond the Pentateuch to include at least the books of the Tanak, if not more, sometimes many more (remember Epiphanius on the seventy-two apocrypha translated by the Seventy-two?). It does not seem, however, that any Late-Antique Christian was trying to correlate the books in the Old Testament canon with the books in the Septuagint translation. And not every Late-Antique Christian broadened the translation in this way; Jerome insisted time and again that the Seventy translators worked on the Pentateuch alone.[128]

What evidence can we cite for a stable Septuagint collection that could have influenced the biblical canon? Greek biblical manuscripts present no such stable collection. Nor do citations or patristic comments on the Septuagint. The canon lists certainly do not encourage this interpretation. What we do have from early Christianity is the insistence that the Septuagint, as opposed to the Hebrew text, is the correct Old Testament for Christians. We will examine this view in subsequent chapters,

---

[128] *Commentary on Ezekiel* 5:12; *Commentary on Micah* 2:9; *Qu. Hebr. Gen.*, prologue.

a view that was dominant in Christian circles all throughout the patristic period. Again, the Fathers routinely insisted that the Septuagint and not the Hebrew Bible was the correct Christian Old Testament. But it is important to notice that their arguments in this regard had to do with the textual form of the Old Testament and not its canon.[129] One of the clearest examples of this sort of reasoning is the Latin author Rufinus of Aquileia, who maintained the narrow canon of Jewish tradition without the deuterocanonical books while also criticizing Jerome for translating the Old Testament from Hebrew rather than the Septuagint.[130] According to many early Christians, the Septuagint was the correct text for the Christian Old Testament, but this view had nothing to do with the scope of the biblical canon.[131]

Rather than the Septuagint influencing the biblical canon, the situation may have been exactly the reverse: the biblical canon influenced the scope of the Septuagint. The deuterocanonical books were read and used in ancient Judaism, not because they were a part of the Septuagint but because they were helpful, edifying, and entertaining. Early Christians read these books for the same reasons. At some point, some early Christians considered these deuterocanonical books to be equal in status to the books of the Tanak, but this was not a universal position. Such disagreement on the Old Testament canon apparently incited Melito in about 170 CE to journey to Palestine to uncover the truth of the matter, though his report did little to settle the issue.[132] It was generally in the West that

---

[129] Scholars often fail to make this distinction, e.g., Ralph Hennings, *Der Briefwechsel zwischen Augustinus und Hieronymus und ihr Streit um den Kanon des Alten Testaments und die Auslegung von Gal. 2, 11–14* (Leiden: Brill, 1994); Mogens Müller, "Die Septuaginta als Teil des christlichen Kanons," in Karrer and Kraus, *Septuaginta*, 708–27 (on Augustine at 711).

[130] On Rufinus's defense of the Septuagint, see the discussion in Gallagher, *Hebrew Scripture in Patristic Biblical Theory*, 197–208. For Rufinus's biblical canon, see Gallagher and Meade, *Biblical Canon Lists*, 216–22.

[131] A caveat in this regard: the Septuagint versions of certain books (books shared with the Jewish canon) contained deuterocanonical material: Esther, Daniel, the Psalter, and 1 Esdras may have been considered the correct text of Ezra instead of (or even in addition to) Ezra-Nehemiah (2 Esdras in Greek manuscripts).

[132] See earlier on Melito; for his canon list, see Gallagher and Meade, *Biblical Canon Lists*, 78–83.

the deuterocanonical books enjoyed equal status with the protocanonical books, while in the East the scope of the Jewish canon exerted greater influence. But the continued use of the deuterocanonical literature among Christians in both East and West led to the expansion of the Septuagint to cover these books. It was not the Septuagint that led to the Christian use of the deuterocanonical books.

5

Text

Textual Pluralism in Ancient Judaism

> The Hebrew Bible . . . has been transmitted to us in a complex
> array of variant forms.
>
> —Eugene Ulrich, *The Dead Sea Scrolls and*
> *the Developmental Composition of the Bible*
> (Leiden: Brill, 2015), 1

Most English Bibles contain for the Old Testament a translation from the
Masoretic Text, a medieval edition of the Hebrew Bible. Translators will also
typically consult other available editions of the Old Testament, especially
the Septuagint, the Dead Sea Scrolls, and the Samaritan Pentateuch and
sometimes the Aramaic Targumim and other ancient translations. English
translators use so many different editions of the Old Testament because
these editions diverge from each other in various ways, and translators
evaluate on a case-by-case basis which edition has the preferred text.[1] This
chapter will introduce the most prominent text forms of the Old Testament
and explore how ancient Jewish readers may have handled the differences
among the texts.

---

[1] See Emanuel Tov, "The Textual Basis of Modern Translations of the Hebrew Bible,"
in *Hebrew Bible, Greek Bible, and Qumran: Collected Studies*, TSAJ 121 (Tübingen: Mohr
Siebeck, 2008), 92–106.

Masoretic Text

The standard scholarly edition of the Hebrew Bible available today, *Biblia Hebraica Stuttgartensia* (BHS), features the Masoretic Text (MT) as its main text (the text at the top of the page), with a critical apparatus attesting other readings from various sources.[2] The reason the main text of BHS contains the MT is because the MT offers us the only extant access to the complete Hebrew Bible (i.e., in the original languages). The main text of BHS actually reproduces the text of one particular Masoretic manuscript, the oldest complete Hebrew Bible manuscript, known as the Leningrad Codex (L or B19a) and dating to the year 1009 CE.

During the second half of the first millennium CE—perhaps beginning about the year 600 and continuing until about 1100—groups of Jewish scholars called Masoretes (from *masorah*, "tradition" or perhaps "enumeration") gathered at different centers for the purpose of preserving the traditions associated with writing and reading the Bible.[3] What became the most important Masoretic tradition was based in the town of Tiberias, on the western shore of the Sea of Galilee. Many manuscripts of the Bible preserve for us the traditions codified by these Tiberian Masoretes, but the earliest examples of these manuscripts go back only to the latter part of the Masoretic period. Most Masoretic manuscripts are actually the work of post-Masoretic scribes.

Masoretic manuscripts contain several important and distinctive features, but the element that most biblical scholars concern themselves with is the

---

[2] K. Elliger and W. Rudolph, eds., *Biblia Hebraica Stuttgartensia* (Stuttgart: Deutsche Bibelgesellschaft, 1977). BHS is gradually being replaced by the fascicles of a new edition: Adrian Schenker et al., eds., *Biblia Hebraica Quinta* (Stuttgart: Deutsche Bibelgesellschaft, 2004–). For an overview of the Masoretic Text, see Emanuel Tov, *Textual Criticism of the Hebrew Bible*, 3rd ed. (Minneapolis: Fortress, 2012), 24–74. For an overview of the *Biblia Hebraica* series, see Tov, 350–57.

[3] For an introduction, see Geoffrey Khan, *A Short Introduction to the Tiberian Masoretic Bible and Its Reading Tradition*, Gorgias Handbooks (Piscataway, NJ: Gorgias, 2012); on the meaning of the term *masorah*, see 1n1. See also Israel Yeivin, *Introduction to the Tiberian Masorah* (Missoula, MT: Scholars Press, 1980). On the time period of Masoretic activity, see §18. And for much more detail on the Tiberian system, see Geoffrey Khan, *The Tiberian Pronunciation Tradition of Biblical Hebrew*, 2 vols. (Cambridge: Open Book, 2020).

consonantal text.[4] The Hebrew alphabet (or alephbet) contains only consonants;[5] the vowel signs found in some Hebrew publications, such as BHS, were invented by the Masoretes themselves and so do not go back to the origins of the biblical text. These vowel signs represent the reading tradition inherited by the Masoretes,[6] and biblical scholars accord this tradition a great deal of weight, but since the biblical books were transmitted for centuries (at least) only in consonantal form, the vowel signs are usually not considered as authoritative as the consonants for determining the text and meaning of Scripture.[7]

The thousands of Masoretic manuscripts all reflect a single tradition so closely that some scholars have concluded that the minor divergences among these manuscripts are irrelevant to the establishment of an earlier (pre-Masoretic) form of the text; as one scholar has put it, the variations among these manuscripts "melt into nothing, and the huge mass of variations does not finally yield a single variant which is significantly, decisively and undoubtedly connected with a pre-medieval tradition."[8] In some ways this strict uniformity of the tradition is unfortunate, since textual scholars rely on variant readings in different manuscripts to reconstruct

---

[4] On the different elements of a Masoretic manuscript, see Khan, *Short Introduction*, 3, who lists eight components: consonantal text, layout, paragraph divisions, accents, vocalization, textual notes, Masoretic treatises, and reading tradition.

[5] Or so it is often said. Some Hebrew letters functioned as vowel markers (*matres lectionis*) very early, by the late eighth century BCE; see William M. Schniedewind, *A Social History of Hebrew: Its Origins Through the Rabbinic Period*, AYBRL (New Haven, CT: Yale University Press, 2013), 14, 115–17.

[6] This online article by Geoffrey Khan provides an introduction to the Tiberian system that became dominant; see "How Was the Hebrew of the Bible Originally Pronounced?," *TheTorah.com*, April 17, 2020, https://www.thetorah.com/article/how-was-the-hebrew-of -the-bible-originally-pronounced.

[7] In the sixteenth century, Christian scholars debated vigorously on the nature and importance of the vowel signs; see Dominique Barthélemy, *Studies in the Text of the Old Testament: An Introduction to the Hebrew Old Testament Text Project*, Textual Criticism and the Translator 3 (Winona Lake, IN: Eisenbrauns, 2012), 13–19. There was likewise debate on this subject between Rabbinites and Karaites (Barthélemy, 245–46, 269–70).

[8] See Moshe H. Goshen-Gottstein, "Hebrew Biblical Manuscripts: Their History and Their Place in the HUBP Edition," *Biblica* 48 (1967): 243–90; repr. in *Qumran and the History of the Biblical Text*, ed. F. M. Cross and S. Talmon (Cambridge, MA: Harvard University Press, 1975), 42–89, at 77; see also Tov, *Textual Criticism*, 38–39; and on the history of this issue, see Barthélemy, *Studies in the Text of the Old Testament*, 29–51.

earlier forms of the text. The many medieval manuscripts of the Hebrew Bible seem to offer little aid in pursuing this goal.

The developed Masoretic system of copying the biblical text aimed at ensuring its perfect preservation. Many rules governed scribal activity, including both the physical features of the scroll—type of writing materials, preparation of parchment, size of the sheets, and so on—and the copying process itself.[9] Scribes endeavored to copy faithfully the wording of the exemplar even in cases where the reading tradition diverged from the written text so that a system of *ketiv/qere* readings arose for passages where what was read (*qere*) differed from what was written (*ketiv*).[10] The Masoretes marked unexpected grammatical forms or terms in order to alert readers and scribes to note well the unusual but correct text.[11] The scribes also counted the verses, words, and sometimes letters in the biblical books.[12] The Talmud already exhibits familiarity with such activity (*b. Qid.* 30a), and some of the notes recording such data are available at the end of the biblical books in Masoretic manuscripts, a practice maintained in BHS. These techniques achieved their goal of preserving the biblical text.[13] We have just noticed that there are no significant variations among the Masoretic manuscripts, and this tradition does preserve an ancient form of the biblical text, as the Dead Sea Scrolls have demonstrated.

The two best representatives of a Masoretic manuscript are the Aleppo Codex (early tenth century) and the Leningrad Codex (early eleventh century). The Aleppo Codex is so named because for several centuries its home was the synagogue in the Syrian city of Aleppo. Prior to the fifteenth century, it had been in Egypt, where the great scholar Moses Maimonides (1138–1204) had seen it and pronounced it the most perfect example of Masoretic activity known to him.[14] Such lofty praise is owing to the fact

---

[9] See Yeivin, *Introduction*, §68.

[10] For an overview, see Yeivin, §§93–107.

[11] Yeivin, §§111–23.

[12] Yeivin, §125.

[13] Perhaps there were other goals for the *masorah*; see David Stern, *The Jewish Bible: A Material History* (Seattle: University of Washington Press, 2017), 71.

[14] At least it would appear that Maimonides was referring to the Aleppo Codex; see Moshe Goshen-Gottstein, "The Authenticity of the Aleppo Codex," *Textus* 1 (1960): 17–58, repr. in *The Canon and Masorah of the Hebrew Bible: An Introductory Reader*, ed. Sid Z. Leiman

that the Masorete responsible for adding vowels, accents, and notes to the Aleppo Codex was none other than Aaron ben Asher, often acclaimed as the preeminent Masoretic scribe.[15] (The scribe who supplied the consonantal text was Shelomoh ben Buyaʿa.)[16] After riots erupted against the Jews in Aleppo in 1948, newspapers reported that the codex was consumed in the fire that destroyed the synagogue, but a decade later the codex was smuggled into Jerusalem, where it currently resides. Unfortunately, the manuscript now lacks almost the entire Pentateuch and several books at its end.[17]

Since the Aleppo Codex is no longer fully extant, the Leningrad Codex now holds the distinction as the world's oldest surviving complete Hebrew Bible. It is housed now in the Russian National Library in St. Petersburg, where it has been since 1863 as part of the Firkovich collection, named for Abraham Firkovich, a Karaite businessman and manuscript hunter who acquired the codex some years earlier from an undisclosed location. A note in the manuscript places it in Damascus in the late fifteenth century. Shemuel ben Yaaqov copied both the consonantal text and the Masorah in Fustat (south of Cairo) in 1008 or 1009.[18] Its 491 pages contain the entire Jewish Bible (463 pages), along

(New York: Ktav, 1974), 773–814. For the statement by Maimonides in English translation, see Paul Kahle, *The Cairo Geniza*, 2nd ed. (Oxford: Oxford University Press, 1959), 107. Hayim Tawil and Bernard Schneider, *Crown of Aleppo: The Mystery of the Oldest Hebrew Bible Codex* (Philadelphia: JPS, 2010), 33: "We can state conclusively" that Maimonides referred to the Aleppo Codex.

[15] On the ben Asher family, see Kahle, *Cairo Geniza*, 75–109. On the Aleppo Codex, see Yeivin, *Introduction*, §§26–28.

[16] Barthélemy, *Studies in the Text of the Old Testament*, 313–30.

[17] On the history of the Aleppo Codex, see Matti Friedman, *The Aleppo Codex: In Pursuit of One of the World's Most Coveted, Sacred, and Mysterious Books* (Chapel Hill, NC: Algonquin, 2012), updated in "The Continuing Mysteries of the Aleppo Codex," *Tablet*, June 30, 2014, at http://www.tabletmag.com/jewish-arts-and-culture/books/176903/aleppo-codex. For a partial response to Friedman, see Yosef Ofer, "The Mystery of the Missing Pages of the Aleppo Codex," *Biblical Archaeology Review*, July/August 2015, 59–62, 70.

[18] See Barthélemy, *Studies in the Text of the Old Testament*, 239; Kahle, *Cairo Geniza*, 131–38. On the date, see Victor V. Lebedev, "The Oldest Complete Codex of the Hebrew Bible," in *The Leningrad Codex: A Facsimile Edition*, ed. D. N. Freedman, et al. (Grand Rapids: Eerdmans, 1998), xxi–xxviii, at xxi–xxii. For more on this codex, see Ben Outhwaite's online articles, "Fragment of the Month" for January 2016 and November 2017, available at http://www.lib.cam.ac.uk/collections/departments/taylor-schechter-genizah-research-unit/fragment-month.

with some Masoretic treatises. In comparison with the Aleppo Codex, the Leningrad Codex is a slightly less precise witness of the Ben Asher tradition.[19]

Samaritan Pentateuch

The Samaritan Pentateuch (SP) is the edition of the Hebrew Pentateuch held sacred by the Samaritan community.[20] The Samaritans do not accept as sacred the other books of the Hebrew Bible. Their Pentateuch contains the same basic content as the Jewish Pentateuch—the two editions of the Torah share a "recognizable shape," as Sidnie White Crawford puts it[21]—but there are also many differences. The most substantial differences consist of a series of forty major expansions in the SP featuring material duplicated from other sections of the Torah. For instance, the Plague Narrative (Exod. 7–12) often represents God commanding Moses to inform Pharaoh of an impending plague. While the MT Plague Narrative will usually follow this command immediately with a report of the plague itself, omitting any reference to Moses's obediently warning Pharaoh according to God's command, the SP narrative closes such gaps, making explicit that Moses did in fact convey God's message to Pharaoh prior to the onset of the plague. Expansions such as these have also been preserved among some of the Dead Sea Scrolls, demonstrating that these changes are not peculiarly Samaritan but that there were ancient Jewish texts attesting the same additional material.[22]

---

[19] See A. Schenker et al., "General Introduction," in *Biblia Hebraica Quinta*, fasc. 18: *Megilloth* (Stuttgart: Deutsche Bibelgesellschaft, 2004), vii–xxvi, esp. xviii–xx; Yeivin, *Introduction*, §30; E. J. Revell, "The Leningrad Codex as a Representative of the Masoretic Text," in Freedman, *Leningrad Codex*, xxix–xlvi.

[20] On the Samaritans, see Gary N. Knoppers, *Jews and Samaritans: The Origins and History of Their Early Relations* (Oxford: Oxford University Press, 2013); Reinhard Pummer, *The Samaritans: A Profile* (Grand Rapids: Eerdmans, 2016).

[21] Sidnie White Crawford, "Interpreting the Pentateuch through Scribal Processes: The Evidence from the Qumran Manuscripts," in *Insights into Editing in the Hebrew Bible and the Ancient Near East*, ed. Reinhard Müller and Juha Pakkala (Leuven: Peeters, 2017), 59–80.

[22] On these expansions, see Molly M. Zahn, *Genres of Rewriting in Second Temple Judaism: Scribal Composition and Transmission* (Cambridge: Cambridge University Press, 2020), esp. 13–16; Magnar Kartveit, *The Origin of the Samaritans* (Leiden: Brill, 2009), 259–312.

Some differences between the SP and the MT apparently owe their existence to ideological emendation—that is, changes in the text aiming to support a particular ideology. Three such changes have featured most prominently in scholarship. The Samaritan version of the Ten Commandments (Exod. 20; Deut. 5) has one more commandment than the Jewish version (but the other commandments are enumerated in such a way that the total still comes to ten). The Samaritan Tenth Commandment, like the other major expansions mentioned previously, draws material from elsewhere in the Pentateuch (Deut. 11:29a; 27:2b–3a, 4a, 5–7; 11:30) to add emphasis to the commandment enjoining the construction of an altar on Mt. Gerizim, the sacred mountain of the Samaritans.[23] The other two differences between the SP and MT often considered by scholars to have been ideologically motivated involve the command at Deuteronomy 27:4 to build an altar and Deuteronomy's cult centralization formula. As for the latter, Deuteronomy contains twenty-one occurrences of a phrase referring to the chosen place of the Lord (e.g., 12:5, etc.). In the MT, the phrase has the future tense, "the place which the Lord will choose," with reference to Jerusalem, the place God will choose at some later time (cf. 1 Kings 8:16, 44; 11:13; etc.). The SP has this phrase in the past tense, "the place which the Lord has chosen," apparently in reference to Shechem (near Mt. Gerizim), chosen before Moses's time (Gen. 12:6; 33:18–20). The difference at Deuteronomy 27:4 concerns the identity of the mountain where the Israelites should construct an altar upon entering the Promised Land. The MT says it should be on Mt. Ebal, but the SP says Mt. Gerizim. Whereas scholars have customarily assumed that the MT preserved the original text for both of these last two differences—the cult centralization formula and the identity of the altar mountain—so that the SP would represent an ideologically altered text, some scholars have taken the opposite view, that the SP in these passages has the original text that was altered in the Jewish version.[24]

---

[23] See Edmon L. Gallagher, "Is the Samaritan Pentateuch a Sectarian Text?," *ZAW* 127 (2015): 96–107; Stefan Schorch, "The So-Called Gerizim Commandment in the Samaritan Pentateuch," in *The Samaritan Pentateuch and the Dead Sea Scrolls*, ed. Michael Langlois (Leuven: Peeters, 2019), 77–97.

[24] See Edmon L. Gallagher, "Cult Centralization in the Samaritan Pentateuch and the Origins of Deuteronomy," *VT* 64 (2014): 561–72.

There are extant about 750 manuscripts of the SP, almost none earlier than the twelfth century.[25] Early Christians were aware of the SP, perhaps in a Greek translation called the *Samareitikon*.[26] But it was unavailable in medieval Europe until 1616, when the adventurer Pietro della Valle acquired a manuscript (produced in 1345/46) in Damascus and brought it to Italy (now in the Bibliothèque Nationale in Paris).[27] This single manuscript became the basis for a great deal of subsequent study of the SP, though over the past century the evidence of other manuscripts has been published. A team of scholars is now producing a large critical edition.[28] An English translation of the SP has also appeared.[29]

Dead Sea Scrolls

Beginning in 1947, bedouin shepherds (and occasionally archaeologists) made a series of manuscript discoveries in the Judean Desert. In eleven different caves surrounding a small community center named Qumran, at the northwest corner of the Dead Sea, around 900 scrolls came to light (or

---

[25] Alan D. Crown, *Samaritan Scribes and Manuscripts*, TSAJ 80 (Tübingen: Mohr Siebeck, 2001), 13.

[26] See Reinhard Pummer, *Early Christian Authors on Samaritans and Samaritanism*, TSAJ 92 (Tübingen: Mohr Siebeck 2002); Pummer, "The Greek Bible and the Samaritans," *Revue des études juives* 157 (1998): 269–358.

[27] See Reinhard Pummer, "The Samaritans and Their Pentateuch," in *The Pentateuch as Torah: New Models for Understanding Its Promulgation and Acceptance*, ed. G. N. Knoppers and B. M. Levinson (Winona Lake, IN: Eisenbrauns, 2007), 237–69. This manuscript—MS Paris BN sam. 2—was printed in the Paris Polyglot of 1632 and the London Polyglot of 1655–57, which became the source for the Samaritan Pentateuch in B. Kennicott, *Vetus Testamentum Hebraicum, cum variis lectionibus*, vol. 1 (Oxford: Clarendon, 1776), though Kennicott had access to a total of eighteen Samaritan manuscripts. It was also a major manuscript for the edition of A. von Gall, *Der Hebräische Pentateuch der Samaritaner* (Giessen: Töpelmann, 1914–18).

[28] See Stefan Schorch, "A Critical *editio maior* of the Samaritan Pentateuch: State of Research, Principles, and Problems," *Hebrew Bible and Ancient Israel* 2 (2013): 100–120. The edition features a diplomatic text of MS Dublin Chester Beatty Library 751, copied in 1225, along with collations of twenty-nine other manuscripts from the twelfth to the fourteenth centuries. The first volumes published are Stefan Schorch, ed., *The Samaritan Pentateuch: A Critical Editio Maior*, vol. 1, *Genesis* (Berlin: de Gruyter, 2021); vol. 3, *Leviticus* (Berlin: de Gruyter, 2018).

[29] Benyamin Tsedaka, *The Israelite Samaritan Version of the Torah: First English Translation Compared with the Masoretic Version* (Grand Rapids: Eerdmans, 2013).

"823 manuscripts that can be categorized"),[30] mostly written in Hebrew, some in Aramaic, and fewer in Greek. These Dead Sea Scrolls included about 210 scrolls of the books now in the Hebrew Bible. In addition to the scrolls from the eleven caves around Qumran, the Judean Desert yielded 41 biblical scrolls from other sites such as Naḥal Ḥever, Wadi at, and Masada.[31] These scrolls—dating to the period between the third century BCE and the early second century CE—provide our best glimpse at the Hebrew Bible at the origins of Christianity and rabbinic Judaism.

One difficulty in surveying the biblical evidence at Qumran is the issue of canon: Which books were considered biblical? The Qumran community left us no canon list, nor did they distinguish in any apparent way the biblical scrolls from the nonbiblical scrolls. They clearly did regard some scrolls as containing the Word of God. For instance, they wrote a series of commentaries (*pesharim*) on the biblical prophetic books that interpreted those prophecies as divine oracles now coming to fulfillment. The Torah also held great weight, as evidenced not just by the large number of scrolls uncovered but, more particularly, by statements attributing its content to God.[32] On the other hand, the community's own compositions—such as the *pesharim* themselves, or the Community Rule, or the Halakhic Letter (4QMMT)—though they might have some sort of divine sanction (see 1QpHab 7.3–5 on Hab. 2:2), were clearly different from the older and more revered scriptures.[33] These examples present the extremes—the

---

[30] Sidnie White Crawford, *Scribes and Scrolls at Qumran* (Grand Rapids: Eerdmans, 2019), 218.

[31] There are many good introductions to the Dead Sea Scrolls; see, e.g., John J. Collins, *The Dead Sea Scrolls: A Biography*, Lives of Great Religious Books (Princeton: Princeton University Press, 2013); James VanderKam and Peter Flint, *The Meaning of the Dead Sea Scrolls: Their Significance for Understanding the Bible, Judaism, Jesus, and Christianity* (New York: HarperCollins, 2002); James C. VanderKam, *The Dead Sea Scrolls and the Bible* (Grand Rapids: Eerdmans, 2012).

[32] Cf., e.g., 1QS 1.1–3; 8.15–16. On the whole question, see VanderKam, *Dead Sea Scrolls and the Bible*, 49–71.

[33] For translations of the scrolls now considered nonbiblical, see Michael Wise, Martin Abegg Jr., and Edward Cook, *The Dead Sea Scrolls: A New Translation* (New York: HarperCollins, 1996). For the *pesher* on Habakkuk (1QpHab), see 79–88; for the Community Rule, 112–36; for the Halakhic Letter, 454–62. Regarding the inspired interpretation at Qumran and its distinction from "Scripture," see the comment of George J. Brooke, "'Canon' in the Light of the Qumran Scrolls," in *The Canon of Scripture in Jewish and Christian Tradition*, ed.

obviously scriptural (the Torah and prophetic literature) and the obviously nonscriptural (the community's own compositions)—but the issue becomes much more difficult when thinking about those works found among the scrolls that some people, but not all groups, have regarded as Scripture. Qumran yielded five copies of the book of Tobit, for instance, a book in the Bible of Roman Catholics, Greek Orthodox, and others, but not in the Bible of Jews or Protestants. Did the Qumran community regard it as Scripture? Ultimately we do not know; we do not even know whether anyone at Qumran thought to ask the question. The same problem accompanies those books now in all Bibles but only poorly represented among the Dead Sea Scrolls: since there is only one tiny fragment of Chronicles, is it possible that the community did not receive it as Scripture? Should we attribute Esther's complete absence from the Dead Sea Scrolls to a willful rejection of its canonicity, to ignorance of its existence, or to a hungry worm that ate the evidence? Such questions must remain open in light of our present lack of data. Despite our frustrating ignorance as to the specific books in the Qumran Bible (if anyone there thought in such terms), our interest here is in the textual form of the books in our Bibles. A scholarly tradition has developed of including within the label "biblical scrolls" all those scrolls containing copies of books in the current Jewish Bible, and we will follow this practice here.[34]

A survey of the biblical scrolls at Qumran drives home two paradoxical points: textual plurality and textual stability. A chart will illustrate:[35]

Philip S. Alexander and Jean-Daniel Kaestli (Prahins: Éditions du Zèbre, 2007), 81–98: "The interpretations may be inspired but they are interpretations, nevertheless" (83).

[34] In her monograph, Crawford dispenses with the term *biblical* and uses instead "classical literature of ancient Israel" (*Scribes and Scrolls at Qumran*, 11) as a way of avoiding the question of whether the Qumran group thought of this literature as sacred (see her note 28). (She is, however, willing to label the classical texts "Scripture"; e.g., 287.) Defining the category based on date of composition rather than later reception entails that the category of "classical" literature does not completely overlap with the category "biblical" (regarding, e.g., Daniel). Here we will maintain the more common categories based on later reception with the acknowledgment that we are not always sure whether the Qumran group attributed biblical (scriptural) status to all the biblical books.

[35] Based on the data presented in Tov, *Textual Criticism*, 108. Tov classifies only 121 scrolls because the remaining ninety or so biblical scrolls are too fragmentary for such analysis. See also the caveats at 107n184. The statistics here differ slightly from those presented earlier in

	Torah (46 Texts)	Remainder (75 Texts)
MT-like	22 (48%)[36]	33 (44%)[37]
Pre-SP	5 (11%)[38]	
LXX *Vorlage*	1 (2%)[39]	5 (7%)[40]
Nonaligned	18 (39%)[41]	37 (49%)[42]

This chart presents one way of understanding the data contributed by the Dead Sea Scrolls.[43] The categories on the left correspond to the text forms we have already discussed, with some necessary nuance. The label

Emanuel Tov, "The Biblical Texts from the Judean Desert—an Overview and Analysis," in *Hebrew Bible, Greek Bible, and Qumran*, 128–54, at 145.

[36] Tov, *Textual Criticism*, 108, does not name the individual scrolls. Instead, he refers to Emanuel Tov, *Scribal Practices and Approaches Reflected in the Texts Found in the Judean Desert*, STJD 54 (Leiden: Brill, 2004), 332–35, where he lists twenty-four MT-like texts: 4QGen-Exod^a, 4QGen^b, 4QGen^c, 4QGen^d, 4QGen^e, 4QGen^f, 4QGen^g, 4QGen^j, 4QpaleoGen-Exod^l, 1QExod, 4QExod^c, 1QpaleoLev, 4QLev^b, 4QLev^c, 4QLev^e, 4QLev-Num^a, 1QDeut^b, 4QDeut^d, 4QDeut^e, 4QDeut^f, 4QDeut^g, 4QDeut^i, 4QDeut^o, 4QpaleoDeut^r. It is not clear to me which two scrolls no longer qualify as MT-like.

[37] Tov, *Textual Criticism*, 108, does not list the scrolls; Tov, *Scribal Practices*, 333–35, includes thirty-four such texts: 4QJosh^b, 4QJudg^b, 1QSam, 4QSam^b, 4QKgs, 1QIsa^b, 4QIsa^a, 4QIsa^b, 4QIsa^d, 4QIsa^e, 4QIsa^f, 4QIsa^g, 4QIsa^h, 4QIsa^m, 4QIsa^o, 4QJer^a, 4QJer^c, 4QEzek^b, 11QEzek, 4QXII^b, 4QXII^f, 4QPs^c, 4QPs^g, 4QPs^m, 4QJob^a, 4QpaleoJob^c, 4QProv^a, 4QProv^b, 2QRuth^a, 2QRuth^b, 4QRuth^a, 4QRuth^b, 1QDan, 4QEzra. It is not clear to me which scroll no longer qualifies as MT-like.

[38] 4QpaleoExod^m, 4QExod-Lev^f, 4QNum^b, 4QRP^a (4Q158), 4QRP^b (4Q364). Tov, *Textual Criticism*, 108: "The [SP]-group was probably popular in Palestine."

[39] 4QDeut^q.

[40] 4QJer^b, 4QJer^d, 4QSam^a, 4QSam^b, 11QPs^a Psalm 151.

[41] Tov, *Textual Criticism*, 109, does not list the scrolls; Tov, *Scribal Practices*, 332–33, includes seventeen such texts: 4QGen^k, 2QExod^b, 4Q[Gen]-Exod^b, 4QExod^d, 4QExod^e, 4QExod-Lev^f, 11QpaleoLev^a, 11QLev^b, 4QDeut^b, 4QDeut^c, 4QDeut^h, 4QDeut^j, 4QDeut^{k1}, 4QDeut^{k2}, 4QDeut^m, 4QDeut^n, 5QDeut. It is not clear to me which additional scroll Tov would now include on this list.

[42] Tov, *Textual Criticism*, 109, does not list the scrolls; Tov, *Scribal Practices*, 333–35, includes forty-one such texts: 4QJosh^a, 4QJudg^a, 4QSam^a, 4QSam^c, 6QpapKgs, 1QIsa^a, 4QIsa^c, 4QIsa^k, 2QJer, 4QEzek^a, 4QXII^a, 4QXII^c, 4QXII^d, 4QXII^e, 4QXII^g, 4QPs^a, 4QPs^b, 4QPs^d, 4QPs^e, 4QPs^f, 4QPs^k, 4QPs^l, 4QPs^n, 4QPs^q, 4QPs^r, 4QPs^x, 8QPs, 11QPs^a, 11QPs^b, 11QPs^c, 11QPs^d, 4QCant^a, 4QCant^b, 6QCant, 4QQoh^a, 4QLam, 4QDan^a, 4QDan^b, 4QDan^c, 4QDan^d, 6QpapDan, 4QChron. It is not clear to me which four scrolls no longer qualify as nonaligned, though probably 4QSam^a is one of them since it is included in the LXX category.

[43] For a comparison of Tov's classifications with those of Armin Lange, see Crawford, "Interpreting the Pentateuch through Scribal Processes," 64–68.

"MT-like"—or, as some scholars prefer, "proto-MT" or "semi-Masoretic"—describes those scrolls that bear a close similarity, though not complete uniformity, to the consonantal text of the MT. The "pre-SP" category includes those scrolls that contain the major expansions attested also by the Samaritan Pentateuch, but without any Samaritan ideological alterations, particularly the Samaritan Tenth Commandment. Scrolls labeled "LXX *Vorlage*" correspond generally, though not perfectly, to the presumed Hebrew text that served as the basis for the LXX translation. Finally, the large nonaligned group of scrolls might in some cases resemble features of the other categories, but no consistent pattern of correspondences can locate these scrolls among the other traditions.

The chart makes clear the two points mentioned above. First, the scrolls at Qumran belong to diverse textual traditions. In the case of Exodus, for instance, the Dead Sea Scrolls preserved examples of the text we normally associate with the SP (again, without the Samaritan Tenth Commandment) and examples of the text we normally associate with the MT. For the books of Samuel and of Jeremiah, the few scrolls attesting either of these books divide among those corresponding to the LXX and those corresponding to the MT.[44] Many of the scrolls of the Psalter vary widely from other known textual traditions and perhaps attest an alternative edition of the book.[45] In fact, many of the Psalter scrolls are probably not Psalter scrolls but just scrolls of one or a few psalms (never existing as a full Psalter).[46] It is significant that the same community owned and apparently used copies of the same biblical book from different textual traditions. Crawford cites this phenomenon as support for her contention that Qumran served as a library used by scholar-scribes: "It was a working library where different forms of the classical text tradition were preserved and used by the scribes

---

[44] See the discussion in Karen H. Jobes and Moisés Silva, *Invitation to the Septuagint*, 2nd ed. (Grand Rapids: Baker, 2015), 188–98.

[45] The issue is debated. See Tov, "Biblical Texts from the Judean Desert," 152–53, who interprets the Psalms scrolls as nonbiblical liturgical collections, against the now dominant view, represented by, e.g., Peter W. Flint, *The Dead Sea Psalms Scrolls and the Book of Psalms*, STDJ 17 (Leiden: Brill, 1997).

[46] Mika Pajunen, "Perspectives on the Existence of a Particular Authoritative Book of Psalms in the Late Second Temple Period," *JSOT* 39 (2014): 139–63; Eva Mroczek, *The Literary Imagination in Jewish Antiquity* (Oxford: Oxford University Press, 2016), ch. 1.

who studied them."[47] The Qumran discoveries have provided a much clearer picture of the textual diversity encountered by ancient readers of Hebrew Scripture than was previously available to us.

But a second point is equally true: the chart above suggests that the textual tradition preserved in the Masoretic Text was prominent or even dominant among all this textual diversity, certainly more prominent than the pre-SP tradition or the text of the presumed LXX *Vorlage*. (Later, we will see how the chart above can be somewhat misleading in this regard.) The only serious rival to the MT-like category, in terms of number of scrolls, is the nonaligned group, which differs from the MT to varying degrees in the different scrolls. While there is certainly textual diversity, there is also some degree of textual stability within the Qumran evidence itself and between the Qumran evidence and the later textual tradition of the Masoretes.

This textual stability becomes more striking when one considers the Judean Desert scrolls from sites other than Qumran. We now have forty-one such biblical scrolls, and all of them correspond to the MT.[48] In fact, Tov equates the text contained in these forty-one scrolls to the text of the Leningrad Codex (L): they "agree with L to such an extent that they are actually identical with that manuscript."[49] He does not mean that these scrolls have no differences from L whatsoever, but they are as close to L as any Masoretic manuscript is:

> The differences between these scrolls and L are negligible, and in fact their nature resembles the internal differences between the medieval manuscripts themselves. Accordingly, the small degree of divergence between L and texts from the Judean Desert, mainly texts outside Qumran, allows us to regard these texts as belonging to the

---

[47] Crawford, *Scribes and Scrolls at Qumran*, 223.

[48] See Tov, *Textual Criticism*, 28–29. Tov writes there of twenty-five non-Qumran texts, but in an email to the author (December 18, 2013), he corrects this to forty-one, referring to the non-Qumran biblical scrolls listed in Emanuel Tov, *Revised Lists of the Texts from the Judaean Desert* (Leiden: Brill, 2010), 126–29. See Edmon L. Gallagher, "The Jerusalem Temple Library and Its Implications for the Canon of Scripture," *Restoration Quarterly* 57 (2015): 39–52, at 44.

[49] Emanuel Tov, "The Text of the Hebrew/Aramaic and Greek Bible Used in the Ancient Synagogues," in *Hebrew Bible, Greek Bible, and Qumran*, 171–88, at 176.

same group, or in our terminology, the inner circle of proto-rabbinic texts. This inner circle contained the consonantal framework of MT one thousand years or more before the time of the Masorah codices. This applies also to the second circle of Masoretic texts [found at Qumran].[50]

This identity relates not just to the words present on the scroll but even to the orthography, the stichographic arrangement of poetic sections, and the sense divisions of the text.[51] Those features make them "inner circle," according to Tov's definitions, equivalent to the Leningrad Codex, whereas a "second circle" of texts (found at Qumran) is close to L but not identical with it. Though Tov's statement quoted above implies that Qumran itself yielded a few manuscripts of the inner circle, Tov's other writings clarify that he does not generally accept this view, but rather that all of the MT-like texts at Qumran were merely close to L and not identical to it (and thus were "second circle").[52]

Not everyone is comfortable with articulating even the evidence from the non-Qumran sites in terms of "identity with MT." Eugene Ulrich, for one, stresses that such language is anachronistic to the period under study, given that ancient Jews would not have thought about their scriptural texts as conforming or diverging from the Masoretic Text. He also stresses that, while the non-Qumran scrolls do bear a strong resemblance, even identity, to the MT, often this identity with the MT is not exclusive but shared with SP and LXX and other texts. (This is how the chart above can be somewhat misleading.) That is, these scrolls sometimes contain text only for books

---

[50] Tov, 176.

[51] Emanuel Tov, "The Dead Sea Scrolls and the Textual History of the Masoretic Bible," in *The Hebrew Bible in Light of the Dead Sea Scrolls*, ed. Nóra Dávid, Armin Lange, Kristin De Troyer, and Shani Tzoref, FRLANT 239 (Göttingen: Vandenhoeck & Ruprecht, 2012) 41–53, at 44–45; on orthography, see Tov, *Textual Criticism*, 29n8.

[52] Tov, "Text of the Hebrew/Aramaic and Greek Bible," 180; cf. *Textual Criticism*, 179; Tov, "Biblical Texts from the Judean Desert," 147. But at *Textual Criticism*, 31, he singles out 4QGen[b] as identical to L. Also see "Dead Sea Scrolls and the Textual History of the Masoretic Bible," 44, where he describes some of the minor differences between the proto-MT Qumran scrolls and L, specifically referring to orthographical and linguistic differences from L contained in 1QIsa[b] and 4QJer[a].

or sections of books in which the MT and SP, for example, do not diverge, so that the scroll is equally close to both traditions. His study of six scriptural scrolls uncovered at Masada finds that in only two cases (MasEzek and MasPs[b]) do the scrolls attest the MT exclusively.[53] But Ulrich does not challenge the notion that all these non-Qumran scrolls attest the same text later preserved in the MT tradition. Indeed, in the same context, he speaks of the "startling fidelity with which the medieval MT preserves a very ancient form of the text."[54]

Ulrich has also pushed forward another way of thinking about the textual diversity of ancient Jewish Scripture, in terms of multiple literary editions of different biblical books. The book of Jeremiah serves as a convenient example: the LXX Jeremiah contains about a sixth less material than the MT Jeremiah, and it features a different sequence for some of the oracles, especially the Oracles against the Nations, comprising MT Jeremiah 46–51 but coming after Jeremiah 25:13 in the LXX.[55] These differences exhibit a pattern throughout the book sufficient to label the variants as not just isolated additions or omissions but part of a distinct literary edition.[56] Both of these editions coexisted in Hebrew at Qumran.[57] Ulrich identifies variant literary editions for many of the books of the Hebrew Bible:

[53] Eugene Ulrich, *The Dead Sea Scrolls and the Developmental Composition of the Bible*, VTSup 169 (Leiden: Brill, 2015), 251–63. See also Ulrich, "The Old Testament Text and Its Transmission," in *The New Cambridge History of the Bible*, vol. 1, ed. James Carleton Paget and Joachim Schaper (Cambridge: Cambridge University Press, 2013), 83–104, at 92–93.

[54] Ulrich, *Dead Sea Scrolls and the Developmental Composition of the Bible*, 256. The context concerns specifically the scrolls MasLev[a] and 1QIsa[b].

[55] There is also a different internal order for the Oracles against the Nations. On the multiple forms of Jeremiah, see Ulrich, 141–50.

[56] For Ulrich's description of variant editions among the biblical texts, see *Dead Sea Scrolls and the Developmental Composition of the Bible*, 41–42. On the LXX as a witness to variant editions, see Jobes and Silva, *Invitation to the Septuagint*, 161–62; Emanuel Tov, "The Nature of the Large-Scale Differences between the LXX and the MT S T V, Compared with Similar Evidence in Other Sources," in *The Earliest Text of the Hebrew Bible: The Relationship between the Masoretic Text and the Hebrew Base of the Septuagint Reconsidered*, ed. A. Schenker (Atlanta: SBL, 2003), 121–43.

[57] MT-like: 4QJer[a], 4QJer[c]; LXX-like: 4QJer[b], 4QJer[d]. A Jeremiah scroll was also found in Cave 2, labeled by Tov "non-aligned."

The Qumran biblical MSS show that at least six books (or possibly ten) of the twenty-four in the Masoretic canon circulated in variant literary editions in the closing centuries of the Second Temple period: Exodus, Numbers, Joshua, Judges(?), Samuel(?), Jeremiah, the Twelve Prophets(?), Psalms, Song, and Lamentations(?). When the study is widened to include the witness of the LXX and SP, seven (or eight) more can be added or become clear: Genesis (chapters 5 and 11), Samuel (at least 1 Samuel 16–17), Kings, Ezekiel, the Twelve Prophets, Job(?), Proverbs, and Daniel. Thus, we have MS evidence that Judaism during the last two and a half centuries while the Second Temple stood knew variant literary editions for half or more of the books that would become Tanakh: thirteen (or up to sixteen) of the traditional twenty-four books.[58]

Such a way of understanding the ancient biblical text is now widely accepted. Scholars would certainly want to argue about how much variation in the manuscripts allows us to talk about variant literary editions, and some would want to dispute whether certain biblical books actually existed in multiple editions, just as Ulrich's question marks in the above quotation exhibit his own uncertainty in some cases. But the basic point is well accepted: a significant number of biblical books did exist in multiple editions in the late Second Temple period.[59]

The Qumran finds have enabled us to see more clearly the confusing array of biblical texts available in antiquity. On the one hand, Jews had access to multiple forms of many books that would become biblical. For each book, the form resembling the later MT was available, but often a form more closely matching the SP or the LXX or some other previously unknown tradition circulated as well. On the other hand, scrolls containing an MT-like text often occupied a prominent place (in terms of number of

---

[58] Eugene Ulrich, "Two Perspectives on Two Pentateuchal Manuscripts from Qumran," in *Emanuel: Studies in Hebrew Bible, Septuagint, and Dead Sea Scrolls in Honor of Emanuel Tov*, ed. Shalom M. Paul, Robert A. Kraft, Lawrence H. Schiffman, and Weston W. Fields (Leiden: Brill, 2003), 453–64, at 460.

[59] VanderKam, *Dead Sea Scrolls and the Bible*, 12–15; Tov, *Textual Criticism*, 186.

scrolls) at Qumran and elsewhere. The text of Jewish Scripture in antiquity was both stable and diverse.[60]

The Septuagint in Jewish Tradition

So far, our discussion in this chapter has revolved around Hebrew texts: their diversity and how people thought about that diversity. Now we turn our attention to Greek texts. Our discussion here can be relatively brief since we have already introduced some of the relevant ideas in previous chapters, and we will continue to think about the reception of the Septuagint as text in subsequent chapters. For now, we want to elaborate on the following points: some Jews thought the Septuagint itself was inspired Scripture and was perfect as it left the hands of the translators; some Jews thought some or all the Greek translations of Scripture were inadequate, so they produced revised versions, beginning before the Common Era; eventually, new Greek versions of the Jewish Bible were produced, sometimes circulating under the names of specific translators, the most famous of whom became Aquila, Symmachus, and Theodotion, whose translations were known to be a closer approximation in Greek to the dominant (proto-MT) Hebrew text in the early Common Era; and some Jews continued to use Greek translations of Scripture throughout the Byzantine era and beyond, and they largely seem to have preferred translations that represented the Hebrew text very closely.

THE INSPIRATION OF THE SEPTUAGINT

Some Jews attributed divine inspiration to the Seventy translators. We have seen this view already in Chapter Two, so here we can be brief. Out of our five main Jewish sources for the story of the translation of the Septuagint, three of them—Philo, the Talmud, and the Letter of Aristeas (but not Aristobulus or Josephus)—explicitly state or strongly imply that God was working through the translators to produce an authoritative Greek version of

---

[60] Crawford, "Interpreting the Pentateuch through Scribal Processes," makes a similar point from the angle of scribal processes.

the Pentateuch. The passage in the Talmud (*b. Meg.* 9a) actually says that God inspired the translators to misrepresent the Hebrew Torah, or at least to alter some details for the pagan king Ptolemy. Philo and the Letter of Aristeas do not share the Talmud's view, but the exact opposite view: God inspired the translators to produce a perfect translation. According to Philo, the Greek Pentateuch produced by the Seventy corresponds to the Hebrew Torah in every way. The theme of inspiration is, admittedly, not as strong in the Letter of Aristeas, but this text still reports on a curse pronounced by the Jewish community of Alexandria against anyone who would dare change a syllable of the translation (§§310–11), presumably because it was without defect.

It is necessary to emphasize two points in relation to this ancient Jewish view of the Septuagint.[61] First, the perfect translation of the Septuagint consisted precisely in its perfect correspondence to the Hebrew text. The idea that the Septuagint was inspired did not represent a rejection of the Hebrew text in theory; certainly, Philo would not have said that the Hebrew text was inferior to the Septuagint, except insofar as he could not read the Hebrew text. In practice, Philo's view allowed him to rely on the Septuagint without bothering with any differences between the Hebrew and Greek texts, because Philo's theory disallowed such difference; the two texts were "sisters, or rather one and the same" (*Mos.* 2.40). Of course, neither did Philo or any of these other Jewish sources on the story of the Septuagint give any attention to divergent Hebrew textual traditions. Judging from these representations of the Greek translation, the Seventy translators produced a perfect translation of the unified Hebrew Torah. Second, this view of an inspired Septuagint applies only to the Greek Pentateuch,[62] not to the Greek translation of Isaiah, Psalms, the wisdom literature, or any other book of the Jewish scriptures. At any rate, I am unaware of any ancient Jewish source attributing inspiration to these non-Pentateuch books. All the Jewish accounts of the translation of the Septuagint tell the story in terms of the Jewish Law alone. No ancient Jewish source ever tells a story

---

[61] I have developed these points more fully in Edmon L. Gallagher, *Hebrew Scripture in Patristic Biblical Theory: Canon, Language, Text* (Leiden: Brill, 2012), 147–52.

[62] This point is also emphasized by Martin Hengel, *The Septuagint as Christian Scripture: Its Prehistory and the Problem of Its Canon* (Edinburgh: T&T Clark, 2002), 75–80.

about the translation of any other book. The Pentateuch stood alone in the minds of some ancient Jews as having been subject to an inspired translation into Greek.

REVISIONS OF GREEK SCRIPTURE[63]

The field of Septuagint studies received a new trajectory and new life more than half a century ago by Dominique Barthélemy's publication of a scroll of the Minor Prophets in Greek found in a cave (the Cave of Horror) in the early 1950s.[64] Sometimes considered a part of the Dead Sea Scrolls, this scroll was not found in one of the eleven caves of Qumran but further south, in a cave near Naḥal Ḥever. The scroll proved so important because it was not a copy of the Septuagint version of the Minor Prophets but a revision of the LXX Minor Prophets. Ancient Jewish revisions of the Septuagint had been an integral part of the discussion of the Septuagint since the early centuries CE. Early Christians were especially familiar with the revisions or translations by Aquila, Symmachus, and Theodotion[65] because Origen included these three translators within his six-column Bible, the Hexapla (about which, see Chapter Seven). It was the Hexapla that made Aquila, Symmachus, and Theodotion the standard set of Jewish alternatives to the Septuagint, known collectively by early Christian writers as "the Three." Each of these scholars produced a version of the Greek Bible closer to the dominant Hebrew text in the first and second centuries CE. That is, the very existence of these translations indicates something like the opposite viewpoint to what we just saw in Philo's account and in the Letter of Aristeas, both of which considered the Septuagint to be perfect

---

[63] See Peter J. Gentry, "Pre-Hexaplaric Translations, Hexapla, Post-Hexaplaric Translations," in *Textual History of the Bible*, vol. 1A, *The Hebrew Bible: Overview Articles*, ed. Armin Lange and Emanuel Tov (Leiden: Brill, 2016), 211–35.

[64] Dominique Barthélemy, *Les Devanciers d'Aquila: Première publication intégrale du texte des fragments du Dodécaprophéton* (Leiden: Brill, 1963). The standard edition of the Naḥal Ḥever scroll today is Emanuel Tov, ed., *The Greek Minor Prophets Scroll from Naḥal Ḥever (8ḤevXIIgr)*, DJD 8 (Oxford: Clarendon, 1990).

[65] Natalio Fernández Marcos, *The Septuagint in Context: Introduction to the Greek Version of the Bible* (Leiden: Brill, 2000), 110: "the figures of Aquila and Symmachus are clearly defined as independent translators, not mere revisers." The situation is different for Theodotion.

(though let me emphasize again that Philo and the author of the Letter of Aristeas were both thinking only of the Greek Pentateuch). Aquila, Symmachus, and Theodotion thought there was room for improvement in the Septuagint. The Greek Minor Prophets Scroll from Naḥal Ḥever published by Barthélemy demonstrated that this tendency to improve on the Greek translations did not start with the Three, but preceded them by decades or centuries. (Thus the title of Barthélemy's book: *Les devanciers d'Aquila*, or *The Predecessors of Aquila*.) The name of the reviser of the Minor Prophets Scroll has not been preserved, so Barthélemy used one of the interesting Greek words that recurs in this version to give a name to the revision: the *kaige* revision.

Such revisions attempted to render Greek Scripture more in line with the dominant Hebrew text (proto-MT), since the Septuagint often diverged from the Hebrew text either because the translator made changes or because he used a base text different from the proto-MT.[66] The Dead Sea Scrolls have helped us see how often the latter scenario must have been the case: Jewish Scripture in the Second Temple period was pluriform. The book of Jeremiah is a prime example displaying drastic differences: the Septuagint is much shorter, and the chapters are arranged differently. Given the evidence of a shorter Hebrew text of Jeremiah found among the Dead Sea Scrolls, there is no doubt that the Septuagint differs from the MT not primarily because the Greek translator made changes but because the translation was based on a shorter text of Jeremiah.[67] In this case, scholars routinely judge the short text of Jeremiah to be the earlier text, later expanded into the form we know from the MT. Jeremiah 10 presents a stark example of how the two texts differ:[68]

---

[66] The standard handbook on these issues is Emanuel Tov, *The Text-Critical Use of the Septuagint in Biblical Research*, 3rd ed. (Winona Lake, IN: Eisenbrauns, 2015). See also the series *Textual History of the Bible*, ed. Armin Lange (Leiden, Brill, 2016–). The phenomenon of the translator deliberately making content changes in the process of translation is the concern of Zahn, *Genres of Rewriting*, ch. 5.

[67] Tov, *Text-Critical Use*, 208–9.

[68] Zahn, *Genres of Rewriting*, 10–13, includes this example as a prototype for scribal rewriting of biblical texts.

MT (NRSV)	LXX (NETS)
1 Hear the word that the LORD speaks to you, O house of Israel.	Hear a word of the Lord that he spoke to you, O house of Israel.
2 Thus says the LORD: DO NOT LEARN THE WAY OF THE NATIONS, OR BE DISMAYED AT THE SIGNS OF THE HEAVENS; FOR THE NATIONS ARE DISMAYED AT THEM.	This is what the Lord says: Do not learn according to the ways of the nations, and do not be afraid of the signs of the sky, because they are afraid of them to their faces,
3 For the customs of the peoples are false: a tree from the forest is cut down, and worked with an ax by the hands of an artisan;	because the precepts of the nations are vain: there is a tree from the forest, cut down, a work of a craftsman, and a molten image.
4 people deck it with silver and gold; they fasten it with hammer and nails so that it cannot move.	They have been beautified with silver and gold; they fastened them with hammers and nails, and they shall not be moved.
	[5a] Wrought silver it is—they will not walk.
5 Their idols are like scarecrows in a cucumber field, and they cannot speak; they have to be carried, for they cannot walk. Do not be afraid of them, for they cannot do evil, nor is it in them to do good.	[b] Raised they will be carried, because they will not walk. Do not be afraid of them, because they shall not do evil, and there is no good in them.
6 There is none like you, O LORD; you are great, and your name is great in might.	
7 Who would not fear you, O King of the nations? For that is your due; among all the wise ones of the nations and in all their kingdoms there is no one like you.	
8 They are both stupid and foolish; the instruction given by idols is no better than wood!	

MT (NRSV)	LXX (NETS)
9 Beaten silver is brought from Tarshish, and gold from Uphaz. They are the work of the artisan and of the hands of the goldsmith; their clothing is blue and purple; they are all the product of skilled workers.	Beaten silver will come from Tharsis, gold of Mophas and a hand of goldsmiths—works of craftsmen all; they will clothe them in blue and purple.
10 But the LORD is the true God; he is the living God and the everlasting King. At his wrath the earth quakes, and the nations cannot endure his indignation.	

In the previous paragraph, I described such differences as drastic, an evaluation that is subject to the eye of the beholder. The description "drastic" applies well, I think, to the textual differences, but whether the message of Jeremiah 10 is drastically altered by the differences between the MT and LXX is more debatable. One might suggest that the longer text (MT) merely draws out or makes explicit what is implied in the shorter text (LXX).

Often the LXX is much closer to the MT but still somewhat different. At Habakkuk 1:8, while the MT describes the horses in the Chaldean army as "swifter than leopards, more menacing than wolves at dusk" (NRSV), the LXX says that these horses "will leap beyond leopards and will be swifter than the wolves of Arabia" (NETS). Here there is little doubt that the Greek translator was using a Hebrew text essentially equivalent to the proto-MT but he interpreted the text differently from the way the Masoretic scribes later did. The end of the quoted phrase—"wolves at dusk" (MT) versus "wolves of Arabia" (LXX)—shows that the Greek translator was looking at a Hebrew text with only consonants and supplied in his reading a different set of vowels from the Masoretic scribes (*erev*, "evening," vs. *arav*, "Arabia"). The Minor Prophets Scroll from Naḥal Ḥever instead assumed the same vowels that the Masoretes would centuries later supply in the text so that the revised Greek version from Naḥal Ḥever says "wolves of evening."[69]

---

[69] Admittedly, there is a gap in the scroll here, but the preserved portion retains some of the letters of the word *evening* ([εσπε]ρας), making it pretty clear what the revised reading

This correction in the Greek Minor Prophets Scroll gives a good example of the types of concerns that the later revisers and translators brought to their work: when the LXX diverged from the dominant Hebrew text (or the dominant interpretation of the dominant Hebrew text), the later revisers and translators often attempted to present a translation more in keeping with this dominant tradition. Scholars call these revisions "Hebraizing." The Greek Minor Prophets Scroll was itself copied during the first century BCE, showing that the desire for Hebraizing revisions of Greek Scripture began in the centuries before Christ, not long after these biblical books were originally translated. In the light provided by the Greek Minor Prophets Scroll, Barthélemy and other scholars have been able to identify similar revisions of the Greek text of many biblical books.[70]

In the first half of the second century CE, Aquila brought this process of Hebraizing revision to its purest (and, sometimes, most incomprehensible) form. He produced a Greek translation of the Jewish scriptures that mirrored as closely as possible the Hebrew text.[71] His translation is quoted on occasion in rabbinic literature,[72] and it was used by more scholarly patristic authors as a window into the text used among Jews. A few decades later, Symmachus produced a translation that was also very close to the Hebrew text but much less literalizing than that of Aquila. Symmachus had the reputation among early Christians of presenting an especially clear translation.[73] The third translator/reviser chosen by Origen in his Hexapla was Theodotion, whose Greek text was much closer to the LXX than was that of Aquila or Symmachus, but still a Hebraizing revision. Scholars used to date

---

was; see Tov, *Greek Minor Prophets Scroll*, 51. At any rate, the Greek Minor Prophets Scroll does not have the word *Arabia*.

[70] Robert A. Kraft, "Reassessing the Impact of Barthélemy's *Devanciers*, Forty Years Later," *Bulletin of the International Organization for Septuagint and Cognate Studies* 37 (2004): 1–28; Gentry, "Pre-Hexaplaric Translations," 213–22 (§1.3.1.2.2).

[71] On the scope of Aquila's translation, as well as that of Theodotion and Symmachus, see Gentry, "Pre-Hexaplaric Translations," 228–29 (§1.3.1.2.6).

[72] Jenny R. Labendz, "Aquila's Bible Translation in Late Antiquity: Jewish and Christian Perspectives," *Harvard Theological Review* 102 (2009): 353–88; Anthony Giambrone, "Aquila's Greek Targum: Reconsidering the Rabbinical Setting of an Ancient Translation," *Harvard Theological Review* 110 (2017): 24–45.

[73] On Aquila and Symmachus, see the account in Fernández Marcos, *Septuagint in Context*, 109–41.

Theodotion to the second half of the second century CE in accordance with a patristic tradition,[74] but given that his Greek text was quoted before that date, more recently scholars have located Theodotion in the first century CE so that he is now thought to be the earliest of the Three.[75]

We do not have complete copies of any of these revisions or newer translations. Aquila, Symmachus, and Theodotion were incorporated into Origen's Hexapla, but we do not have a copy of the Hexapla either. All these texts have been lost in the course of time. We do have some fragmentary remains of the Hexapla and of the individual translations, but mostly we rely on quotations of these Greek versions in ancient Christian writings, and sometimes manuscripts of the LXX provide marginal readings attributed to these other versions.[76]

These revisions are important for our purposes in a couple of ways. First, they demonstrate that some users of Greek Scripture were unsatisfied with the Old Greek translations and desired something closer to the dominant Hebrew text. Second, they complicate the study of the New Testament quotations of the Old Testament, a topic we will explore in our next chapter. It is true that the apostles quoted the Septuagint, but they did not quote the Septuagint always. There were other Greek texts available in the first century in addition to the Septuagint, and sometimes these versions came into the hands of the apostles. When a quotation does not match the Old Greek, it could possibly have been altered by the apostle himself, but we also must consider whether the apostle was quoting from an available Greek text that had undergone revision.

---

[74] Epiphanius, *On Weights and Measures* 17.

[75] For an account of Theodotion, see Fernández Marcos, *Septuagint in Context*, 141–54. On the date of Theodotion, see also Gentry, "Pre-Hexaplaric Translations," 225–27 (§1.3.1.2.4): "We should place the person and work of Theodotion at the same time as the Greek Minor Prophets Scroll (8ḤevXII gr [. . .]), prior to Aquila, probably sometime in the early first century C.E. or perhaps even late first century B.C.E. There is no basis or need to speak of a proto-Theodotion or Ur-Theodotion" (226).

[76] For information on the remains of the Three and the Hexapla, see Chapter Seven and the relevant chapters in Fernández Marcos, *Septuagint in Context*.

JEWISH USE OF GREEK SCRIPTURE
DURING THE FIRST MILLENNIUM CE

To round out this portrait of the text of Scripture among ancient Jews, we can briefly extend our timeline to Late Antiquity and the medieval era,[77] periods that will be important in our subsequent examination of the Septuagint among Christians. As always, the topic is rather complex, and the sparse evidence defies scholarly consensus. What is clear is that some Greek-speaking Jews continued to use Greek Scripture for centuries after the point that the Septuagint became most closely associated with Christians. What version of the Greek scriptures did Jews use during this period? The old scholarly consensus was that the Jews abandoned the Septuagint around the second century CE because Christians began using it and because Jews preferred a translation closer to the Hebrew text, a translation such as Aquila's.[78] More recently, scholars have questioned this view, and indeed, it is strange to think that Jews would forfeit the Septuagint because another group was using it.[79] The evidence we have for Jewish use of Scripture in Late Antiquity is not abundant or conclusive: inscriptions point in multiple directions, showing that Jews sometimes used the Septuagint, sometimes Aquila; manuscripts of the Septuagint or even of Aquila are hard to identify as Jewish copies as opposed to Christian ones.[80] De Lange finds that Byzantine Jews mostly used either Aquila's translation or a translation similar to Aquila's but also sometimes the Septuagint.[81] On the other hand, Origen says about Aquila that he is "believed among Jews to have translated

---

[77] See further Gallagher, *Hebrew Scripture in Patristic Biblical Theory*, 164–73; and Nicholas de Lange, *Japheth in the Tents of Shem: Greek Bible Translations in Byzantine Judaism* (Tübingen: Mohr Siebeck, 2015). See also my review of de Lange's monograph at "Review of Biblical Literature," SBL Central, July 2018, https://www.sblcentral.org/API/Reviews/11159_12428.pdf.

[78] E.g., Jellicoe, *The Septuagint and Modern Study* (Oxford: Oxford University Press, 1968), 74–76.

[79] See especially here Tessa Rajak, *Translation and Survival: The Greek Bible of the Ancient Jewish Diaspora* (Oxford: Oxford University Press, 2009), 278–313.

[80] Gallagher, *Hebrew Scripture in Patristic Biblical Theory*, 165–67; Edmon L. Gallagher, "The Religious Provenance of the Aquila Manuscripts from the Cairo Genizah," *Journal of Jewish Studies* 64 (2013): 283–305.

[81] De Lange, *Japheth in the Tents of Shem*, who throughout emphasizes the continued use of Greek Scripture in Byzantine Judaism, especially Greek Scripture in the tradition of

Scripture more zealously, whose translation those not knowing the language of the Hebrews have become especially accustomed to use, considering it the most successful of all."[82] Then again, the proclamation by the emperor Justinian in the year 553 concerning the Greek translation that Jews should read (*Novella* 146)—he encourages them to read the Septuagint but allows also Aquila—has been interpreted as evidence that some Jews in the sixth century preferred to use the Septuagint.[83]

The scanty evidence fails to answer our question fully, but it seems that some Jews in Late Antiquity continued to use the Septuagint (sharing this translation with Christians). Other Jews adopted Aquila's translation or, possibly, another. We can approach the question from a different angle. We have seen that some ancient Jews, particularly Philo, regarded the Septuagint as inspired. Might this high view of the Septuagint have continued into Late Antiquity and beyond? Perhaps, but I do not believe we have explicit evidence for it. Remember that for Philo—and for all Jews who transmit the translation legend—the Septuagint was restricted to the Pentateuch. A view of the inspiration of the Septuagint, such as Philo held, would not have entailed a theoretical adherence to the LXX of Isaiah or Proverbs or any other book besides the Pentateuch. Even for Philo, the inspiration of the Septuagint manifested itself in its perfect representation of the Hebrew text; that is, Philo's theory was that the Seventy translators were inspired specifically to create a translation that reproduced in Greek the Hebrew text in every way, a belief sustained, in part, by Philo's inability to compare the two texts because he lacked Hebrew. It may be that this idea about the LXX Pentateuch's mirroring the Hebrew Torah became less compelling among Jews after the time of Aquila.[84] We will see that a similar development occurred in Christian circles in the wake of Origen's text-critical labors.

Aquila, with some evidence pointing toward continued use of a traditional Septuagintal form (see, e.g., 110, 114).

[82] Origen, *Epistle to Africanus* 4.

[83] De Lange, *Japheth in the Tents of Shem*, 60–67.

[84] Kristin De Troyer, "The Septuagint," in *The New Cambridge History of the Bible*, vol. 1, ed. James Carleton Paget and Joachim Schaper (Cambridge: Cambridge University Press, 2013), 267–88, at 279: "it seems more plausible to emphasise that the Jewish comparison between the texts of the Septuagint and the Hebrew texts led them to value the pre-masoretic text more than the Septuagint."

Conclusion

It has become commonplace to talk about the pluriformity of Jewish Scripture in the Second Temple period; we have seen in this chapter why that view has taken hold. At the same time, there seems to have been—even at Qumran and certainly among the non-Qumran scrolls found in the Judean Desert—a dominant Hebrew textual tradition, at least for most biblical books, that later became the only Hebrew textual tradition among Jews, codified in the Masoretic Text. The Septuagint was sometimes translated from Hebrew texts in this dominant textual tradition and sometimes translated from other Hebrew texts. Some Jews considered the LXX Pentateuch an inspired text, but no Jew on record states that the Greek form of the other biblical books was inspired. Even the view that the Septuagint was inspired, as represented by Philo, entailed that the Greek text was a perfect match to the Hebrew text. While the original Greek translations for some books of the Bible were translated in a dynamic way (i.e., not very literally), the Hebraizing revisions that quickly appeared indicate that Jewish users of Greek Scripture often wanted a translation very closely resembling the dominant Hebrew text. Alongside the pluriform Jewish Scripture there was an ideal and a desire for uniformity. The Christian adoption of Jewish Scripture compelled Christians to deal with these same issues.

6

Apostles

The LXX in the New Testament

Let that translation be the true one which the apostles approved.

—Jerome, *Preface to the Gospels*[1]

The New Testament was written in Greek. By my count, it quotes the Old Testament 344 times,[2] always in Greek. The one partial exception is the Cry of Dereliction at the Crucifixion, "Eloi, Eloi, lama sabachthani" (Mark 15:34; cf. Matt. 27:46), a quotation of Psalm 22:1 in Aramaic. But the Gospels neither mark these words as a quotation (i.e., they do not introduce it with something like "Jesus said, it is written . . .") nor leave them in Aramaic only, since they immediately provide a Greek translation. Every other quotation of the Old Testament is in Greek; what Greek version of the scriptures were the New Testament writers quoting?

---

[1] Jerome, *Preface to the Gospels*, in *Biblia Sacra iuxta vulgatam versionem*, ed. R. Weber and R. Gryson, 5th ed. (Stuttgart: Deutsche Bibelgesellschaft, 2007), 1515 line 19.

[2] See the "Index of Quotations" in *The Greek New Testament*, ed. B. Aland et al., 5th ed. (Stuttgart: Deutsche Bibelgesellschaft, 2014), 857–60. Estimates can vary widely; according to Henry Barclay Swete, *An Introduction to the Old Testament in Greek*, 2nd ed. (Cambridge: Cambridge University Press, 1914), 386, there are 160 quotations, whereas 312 quotations/ allusions are closely analyzed in Gleason L. Archer and Gregory Chirichigno, *Old Testament Quotations in the New Testament* (Chicago: Moody Press, 1983). For surveys of our subject, see Swete, *Introduction*, 381–405; Natalio Fernández Marcos, *The Septuagint in Context: Introduction to the Greek Version of the Bible* (Leiden: Brill, 2000), 320–37; Martin Karrer, "The Septuagint Text in Early Christianity," in *Introduction to the Septuagint*, ed. Siegfried Kreuzer (Waco, TX: Baylor University Press, 2019), 613–26.

The easy answer is that they were quoting the Septuagint, and that is the answer that is often given. That was the answer given as early as we have record of such questions being asked and answered. The first Christian to mention the Septuagint, Justin Martyr in the mid-second century, did not directly address our question. A few decades later, Irenaeus of Lyons did build an argument for the authority of the Septuagint in part on the basis of the apostolic use of this translation. Irenaeus mentioned the alternative translations of Theodotion and Aquila (*Haer.* 3.21.1), but he nonchalantly claimed that the apostles used the Septuagint: "They agree with the above-mentioned translation, and the translation agrees with the tradition of the apostles. For Peter and John and Matthew and Paul, and the rest after them, and also the followers of these, preached all the prophetical writings, just as they are contained in the translation of the elders" (*Haer.* 3.21.3).[3] Irenaeus's argument is especially directed at the proper wording for Isaiah 7:14, and particularly one word—whether the Hebrew עלמה (*almah*) is better rendered by the Septuagint with παρθένος (*parthenos*, "virgin") or by the newer translations with νεᾶνις (*neanis*, "young woman"). If the question is whether the New Testament use of Isaiah 7:14 agrees more with the Septuagint or with Aquila and/or Theodotion on the translation of *almah*, the answer—for the one New Testament passage that quotes this verse (Matt. 1:23)—is the Septuagint.

Our question is somewhat broader, however, and when one takes into account the variety of Old Testament quotations in the New Testament, and the variety of textual forms of the Old Testament available in the first century (as surveyed in the previous chapter), the Septuagint might still be the right answer, but one must reckon with numerous caveats. In subsequent chapters we will look at how this issue played out in the early centuries after the New Testament, but for now, we can say that some ancient Christians also recognized the difficulties of a flat assertion that the New Testament quoted the Septuagint. In the late fourth century, Jerome even reversed the normal claim and insisted instead that the apostles quoted the

---

[3] The translation is in St. Irenaeus of Lyons, *Against the Heresies*, Book 3, trans. Dominic J. Unger and Irenaeus M. C. Steenberg, Ancient Christian Writers 64 (New York: Newman, 2012), 99.

Hebrew Bible, or they quoted the Septuagint only if it shared the wording of the Hebrew Bible.[4] Though no modern scholar would follow Jerome in these claims—and Jerome himself sometimes issued his own caveats on this issue—Jerome was not without evidence, even if he exaggerated its significance. The point is that the issue of the textual form of the Old Testament that appears in the New Testament quotations has no easy solution.

In this chapter we will observe some of the issues revolving around the New Testament quotations of the Old Testament. With nearly 350 quotations to consider, we certainly will not comprehensively study the textual form employed by the New Testament writers, but we will investigate a representative sampling of the quotations and the difficulties they present. We will see why almost all early Christians and many modern scholars have assumed that the New Testament writers routinely quoted the Septuagint, but we will also find quotations that give credence to Jerome's view. We will not try to solve all the problems, but we do want to get a lay of the land here, a broad understanding of the ways that the New Testament quotations agree with or diverge from the Septuagint.

Methodological Warnings

In such an investigation, the researcher encounters numerous problems at the very foundation of the enterprise. How do we know what the Septuagint says, what words its text contains? How do we know what the Septuagint's Hebrew *Vorlage* said? How do we know what the apostles actually wrote? We do not possess the original copies of any of these writings. We do have modern scholarly editions for the Septuagint (most of it), the Hebrew Bible (at this point, just a diplomatic edition of the Leningrad Codex),[5]

---

[4] E.g., Jerome, *Epist.* 57.11; see Chapter Nine.

[5] Except for the book of Proverbs, which is available in an eclectic edition, edited by Michael V. Fox, *Proverbs: An Eclectic Edition with Introduction and Textual Commentary* (Atlanta: SBL, 2015). This is the first published volume of The Hebrew Bible: A Critical Edition, under the general editorship of Ronald Hendel. For orientation to the textual theories enacted in this series, see Ronald Hendel, *Steps to a New Edition of the Hebrew Bible* (Atlanta: SBL, 2016).

and the New Testament (a critically reconstructed text), but all these scholarly editions are based on manuscripts that may or may not represent the original form of the passage we are examining. These modern editions are all preliminary, and all modern editions will always be preliminary, until archaeologists unearth the original copy of a biblical writing. As long as modern editions are based on later manuscripts, these editions will always be subject to revision based on further research or discoveries or simply different opinions on how to interpret the available evidence. All this means that, when we look at a particular quotation in the New Testament, we need to account for the possibility that we do not know exactly what the original wording of the New Testament was. And when we look in the Septuagint to compare the quotation, we do not know either the original wording of the Septuagint or the wording of the copy of the Septuagint that was available to the New Testament author. And when we compare the Hebrew text, we are invariably (and necessarily) looking first at the Masoretic Text, which may not represent the Hebrew text available to the Septuagint translator, to later revisers, or (possibly) to the New Testament author. The easiest way to mitigate our ignorance in these areas is to pay attention to the apparatus in a critical edition of the text, where readings of various manuscripts and other witnesses are recorded for just such a purpose.[6]

Paul

Paul's letters are the earliest documents we have from a Christian. The thirteen letters in the New Testament that bear Paul's name contain many quotations of the Old Testament, around a hundred or more, depending on what counts as a quotation (i.e., Does it have to have an introductory formula, such as "it is written"? How close of a verbal parallel counts as a quotation?). The vast majority of these quotations appear in the four major letters of Romans, 1–2 Corinthians, and Galatians. Perhaps more than any other New Testament writer, Paul quotes Scripture according to a

---

[6] For a treatment of these issues, see R. Timothy McLay, *The Use of the Septuagint in New Testament Research* (Grand Rapids: Eerdmans, 2003).

variety of textual forms. At the turn of the twentieth century, Henry Barclay Swete recognized that a majority of the Pauline quotations "are taken from the LXX. without material change," whereas "a smaller proportion shew important variants," and in "other passages St Paul departs still further from the LXX., quoting freely, or paraphrasing, or fusing two distinct passages into a single citation, or occasionally deserting the Alexandrian version altogether."[7] More recently, Moisés Silva analyzed 107 quotations in all thirteen canonical Pauline letters and provided the following breakdown:[8]

Paul = LXX = MT: forty-two quotations (39 percent)

Paul = MT ≠ LXX: seven quotations (6.5 percent)

Paul = LXX ≠ MT: seventeen quotations (16 percent)

Paul ≠ LXX or MT: thirty-one quotations (29 percent)

Debated: ten quotations (9 percent)

This analysis presents only a rough generalization. We have seen that Swete found quotations that would not easily fit into any of these categories. Other scholars locate certain quotations in different categories,[9] but the major impression is the same: Paul mostly used the Septuagint, but not always.

As an example of a Pauline quotation that corresponds to the Septuagint against the MT, see Romans 15:12:

---

[7] Swete, *Introduction*, 400; Swete provides examples for each category. For an analysis emphasizing the infrequency of Paul's reliance on the LXX, see Michael L. Satlow, "Paul's Scriptures," in *Strength to Strength: Essays in Appreciation of Shaye J. D. Cohen*, ed. Michael L. Satlow (Providence, RI: Brown Judaic Studies, 2018), 257–73.

[8] Moisés Silva, "Old Testament in Paul," in *Dictionary of Paul and His Letters*, ed. G. F. Hawthorne and R. P. Martin (Leicester: InterVarsity, 1993), 630–42, esp. 631. For a justification for focusing on the entire canonical witness to Paul rather than only the undisputed letters, see Luke Timothy Johnson, *Constructing Paul: The Canonical Paul, Volume 1* (Grand Rapids: Eerdmans, 2020), 33–41, 62–92.

[9] See the major studies by Dietrich-Alex Koch, *Die Schrift als Zeuge des Evangeliums: Untersuchungen zur Verwendung und zum Verständnis der Schrift bei Paulus* (Tübingen: Mohr Siebeck, 1986); Christopher D. Stanley, *Paul and the Language of Scripture: Citation Technique in the Pauline Epistles and Contemporary Literature* (Cambridge: Cambridge University Press, 1992).

καὶ πάλιν Ἡσαΐας λέγει· ἔσται ἡ ῥίζα τοῦ Ἰεσσαὶ καὶ ὁ ἀνιστάμενος ἄρχειν ἐθνῶν, ἐπ᾽ αὐτῷ ἔθνη ἐλπιοῦσιν.

And again Isaiah says: "There will be the root of Jesse and the one rising to rule the nations; upon him the nations will hope."

Here Paul quotes Isaiah 11:10:

Καὶ ἔσται ἐν τῇ ἡμέρᾳ ἐκείνῃ ἡ ῥίζα τοῦ Ιεσσαι καὶ ὁ ἀνιστάμενος ἄρχειν ἐθνῶν, ἐπ᾽ αὐτῷ ἔθνη ἐλπιοῦσιν, καὶ ἔσται ἡ ἀνάπαυσις αὐτοῦ τιμή.

And there will be in that day the root of Jesse and the one rising to rule the nations; upon him the nations will hope, and his rest will be honor.

In the MT, where the LXX has καὶ ὁ ἀνιστάμενος ἄρχειν ἐθνῶν ("the one rising to rule the nations"), we find instead אשר עמד לנס עמים, "who stands as a banner of the nations." Wagner interprets the LXX rendering as interpretive rather than as based on a different Hebrew *Vorlage*.[10] Whatever the reason for the distinctive LXX version of Isaiah 11:10, Paul's exegesis clearly depended on it, whether or not he knew of any other version.

Paul also quotes the Old Testament in forms resembling more the MT than the LXX (e.g., Rom. 11:4, quoting 1 Kings 19:18), perhaps in reliance on revised Greek texts, and sometimes Paul's quotations match no independently known form of the text (e.g., 1 Cor. 15:55, quoting Hosea 13:14).[11] And then there are the problematic quotations, the source of which is unknown (e.g., 1 Cor. 2:9).[12]

---

[10] J. Ross Wagner, *Heralds of the Good News: Isaiah and Paul in Concert in the Letter to the Romans* (Leiden: Brill, 2003), 322.

[11] See Katja Kujanpää, "Adjusted to the Argument: Tracing Paul's Motives for Modifying the Wording of Scriptural Quotations," in *From Scribal Error to Rewriting: How Ancient Texts Could and Could Not Be Changed*, ed. Anneli Aejmelaeus, Drew Longacre, and Natia Mirotadze (Göttingen: Vandenhoeck & Ruprecht, 2020), 201–19.

[12] Briefly reviewed in Wolfgang Kraus, "The Significance of Septuagint Quotations in the New Testament against the Background of Old Testament Textual History," in Kreuzer,

Wagner proposes three quotations of Isaiah in Romans in which Paul's exegetical point depended on the Septuagint.[13] One we have already seen: Isaiah 11:10 in Romans 15:12. The other two are briefly examined below:

Romans 9:33

As it is written, "See, I am laying in Zion a stone that will make people stumble, a rock that will make them fall, and whoever believes in him will not be put to shame."

καθὼς γέγραπται· ἰδοὺ τίθημι ἐν Σιὼν λίθον προσκόμματος καὶ πέτραν σκανδάλου, καὶ ὁ πιστεύων ἐπ᾽ αὐτῷ οὐ καταισχυνθήσεται.

Isaiah 28:16

Therefore thus says the Lord, See, I will lay for the foundations of Sion a precious, choice stone, a highly valued cornerstone for its foundations, and the one who believes in him will not be put to shame.

διὰ τοῦτο οὕτως λέγει κύριος Ἰδοὺ ἐγὼ ἐμβαλῶ εἰς τὰ θεμέλια Σιων λίθον πολυτελῆ ἐκλεκτὸν ἀκρογωνιαῖον ἔντιμον εἰς τὰ θεμέλια αὐτῆς, καὶ ὁ πιστεύων ἐπ᾽ αὐτῷ οὐ μὴ καταισχυνθῇ.

The issue is the final phrase of Isaiah 28:16 and its quotation in Romans 9:33 (reappearing in Romans 10:11): ὁ πιστεύων ἐπ᾽ αὐτῷ οὐ καταισχυνθήσεται, "whoever believes in him will not be put to shame." Though Paul's wording does not precisely match the LXX,[14] it does correspond to the LXX in one of the ways in which the LXX departs from the MT: ἐπ᾽ αὐτῷ, "in him."[15] The MT instead says, "One who trusts will not panic." Arguably, "in him" is an important part of the verse for the apostle, and it appears not in the MT but in the LXX.

Introduction to the Septuagint, 627–40, at 627–28. As for 1 Corinthians 2:9, the source might be Isaiah 64:4 (v. 3 in MT), which is the traditional explanation, followed by Archer and Chirichigno, *Old Testament Quotations in the New Testament*, 132–33. John Calvin held the same view on 1 Corinthians 2:9, which showed that the apostles "paid more attention to the [subject] matter than to the words"; John Calvin, *Commentary on the Book of the Prophet Isaiah* (repr.; Grand Rapids: Eerdmans, 1956), 4.364.

[13] Wagner, *Heralds of the Good News*, 344 with note 6.

[14] Which is why Silva, "Old Testament in Paul," 631, puts Romans 9:33 in the unaligned category (Paul ≠ LXX ≠ MT).

[15] According to the apparatus in Joseph Ziegler, ed., *Isaias*, 3rd ed., Septuaginta 14 (Göttingen: Vandenhoeck & Ruprecht, 1983), 218, these words are obelized in Ra 88 and absent from some witnesses of the Origenian recension.

Next, Isaiah 52:15 in Romans 15:21:

Romans 15:21

But as it is written, "Those who have never been told of him shall see, and those who have never heard of him shall understand."

ἀλλὰ καθὼς γέγραπται· οἷς οὐκ ἀνηγγέλη περὶ αὐτοῦ ὄψονται, καὶ οἳ οὐκ ἀκηκόασιν συνήσουσιν.

Isaiah 52:15

So shall many nations be astonished at him, and kings shall shut their mouth, because those who were not informed about him shall see and those who did not hear shall understand.

οὕτως θαυμάσονται ἔθνη πολλὰ ἐπ᾽ αὐτῷ, καὶ συνέξουσι βασιλεῖς τὸ στόμα αὐτῶν· ὅτι οἷς οὐκ ἀνηγγέλη περὶ αὐτοῦ, ὄψονται, καὶ οἳ οὐκ ἀκηκόασι, συνήσουσι.

What is especially relevant in this case is the clause οἷς οὐκ ἀνηγγέλη περὶ αὐτοῦ ὄψονται, "those who have never been told of him shall see." Here Paul's language matches the LXX precisely, whereas the MT has "that which had not been told them they shall see."[16] In other words, the MT's להם ("to them") is rendered in the LXX with περὶ αὐτοῦ ("about him"), which more easily allows for a reference to Christ. Not surprisingly, that is how Paul takes it, since he quotes this passage in reference to his own preaching ministry:

> Thus I make it my ambition to proclaim the good news, not where Christ has already been named, so that I do not build on someone else's foundation, but as it is written, "Those who have never been told of him shall see." (Rom. 15:20–21)

These passages present just a few examples of how the wording of the LXX, as opposed to the MT, was important for Paul. But I have already mentioned that Paul's use of the LXX is not universal in his letters, and even some of these examples above show the apostle alternately departing from and agreeing with the LXX. Just to drive home the point that Paul cited

---

[16] The difference is small enough that Silva, "Old Testament in Paul," 631, puts this verse in the unanimous category (Paul = LXX = MT).

not just one textual tradition but a variety, I mention here the quotation of Deuteronomy 32:35 in Romans 12:19:

Romans 12:19

For it is written, "Vengeance is mine, I will repay, says the Lord."

γέγραπται γάρ· ἐμοὶ ἐκδίκησις, ἐγὼ ἀνταποδώσω, λέγει κύριος.

Deuteronomy 32:35

In a day of vengeance, I will repay.

ἐν ἡμέρᾳ ἐκδικήσεως ἀνταποδώσω.

Vengeance is mine, and recompense.

לִי נָקָם וְשִׁלֵּם.

To undergird his admonition against revenge, the apostle quotes Deuteronomy 32:35 in a form combining elements from the MT (the first bit) and the LXX (the second bit). The LXX's translation "in a day of vengeance" corresponds to the reading in the Samaritan Pentateuch (ליום for MT's לי). Carmel McCarthy, the editor for BHQ Deuteronomy, judges the MT in this verse corrupt and the LXX/SamP reading more original.[17] The writer of Hebrews quotes the passage (10:30) in precisely the same form as Paul.[18] McCarthy points out that other witnesses also attest to the mixed form of the verse similar to what we find in the New Testament quotations, including Symmachus, the Vulgate, the Syriac, and the Targumim.

Hebrews

The Epistle to the Hebrews quotes Scripture thirty-seven times, almost always the Psalms (eighteen times), the Pentateuch (eleven times), and the Prophets (seven times). These quotations have received a great deal

---

[17] Carmel McCarthy, ed., *Deuteronomy*, BHQ 5 (Stuttgart: Deutsche Bibelgesellschaft, 2007), 150*–51*.

[18] This reading is similar to that of Symmachus as recorded in the Syro-Hexapla; reported in the second apparatus of John William Wevers, ed., *Deuteronomium*, Septuaginta 3.2 (Göttingen: Vandenhoeck & Ruprecht, 1977), 356.

of attention, including in terms of their textual form.[19] Hebrews uses the LXX text form more consistently than does any other portion of the New Testament. One particularly important example, and the only one we will examine here, is the quotation of Psalm 40 (LXX Psalm 39) in Hebrews 10. There are a few minor differences in this quotation between Hebrews and the LXX—such as ᾔτησας (you requested) in LXX Psalm 39:7 (Eng. Ps. 40:6) as opposed to εὐδόκησας (you desired) in Hebrews in 10:6—but it is again clear in this passage that Hebrews is quoting the Septuagint.[20] There is one significant textual issue, however, that has generated significant discussion, an issue found in the second clause of the quoted material in Hebrews 10:5: σῶμα δὲ κατηρτίσω μοι (a body you prepared for me). The corresponding line in the Hebrew text of the Psalm reads אזנים כרית לי (ears you have dug for me).

The problems are obvious: first, what in the world does "ears you have dug for me" mean and, second, why does Hebrews 10:5 contain nothing about ears but a statement about a body? And what about the LXX reading? Here there continues to be debate. The most authoritative version of LXX Psalms prints the text of this line as ὠτία δὲ κατηρτίσω μοι, "ears you prepared for me," but the editor (Rahlfs) can cite no Greek manuscript in support, only some Latin evidence.[21] Some scholars fault Rahlfs and argue instead that the original Greek translation had "body," in agreement with the Septuagint manuscripts. In any case, no scholar seems to imagine that

---

[19] E.g., Radu Gheorghita, *The Role of the Septuagint in Hebrews: An Investigation of Its Influence with Special Consideration to the Use of Hab 2:3–4 in Heb 10:37–38* (Tübingen: Mohr Siebeck, 2003); Gert J. Steyn, *A Quest for the Assumed LXX Vorlage of the Explicit Quotations in Hebrew* (Göttingen: Vandenhoeck & Ruprecht, 2011); Georg A. Walser, *Old Testament Quotations in Hebrews: Studies in Their Textual and Contextual Background* (Tübingen: Mohr Siebeck: 2013).

[20] There are also a few other differences; see Karen H. Jobes and Moisés Silva, *Invitation to the Septuagint*, 2nd ed. (Grand Rapids: Baker, 2015), 216–19.

[21] Alfred Rahlfs, ed., *Psalmi cum Odis*, Septuaginta 10 (Göttingen: Vandenhoeck & Ruprecht, 1931), 143. Unlike other volumes in this series, this edition of Psalms is preparatory and does not present all the relevant evidence. A new, multidecade project is underway in Göttingen, under the leadership of Reinhard Gregor Kratz and Felix Albrecht, aiming at a new edition of the Greek Psalter; for a description see Felix Albrecht, "Report on the Göttingen Septuagint," *Textus* 29 (2020): 201–20.

the Septuagint translated from a Hebrew text different from the MT.[22] It has been proposed that *ears* became *body* through a copying error in the Greek manuscripts, but *body* might also be explained as an interpretation of "ears," on the assumption that "ears" is a metonymy or synecdoche, part for the whole. "Ears you have dug for me" might mean something like "you have opened my ears" so that I might obey (with my whole body, not just my ears). The Midrash interprets the line in light of the general biblical theme that God prefers obedience to sacrifice.[23] Even so, scholars debate various possibilities to explain the reading in Hebrews. Did the original Greek Psalter have "body," as reflected in the quotation in Hebrews? Or perhaps the Greek Psalter originally had "ears," but the author of Hebrews had access to a copy of the Greek Psalter with "body." Or maybe the author of Hebrews himself introduced the reading "body" (because of a part-for-whole interpretation), and this new reading subsequently influenced the textual transmission of the Psalms. It is difficult to judge among these possibilities. On the one hand, the Greek Psalter is usually a very literal translation, which makes it difficult to imagine that the translator would alter the reading so drastically as to go from "ears" to "body." On the other hand, the writer of Hebrews usually quotes the LXX rather precisely, making it unlikely that he himself introduced the reading "body." Moreover, scholars have found that the often-hypothesized influence of the New Testament on the transmission history of the LXX is not really borne out by the evidence, a point against the notion that the newly introduced reading "body" in Hebrews would have influenced LXX manuscripts of the Psalms.[24]

The difficulties surrounding this example continue to provoke divergent scholarly solutions, and I have no new proposal to make, nor do I care here even to support a particular viewpoint.[25] Even so, this unusually difficult

---

[22] On a proposal to emend the Hebrew text, see Walser, *Old Testament Quotations*, 92–93.

[23] William G. Braude, trans., *The Midrash on Psalms*, 2 vols. (New Haven, CT: Yale University Press, 1959), 1.435.

[24] Martin Karrer, "LXX Psalm 39:7–10 in Hebrews 10:5–7," in *Psalms and Hebrews: Studies in Reception*, ed. Dirk J. Human and Gert Jacobus Steyn (London: Bloomsbury, 2010), 126–46, at 142.

[25] For helpful discussions, see Karrer, "LXX Psalm 39:7–10 in Hebrews 10:5–7," 137–45; Jobes and Silva, *Invitation to the Septuagint*, 216–19; Walser, *Old Testament Quotations*, 90–140; Christian-Bernard Amphoux and Gilles Dorival, "'Des oreilles, tu m'as creusées'

example should not distract us from the main point that the writer of Hebrews routinely quoted the Septuagint, whether or not he felt free on occasion (as Paul did) to adjust its wording.

Gospels

As with Paul, there are also a variety of text forms employed in the Gospels. Perhaps unexpectedly, the Old Testament quotations attributed to Jesus are almost wholly Septuagintal, and sometimes the point Jesus wants to make is apparently dependent on the particular form of the cited verse preserved in the LXX.[26] A good example of the latter phenomenon is the citation of Psalm 8:3 (verse 2 in English) at Matthew 21:16: "Out of the mouths of infants and nursing babes you have prepared praise [αἶνος] for yourself," as Jesus quotes it, in precise agreement with the LXX. The MT has "strength" [עֹז] instead of "praise." Jesus cites the passage because some children were praising him.

On the other hand, the editorial quotations (i.e., not spoken by one of the characters in the story) from the Evangelists sometimes depart from the main LXX tradition. This statement is more true in relation to the first and fourth Gospels than the second and third: Mark, in fact, contains only a single editorial quotation (only Mark 1:2-3), whereas Luke contains only

---

ou 'un corps, tu m'as ajusté'? À propos du Psaume 39 (40 TM), 7," in Φιλολογία: *Mélanges offerts à Michel Casevitz*, ed. Pascale Brillet-Dubois and Edith Parmentier (Lyon: Maison de l'Orient et de la Méditerranée, 2006), 315–27.

[26] Richard N. Longenecker, *Biblical Exegesis in the Apostolic Period*, 2nd ed. (Grand Rapids: Eerdmans, 1999), 41–50; Longenecker mentions three citations for which Jesus's point is dependent on the LXX text form: Matthew 15:8–9 (Isa. 29:13); Matthew 21:16 (Ps. 8:3); Luke 4:18 (Isa. 61:1). But see the qualifications in Karrer, "Septuagint Text in Early Christianity," 618–20. Already, E. W. Grinfield, *An Apology for the Septuagint: In Which Its Claims to Biblical and Canonical Authority Are Briefly Stated and Vindicated* (London: William Pickering, 1850), 30–31: "Out of thirty-seven quotations made by Jesus himself from the Old Testament, thirty-three agree almost *verbatim* with the LXX, two agree with the Hebrew, and differ from the LXX, one differs from both, and one agrees partially with both. Only six agree exactly with the Hebrew. From this enumeration, it is plain, that our Lord constantly used and quoted the version." See also 185, where Grinfield recognizes the different character of the quotations in the mouth of Jesus and the editorial quotations.

a few more and relies typically on the LXX (Luke 3:4–6; 4:18–19; cf. also 2:23–24). There are difficulties, of course: Luke's quotation of Isaiah 61 at Luke 4:18–19 is not a precise reproduction of the Old Greek (he omits from Isa. 61:1 the bit about the "brokenhearted," and he draws "let the oppressed go free," the last phrase of Luke 4:18, from Isa. 58:6), but his inclusion of the phrase "sight to the blind" shows his reliance on the LXX rather than some other form of Isaiah.[27] As for John, there are the following seven editorial quotations to consider: 2:17 (Ps. 69:9); 12:15 (Zech. 9:9); 12:38 (Isa. 53:1); 12:40 (Isa. 6:9–10); 19:24 (Ps. 22:18); 19:36 (Exod. 12:46); and 19:37 (Zech. 12:10). Maarten Menken's thorough study of the quotations in the Gospel of John well illustrates the complexity. As a general rule, Menken concludes, "it is evident that the LXX is the Bible of the fourth evangelist."[28] He then qualifies this statement:

> The evangelist's use of the LXX does not exclude an occasional recourse to the Hebrew text. We saw that—apart from minor influences of the Hebrew on details, especially the case of 7:38—the quotations in 12:40 and 13:18 are independent translations, apparently by the evangelist himself, from the Hebrew (except for the last three words of 12:40, which come from the LXX). The quotation in 19:37 comes from a current early Christian translation of the Hebrew text instead of from the LXX.[29]

Colton Moore has shown that John's use of Zechariah has affinities with the textual form preserved in Theodotion's translation.[30] The Septuagint was influential but not exclusively so.

---

[27] For comment on this quotation, see David W. Pao and Eckhard J. Schnabel, "Luke," in *Commentary on the New Testament Use of the Old Testament*, ed. G. K. Beale and D. A. Carson (Grand Rapids: Baker, 2007), 287–90.

[28] Maarten J. J. Menken, *Old Testament Quotations in the Fourth Gospel: Studies in Textual Form* (Kampen: Kok Pharos, 1996), 206.

[29] Menken, *Old Testament Quotations*, 205; similarly, Richard Bauckham, *Gospel of Glory: Major Themes in Johannine Theology* (Grand Rapids: Baker, 2015), who repeatedly asserts that the Fourth Evangelist had recourse to the Hebrew Bible (e.g., 132, 154, 156–57).

[30] Colton Moore, "Theodotion Zechariah in the Fourth Gospel," *Novum Testamentum* 63 (2021): 221–28.

Now to Matthew, which contains more quotations than any of the other Gospels, almost as many as all three of the others put together (depending on how a count is made). Most of these quotations are on the lips of Jesus or one of the other characters in the Gospel, but there are eleven editorial quotations: 1:23 (Isa. 7:14); 2:15 (Hosea 11:1); 2:18 (Jer. 31:15); 2:23 (???); 3:3 (Isa. 40:3); 4:15–16 (Isa. 9:1–2); 8:17 (Isa. 53:4); 12:18–21 (Isa. 42:1–4); 13:35 (Ps. 78:2); 21:5 (Zech. 9:9); and 27:9–10 (Zech. 11:12–13). These quotations sometimes correspond to the Septuagint and sometimes depart from it. A clear case of departure from the Septuagint is the quotation of Hosea 11:1 in Matthew 2:15:

Matthew 2:15

Out of Egypt I called my son.   ἐξ Αἰγύπτου ἐκάλεσα τὸν υἱόν μου.

Hosea 11:1 LXX

Out of Egypt I called his children.   ἐξ Αἰγύπτου μετεκάλεσα τὰ τέκνα αὐτοῦ.[31]

Hosea 11:1 MT

And out of Egypt I called my son.   וממצרים קראתי לבני.

Here, Matthew follows a reading closer to the MT than to the LXX.[32] The reading of the LXX makes sense in its Hosea context, as the nation Israel could be thought of as God's son (MT; cf. Exod. 3:22–23) or the children of Israel (LXX's "his children"). But the LXX reading does not really work for Matthew's purposes.

The most famous and controversial quotation in Matthew's Gospel is the so-called prophecy of the virgin birth at 1:23 (Isa. 7:14), which was generating controversy already in the second century, as we saw at the beginning of this chapter. The controversy has concerned the translation of the Hebrew word עלמה, translated in the LXX with παρθένος, "virgin." It is perhaps understandable that attention should be focused on this word, but

---

[31] Some of the daughter versions of the Septuagint contain the reading "my son"; see Joseph Ziegler, ed., *Duodecim Prophetae*, 3rd ed., Septuaginta 13 (Göttingen: Vandenhoeck & Ruprecht, 1984), 172. This verse has also been preserved in the columnar arrangement of the Hexapla, in Ra 86, and presented as such in Ziegler's second apparatus.

[32] Maarten J. J. Menken, *Matthew's Bible: The Old Testament Text of the Evangelist* (Leuven: Leuven University Press, 2004), 133–42.

Matthew's attention seems to be directed elsewhere, to the word Ἐμμανουήλ (Immanuel), which Matthew translates as "God with us." The presence of Jesus with his disciples is a special theme of Matthew's Gospel.[33] At any rate, Matthew's quotation of Isaiah 7:14 does not follow the LXX unvaryingly:

Matthew 1:23

Look, the virgin shall conceive and bear a son, and they shall name him Emmanuel.	ἰδοὺ ἡ παρθένος ἐν γαστρὶ ἕξει καὶ τέξεται υἱόν, καὶ καλέσουσιν τὸ ὄνομα αὐτοῦ Ἐμμανουήλ.

Isaiah 7:14

Therefore the Lord himself will give you a sign. Look, the virgin shall be with child and bear a son, and you shall name him Emmanouel.	διὰ τοῦτο δώσει κύριος αὐτὸς ὑμῖν σημεῖον· ἰδοὺ ἡ παρθένος ἐν γαστρὶ ἕξει καὶ τέξεται υἱόν, καὶ καλέσεις τὸ ὄνομα αὐτοῦ Εμμανουηλ.

The only difference in the quotation is that Isaiah (LXX) says "you (sing.) shall name him," whereas Matthew has "they shall name him."[34] This is not an instance when Matthew's quotation corresponds better to the Hebrew text, which for this term is ambiguous but is traditionally understood among Jews to mean "she shall name him"—that is, the mother would supply the name.[35] Matthew has apparently adjusted the wording of the quotation to fit the situation with Jesus, who was not actually named Immanuel, either by his mother or by King Ahaz (the "you" addressed by Isaiah). Rather, Matthew presents this title Immanuel as something that "they" would call

---

[33] Richard B. Hays, *The Moral Vision of the New Testament: Community, Cross, New Creation; A Contemporary Introduction to New Testament Ethics* (New York: HarperCollins, 1996), 104–6.

[34] A few LXX witnesses have "he/she will call," and many have "you (pl.) will call," including Marchalianus (Q) and Lucianic manuscripts and others. Then again, a good many LXX manuscripts (but none of the majuscules) attest Matthew's reading, "they will call." In Matthew, Bezae reads "you will call." As for other variants in this verse, several LXX manuscripts have λήμψεται rather than ἕξει, including Origenian and Lucianic manuscripts, and a number of Church Fathers.

[35] See Amy-Jill Levine and Marc Zvi Brettler, *The Bible with and without Jesus: How Jews and Christians Read the Same Stories Differently* (San Francisco: HarperOne, 2020), 268.

him: the people would come to know Jesus as "God with us."[36] (For further reflections on this quotation, see the Epilogue.)

Acts

As in Luke's Gospel, so also in Acts the Septuagint has had a profound influence and is regularly quoted. There are about forty quotations, almost all of them in the major speeches: Peter's two sermons in Acts 2–3, Stephen's speech in Acts 7, and Paul's speech in Acts 13. Otherwise, Peter quotes Psalm 69:25; 109:8 at Acts 1:20, and he quotes Psalm 118:22 at Acts 4:11; the apostles quote Psalm 2:1–2 in their prayer at Acts 4:25–26; James quotes Amos 9:11–12 at Acts 15:16–17; and Paul quotes Exodus 22:28 before the Sanhedrin (Acts 23:5), and he quotes Isaiah 6:9–10 to the Roman Jews (Acts 28:26–27). There is only one editorial quotation in Acts, when the narrator reports that the Ethiopian eunuch had been reading Isaiah 53:7–8 (Acts 8:32–33).

An interesting case is James's quotation of Amos at the Jerusalem Council in Acts 15. The apostles and elders have convened to discuss the issue of the circumcision of Gentiles: is the practice required for those who express faith in Jesus (Acts 15:1–2)? Eventually James speaks, explaining that God's desire "to take from among them [the Gentiles] a people for his name . . . agrees with the words of the Prophets, as it is written" in Amos. James quotes Amos thus:

---

[36] For a thorough treatment, see Menken, *Matthew's Bible*, 117–31, who argues that Matthew presented the quotation as he found it in his source. On the use of παρθένος in the LXX here, see Andrew T. Lincoln, *Born of a Virgin? Reconceiving Jesus in the Bible, Tradition, and Theology* (Grand Rapids: Eerdmans, 2013), 74–77; H. G. M. Williamson, *Isaiah 6–12*, ICC (London: T&T Clark, 2018), 139.

Acts 15:16-17

After this I will return, and I will rebuild the dwelling of David, which has fallen; from its ruins I will rebuild it, and I will set it up, so that all other peoples may seek the Lord—even all the Gentiles over whom my name has been called. Thus says the Lord, who has been making these things.

μετὰ ταῦτα ἀναστρέψω καὶ ἀνοικοδομήσω τὴν σκηνὴν Δαυὶδ τὴν πεπτωκυῖαν καὶ τὰ κατεσκαμμένα αὐτῆς ἀνοικοδομήσω καὶ ἀνορθώσω αὐτήν, ὅπως ἂν ἐκζητήσωσιν οἱ κατάλοιποι τῶν ἀνθρώπων τὸν κύριον καὶ πάντα τὰ ἔθνη ἐφ᾽ οὓς ἐπικέκληται τὸ ὄνομά μου ἐπ᾽ αὐτούς, λέγει κύριος ποιῶν ταῦτα.

Amos 9:11-12

On that day I will raise up the tent of Dauid that is fallen and rebuild its ruins and raise up its destruction, and rebuild it as the days of old in order that those remaining of humans and all the nations upon whom my name has been called might seek out me, says the Lord who does these things.

ἐν τῇ ἡμέρᾳ ἐκείνῃ ἀναστήσω τὴν σκηνὴν Δαυιδ τὴν πεπτωκυῖαν καὶ ἀνοικοδομήσω τὰ πεπτωκότα αὐτῆς καὶ τὰ κατεσκαμμένα αὐτῆς ἀναστήσω καὶ ἀνοικοδομήσω αὐτὴν καθὼς αἱ ἡμέραι τοῦ αἰῶνος, ὅπως ἐκζητήσωσιν οἱ κατάλοιποι τῶν ἀνθρώπων καὶ πάντα τὰ ἔθνη, ἐφ᾽ οὓς ἐπικέκληται τὸ ὄνομά μου ἐπ᾽ αὐτούς, λέγει κύριος ὁ θεὸς ὁ ποιῶν ταῦτα.

This quotation has received much attention.[37] A close comparison of the text in Acts to the LXX shows some differences but generally close alignment. The significance of the agreement between Acts and LXX Amos becomes clear when one looks at the MT of Amos, which is significantly different (see the figure "Amos 9:11–12 in the MT and LXX"). The main difference comes at Amos 9:12, where the MT has "remnant of Edom" and the LXX has "those remaining of humans," but the entire sentence is reworded so that the MT comes across as very militaristic, pronouncing judgment upon the enemy Edom, whereas the LXX comes off as welcoming the foreigner into the people of God. It is no wonder that Luke presents James as quoting the LXX of Amos; had he used the MT, he could not have easily made his point about God wanting to include the Gentiles within his people.

---

[37] For instance, Luke Timothy Johnson, *Septuagintal Midrash in the Speeches of Acts* (Milwaukee: Marquette University Press, 2002), 17–18; McLay, *Use of the Septuagint in New Testament Research*, ch. 1.

Amos 9:11–12 in the MT (NRSV) and LXX (NETS) and Its Quotation by James at the Jerusalem Council in Acts 15:16–18 (NRSV)

NRSV (MT)	NETS (LXX)	Acts 15:16–18 (NRSV)
On that day I will raise up	On that day I will raise up	After this I will return, and I will rebuild
the booth of David that is fallen,	the tent of Dauid that is fallen	the dwelling of David, which has fallen;
and repair its breaches,	and rebuild its ruins	from its ruins I will rebuild it,
and raise up its ruins,	and raise up its destruction,	and I will set it up,
and rebuild it as in the days of old;	and rebuild it as the days of old	
in order that they may possess the remnant of Edom	in order that those remaining of humans	so that all other peoples .may seek the Lord—
and all the nations who are called by my name,	and all the nations upon whom my name has been called might seek out me,[38]	even all the Gentiles over whom my name has been called.
says the LORD who does this.	says the Lord.	Thus says the Lord, who has been making these things known from long ago.

It might be valuable to spend a little more time on this quotation. How is it that the LXX reads so differently from the MT? Scholars allow for the possibility that the LXX attests a Hebrew text different from the MT or, on the other hand, that the translator had the same consonantal text in front

---

[38] The note in NETS reveals that "me" is lacking in the Greek text, which does not have an explicit object for the verb "seek out." The "me" is present in the Lucianic manuscripts and others, according to the apparatus in Ziegler, *Duodecim Prophetae*, 204.

of him as is preserved in MT, but he interpreted his text differently. There are three main differences between the MT and LXX for Amos 9:12:[39]

1. Possess (MT) vs. seek (LXX). The MT has the word ירש (*yarash*), a common word (230×) that means "possess." The LXX's use of ἐκζητέω seems to correspond to a Hebrew text not with ירש (*yarash*) but with דרש (*darash*), also a common word (164×) and one meaning "seek."

2. Edom (MT) vs. mankind (LXX). Anyone who knows Hebrew can easily imagine what has happened. A Hebrew text written without vowels might contain a word that could be read either as Edom or as *adam*, which is the name for the man in the early chapters of Genesis precisely because it is a Hebrew word meaning "mankind." In a Hebrew text with only consonants, the word *Edom* and the word *adam* would often look identical (אדם) and a reader would decide which word was intended based on context. In this particular example, it looks like the context led some people to think of Edom and other people to think of mankind. Now, it is not quite that simple, because the MT has a letter (a *waw*) in our word that functions like a vowel (a *mater lectionis*) so that the word (אדום) has to be read as *Edom*, or at least with an o-vowel in the second syllable. That means the LXX translator either had a Hebrew text slightly different from our MT (missing the *waw*) or ignored the *waw* or overlooked it or thought it was wrong. Or, just maybe, the translator thought he was offering the sense of the passage despite departing from the literal wording.

3. Object (MT) vs. subject (LXX). This point again has to do with the reading Edom/mankind. In the MT, *Edom* functions as the object of the verb (possess), whereas in the LXX, *mankind* functions as the subject of the verb (seek). Sometimes in Hebrew a reader has to take a guess about whether a particular noun is the subject or object of the verb, but the MT clearly presents *Edom* as the object of the verb because it includes a little word (את, *et*) that signals the direct object. The LXX translator, however, apparently either had a Hebrew text

---

[39] There is a brief treatment in Anthony Gelston, ed., *The Twelve Minor Prophets*, BHQ 13 (Stuttgart: Deutsche Bibelgesellschaft, 2010), 88*.

lacking this little word, or he ignored it, or he interpreted it differently from its normal function.[40] Again, the translator may have felt that he was offering the sense of the passage without adhering strictly to the words.

As I have suggested, it is possible that the translator understood the passage to say something about "possessing Edom" but interpreted the expression as a synecdoche in light of the biblical theme of the conversion of the nations (cf. Mic. 4:1–4; etc.). That is, the translator may have intended his translation to clarify the meaning of the passage. Presumably the translator's rendering would not be the origin of this way of reading the end of Amos; that is, presumably, the translator had encountered the Minor Prophets in Hebrew previously and may have been a part of a community that routinely interpreted the ending of Amos in this creative way. This way of understanding the translator's work aligns with the analysis of Timothy McLay:

> With regard to Amos 9:12 we note that there are other cases where consonants have been confused in the translation of the Minor Prophets, but the fact that this variant involves three changes means that the alteration was probably not simply a case of misreading the consonantal text. In addition, the theology that *the rest/remainder of the peoples* would seek the Lord after the restoration of the people of Israel is a minor theme of the twelve prophets (see also Zech. 8:20–23; Mic. 7:17). Therefore, it is possible that reading the following clause *and all the nations over whom my name has been called* as parallel with the clause in question influenced the translator's understanding of the text.[41]

---

[40] "In certain instances אֵת serves apparently to introduce or to emphasize a nominative"; E. Kautzsch and A. E. Cowley, ed., *Gesenius' Hebrew Grammar*, 2nd ed. (Oxford: Clarendon, 1910), 165 at §117i. This idea is mentioned in regard to our passage by Wolfgang Kraus, "The Role of the Septuagint in the New Testament: Amos 9:11–12 as a Test Case," in *Translation Is Required: The Septuagint in Retrospect and Prospect*, ed. Robert J. V. Hiebert (Atlanta: SBL 2010), 171–90, at 181.

[41] McLay, *Use of the Septuagint in New Testament Research*, 23.

We do not know what led the translator to render the passage the way he did. Perhaps he had a Hebrew text slightly different from our Hebrew text, although no such Hebrew text is extant.[42] Perhaps he misread his Hebrew and interpreted it along the lines of a wider biblical theme (the conversion of the nations). Or perhaps he arrived at this interpretation intentionally, through no misreading. Whatever the case, at the Jerusalem Council (as narrated by Luke), James found in the LXX Amos 9:12 confirmation for the events he himself had witnessed.[43] God was now calling a people for himself out of the nations, as Amos had predicted so long beforehand.

Conclusion

As Jerome said in the epigraph to this chapter, "Let that translation be the true one which the apostles approved." But which translation is that? If one were to pick a single textual tradition as the dominant one used in the New Testament, certainly the LXX must be the pick. The Septuagint was enormously influential on the New Testament, in terms of its theological expression and specifically in the quotations of the Old Testament that we find in abundance in early Christian literature. When early Christians began to reflect on the best Old Testament text—that is, when they found themselves in dispute with Jews (Justin Martyr) or other Christians (Irenaeus) in regard to the proper interpretation of some Old Testament passages subject to varying translations—they followed the principle later articulated by Jerome: they adopted the text used by the apostles, which often led directly to the LXX.

---

[42] None of the Dead Sea Scrolls preserve these verses from Amos, and even the Greek Minor Versions (Aquila, Symmachus, and Theodotion) are unattested for Amos 9:11–12, as reported in the second apparatus in Ziegler, *Duodecim Prophetae*, 204–5. But the text as preserved in MT is already attested by the Wadi Murabbaat Scroll from the end of the first century CE, at least in terms of the second and third aspect highlighted earlier (the *waw* in Edom and the *et*); the verb is lost in a lacuna. See the edition of J. T. Milik in *Les Grottes de Murabba'ât: Texte*, DJD 2 (Oxford: Clarendon, 1961), 188.

[43] Kraus comments on some attempts to find the source of James's quotation in a text other than the LXX; "Role of the Septuagint in the New Testament," 184.

And yet we have seen that this way of representing the apostolic quotations does not tell the whole story. There are plenty of quotations that depart from the LXX, some of which align better with the MT, many that do not. Jerome knew well this complicated textual picture, and it is most likely that his comment approving the apostolic selection of Old Testament text was intended not as an endorsement of the LXX—as his contemporaries might have interpreted it and as many modern scholars have assumed—but rather as a subtle nod toward the argument he was already at that time developing, that the apostolic quotations conformed to the Hebrew text. Any such simple evaluation is bound to be overly simplistic, Jerome's even more so than the view he was opposing.

In the centuries after the apostles, the New Testament quotations became the foundational element of a theory of the best text of the Old Testament. Sometimes the Church Fathers simply assumed that the apostles quoted the Septuagint; sometimes they encountered New Testament quotations that did not easily fit that narrative, so they devised various explanations to account for such data. Some Church Fathers did not look at the Septuagint as a sacrosanct text. Jerome argued this position more forcefully than any of the other Fathers in the first several centuries. But no matter what position was advocated, at the heart of the argument was always the practice of the apostles.

The Text of the Septuagint among the Fathers

Here we move into Christianity after the New Testament and up to the early fifth century. If we had to isolate one main character in this section, it would probably be Origen, the Greek writer born around 185 CE in Alexandria who almost single-handedly pioneered Christian theology and Christian textual scholarship before he died in the early 250s CE in Caesarea. Though no single chapter below is dedicated to Origen, he features prominently in Chapters Seven and Eight and sets the stage for Chapters Nine and Ten. Origen's work on the text of the LXX (Chapter Seven) and his views on its authority (Chapter Eight) dominate the subsequent reception of the translation.

The first two chapters in this section deal with the Greek Christian world, while the last two chapters turn to the Latin world. The main players in Chapters Seven and Eight include the second-century authors Justin Martyr and Irenaeus of Lyons; Origen in the third century; and in the fourth century we encounter Eusebius of Caesarea, the famed church historian; Eusebius of Emesa; Basil of Caesarea and his brother Gregory of Nyssa; and Epiphanius of Salamis; and in the fifth century, Theodoret of Cyrus. When we turn our attention to Latin writers, we devote one chapter a piece to the two most important Latin biblical interpreters in the patristic era—or any other era, for that matter: Jerome, the Bible translator and commentator who died around 420 CE, and his younger contemporary Augustine, the great bishop of Hippo in North Africa whose works continue to inspire and challenge theologians.

Throughout the patristic era, the LXX was the Christian Old Testament, both in Greek and in Latin (the latter being a translation of a translation). In this section we examine their text-critical work on the LXX (Chapters Seven and Nine) and especially their thoughts on the LXX. Most patristic writers affirmed the divine inspiration of the LXX, but here we want to press beyond that affirmation to the way these Christians imagined the relationship between the Greek translation and the Hebrew texts circulating among Jews. We are especially interested in how they thought about the many passages in which the LXX and the Hebrew contain different texts. Sometimes the Fathers declared the LXX correct and the Hebrew at fault, and sometimes they took the opposite approach, but it was often an issue they felt compelled to address.

7

Varietas

Patristic Textual Criticism on the LXX

Alexandria and Egypt praise Hesychius as the authority in their Septuagint, [the territory from] Constantinople all the way to Antioch approves the exemplars of the martyr Lucian, and the provinces between those read Palestinian codices that were worked over by Origen and that Eusebius and Pamphilus disseminated, and the entire world fights among itself due to this *trifaria varietas.*

—Jerome, *Preface to Chronicles from the Hebrew*[1]

Jerome wrote the above words in the year 396, explaining the *trifaria varietas* or "threefold variety" into which LXX manuscripts could be divided.[2] Greek-speaking Christians in the fourth century had options when it came to which Old Testament version they would read. Actually, "version" is not the right word; Jerome was talking about recensions. All three of the editions that Jerome named were recensions of the Septuagint. Origen and Hesychius and Lucian all started with the Septuagint and revised it

---

[1] *Biblia Sacra iuxta vulgatam versionem*, ed. R. Weber and R. Gryson, 5th ed. (Stuttgart: Deutsche Bibelgesellschaft, 2007), 546, lines 9–12.

[2] On the date, see J. N. D. Kelly, *Jerome: His Life, Writings, and Controversies* (New York: Harper & Row, 1975), 190. This dating is established by Jerome's statement in his preface that he had recently written *De optimo genere interpretandi* (i.e., *Epist.* 57 to Pammachius, dating to 395). For that statement in Jerome's preface, see Weber and Gryson, *Biblia Sacra*, 546 line 21.

in some way; they did not produce new translations from the Hebrew. (Even *recension* might not be the right word; maybe *edition* would be more appropriate.) Perhaps none of them even knew Hebrew, or probably not any more than the letters of the alphabet. Different reasons compelled them to issue their own editions of the Septuagint. In Chapter Five, we saw that there had already been significant recensional activity in the Greek Old Testament even before the birth of Christianity, an activity that continued into the second century CE among Jews. These texts circulated among Christians—texts that were generally much closer to the by-now standard form of the Hebrew text, the proto-MT—leading to some concerns about the obvious differences among these editions of the Greek Old Testament. Which one was the true text? In the next chapter, we will look at how early Christians thought about that question and what answers they devised. Here we will look at the actual recensions that Christians developed, partly in response to the variety of texts confronting them. But revising the Septuagint toward the Hebrew—which is not necessarily the way Origen or others would have described their own activities, as we will see—was not the only motivation for Christian recensional activity. Another problem some Christians perceived with the Septuagint is that it did not compare favorably with Greek literature. The Septuagint was sometimes thought to exhibit poor literary quality, and some Christians (this aim is especially associated with Lucian) sought to help the Septuagint out on this score, to improve its vocabulary and literary style. On the other hand, Hesychius is more of a mystery.

We do not actually have any of these recensions as such. There are no manuscripts labeled "Origen's Recension" or "Lucian's Recension" or "Hesychius's Recension." The closest thing to that are the colophons (editorial notes at the close of a book) in some manuscripts. We will meet some of these colophons in this chapter. For the most part, though, the recensions are disguised as regular Septuagint manuscripts, meaning that scholars must investigate the textual profile of individual manuscripts to determine whether they belong to one of these recensions. Greek manuscripts often have a mixed character, featuring one biblical book according to one recension, and another biblical book with a different textual profile. The identification of the individual recensions constituting Jerome's *trifaria varietas* has occupied generations of Septuagint scholars.[3]

In this chapter, we will see what scholars think they know about these recensions. We will spend most of our time on Origen because he is by far the most famous of the three, his recension has been the most investigated, and his work has had the most widespread impact on the textual transmission of the Septuagint. Lucian will attract less of our attention and Hesychius much less than Lucian. But first we need to understand which texts, besides the Septuagint, were available to Christians in the second through fourth or fifth centuries. Our emphasis is especially on textual options in Greek and to some extent we will look at Latin evidence, but we will not venture into other languages in which Christians read Scripture.

Old Testament Versions Available to Early Christians[4]

The earliest Christians who mention the Septuagint—rather than simply quoting its text, as we find in the New Testament and Apostolic Fathers—do so in a context in which they contrast the Septuagint with other translations. Justin Martyr defends what he thinks is the reading of the Septuagint against other translations proposed by Jews, discussing several such passages, but he names no translator apart from the Seventy.[5] In the late second century CE,

---

[3] See the chapter called "The *Trifaria Varietas*" in Sidney Jellicoe, *The Septuagint and Modern Study* (Oxford: Oxford University Press, 1968), 134–71 (and also 344–48). For a treatment and rejection of Jerome's schema, see S. Kreuzer, "'*Et a plerisque nunc loukianeios dicitur*': Jerome's Statements on the Greek Biblical Texts and Modern Septuagint Scholarship," *Zeitschrift für die alttestamentliche Wissenschaft* 130 (2018): 69–85; a more positive use of Jerome's schema is found in Felix Albrecht, "Von der *hebraica veritas* zur *vera graecitas*: Origenes—Hesych—Lukian," *Biblische Notizen* 184 (2020): 105–41.

[4] Much of the material in this chapter was originally written for my essay in *Textual History of the Bible*, ed. Armin Lange, vol. 3 (Leiden: Brill, forthcoming).

[5] For Justin's comments on Isaiah 7:14, see his *Dial.* 43.8; 67–68, 71, 84. Justin also mentions textual divergence in regard to the following biblical verses: Jeremiah 11:19 (*Dial.* 72); Psalm 96:10 (*Dial.* 73); Genesis 49:10 (*Dial.* 120.4); Psalm 82:7 (?; *Dial.* 124.3–4); Deuteronomy 32:8 (*Dial.* 131.1); Isaiah 3:9 (*Dial.* 137.3). Some of Justin's comments on these textual issues are difficult to reconcile with our manuscripts of the Septuagint, so Justin must have

Irenaeus of Lyons names two translators who have published what Irenaeus regards as inferior translations compared with the Septuagint, especially in regard to Isaiah 7:14, a verse quoted in the New Testament (Matt. 1:23), as we saw in the previous chapter:

> So God became man and the Lord himself saved us, giving us the sign of the virgin [τὸ τῆς παρθένου σημεῖον], but not as some say, who at the present time venture to translate the Scriptures, ἰδοὺ ἡ νεᾶνις ἐν γαστρὶ ἕξει καὶ τέξεται υἱόν, "behold a young woman shall conceive and bear a son," as Theodotion the Ephesian translated it and Aquila from Pontus, both of them Jewish proselytes, whom the Ebionites follow and aver that he was begotten by Joseph. (*Haer.* 3.21.1, preserved in Eusebius, *Hist. eccl.* 5.8.10)[6]

Not long after Irenaeus, another translator, Symmachus, would achieve notoriety in Christian circles, starting with the use of his translation by Origen. Aquila, Symmachus, and Theodotion are the three translators included by Origen in his Hexapla, and so they became for Christians the standard non-Septuagintal translators, known collectively as "the Three." Christian authors, due to Origen's labors, were also familiar with other Greek versions, called the *Quinta*—that is, the "fifth" version, after the LXX and the Three—the *Sexta* (sixth), and the *Septima* (seventh). None of these versions has come down to us except in fragments. The Three were included in Origen's Hexapla, which also has not survived. We mostly rely on patristic quotations of the Three, and sometimes the other versions, along with a few scraps preserving parts of some of the translations. Scholars debate many issues regarding each of these versions, in some cases even their existence.[7]

It is generally agreed now that Aquila's translation in the second quarter of the second century can be described as isomorphic, and his translation

---

misread the evidence. See O. Skarsaune, *The Proof from Prophecy: A Study in Justin Martyr's Proof-Text Tradition* (Leiden: Brill, 1987).

[6] Text and translation taken from Eusebius, *The Ecclesiastical History*, vol. 1, trans. Kirsopp Lake, Loeb Classical Library (Cambridge, MA: Harvard University Press, 1926), 458–59.

[7] See the relevant chapters in Natalio Fernández Marcos, *The Septuagint in Context: Introduction to the Greek Version of the Bible* (Leiden: Brill, 2000).

technique was an extreme example of a tradition that preceded him by some centuries aimed at revising the Septuagint toward the reigning Hebrew text.[8] Despite Christian confusion regarding the date of Theodotion, this translator actually preceded Aquila and was a part of this earlier tradition (the *kaige* tradition). Symmachus, in the later second century CE, followed the proto-MT but produced more pleasing Greek than his predecessors. Patristic authors often attribute to him an especially clear translation.[9] In Chapter Five, we mentioned these translators within the context of the textual situation in ancient Judaism.

Early Christians had access to a few other biblical texts besides those named above. Some were familiar with the *Samareitikon*, an edition of the Septuagint aligned toward the Samaritan Pentateuch.[10] A Greek transcription of the Hebrew text of the proto-MT also existed, available in the Hexapla and perhaps preexisting the Hexapla.[11] Finally, some patristic authors could access the Hebrew text directly. Jerome is the prime example here, but the tradition also attributes to Origen's Hexapla a Hebrew column in Hebrew letters, and scholars tend to affirm this tradition.[12] That is not to say that Origen could work with the Hebrew text to any great extent,

---

[8] The seminal study here is Dominique Barthélemy, *Les devanciers d'Aquila*, VTSup 10 (Leiden: Brill, 1963).

[9] See Adam Kamesar, *Jerome, Greek Scholarship, and the Hebrew Bible: A Study of the Quaestiones Hebraicae in Genesim* (Oxford: Clarendon, 1993), 37–38.

[10] See Reinhard Pummer, *Early Christian Authors on Samaritans and Samaritanism*, TSAJ 92 (Tübingen: Mohr Siebeck 2002); Reinhard Pummer, "The Greek Bible and the Samaritans," *Revue des études juives* 157 (1998): 269–358. Might the *Samareitikon* have featured within Origen's Hexapla? See Anthony Grafton and Megan Hale Williams, *Christianity and the Transformation of the Book: Origen, Eusebius, and the Library of Caesarea* (Cambridge, MA: Harvard University Press, 2006), 95–96.

[11] On whether Origen commissioned the Greek transcription or acquired a preexisting text, see Benjamin Paul Kantor, "The Second Column (Secunda) of Origen's Hexapla in Light of Greek Pronunciation" (PhD diss., University of Texas at Austin, 2017), 10–47. Kantor considers it more likely that Origen acquired a preexisting transcription.

[12] See especially R. G. Jenkins, "The First Column of the Hexapla: The Evidence of the Milan Codex (Rahlfs 1098) and the Cairo Genizah Fragment (Rahlfs 2005)," in *Origen's Hexapla and Fragments: Papers Presented at the Rich Seminar on the Hexapla, Oxford Centre for Hebrew and Jewish Studies, 25th July–3rd August 1994*, ed. Alison Salvesen (Tübingen: Mohr Siebeck, 1998), 88–102. Or, more conveniently, see Benjamin Kantor, *The Oldest Fragment of Origen's Hexapla: T-S 12.182*, March 2019, https://doi.org/10.17863/CAM.45329.

nor other patristic writers either, aside from Jerome.[13] Jerome also attests on occasion to acquaintance with Hebrew manuscripts of the Samaritan Pentateuch.[14]

Origen

The first great scholar that Christians produced was Origen, born in Alexandria about 185 and based at Caesarea from about 230. Much of what we know about Origen's life is owing to the narrative supplied by his fourth-century admirer Eusebius of Caesarea, the great church historian, who dedicated much of book 6 of his *Ecclesiastical History* to Origen.[15] According to Eusebius, Origen's father was martyred in about the year 202 (*Hist. eccl.* 6.2.12–13), and Origen himself died around 254 due to injuries sustained during the persecution under Emperor Decius.[16] In the meantime, he generated an enormous body of scholarship dedicated to the exposition of the Christian scriptures. He was nicknamed "Adamantius" (*Hist. eccl.* 6.14.10) because he wrote day and night like he was running out of time.[17] He paid particular attention to the textual form of the Old Testament, producing a research tool called the Hexapla that displayed many textual difficulties among a variety of witnesses to the Old Testament and would prove to be seminal not only to the subsequent textual transmission of the Septuagint

---

[13] The classic article that tends to paint patristic knowledge of Hebrew in a rather negative light is C. J. Elliott, "Hebrew Learning among the Fathers," in *Dictionary of Christian Biography*, ed. W. Smith and H. Wace, 4 vols. (London: John Murray, 1877–1887), 2.851–72. On Origen, see N. R. M. de Lange, *Origen and the Jews: Studies in Jewish-Christian Relations in Third-Century Palestine* (Cambridge: Cambridge University Press, 1976), 21–23; Kantor, "Second Column," 11–39.

[14] See his *Comm. Gal.* 3:10, commenting on Deut. 27:26; see the discussion in Edmon L. Gallagher, *Hebrew Scripture in Patristic Biblical Theory: Canon, Language, Text* (Leiden: Brill, 2012), 199–200.

[15] For modern accounts of Origen's biblical scholarship, see Grafton and Williams, *Christianity and the Transformation of the Book*; Ronald E. Heine, *Origen: Scholarship in the Service of the Church* (Oxford: Oxford University Press, 2010); Peter W. Martens, *Origen and Scripture: The Contours of the Exegetical Life* (Oxford: Oxford University Press, 2012).

[16] Heine, *Origen*, 219.

[17] On Origen's works, see Jerome, *Epist.* 33, an incomplete list, on which see Pierre Nautin, *Origène: Sa vie et son œuvre* (Paris: Beauchesne, 1977), 214.

but to the way Christians thought about the Septuagint and other Old Testament texts.

Most of Origen's works have been lost. Origen was a speculative theologian who lived before the Christian councils that in the fourth century would articulate orthodox Christian belief, so some of the ideas he proposed were later misunderstood and/or viewed with suspicion, so much so that eventually, three centuries after his death, the Second Council of Constantinople condemned him in the year 553.[18] One of the effects of this condemnation is that most of Origen's works were no longer copied. The Hexapla suffered the same fate as many of his other writings but probably for different reasons. Its immensity probably discouraged copyists from making a full reproduction of the original Hexapla that resided in the library at Caesarea, so the only full copy of the Hexapla that ever existed likely perished during the seventh century when the city was captured alternately by Persians and Arabs.[19]

What is the Hexapla? In the sources available to us, Origen never uses the term *Hexapla* (τὰ Ἑξαπλᾶ, "sixfold"), and some scholars doubt whether our sources ever present Origen describing the multicolumn Bible. The earliest certain description of the Hexapla is from Eusebius:

> And so accurate was the examination that Origen brought to bear upon the divine books, that he even made a thorough study of the Hebrew tongue, and got into his own possession the original writings in the actual Hebrew characters, which were extant among the Jews. Thus, too, he traced the editions of the other translators of the sacred writings besides the Seventy; and besides the beaten track of translations, that of Aquila and Symmachus and Theodotion, he discovered certain others, which were used in turn, which, after lying hidden for a long time, he traced and brought to light, I know not from what recesses. With regard to these, on account of their obscurity (not knowing whose in the world they were) he merely indicated this:

---

[18] On the first wave of the Origenist Controversy, see Elizabeth A. Clark, *The Origenist Controversy: The Cultural Construction of an Early Christian Debate* (Princeton: Princeton University Press, 1992).

[19] See Andrew Carriker, *The Library of Eusebius of Caesarea* (Leiden: Brill, 2003), 28–29.

that the one he found at Nicopolis, near Actium, and the other in such another place. At any rate, in the Hexapla of the Psalms, after the four well-known editions, he placed beside them not only a fifth but also a sixth and a seventh translation; and in the case of one of these he has indicated again that it was found at Jericho in a jar in the time of Antoninus the son of Severus. All these he brought together, dividing them into clauses [διελών τε πρὸς κῶλον] and placing them one against the other [καὶ ἀντιπαραθεὶς ἀλλήλαις], together with the actual Hebrew text [μετὰ καὶ αὐτῆς τῆς Ἑβραίων σημειώσεως];[20] and so he has left us the copies of the Hexapla, as it is called.[21] He made a further separate arrangement of the edition of Aquila and Symmachus and Theodotion together with that of the Seventy, in the Tetrapla. (*Hist. eccl.* 6.16)[22]

A reader of Eusebius can only with difficulty imagine what the Hexapla looked like. But other fourth-century CE Christians—who, like Eusebius, probably saw the original Hexapla in the library of Caesarea[23]—provide more precise descriptions (Jerome, Rufinus, Epiphanius).[24] Moreover, a couple of palimpsest fragments of the Hexapla, both containing portions of the Psalter, turned up at the end of the nineteenth century: one from the Cairo Genizah, now in Cambridge (Ra 2005), the other from Milan (Ra 1098).[25] The six columns included (1) the Hebrew text, (2) a transliteration

---

[20] Compare the translation of Jeremy M. Schott in Eusebius of Caesarea, *The History of the Church: A New Translation* (Oakland: University of California Press, 2019), 300: "along with the Hebrew signifiers themselves." The Greek is a good deal more ambiguous than is Oulton's translation quoted in the text.

[21] Rufinus translates *et propter huiuscemodi compositionem exemplaria ipsa nominavit* Ἑξαπλᾶ, *id est sextiplici ordine scripta* "and because of its composition in this manner, he named those copies *Hexapla*, that is, written in sixfold order"; text ed. T. Mommsen in E. Schwartz, ed., *Eusebius Werke*, vol. 2, *Die Kirchengeschichte*, Part 2: *Die Bücher VI bis X* (Leipzig: Hinrichs, 1908), 555.

[22] Translation by J. E. L. Oulton, *Eusebius: The Ecclesiastical History*, vol. 2, Loeb Classical Library (Cambridge, MA: Harvard University Press, 1932), 51–53.

[23] See Grafton and Williams, *Christianity and the Transformation of the Book*, 89–95.

[24] See Jerome, *Comm. Tit.* 3.9; *Comm. Ps.* 1.4; Epiphanius, *Pan.* 64.3.5; *Mens.* 510–35; Rufinus, *Eccl. Hist.* 6.16.4.

[25] See the descriptions in Grafton and Williams, *Christianity and the Transformation of the Book*, 96–102. One should also note that Ra 86 contains a marginal reading with Hosea

of the same into Greek letters, and the translations of (3) Aquila, (4) Symmachus, (5) the LXX, and (6) Theodotion. Grafton and Williams estimate that the entire Hexapla would have occupied forty codices of four hundred leaves (eight hundred pages) each.[26] It would have been a work of enormous labor and expense, and of little practical value for most people, so that—as we have already surmised—it is doubtful whether a complete second copy of the Hexapla was ever made, though partial copies were obviously made, judging from the existing fragments.[27]

Origen's work on the text of the Septuagint affected the entire subsequent history of the translation. Nearly every aspect of Origen's textual scholarship continues to be debated, including the form it took and its aims. All scholars accept at least two points: that Origen created a multicolumn Old Testament called (at least, by later writers) the Hexapla and that he had a hand in creating a recension of the LXX that featured critical signs indicating quantitative differences between the standard LXX and the Hebrew text available to him. These critical signs—especially the asterisk and the obelus (a horizontal line)—had been developed in pre-Christian Alexandrian scholarship of pagan authors such as Homer as a way of marking passages that were problematic in some way. Origen adopted (and adapted) this system for his text-critical work on the LXX. He marked with an obelus those passages in the LXX that had no corresponding text in the Hebrew Bible (i.e., LXX pluses), and for the minuses in the LXX vis-à-vis the Hebrew text, Origen incorporated into the LXX material from later translators (especially Theodotion, according to Jerome)[28] and signaled such interpolations

---

11:1 in Hexaplaric (multicolumn) format; and Ra 113 has two lines in the heading of the book of Psalms.

[26] Grafton and Williams, *Christianity and the Transformation of the Book*, 105; see also Fernández Marcos, *Septuagint in Context*, 210n24. This is a better guess than the "fifteen large volumes" of Jellicoe, *Septuagint and Modern Study*, 127.

[27] A point emphasized by Reinhart Ceulemans, "Greek Christian Access to 'The Three,' 250–600 CE," in *Greek Scripture and the Rabbis*, ed. Timothy Michael Law and Alison Salvesen (Leuven: Peeters, 2014), 165–91.

[28] E.g., Jerome, *Preface to the Pentateuch*; *Preface to Chronicles* (*iuxta Hebraeos*), in Weber and Gryson, *Biblia Sacra*, 546, lines 12–16; *Preface to Job*; *Epist.* 112.19. But at *Comm. Isa.* 1.2.22, Jerome says that some text inserted by Origen into the LXX under asterisk derives from Aquila. Origen himself (*Comm. Matt.* 15.14) says only that he pulled the asterisked material from the other versions, without further specification. On the additions in Codex

by means of an asterisk. Scholars debate whether Origen used the critical signs in the LXX (fifth) column of the Hexapla itself—so that this fifth column would not have corresponded to the traditional LXX but rather to a reworked, Hebraized edition of the LXX—or rather whether Origen left the LXX untouched in the Hexapla and subsequently produced a stand-alone edition of the LXX marking the differences from the Hebrew text with these critical signs. The few fragmentary copies of the Hexapla preserved for us do not contain the critical signs, and usually the manuscripts containing portions of the stand-alone edition (the Origenian or Hexaplaric recension) do not contain the critical signs either, probably because scribes did not understand them or care for them. But we are not without sources, particularly for the recension, and painstaking research has further revealed the methods employed by Origen in editing the Old Testament text.

In two well-known passages, both from late in his career, Origen explains his text-critical labors on the LXX. While scholars have usually assumed that Origen was describing his work on the Hexapla, some scholars believe that he was rather describing a subsequent work, a recension of the LXX for which the Hexapla provided the essential critical tool. Both of these passages mention the critical signs marking deviations between the Hebrew text and Greek text. The question is essentially whether the fifth column (LXX column) of the Hexapla featured the asterisks and obeli, or whether that column contained the common LXX without quantitative alteration.

The earlier passage is in a letter Origen wrote to a fellow Christian named Julius Africanus, in response to Africanus's own letter criticizing Origen's use of the story of Susanna, one of the deuterocanonical additions to Daniel. Origen's letter constitutes a sustained critique of Africanus's position, which is essentially that Christians should excise the story of Susanna from their Bibles on the grounds that it is not a genuine part of the book of Daniel. Origen assures his correspondent that he himself is fully aware of the textual difficulties of the Greek Old Testament. He notes that he has engaged in extensive research on the differences between the Hebrew copies and the Greek copies of various Old Testament books. After mentioning several

---

Marchalianus (Q), see F. Schironi, "*P.Grenf.* 1.5, Origen, and the Scriptorium of Caesarea," *Bulletin of the American Society of Papyrologists* 52 (2015): 181–223, at 202 (mostly Theodotion).

examples of such differences (e.g., in Daniel, Esther, Job), he brings up a statement in Genesis: at Genesis 1:8, the Hebrew text says that immediately before the end of the second day of Creation Week, God named the firmament "heaven," whereas the LXX also has the additional comment that "God saw that it was good" before drawing Day Two to a close. It is in this context that Origen describes his methods for dealing with such differences between Greek and Hebrew:

> And in Genesis this statement: "God saw that it was good," in the case of the firmament is not found among the Hebrews [cf. Gen. 1:8]. And this is no ordinary problem among them.[29] And one can find other passages in Genesis, to which I have affixed the signs called *obeloi* among the Greeks, in order that such might be known to us. And again (I have affixed) asterisks to those passages present in the Hebrew but not found among us. (*Ep. Afr.* 7)

Origen says here that in such a case as Genesis 1:8, in which the LXX contains a line absent from the Hebrew, he marks such a line with an obelus, using an asterisk for the opposite situation.

The other passage in which Origen talks about his text-critical procedure is in his *Commentary on Matthew*. While commenting on Jesus's encounter with the rich young man (Matt. 19:16–22), Origen has occasion to mention a text-critical difficulty in the Gospel, which leads him to a discussion of his work on the text of the LXX:

> But now it is evident that much variation has arisen among the copies [of Matthew], whether because of the carelessness of some copyists, or because of the daring of some rogues, or because of those who are unwilling to undertake the correction of what has been written, or even because they add or remove things according to their own judgment in the process of correction. So then, God willing, we have been able to heal the discord in the copies of the Old Testament, using as a criterion the other editions. For regarding

---

[29] De Lange (*Lettre à Africanus*, 531n3) cites *Gen. Rab.* 4.6.

the things that the discord of the copies put in doubt among the Seventy, we made a judgment from the other editions and preserved what agreed with them. And some things we obelized since it did not exist in the Hebrew (though we did not dare to eliminate them completely), and other things we added with an asterisk, to make it clear that though they did not exist among the Seventy we added them from the other editions in harmony with the Hebrew, and the one who wants to can accept them, whereas whoever is offended by such a thing can do what he wants concerning the acceptance of them or not.[30]

The interpretation of all these passages is difficult and controversial. As I mentioned earlier, it was long assumed that Origen's description of his text-critical work on the LXX was a description of the Hexapla, or more specifically, the fifth (LXX) column of the Hexapla.[31] The idea has become more common over the previous generation—though it perhaps is still not the consensus view—that the fifth column of the Hexapla did not contain the critical text of Origen (with critical signs) but rather the common LXX text. If that is the case, then Origen's two descriptions of his text-critical work, where he mentions the employment of the obelus and asterisk, would be descriptions of a subsequent edition of the LXX.[32] Arguments in favor of this latter view include

---

[30] Translation adapted from Grafton and Williams, *Christianity and the Transformation of the Book*, 125; see also Fernández Marcos, *Septuagint in Context*, 209n21; Francesca Schironi, "The Ambiguity of Signs: Critical Σημεῖα from Zenodotus to Origen," in *Homer and the Bible in the Eyes of Ancient Interpreters*, ed. Maren R. Niehoff, Jerusalem Studies in Religion and Culture (Leiden: Brill, 2012), 87–112, at 101.

[31] This is the position assumed by Jellicoe, *Septuagint and Modern Study*, 123–24, 135, though he also discusses an alternative proposal, and considers it an open question (139). Heine, *Origen*, 76, still takes this position.

[32] This is the view of Grafton and Williams, *Christianity and the Transformation of the Book*, 116–17; John D. Meade, "Hexapla," in *The Dictionary of the Bible and Ancient Media*, ed. Tom Thatcher et al. (London: Bloomsbury, 2017), 170–72; Schironi, "*P.Grenf.* 1.5," and for references to scholars on either side of the debate, see 194nn31–32. See also the helpful discussion in Olivier Munnich, "Lex Hexaples d'Origène à la lumière de la tradition manuscrite de la Bible grecque," in *Origeniana Sexta: Origène et la Bible/Origen and the Bible*, ed. Gilles Dorival and Alain Le Boulluec (Leuven: Peeters, 1995), 167–85, esp. 174–77, who argues (based on evidence in Ra 344) that the fifth column of the Hexapla contained the Origenian recension. See also Peter J. Gentry, "Did Origen Use the Aristarchian Signs in the Hexapla?,"

especially the fact that critical signs marking quantitative differences among the various texts in a synoptic edition like the Hexapla seem rather pointless. Critical signs in an edition of a single text would be more helpful, and this corresponds to the limited manuscript evidence we have (see the figure "The Hexapla in Extant Sources"): on the one hand, single-language manuscripts with critical signs; on the other hand, manuscripts of the Hexapla without critical signs. In this scenario, the Hexapla would have been largely a study tool, a project preliminary to the creation of an improved text.[33]

The Hexapla in Extant Sources

Manuscripts preserving parts of the columnar presentation of the Hexapla:

- Ra 2005. Thirteen verses from Psalm 32. Genizah Fragment (CUL T-S 12.182), published by Charles Taylor in 1900.[34] A single palimpsest leaf (overwriting being medieval Hebrew poetry). The underwriting majuscule dated by Taylor to the eighth century. Extant Columns: Transliteration, Aquila, Symmachus, LXX, Theodotion. Jenkins has shown that this manuscript originally contained a Hebrew column before it was palimpsested.[35] The Tetragrammaton is written ΠΙΙΙΙ.

- Ra 1098. One hundred forty-eight verses from Psalms 17–88. Milan Fragment (Biblioteca Ambrosiana, O 39), announced by Giovanni Mercati in 1896, published in 1958.[36] Forty-four pages. Palimpsest, the overwriting of a thirteenth/fourteenth-century Octoechos manuscript

---

in *XV Congress of the International Organization for Septuagint and Cognate Studies, Munich 2013*, ed. W. Kraus, M. N. van der Meer, and M. Meiser (Atlanta: SBL, 2016), 133–48.

[33] On Origen's purposes for creating the Hexapla, see T. M. Law, "Origen's Parallel Bible: Textual Criticism, Apologetics, or Exegesis?," *Journal of Theological Studies* 59 (2008): 1–21.

[34] Charles Taylor, *Hebrew-Greek Cairo Genizah Palimpsests from the Taylor-Schechter Collection: Including a Fragment of the Twenty-Second Psalm According to Origen's Hexapla* (Cambridge: Cambridge University Press, 1900).

[35] Jenkins, "First Column of the Hexapla."

[36] G. Mercati, *Psalterii Hexapli Reliquiae* (Vatican City: Bybliotheca Vaticana, 1958).

housed in the Biblioteca Ambrosiana. Underwriting Greek minuscule of ninth century. Columns: Transliteration, Aquila, Symmachus, LXX, Theodotion (actually, Quinta). This manuscript never contained a Hebrew column.

- Ra 86. See Hosea 11:1 for columnar presentation. Rome, Biblioteca Vaticana, Barberiniana gr. 549, ninth–tenth century CE.[37]

- Ra 113. See heading of the Psalter. Milan, Biblioteca Ambrosiana, B 106 sup, ca. 966 CE. Marginal notes in a twelfth-century CE hand cite two lines, in the heading of the book of Psalms.[38]

- Ra 271.[39] Flyleaf contains (1) beginning of Psalm 1, (2) Hebrew alphabet, (3) LXX Psalm 111:1a in the *Secunda* and LXX.

Manuscripts preserving critical signs:

- G = Colberto-Sarravianus. Fifth century. Heptateuch. Leiden, University Library, Voss. Gr. Q. 8; and Paris, Bibliothèque Nationale, Gr. 17; and St. Petersburg, Public Library, Gr. 3.[40]

- Q = Marchalianus. Sixth century. Prophets. Vat. Gr. 2125.[41]

- P. Grenf. 1.5. Third/fourth century. Ezekiel 5:12–6:3.[42]

---

[37] Digital images available online: "Manuscript—Barb.gr.549," DigiVatLib, last accessed April 27, 2021, https://digi.vatlib.it/view/MSS_Barb.gr.549. See fol. 17v. This section is also presented in the second apparatus of the Göttingen edition: Joseph Ziegler, ed., *Duodecim Prophetae*, 3rd ed., Septuaginta 13 (Göttingen: Vandenhoeck & Ruprecht, 1984), 172.

[38] See Albrecht, "Von der *hebraica veritas* zur *vera graecitas*," 16–17.

[39] Digital images available online: "Manuscript—Vat.gr.1747," DigiVatLib, last accessed April 27, 2021, https://digi.vatlib.it/view/MSS_Vat.gr.1747. See image 3 (right side). Analyzed by Albrecht, "Von der *hebraica veritas* zur *vera graecitas*," 17–19. This flyleaf was noticed already in 1899 by Mercati but was unpublished until Albrecht. The last page of Albrecht's article actually provides a much clearer picture than what is available on the Vatican's website.

[40] See Swete, *Introduction*, 137–38; Jellicoe, *Septuagint and Modern Study*, 194.

[41] Digital images available online: "Manuscript—Vat.gr.2125," DigiVatLib, last accessed April 27, 2021, https://digi.vatlib.it/view/MSS_Vat.gr.2125. See Schironi, "*P. Grenf.* 1.5," who points out that Q uses the asterisk not only to mark material taken from the Three but also to mark inverted lines, a use not deriving from Origen. She also notes, "In general, Q does not display many *obeloi*" (204). She cites (204n62) some examples of obeloi: image 405 at Jeremiah 19:13, where they mark additions, "thus not according to Origen's system."

[42] The fundamental study is Schironi, "*P.Grenf.* 1.5."

- 88 = Codex Chisianus. Tenth century. Vat. Chigiani R. VII. 45.[43]

- Syro-Hexapla, esp. Codex Syro-Hexaplaris Ambrosianus. Eighth century. Bibl. Ambr. C 313 inf.

Just as scholars debate the nature of the Hexapla's fifth column, they debate everything else about the Hexapla. First, the overall purpose behind the Hexapla is debated, a topic we will address a little later. Was there actually a Hebrew (first) column? Our preserved copies do not have the Hebrew column, and its existence in the original Hexapla has been doubted, but—as we have seen—scholars now seem to agree that it was there. What was the purpose of the transliterated Hebrew (second) column? Did it precede the creation of the Hexapla, or did Origen himself commission its creation?[44] What was in the sixth column? It was not always Theodotion's text; in the Hexapla fragments from Milan (Ra 1098), the sixth column contains the Quinta.[45] And finally, what about the Tetrapla? In the passage quoted above from Eusebius (*Hist. eccl.* 6.16), the church historian says that Origen, following his work on the Hexapla, created something called a "Tetrapla," which Eusebius described thus: "He made a further separate arrangement of the edition of Aquila and Symmachus and Theodotion together with that of the Seventy." The name *Tetrapla* (fourfold) has often led scholars to think that it must be some kind of pared-down version of the Hexapla, perhaps containing only the four Greek columns. Peter Gentry and John Meade have argued that Eusebius's description of the Tetrapla actually applies to the independent recension of the LXX created by Origen; that is, the Tetrapla is the Origenian edition of the LXX, a one-column text—just the LXX—with asterisks marking passages included from Theodotion and

---

[43] Schironi, "*P.Grenf.* 1.5," 199n53, calls this manuscript's preservation of signs "less accurate and precise."

[44] On these questions, see Fernández Marcos, *Septuagint in Context*, 215–20; Kantor, "Second Column."

[45] Jellicoe, *Septuagint and Modern Study*, 94; Schironi, "*P.Grenf.* 1.5," 195.

obeloi indicating pluses in the LXX vis-à-vis the Hebrew, and with marginal notes signaling readings from the Three, very similar to the Syro-Hexapla.[46]

In the *Commentary on Matthew* 15.14, Origen describes his text-critical work as involving two elements: first, where there was discord among the copies of the LXX, he decided upon the correct reading with the aid of the other editions (Aquila, Symmachus, and Theodotion); second, where there was a quantitative difference between the LXX and the Hebrew, Origen employed critical signs to indicate the difference, filling in minuses in the Septuagint from the other editions. Manuscripts of Origen's text reveal additional changes: adapting the spelling of proper names toward the Hebrew and altering the word order toward the Hebrew.[47]

While Origen's text-critical work significantly influenced the subsequent history of the transmission of the Septuagint, it did so in no uniform manner. The Hexapla itself is largely lost, preserved now in only the fragments mentioned earlier (see the figure "The Hexapla in Extant Sources"). A few Septuagint manuscripts preserve Origen's critical signs (again, the figure "The Hexapla in Extant Sources"), the earliest such manuscript being Ra 922 (third or fourth century CE). Readings of the Three are preserved more often in scattered comments of Christian authors and as marginalia in biblical manuscripts, as well as in a few independent manuscripts (Aquila: Ra oS-1, oS-2; Symmachus: oS-3). The authoritative edition of such material is still that of Field from 1875,[48] while the ongoing Göttingen editions of

---

[46] See, e.g., Peter J. Gentry, "Pre-Hexaplaric Translations, Hexapla, Post-Hexaplaric Translations," in *Textual History of the Bible*, vol. 1A, *The Hebrew Bible: Overview Articles*, ed. Armin Lange and Emanuel Tov (Leiden: Brill, 2016), 211–35, at 231–32 (§1.3.1.2.7); Meade, "Hexapla," 171. Jellicoe, *Septuagint and Modern Study*, 124, considered the possibility "that Origen, some time after compiling the Hexapla, composed a recension of the Greek Old Testament and that this manuscript, and not the fifth column, provided the archetype of the Syro-Hexaplar and those Greek manuscripts which embody the critical symbols."

[47] For the order of words, see J. W. Wevers, *Text History of the Greek Genesis*, Mitteilungen des Septuaginta-Unternehmens (Göttingen: Vandenhoeck & Ruprecht, 1974), 59–61; for proper names, see J. W. Wevers, *Text History of the Greek Numbers*, Mitteilungen des Septuaginta-Unternehmens (Göttingen: Vandenhoeck & Ruprecht, 1982), 61. See also Gallagher, *Hebrew Scripture in Patristic Biblical Theory*, 178–89. For these characteristics in Ra 922, see Schironi, "*P.Grenf.* 1.5," 189.

[48] F. Field, *Origenis Hexaplorum quae supersunt sive veterum interpretum graecorum in totum Vetus Testamentum fragmenta* (Oxford: Clarendon, 1875).

the Septuagint contain updated collections in their second apparatus.[49] An updating of Field's work is in progress under the auspices of the Hexapla Institute (hexapla.org).[50]

What was Origen's purpose in his work on the text of the Septuagint? Or, to ask a somewhat different question, why did he create the Hexapla? The massive undertaking is well described by Grafton and Williams:

> Complex, difficult to produce, and extremely expensive, its execution would have required tremendous resources, both in terms of patronage and in terms of learning and labor. Furthermore, in order to incorporate a foreign, barbarian tongue, written in a non-Greek alphabet, into his great compilation, Origen would have had to turn outside the Greek Christian community for key components of the work—whether these were available in the form of preexisting texts or Jewish scholars willing to cooperate in this Christian undertaking. No exaggeration is needed to make clear how impressive an accomplishment the Hexapla was. Yet its form, its contents, and above all its purpose remain unclear.[51]

Origen's purpose was debated even in antiquity, partly because he himself gave contrary accounts of his aims. Such a large project probably arose from multiple motivations and fulfilled multiple purposes.[52] In his *Letter to Africanus*, Origen characterizes his textual work as aimed at helping Christians understand where their Bible differs from that of Jews so that they may more effectively engage Jews in religious discussions (an apologetic motive). In his commentaries and homilies, Origen often cited not just the LXX but also readings from other editions in order to help him arrive at a meaning for a biblical passage, and so that we can say there was an exegetical

---

[49] On the history of the collection of the Hexaplaric readings, see Jellicoe, *Septuagint and Modern Study*, 127–29.

[50] The inaugural volume is John D. Meade, *A Critical Edition of the Hexaplaric Fragments of Job 22–42*, Origen's Hexapla: A Critical Edition of the Extant Fragments (Leuven: Peeters, 2020). There are plans also to launch an online edition.

[51] Grafton and Williams, *Christianity and the Transformation of the Book*, 86–87.

[52] Law, "Origen's Parallel Bible," 1–21.

effect of the Hexapla, whether or not Origen began the project with such an intention. Finally, there was a text-critical motive: Origen apparently thought that the text of the LXX had suffered at the hands of scribes, and he wanted to restore the LXX to its original purity, which he thought he could do by comparing it with the Hebrew text and other versions closer to the Hebrew. In his *Commentary on Matthew* 15.14, he says, "We have been able to heal [ἰάσασθαι] the discord in the copies of the Old Testament, using as a criterion the other editions."[53]

Our next chapter will delve further into the theory behind such textual intervention. For now, we note that the outcome of Origen's work was, on the whole, a Hebraized LXX. He himself says that he placed critical marks in the LXX to indicate its quantitative differences from the Hebrew text—that is, where the Hebrew text had more or less material than the LXX. To fill in the gaps where the LXX had less material than the Hebrew, Origen inserted Theodotion with an asterisk. There were plenty of differences between the LXX and the Hebrew text that did not fit the category of quantitative differences, and in these cases, Origen sometimes left the LXX as he found it. But he apparently intervened in the text even more than he acknowledged: we briefly mentioned earlier that he revised the spelling of proper names to agree more closely with their Hebrew spelling, and he adapted the word order of the LXX to match the Hebrew. This latter move seems more or less required for the production of the Hexapla, which—according to our extant fragments—features one Hebrew word per line in a column, and the subsequent columns would need to be arranged in accordance with the Hebrew, to facilitate comparison. Eusebius may indicate this procedure when he says about Origen's work on the Hexapla that it involved "dividing them into clauses [διελών τε πρὸς κῶλον] and placing them one against the other [καὶ ἀντιπαραθεὶς ἀλλήλαις]" (*Hist. eccl.* 6.16, quoted above).[54] The Origenian recension of the Septuagint did not match the Hebrew text in every way, but the general outcome was that Origen left the Septuagint text much closer to the Hebrew than he found it.

---

[53] On the purpose of Origen's textual labors, see Kamesar, *Jerome*, 1–28; Grafton and Williams, *Christianity and the Transformation of the Book*, 117–30.

[54] See Grafton and Williams, *Christianity and the Transformation of the Book*, 104, 108–9, 115–16, 325n46.

Eusebius and Pamphilus

Before moving to Lucian's text-critical work, we should observe the ancient evidence connecting Origen's LXX text with two later disciples. In the passage from Jerome (the epigraph to this chapter) in which he lays out the three Christian recensions of the Septuagint, the *trifaria varietas*, he links the Origenian recension to Eusebius and Pamphilus: "Codices that were worked over by Origen and that Eusebius and Pamphilus disseminated."

Eusebius is, of course, the famous church historian whose floruit covered most of the first half of the fourth century CE. Pamphilus came from Berytus to Caesarea in the late third century and was martyred in the year 310.[55] Together they wrote the *Apology for Origen* in six books, of which only the first book survives, and that only in Rufinus's Latin translation. It is not clear what role these two disciples of Origen played in the creation or dissemination of the Origenian recension, but Jerome's comment is not the only one linking the text to the two scholars.[56] Primarily there are also a number of colophons in Greek manuscripts (Codex Sinaiticus, Codex Marchalianus) and the Syro-Hexapla. The colophon to the book of Esther in Codex Sinaiticus says this:

> Collated against an extremely old copy corrected in the hand of the holy martyr Pamphilus. At the end of this very old book (which begins with the First Book of Kingdoms and ends at Esther) is the signature, in its distinctive form, of Pamphilus himself, reading thus:
>
>> Copied from and corrected against the Hexapla of Origen as corrected by himself. Antoninus the confessor collated; I, Pamphilus, corrected the volume in prison, with the great favour and enlargement of God. And if it is not too much to say, to find a copy to match this one would not be easy.

---

[55] Timothy D. Barnes, *Constantine and Eusebius* (Cambridge, MA: Harvard University Press, 1981), 153–54. On Pamphilus and his biblical scholarship, see Grafton and Williams, *Christianity and the Transformation of the Book*, 178–94.

[56] See the sources collected by Peter J. Gentry, *The Asterisked Materials in the Greek Job* (Atlanta: Scholars Press, 1995), 8–9n19; and see Nautin, *Origène*, 354–58.

The same very ancient book disagrees with this volume in the proper names.[57]

The colophon to Ezekiel in Codex Marchalianus reads thus:

Copied from the Hexapla according to the editions and corrected from Origen's own Tetrapla, which was corrected and annotated in his hand. I Eusebius added the scholia from this source. Pamphilus and Eusebius corrected.[58]

Such work arising from Origen's textual labors characterized those scholars who followed in his wake. Aside from Jerome, we have little evidence of Christian scholars engaging directly with the Hebrew text, even for those authors reputed to know Hebrew (such as Epiphanius of Cyprus)[59] or whose native language was another Semitic language (e.g., Eusebius of Emesa).[60] Christian scholars continued to be interested in the Hebrew text, and they typically used the Hexapla or other literature derivative of

---

[57] Translation from D. C. Parker, *Codex Sinaiticus: The Story of the World's Oldest Bible* (Peabody, MA: Hendrickson, 2010), 81. Images of this colophon along with a transcription can be found at the Codex Sinaiticus website (www.codexsinaiticus.org).

[58] Translation from Grafton and Williams, *Christianity and the Transformation of the Book*, 342n23. See also their discussion of the colophons on 184–94, with the presentation of the colophons (often in Greek with English translation) in the notes (340–42). Digital images of Codex Marchalianus are available here: "Manuscript—Vat.gr.2125," DigiVatLib, last accessed April 27, 2021, https://digi.vatlib.it/view/MSS_Vat.gr.2125. The relevant colophon appears on the bottom of image 568 immediately before the beginning of the book of Ezekiel. (On this placement, see Schironi, "*P.Grenf.* 1.5," 198n50.)

[59] Jerome (*Adv. Ruf.* 3.6; cf. 2.22) refers to Epiphanius as *pentaglossus*, "knowing five languages" (Greek, Latin, Syriac, Hebrew, Egyptian). For a skeptical evaluation of Epiphanius's knowledge of Hebrew and Aramaic, see Jürgen Dummer, "Die Sprachkenntnisse des Epiphanius," in *Die Araber in der alten Welt*, ed. F. Altheim and R. Stiehl, vol. 5.1 (Berlin: de Gruyter, 1968); repr. in J. Dummer, *Philologia Sacra et Profana: Ausgewählte Beiträge zur Antike und zu ihrer Wirkungsgeschichte* (Stuttgart: Steiner, 2006), 29–72, esp. 35–47.

[60] R. B. ter Haar Romeny, *A Syrian in Greek Dress: The Use of Greek, Hebrew, and Syriac Biblical Texts in Eusebius of Emesa's Commentary on Genesis* (Leuven: Peeters, 1997). Ter Haar Romeny argues that Eusebius used the Syriac Bible as an avenue toward understanding the Hebrew text.

the Hexapla in order to access its readings.[61] That disposition may include Lucian as well.

Lucian

According to some ancient sources, especially Jerome, an edition or recension of the Septuagint is associated with Lucian of Antioch, martyred in 312 CE. About him we have little information. Eusebius mentions him in two passages:

> Of the martyrs at Antioch the best in his entire life was Lucian, a presbyter of that community; the same who in Nicomedia, where the emperor was, proclaimed the heavenly kingdom of Christ, first by word of mouth in an Apology, and afterwards also by deeds. (*Hist. eccl.* 8.13.2)

> Lucian, a most excellent man in every respect, of temperate life and well versed in sacred learning, a presbyter of the community at Antioch, was brought to the city of Nicomedia, where the Emperor was then staying; and, having made his defence before the ruler on behalf of the doctrine which he professed, he was committed to prison and put to death. (*Hist. eccl.* 9.6.3)

Neither of these brief notices mentions anything about a revision of the Greek Bible. Jerome's entry on Lucian in *On Illustrious Men* (§77) is equally brief, but he does mention that Lucian "labored in the study of the scriptures so much that now some exemplars of the Scriptures are called Lucianic." We saw earlier that Jerome mentioned the Lucianic recension of the Greek Bible in his *Preface to Chronicles* (*iuxta Hebraeos*, 396 CE) as dominant in the area from Constantinople to Antioch. In his *Preface to the Gospels* (384 CE), Jerome makes a disparaging comment on the Lucianic exemplars.[62] Jerome

---

[61] Ceulemans, "Greek Christian Access."
[62] Weber and Gryson, *Biblia Sacra*, 1515, lines 23–27.

also mentions Lucian in connection with the Greek Bible in his *Epistle* 106.2 to Sunnia and Fretela (403 CE):

> I mention briefly so that you know that there is one edition which Origen and Eusebius of Caesarea and all Greek editors call *koine*—that is, common—and vulgate and is called now by many Lucianic; another edition of the Seventy translators, which is found in the codices of the Hexapla and has been translated faithfully by us into the Latin language and is sung at Jerusalem and in the churches of the east.

> Now the *koine*, that is, common, is the same edition as the Septuagint. But this distinguishes them, that the *koine* is the old edition corrupted in respect of places and times and the will of scribes.

Some later writers also mention Lucian's work on the biblical text,[63] but, oddly, the writers from Antioch who used this distinctive biblical text say nothing of it.[64]

It was Ceriani who in 1863 identified the manuscripts preserving the Lucianic text for the historical books.[65] As Siegfried Kreuzer notes, "The identification became possible because of the rich material in the

---

[63] The *testimonia* are most conveniently accessed through Fernández Marcos, *Septuagint in Context*, 223–26; see also Bruce M. Metzger, "The Lucianic Recension of the Greek Bible," in *Chapters in the History of New Testament Textual Criticism* (Leiden: Brill, 1963), 1–41, at 3–7; Anna Kharanauli, "Origen and Lucian in the Light of Ancient Editorial Techniques," in *From Scribal Error to Rewriting: How Ancient Texts Could and Could Not Be Changed*, ed. A. Aejmelaeus, D. Longacre, and N. Mirotadze (Göttingen: Vandenhoeck & Ruprecht, 2020), 15–52, at 40–42.

[64] As pointed out by R. Devreesse, *Introduction à l'étude des manuscrits grecs* (Paris: Imprimerie Nationale, 1954), 118, naming John Chrysostom, Theodore of Mopsuestia, and Theodoret of Cyrus. This point is also taken up by Dominique Barthélemy, *Études d'histoire du texte de l'Ancien Testament* (Fribourg: Éditions Universitaires, 1978), 250–52.

[65] A. M. Ceriani, *Pentateuchi Syro-Hexaplaris quae Supersunt*, Monumenta sacra et profana 2.2 (Milan: Bibliotheca Ambrosiana, 1864), xxiv; see also A. M. Ceriani, "Le recensioni dei LXX e la versione latina detta Itala," *Rendiconti del reale Istituto Lombardo* 19 (1886): 206–13. For the history of research, see J.-H. Kim, *Die hebräischen und griechischen Textformen der Samuel- und Königbücher: Studien zur Textgeschichte ausgehend von 2Sam 15,1–19,9*, BZAW (Berlin: de Gruyter, 2009), 4–32.

Holmes-Parsons edition.[66] There it could be seen that the manuscripts 19, 82, 93, 108 (and 127 [not yet fully available to Holmes and Parsons]) present a common text form that evidently also was the biblical text of the Antiochene fathers, especially Theodoret."[67]

Lucianic Manuscripts

The five manuscripts preserving the Lucianic text in the books of Samuel and Kings are the following. They are sometimes identified by the sigla used in the Brooke-McLean edition boc_2e_2,[68] but here we use the Rahlfs number:

19, Rome, twelfth century (Brooke-McLean b′, and with 108 known as b)

82, Paris, twelfth century[69] (Brooke-McLean o)

93, London, thirteenth century[70] (Brooke-McLean e_2)

108, Rome, thirteenth century (Brooke-McLean *b*, and with 19 known as b)

127, Moscow, tenth century CE (Brooke-McLean c_2)

---

[66] Robert Holmes and James Parsons, *Vetus Testamentum Graecum cum variis lectionibus*, 5 vols. (Oxford: Clarendon, 1798–1827).

[67] S. Kreuzer, "Translation and Recensions: Old Greek, Kaige, and Antiochene Text in Samuel and Reigns," in *The Bible in Greek: Translation, Transmission, and Theology of the Septuagint* (Atlanta: SBL, 2015), 154–74, at 156–57. In addition to Theodoret, other writers important for the identification of the Lucianic text are Eustathius, Asterius, Diodore, John Chrysostom, and Theodore of Mopsuestia.

[68] Alan E. Brooke and Norman McLean, *The Old Testament in Greek according to the Text of Codex Vaticanus* (Cambridge: Cambridge University Press, 1906–1940).

[69] Online digital images: "Coislin 3," BNF Gallica, last accessed April 27, 2021, https://gallica.bnf.fr/ark:/12148/btv1b11004824x.r=coislin%203?rk=21459;2.

[70] Online digital images: "Royal MS 1 D II," British Library, last accessed April 27, 2021, http://www.bl.uk/manuscripts/FullDisplay.aspx?ref=Royal_MS_1_D_II.

The Lucianic text has not been identified in the Pentateuch.[71] It is known most distinctly in the historical books, and it is for these books alone that a critical edition of the Lucianic (or Antiochene) text has been published.[72] Scholars have identified Lucianic readings also for the wisdom and prophetic books.[73]

The frequently cited characteristics of the Lucianic text are described by one of the editors of the critical text in this way:

> In general, it can be stated that it tends to fill the gaps in the LXX in respect of the Hebrew text on the basis of additions taken from "the three," particularly from Symmachus. This procedure, combined with a certain freedom in handling the text, often gives rise to a series of doublets that are not in the LXX. It also inserts a series of interpolations (proper names instead of corresponding pronoun, possessive pronouns, articles, conjunctions, making implicit subjects or objects explicit, etc.) which tend to clarify the sense or minimise incorrect grammar. It often resorts to changing a synonym, in most cases without it being possible to discover the reason for the change. At other times one notices a tendency to replace Hellenistic forms with Attic forms due to the influence of the grammarians of the time. There are also many grammatical and stylistic changes: of preposition, of simple to compound verbs, of person, number, etc.[74]

Controversy surrounds discussions of the nature of the Lucianic text. Many scholars agree that the label "Lucianic recension" is misleading, whether in regard to the word *recension* (if it implies a coherent revision toward a Hebrew text) or the attribution to Lucian—or both.[75] According

---

[71] Fernández Marcos, *Septuagint in Context*, 226–30.

[72] Natalio Fernández Marcos and J. R. Busto Saiz, *El texto antioqueno de la Biblia griega*, 3 vols., Textos y Estudios Cardenal Cisneros (Madrid: Consejo Superior de Investigaciones Científicas, 1989, 1992, 1996). The three volumes cover the books of Samuel, Kings, and Chronicles.

[73] The relevant volumes of the Göttingen Septuagint each have sections of their *Enleitungen* devoted to the Lucianic text. See also Barthélemy's comments on these sections in his *Études*, 243–45.

[74] Fernández Marcos, *Septuagint in Context*, 230.

[75] Barthélemy rejects both words as an apt description; *Études*, 245–47 (on the term *recension*), 248–54 (on the attribution to Lucian); see also 271.

to Fernández Marcos, "It is probable that the revision was not the work of one person, was not uniform, and, although there are a set of common features, the level of intervention varies from book to book."[76] Given the association of this text with the Antiochian Fathers, the label Antiochian or Antiochene Text has become a common designation.[77] Still, some scholars are more open to the idea that Lucian himself performed some of the work of recension.[78]

Often the Antiochene Text is described as containing multiple layers: an early stratum preceding Lucian and attested in the New Testament, Josephus, and other sources (i.e., the proto-Lucianic recension or text) and a later layer resulting from a recension in the time period of Lucian.[79] The proto-Lucianic text is often characterized as Hebraizing (but not toward the proto-MT), whereas the later layer is characterized as aiming for Greek stylistic revision.[80] Neither of these characteristics is carried through consistently, so that lack of consistency has become one of the hallmarks in descriptions of the Antiochene Text—thus Rahlfs's famous description: "The main characteristic of this recension is the lack of a clear principal."[81]

This description has suffered attacks from both sides, though it is still the most common way of seeing the Antiochene Text. On the one hand, Barthélemy argued that the Antiochene Text is hardly recensional at all and rather represents the Old Greek, at least in the books of Kingdoms

---

[76] Natalio Fernández Marcos, "The Antiochene Edition in the Text History of the Greek Bible," in *Der Antiochenische Text der Septuaginta in seiner Bezeugung und seiner Bedeutung*, ed. S. Kreuzer and M. Sigismund (Göttingen: Vandenhoeck & Ruprecht, 2013), 57–73, at 63.

[77] Henry Barclay Swete, *An Introduction to the Old Testament in Greek*, 2nd ed. (Cambridge: Cambridge University Press, 1914), 80, already used the term.

[78] Albrecht, "Von der *hebraica veritas* zur *vera graecitas*," 113–32.

[79] See the summary by Kristin De Troyer, "The Septuagint," in *The New Cambridge History of the Bible*, vol. 1, ed. James Carleton Paget and Joachim Schaper (Cambridge: Cambridge University Press, 2013), 267–88, 282–86.

[80] See the description in Eugene C. Ulrich, *The Qumran Text of Samuel and Josephus* (Chico, CA: Scholars Press, 1978), 257–59.

[81] Alfred Rahlfs, *Lucians Rezension der Königsbücher*, Septuaginta-Studien 3 (Göttingen: Vandenhoeck & Ruprecht, 1911), 293: "der Hauptcharakter dieser Rezension ist das Fehlen eines klaren Prinzips." Often quoted, e.g., Kharanauli, "Origen and Lucian," 40. Jellicoe, *Septuagint and Modern Study*, 158, voices a different perspective: "The characteristics of Lucian's work are quite distinctive, and the revision was made with clearly identifiable objects in view."

(especially 2 Kingdoms).[82] This position has been taken up and strengthened by Kreuzer.[83] In this scenario, there is little room left for a fourth-century revision. On the other hand, Kauhanen and others have argued that the evidence for the proto-Lucianic recension (i.e., the links between the Antiochene Text and pre-Lucianic sources such as Josephus, Qumran, and the Vetus Latina) is coincidental or illusory, thus dispensing with the hypothesized early layer.[84] Hugo prefers the traditional and still dominant description of multiple layers: "The Antiochene tradition consists of two textual layers: the so-called 'proto-Lucianic' text, which is very close to the original LXX, and an Antiochene revision" (citing Barthélemy in support).[85]

Any point we try to draw in regard to the Antiochene Text for Christian text-critical work on the Septuagint will be controversial. If Kreuzer is right in his update of Barthélemy's position, the Antiochene Text gives essentially no information about Christian textual criticism. If Kauhanen is right, then most of the distinctive features of the Antiochene Text can be attributed to Christian text-critical work, whether to Lucian of Antioch specifically or to others working close to that time and place. If the more prominent description is right—that the Antiochene Text evidences multiple layers: an early form of the text revised by *kaige* and a later recension from the time of Lucian—then this Christian text-critical work on the Septuagint would evince a concern for better Greek, including Atticizing word choices and added words to clarify the meaning. Brock suggested that this text was designed for public reading.[86]

---

[82] Barthélemy, *Devanciers*, 126–27; with additional nuance at *Études*, 243–54.

[83] Kreuzer, *Bible in Greek*, 113–230.

[84] Tuukka Kauhanen, *The Proto-Lucianic Problem in 1 Samuel* (Göttingen: Vandenhoeck & Ruprecht, 2012). See also the critique of Kreuzer by Kauhanen and Law along with the rejoinder by Kreuzer; T. M. Law and Tuukka Kauhanen, "Methodological Remarks on the Textual History of Reigns: A Response to Siegfried Kreuzer," *Bulletin of the International Organization for Septuagint and Cognate Studies* 43 (2010): 73–87; Siegfried Kreuzer, "A Reply to T. M. Law and T. Kauhanen, 'Methodological Remark . . . ,'" *Bulletin of the International Organization for Septuagint and Cognate Studies* 43 (2010): 89–95. A seminal paper in this vein is S. P. Brock, "Lucian *Redivivus*: Some Reflections on Barthélemy's *Les Devanciers d'Aquila*," *Studia Evangelica* 5 (1968): 176–81.

[85] Philippe Hugo, "Basileion I and II/1–2 Kingdoms/1–2 Samuel," in *Introduction to the Septuagint*, ed. Siegfried Kreuzer (Waco, TX: Baylor University Press, 2019), 173–94, at 186; citing Barthélemy, *Études*, 224.

[86] S. Brock, *The Recension of the Septuaginta Version of I Samuel*, Quaderni di Henoch (Turin: Silvio Zamorani, 1996), 252–53.

On a maximal understanding of Lucian's contribution to the Antiochene Text, it is probable that Lucian worked solely on the basis of Greek manuscripts with little knowledge of Hebrew (despite his native Syriac).[87] He would have used the Hexaplaric texts to revise his Greek text toward the Hebrew while also attempting to polish the Greek and improve its readability.

Hesychius

Here we can be brief because there is not much to say. Jerome mentioned an Egyptian edition of the Septuagint circulating under the name of Hesychius. As Swete said long ago, "It is not easy to ascertain who this Hesychius was."[88] Not only is the figure of Hesychius himself mysterious, but a distinctive Septuagint text able to be associated with him or Egypt is difficult to isolate, so Kreuzer can say, "The idea of a Hesychian recension today is largely dismissed."[89] Scholars have debated whether any such text can be ascertained from our manuscripts, with some scholars being somewhat more positive about the prospect.[90] To the extent that such a text has been identified, it seems to have little concern for revision toward the Hebrew text but more interest in improving the Greek.[91] Some editions of the Göttingen Septuagint, especially in the Prophets, include a section on an Egyptian (or, even, an Alexandrian) text.[92]

---

[87] Jellicoe, *Septuagint and Modern Study*, 161–62.

[88] Swete, *Introduction*, 79.

[89] Kreuzer, *Bible in Greek*, 114n5; see also Anneli Aejmelaeus, "Textual History of the Septuagint and the Principles of Critical Editing," in *The Text of the Hebrew Bible and Its Editions: Studies in Celebration of the Fifth Centennial of the Complutensian Polyglot*, ed. Andrés Piquer Otero and Pablo A. Torijano Morales (Leiden: Brill, 2016), 160–79, at 163.

[90] Felix Albrecht, "Die alexandrinische Überlieferung und die Rezension des Hesych von Alexandrien in den Prophetenbüchern der Septuaginta," in *Die Septuaginta: Orte und Intentionen: 5. Internationale Fachtagung veranstaltet von Septuaginta Deutsch (LXX.D), Wuppertal 24.–27. Juli 2014*, ed. S. Kreuzer, M. Meiser, and M. Sigismund (Tübingen: Mohr Siebeck 2016), 337–62.

[91] Fernández Marcos, *Septuagint in Context*, 239–46.

[92] On the prophetic books, see Albrecht, "Die alexandrinische Überlieferung," who focuses on Codex Alexandrinus. The publication in the Göttingen Septuagint series on Ecclesiastes includes a section on an Egyptian text, for which Codex Vaticanus is a primary witness and Greek stylistics is a primary concern; Peter John Gentry, ed., *Ecclesiastes*, Septuaginta

Conclusion

Christians were not always content to leave the text of the Greek Old Testament as they found it. Fundamentally, this desire to revise or correct the biblical text simply resulted from the nature of ancient books: hand-copied and therefore always faulty to some degree. Any decent secondary school teacher (*grammatikos*) in antiquity would train students, as one of the first steps in interpreting works of literature, that they must ensure a good quality text.[93] Origen, Lucian, and perhaps Hesychius moved a good deal beyond that basic activity. Origen and the scholars behind the Antiochene Text found the differences between the traditional Septuagint and the standard Hebrew Bible to be problematic, requiring patient attention and careful work. We have also observed the desire to improve the literary quality of the Greek Old Testament. These issues would continue to influence Christian reception of the Septuagint, and our next chapter will explore especially patristic theories about the best text of the Old Testament and what the relationship between the Septuagint and the Hebrew Bible ought to be. This chapter has shown that, even as Christians proclaimed the Septuagint to be the inspired text of the Old Testament for the church, their reading of Scripture continued to be influenced by the Hebrew Bible.

11.2 (Göttingen: Vandenhoeck & Ruprecht, 2019), 54–57; see further Peter J. Gentry, "Special Problems in the Text History of Ecclesiastes," in *XIII Congress of the International Organization for Septuagint and Cognate Studies*, ed. M. K. H. Peters (Atlanta: SBL, 2008), 137–57.

[93] See, briefly, H. I. Marrou, *A History of Education in Antiquity* (New York: Sheed & Ward, 1956), 230; Martens, *Origen and Scripture*, 42–44.

8

Theory

The Relationship between the
LXX and the Hebrew Bible in
Early Christian Thought

But Ptolemy, wishing to make trial of them in his own way, and being afraid lest they should have made some agreement to conceal by their translation the truth in the Scriptures, separated them from one another and commanded them all to write the same translation. And this he did in the case of all the books. But when they came together to Ptolemy, and compared each his own translation, God was glorified and the Scriptures were recognized as truly divine, for they all rendered the same things in the same words and the same names, from beginning to end, so that even the heathen who were present knew that the Scriptures had been translated by the inspiration of God.

—Irenaeus, *Against Heresies* 3.21.2[1]

The Church Fathers in the second century and later argued that the Septuagint was an inspired translation, necessarily superior to any other version. In Chapter Two, we saw how the story of the translation developed in

---

[1] Quoted from Eusebius, *Ecclesiastical History*, vol. 1, trans. Kirsopp Lake, Loeb Classical Library (Cambridge, MA: Harvard University Press, 1926), 461.

Jewish circles, including Philo's view that the translators produced a perfect translation due to their communion with the spirit of Moses. Christians adopted this view and expanded it. Philo's comments were directed at the Greek Pentateuch specifically; Christians understood the entire Greek Old Testament to derive from the Seventy translators so that it is all inspired. Christians also assumed that the Hebrew Bible was inspired. How could they not? Their own Old Testament demanded the view that God spoke through the ancient Israelite prophets, and they knew these prophets had spoken and written Hebrew, as affirmed again each time they told the story about Seventy-two Jewish elders translating the scriptures from Hebrew into Greek. So what about all the times that the Hebrew Bible and the Septuagint disagree? How could they both be inspired? Early Christian scholars thought about this question, and they developed answers. This chapter explores patristic textual theory.

Jewish believers in Jesus had been using Greek translations of Scripture already for a century before any of them acknowledged the fact in writing.[2] We have seen in previous chapters that, beginning in the second century, Christian writers acknowledged certain differences between the Septuagint and other available Greek texts of Scripture. Justin Martyr, the first Christian writer to mention the Septuagint, transmitted a version of the translation legend in his *First Apology* (ch. 31) and—in his *Dialogue with Trypho* (esp. chs. 70–73)—promoted the authenticity of the original translation against competing translations. Not long after Justin, Irenaeus of Lyons (*Haer.* 3.21.1–3) more explicitly attacked later Jewish translations as inferior to the Septuagint, a position Irenaeus supported through several arguments, including his own retelling of the translation legend. The Christian expansion of the work of the Seventy to include all Greek Jewish Scripture and not just the Pentateuch allowed them to defend the authority of the Greek form of the prophetic books. When the Fathers encountered differences between their manuscripts of the Septuagint and other Greek translations, they explained these differences in various ways, but they rarely

---

[2] Much of the following material was originally written for my essay "The Septuagint in Patristic Sources," in *The T&T Clark Handbook of Septuagint Research*, ed. William A. Ross and W. Edward Glenny (London: T&T Clark, 2021), 255–67.

questioned the authority of the Seventy translators, whom they thought God had inspired to make the Hebrew scriptures available to the world. Jerome's promotion of the alternative view that the Seventy were mere translators, not prophets, and that their translation sometimes contained mistakes, caused controversy throughout the West, particularly with his erstwhile friend Rufinus of Aquileia and his correspondent Augustine of Hippo. Eventually Jerome's own translation, later christened the Vulgate, replaced the Septuagint as the Old Testament in the Latin-speaking West. But Jerome's work had no similar effect in the East, and the Greek Orthodox Church continues to use primarily the Septuagint as its Old Testament.[3]

The Septuagint Translation Legend

Christians adopted several elements of the translation story as it circulated among Jews (discussed more fully in Chapter Two above): in the early Ptolemaic era, seventy-two Jewish sages produced a wonderfully accurate translation. Christians largely ignored or reinterpreted the Jewish statements that the Seventy translators worked on the Jewish Law, apparently understanding the term *law* as encompassing not just the Pentateuch but the entire Old Testament (in line with some New Testament passages; cf. John 10:34; 1 Cor. 14:21; etc.).

Most patristic accounts of the translation echoed Philo's belief in the divine inspiration of the Septuagint, and they regarded the Septuagint as a supremely accurate rendering of the Hebrew Bible, though they usually refrained from following Philo completely in his assertion that the Hebrew and the Greek represent the exact same text; Christians recognized ambiguities and difficulties in the Septuagint that, they surmised, did not exist in the Hebrew text.[4] Justin actually did not mention the inspiration of the translation, but his entire discussion, both in the *First Apology* (ch. 31) and in the *Dialogue with Trypho* (ch. 71), presupposed that the translation of the

---

[3] Eugen J. Pentiuc, *The Old Testament in Eastern Orthodox Tradition* (Oxford: Oxford University Press, 2014), 62–100.

[4] Pentiuc, *Old Testament in Eastern Orthodox Tradition*, 97–99, and see below on Epiphanius especially.

Seventy accurately represented the original Hebrew prophecies. In Justin's mind, the Jewish leaders contemporary with him were at fault for refusing to acknowledge the accuracy of the ancient translation and proposing a revised translation/interpretation, particularly with regard to Isaiah 7:14, a verse that should read *virgin* (παρθένος), rather than *young woman* (νεᾶνις). It was essential to Justin's argument that the ancient Hebrew prophecies agreed completely with his Greek Bible in their predictions of the Christ.

Irenaeus argued extensively for the inspiration of the Septuagint. Whether or not Philo imagined that the Seventy translators worked independently from one another, Irenaeus certainly did, asserting that King Ptolemy desired to test the translators by separating them and demanding each to produce a translation (see the epigraph above). Comparison of the seventy-two translations showed that they all contained the same words, proving not only that the translators produced an accurate translation but much more that "the Scriptures had been translated by the inspiration of God" (κατ᾽ ἐπίπνοιαν τοῦ θεοῦ εἰσιν ἑρμηνευμέναι αἱ γραφαί; *Haer.* 3.21.2; *apud* Eusebius, *Hist. eccl.* 5.8.14). This story of separated translators producing identical results was repeated many times—with some variations—by patristic authors, such as Clement of Alexandria (*Strom.* 1.22), Ps.-Justin (*Cohort. Graec.* 13), Epiphanius (*Mens.* 17), John Chrysostom (*Hom. Matt.* 5.2), and Theodoret of Cyrus (*Comm. Isa.* 7:14).[5] It was Jerome who pointed out that the earliest Jewish sources, Aristeas and Josephus, in fact said nothing about the separation of the translators (*Praef. in Pent.*). Jerome's caution seems to have made little impact on his contemporaries; even Augustine, who initially seemed not completely convinced of the miracle story (*Doctr. chr.* 2.15.22), later affirmed it more confidently (*De civitate dei* [*Civ.*] 18.43).

---

[5] For collection of sources in translation and analysis, see Abraham Wasserstein and David J. Wasserstein, *The Legend of the Septuagint: From Classical Antiquity to Today* (Cambridge: Cambridge University Press, 2006), 95–131. Many of the sources in their original languages were collected by Paul Wendland, ed., *Aristeae ad Philocratem Epistula cum ceteris de origine versionis LXX interpretum testemoniis* (Leipzig: Teubner, 1900), 121–66 (Jewish testimonia on 87–121).

THE APOSTLES AND THE SEPTUAGINT
IN PATRISTIC THOUGHT

In Chapter Six, we saw that the textual form of Old Testament quotations in the New Testament is a complex topic defying simple solutions. Nevertheless, patristic authors often considered the matter rather straightforward: the apostles quoted the Septuagint.[6] This interpretation so dominated patristic thought that hardly anyone felt the need to justify it through detailed comparison of texts. At most, an author might compare Matthew 1:23 with Isaiah 7:14 in its available versions (Justin, *Dial.* 67, 71; Irenaeus, *Haer.* 3.21.1). Jerome, again, sought to complicate the picture by pointing to several New Testament quotations that did not match the Septuagint, such as Hosea 11:1, quoted in Matthew 2:15. Jerome claimed to have found the *Vorlage* for these quotations in the Hebrew text, as we will see more fully in the next chapter. Not everyone found Jerome's argument convincing (e.g., Rufinus, *Apol. Hier.* 2.37–38),[7] but Augustine, for one, did come to acknowledge that the apostles quoted both the Septuagint and the Hebrew text (*Clv.* 18.44; see Chapter Ten).

EXEGESIS

The Septuagint (as traditionally understood) served as the textual basis for patristic interpretation, usually without recourse to any other textual witness. Early Christian exegetes did not, as a rule, bother with Hebrew at all, even to the point of treating the Greek text as the original text. To cite an oft-discussed example, some interpreters saw in the 318 men taken by Abram in search of Lot (Gen. 14:14) a reference to the name of Jesus, because in Greek the number 18 is written with the first two letters of Ἰησοῦς (Jesus), and the number 300 is written with the Greek letter T (*tau*), resembling a cross (Barn 9.7–8; Clement of Alexandria, *Strom.* 6.85). This sort of interpretation could not have occurred to a reader of Hebrew. Whereas

---

[6] Adam Kamesar, *Jerome, Greek Scholarship, and the Hebrew Bible: A Study of the Quaestiones Hebraicae in Genesim* (Oxford: Clarendon, 1993), 29–34.

[7] Edmon L. Gallagher, *Hebrew Scripture in Patristic Biblical Theory: Canon, Language, Text* (Leiden: Brill, 2012), 203–5.

patristic interpretation of many biblical passages might have arrived at the same basic results regardless of the textual form used because "the Septuagint and the Hebrew are either the same or similar" (as Jerome asserts near the end of the preface to the first book of his *Commentary on Isaiah*),[8] there are many passages for which a Greek text as opposed to the Hebrew text—or, alternatively, the Septuagint as opposed to other Greek translations (such as the Three)—could suggest distinctive avenues for interpretation. For example, Origen began his *Exhortation to Martyrdom* (ca. 235 CE) with an exposition of the Septuagint text of Isaiah 28:9–11, where the Hebrew and Greek texts diverge significantly: the MT has "precept upon precept" (צו לצו) where the Septuagint reads "receive affliction upon affliction" (θλῖψιν ἐπὶ θλῖψιν προσδέχου), a reading that makes this verse relevant to the theme of martyrdom. Readers of the Septuagint learn in Genesis 14:13 that Abraham is an emigrant (περάτης), whereas the Hebrew text calls him a Hebrew (cf. Philo, *Migr.* 20).[9] The Septuagint of Genesis 5:24 presents a fairly straightforward translation, but the use of μετατίθημι (God transferred [μετατίθημι] him) gave rise to the tradition of making Enoch a model of repentance (cf. Sir. 44:16), an idea hardly derivable from the Hebrew.[10] One can also gain a sense of what early Christians made of the distinctive interpretive possibilities of the Greek and Hebrew by perusing Jerome's commentaries on the Hebrew prophets, which often present alternative interpretations for the Hebrew text and for the Septuagint.

After presenting five pages of excerpts of patristic interpretations based especially on the Septuagint,[11] Swete emphasizes two points: first, the peculiar wording of the Septuagint shaped the Christian imagination in liturgy

---

[8] See also Gilles Dorival, "Textes des écritures et exégèse patristique: Des relations complexes," in *La reception du livre de Qohélet, 1er–XIIIe siècle*, ed. L. Mellerin (Paris: Cerf, 2016), 22–23.

[9] Further references at Marguerite Harl, *La Genèse*, 3rd ed., La Bible d'Alexandrie (Paris: Cerf, 2010), 159; Aaron P. Johnson, *Ethnicity and Argument in Eusebius' Praeparatio Evangelica* (Oxford: Oxford University Press, 2006), 115.

[10] These examples are taken from Marguerite Harl, "La Septante chez les Pères grecs et dans la vie des chrétiens," in *La bible grecque des Septante: Du judïsme hellénistique au christianisme ancien*, ed. Gilles Dorival, Marguerite Harl, and Olivier Munnich (Paris: Cerf, 1988), 289–320, at 292–3; see also 304–11.

[11] Henry Barclay Swete, *An Introduction to the Old Testament in Greek*, 2nd ed. (Cambridge: Cambridge University Press, 2014), 464–71.

and Bible study; and, second, the Greek version contributed its language to theological formulation in these crucial early centuries. He points out how critical was the wording of LXX Proverbs 8:22, κύριος ἔκτισέν με ἀρχὴν ὁδῶν αὐτοῦ εἰς ἔργα αὐτοῦ, "the Lord created me as a beginning of his ways for his works." Since the speaker of this line, ostensibly divine Wisdom, was universally acknowledged among Christian exegetes to be the preincarnate Christ (cf. 1 Cor. 1:24), this verse could be used to demonstrate that the Son is a created being.[12] Those inimical to such an idea devised various explanations, the most popular being Athanasius's proposal that the apparent reference to the creation of Christ pointed to the birth of Jesus from Mary (*Or.* 2.44–56). Other interpreters compared different textual traditions. Eusebius of Caesarea pointed out, in part, that Aquila, Symmachus, and Theodotion each used in Proverbs 8:22 not κτίζω, "create," but κτάομαι, "acquire," a verb also appearing in LXX Genesis 4:1 in the context of giving birth (*Eccl. Theol.* 3.2).[13] According to Eusebius, these alternative translations clarify what is apparently a special use of κτίζω in Proverbs 8:22, which does not mean "create" but—in light of the translations of the Three—something more like "acquire."[14] Likewise, in the view of Epiphanius of Salamis, misunderstanding of this passage resulted from the failure to appreciate the Hebrew terms (τὰς λέξεις τὰς Ἑβραϊκάς; *Pan.* 69.25.1–9).[15] The wording of the Septuagint could be reinterpreted but not abandoned, and the versions of the Three could help explain its more peculiar elements or otherwise be enlisted for Christian exegesis.[16]

There were also other times that patristic exegetes acknowledged the Hebrew origins of their scriptures. The etymology of Hebrew proper names

---

[12] Manlio Simonetti, *Biblical Interpretation in the Early Church: An Historical Introduction to Patristic Exegesis* (Edinburgh: T&T Clark, 1994), 127–28.

[13] Eusebius sometimes viewed the *recentiores*, particularly Symmachus, as clearer than the Septuagint; Dominique Barthélemy, *Études d'histoire du texte de l'Ancien Testament* (Göttingen: Vandenhoeck & Ruprecht, 1978), 179–93.

[14] Mark DelCogliano, "Basil of Caesarea on Proverbs 8:22 and the Sources of Pro-Nicene Theology," *Journal of Theological Studies* 59 (2008): 183–90.

[15] Andrew S. Jacobs, "Epiphanius of Salamis and the Antiquarian's Bible," *Journal of Early Christian Studies* 21 (2013): 437–64, at 449.

[16] Kamesar, *Jerome*, 35–38; Alison Salvesen, "The 'Three' in Early Christian Commentary: The Case of the 'Song of the Vineyard' (Isaiah 5:1–7)," *Journal of the Septuagint and Cognate Studies* 48 (2015): 72–85.

was an enduring part of Greco-Latin biblical exegesis, going back to Philo and before.[17] Origen and Jerome used Hebrew etymologies extensively in their exegesis, a practice that continued throughout the Middle Ages owing to the wide influence of Jerome's work *On Hebrew Names*.[18] As Augustine said, "Many Hebrew names that are not interpreted by the authors of these books undoubtedly provide no meager power and assistance in solving the enigmas of the Scriptures, if someone can interpret them" (*Doctr. chr.* 2.16.23).

Such (mediated) use of the Hebrew text does not lead any of these authors to reject or even criticize the LXX, but—at least sometimes—the LXX must be interpreted in light of the original Hebrew text. At Proverbs 8:22, κτίζω should be interpreted not in terms of its usual definition but more in terms of κτάομαι, as the Hebrew text reveals. Our Christian authors would claim that the Seventy had used an unusual and unclear, but still correct, definition of κτίζω in this instance and that knowledge of the Hebrew text clarifies the intended sense. On the other hand, not all Christians approached the Septuagint quite so reverently, particularly the Antiochene school of biblical exegesis. They still used the Septuagint, but they did not seem to think of it as sacrosanct. One of the early Antiochene exegetes, Eusebius of Emesa (d. ca. 360), did not believe in the infallibility of the LXX. While he did not know Hebrew, he used his native Syriac—a close relative of Hebrew, as he knew—to aid his biblical exegesis. Because he grew up with the Syriac Peshitta as his Bible, he did not consider the LXX to be a special part of the divine economy.[19] In his study of the Genesis portion of Eusebius's *Commentarii in Octateuchum*, Haar Romeny has demonstrated that several comments from Eusebius reveal that "the

---

[17] On patristic use of etymology, see Michael Graves, *The Inspiration and Interpretation of Scripture: What the Early Church Can Teach Us* (Grand Rapids: Eerdmans 2014), 65–70. On Philo, see Lester L. Grabbe, *Etymology in Early Jewish Interpretation: The Hebrew Names in Philo* (Atlanta: Scholars Press, 1988).

[18] On Origen, see Marguerite Harl, ed., *Origène. Philocalie, 1–20 Sur Les Écritures*, SC 302 (Paris: Cerf, 1983), 447–57; on Jerome, see Kamesar, *Jerome*, 103–26; on medieval exegetes, see Eyal Poleg, "The Interpretation of Hebrew Names in Theory and Practice," in *Form and Function in the Late Medieval Bible*, ed. Eyal Poleg and Laura Light (Leiden: Brill, 2013), 217–36.

[19] R. B. ter Haar Romeny, *A Syrian in Greek Dress: The Use of Greek, Hebrew, and Syriac Biblical Texts in Eusebius of Emesa's Commentary on Genesis* (Leuven: Peeters, 1997), 109.

reading of the Hebrew was decisive for Eusebius" so that he preferred, at times, the Hebrew or the Syrian to the LXX.[20] Like Philo before him, Eusebius recognized that translation cannot be both word-for-word and sense-for-sense, and (unlike Philo) he made no exception for the LXX.[21] The very first verse of the Bible elicits the judgment that the Seventy have mistranslated the Hebrew with the word ἐποίησεν (made), whereas they should have put ἔκτισε (created).[22] Eusebius's own ignorance of Hebrew and his use of Greek for his own composition meant that the LXX always served as the base text of his exegesis, but he was willing to correct the LXX and recognized the ultimate authority of the Hebrew text: "He did not use the term 'Hebrew truth,' but it is clear that the Hebrew text, as the basis of the translations, was the criterion."[23]

Eusebius of Emesa was unusual. Most Christians writing in Greek accepted the Septuagint as an inspired translation, as essentially an original text. And yet, through investigation of biblical etymologies and from their use of the Three for help in interpreting difficult expressions in the Septuagint, Christians were always aware of the Hebrew origins of their Scripture, and they recognized that the Septuagint did not always correspond to the Hebrew Bible. How did they think through such issues?

---

[20] Romeny, 110. Romeny also prints the preserved Genesis fragments of Eusebius's *Commentarii* that deal with this issue, along with a translation and discussion. Eusebius prefers the Hebrew over the LXX at frg. v, xix, xxv, xl; and the Syrian over the LXX at frg. v, xxiii, xxv, xxxix, lviii, lxix.

[21] See the introduction to his *Comm. Oct.* as presented and discussed by Haar Romeny, *Syrian in Greek Dress*, 156–69.

[22] See the fragment and the discussion at Romeny, *Syrian in Greek Dress*, 169–74.

[23] Romeny, 108. For a comparison of Eusebius with Origen, see Romeny, 117–20; for a comparison with Jerome, see Romeny, 124–31. According to Romeny, the LXX was the "point of departure" for Eusebius (112), but "recognition of the priority of the Hebrew text" was "his starting-point" (139).

Textual Theory among Greek
Patristic Authors[24]

Often, they did not think about such issues at all, if Jerome can be believed, who claimed that even "learned men" (*diserti homines*) were unaware that the scriptures had been translated from Hebrew.[25] But what about the Fathers who promoted the inspiration of the LXX and reflected on its relationship to the Hebrew text? Perhaps most famously, Augustine—the great Latin Church Father of the late fourth and early fifth century—asserted that the LXX was inspired even in its divergences from its Hebrew *Vorlage* (*Civ.* 18.42–44), a view that has found some support among modern proponents of the theological value of the LXX[26] and that will occupy us in Chapter Ten. Scholars have sometimes thought that Augustine's view may be indicative of the earlier patristic view, especially in the belief that a substantive gap separates the Greek Bible from the Hebrew Bible. About the biblical text in the church of the patristic age, Mogens Müller has written, "The Hebrew Bible text was devalued or even rejected, either because it was taken to be a forgery, or because it was the Jewish Bible. Since the Septuagint was considered to be inspired, there was no need to vindicate it in relation to the wording of the Hebrew text."[27]

---

[24] Much of what follows is from my essay "The Septuagint's Fidelity to Its *Vorlage* in Greek Patristic Thought," in *XIV Congress of the IOSCS, Helsinki, 2010*, ed. M. K. H. Peters (Atlanta: SBL, 2013), 663–76. See also my *Hebrew Scripture in Patristic Biblical Theory*, ch. 5.

[25] For this statement from Jerome, cf. the edition by Rudolf Helm, *Eusebius Werke VII: Die Chronik des Hieronymus*, GCS 47 (Berlin: Akademie-Verlag, 1956), 3, lines 14–15; and see Megan Hale Williams, *The Monk and the Book: Jerome and the Making of Christian Scholarship* (Chicago: University of Chicago Press, 2006), 47.

[26] Pierre Benoit, "L'inspiration des Septante d'après les Pères," in *L'homme devant Dieu: Mélanges offerts au père Henri de Lubac*, 3 vols., Théologie 56–58 (Paris: Aubier, 1963–64), 1.169–87, at 185, where he calls Augustine's "double inspiration" position "une vue singulièrement profonde et vraie." See also Dominique Barthélemy, "La place de la Septante dans l'Église," in *Études d'histoire du texte de l'Ancien Testament* (Göttingen: Vandenhoeck & Ruprecht, 1978), 111–26 (119–20); repr. from *Aux grands carrefours de la révélation et de l'exégèse de l'Ancien Testament* (Paris: Desclée de Brouwer, 1967), 13–28.

[27] Mogens Müller, *The First Bible of the Church: A Plea for the Septuagint* (Sheffield: Sheffield Academic, 1996), 78; this is at the conclusion of Müller's investigation of patristic views that he labels "Graeca Veritas," 68–78.

However, it is not at all clear that Greek authors maintained this position. The one Father that seems to give the most explicit support to this view is Epiphanius, whose complex comments merit an extended discussion (see below). On the whole, the Fathers denied that their Greek Bible diverged at all from the original Hebrew, so we must respond to Müller by saying that the Fathers consistently sought to vindicate the LXX in relation to the wording of the Hebrew text. We will see that some of their arguments for establishing the authority of the LXX work only by uniting the Greek with the Hebrew. We have several times already observed the common belief that God inspired the Seventy translators specifically for the purpose of rendering an accurate translation of the original Hebrew scriptures. We will briefly survey the opinions of the second-century Fathers before turning to Origen and the way that his work altered the debate, and then we will investigate the views of the Greek Fathers who followed Origen.

BEFORE ORIGEN

Because patristic writers of the second century adopted Philo's view that the LXX corresponded perfectly with the Hebrew text, they felt compelled to demonstrate the superiority of the LXX over the translations produced by Aquila, Symmachus, and Theodotion. The second-century authors provided little indication that they investigated the new versions to any great extent. Justin and Irenaeus—the only pre-Origen Christians whose comments on these textual differences are preserved for us (but cf. Tertullian, *Marc.* 3.13; *Jud.* 9.8)—regarded the new translations, or at least the proposed translation of Isaiah 7:14 with the wording νεᾶνις (young woman) in place of παρθένος (virgin), as at best inaccurate and at worst the willful perversion of Scripture designed merely to score points against Christians. Neither Justin nor Irenaeus seemed to consider seriously the possibility that the wording of the Septuagint might diverge from the Hebrew. Irenaeus knew that the Septuagint must be the correct translation because the Jews themselves translated it (*Haer.* 3.21.1), the miracle story (seventy-two translators separated into different cells; seventy-two identical translations) demonstrated its authority (3.21.2), the translation long preceded the coming of Christ so that there was no possibility of Christian bias, and the apostles used the

Septuagint (3.21.3). Justin did not mention the miracle story or the apostolic use of the Septuagint, but he stressed that the Jews themselves produced the Septuagint in ages long past, and the newer translations or interpretations resulted from anti-Christian prejudice (cf. *Dial.* 68–73). Justin and Irenaeus insisted that the Septuagint alone accurately represented the Hebrew text.

ORIGEN

Origen knew better. His enormous research project known as the Hexapla demonstrated numerous differences between the Hebrew text as Origen knew it and the Septuagint as it existed in the early third century. A detailed inspection of the columns of the Hexapla would of course reveal many differences of translation such as those Justin and Irenaeus observed in Isaiah 7:14, though the Hexapla itself could not clarify for the reader without Hebrew which of the Greek translations most accurately reflected the first column. But a mere glance at this parallel Bible sufficed to expose the quantitative differences among the editions (cf. Origen, *Ep. Afr.* 4–5)—that is, where the Septuagint had more or less material than the Hebrew text—in which cases Aquila, Symmachus, and Theodotion almost always matched the Hebrew text. One who had seen the Hexapla could not claim that the Septuagint and not the Three best conformed to the Hebrew Bible.

Origen's views on this matter are complex and subject to varying interpretations. At times he seemed to advocate a Septuagint revised according to the Hebrew text, as when he wrote about "healing" the text of the Septuagint (*Comm. Matt.* 15.14; quoted in the previous chapter), or in his adapting the Greek word order toward the Hebrew word order, or correcting the spelling of proper names. These aspects of Origen's textual theory suggest that he believed that the Septuagint textual tradition had suffered corruption and he could restore it to its original form by revising it toward the Hebrew text, a theory that he worked out in practice with his Hexapla and the Septuagint recension resulting from it. But elsewhere Origen argued stridently against the suggestion by Julius Africanus that questions surrounding quantitative differences between the Septuagint and the Hebrew Bible should be decided in favor of the latter. He did not rely on the miraculous legend of the origins of the Septuagint, a story that never appears in his extant writings. Instead, he argued for the authority of the translation from his confidence that divine Providence had ensured that the church had the correct Bible, regardless of these textual issues (*Ep. Afr.* 8).[28] These were cases, apparently, in which Origen did not think the Septuagint had suffered corruption. Origen offered a detailed explanation for why the Septuagint sometimes contained more material than the Hebrew Bible: the Jewish leaders had excised narratives unflattering to themselves (*Ep. Afr.* 13–15). His argument implied that the Hebrew Bible itself may have suffered in transmission, in which case its differences from the Septuagint could hardly encourage revision toward the corrupt Bible of the Jews.

Whereas Justin and Irenaeus had assumed that the Septuagint corresponded more closely to the Hebrew text than did the later Jewish translations, Origen's work demonstrated that the Septuagint diverged from the Hebrew Bible often. As just discussed, he entertained multiple explanations for this potentially troubling situation: sometimes he regarded the Septuagint, sometimes the Hebrew Bible, as textually suspect. In both cases, Origen's underlying assumption was apparently that the original Septuagint constituted a faithful translation of its *Vorlage*. There were also occasions when Origen claimed that what might at first blush appear to be a difference did not, upon critical examination, turn out to be so. Such is the case for παρθένος and νεᾶνις at Isaiah 7:14, the difference that had so troubled earlier Christians. While Justin and Irenaeus had rejected the reading νεᾶνις as patently inaccurate, Origen interpreted these two translation options as synonyms in the biblical idiom, both meaning (or, at least, allowing for the meaning) "virgin" (*Cels.* 1.34–35), an argument that became standard in later patristic writings.[29]

Origen also proposed a further explanation for observed textual differences: he sometimes attributed to the Seventy translators a desire to highlight certain aspects of biblical religion by putting forward a turn of phrase

---

[28] Here I use the paragraph numbering of Nicholas de Lange, ed., *Origène, La Lettre à Africanus sur l'histoire de Suzanne*, in *Origène, Philocalie, 1–20: Sur les Écritures*, ed. Marguerite Harl, SC 302 (Paris: Cerf, 1983), 469–578.

[29] Adam Kamesar, "The Virgin of Isaiah 7:14: The Philological Argument from the Second to the Fifth Century," *Journal of Theological Studies* 41 (1990): 51–75.

not precisely equivalent to what they found in their Hebrew *Vorlage*.[30] For example, some prophecies of Christ, which appear with the future tense in the Hebrew text and in the Three, are rendered by the Seventy in the past tense.[31] Origen suggested that the Seventy wanted to represent God as omniscient (*Sel. Ps.* 2:1, PG 12.1104c), whereas the Three translated "more clearly" (σαφέστερον; *Sel. Ps.* 42:3, PG 12.1420d). Sometimes the Seventy offered spiritual rather than literalizing translations, such as might be the case at Psalm 3:8 when they (perhaps) substituted the term *without cause* for the more literal *cheek* (*Sel. Ps.* 3:8, PG 12.1129b–c), in which case, Origen said, the translators would have "avoided the poverty of the letter" (τὸ εὐτελὲς περιϊσταμένους . . . τῆς λέξεως).[32] In his *Commentary on Romans* (a work preserved in Rufinus's Latin translation), Origen recognized that Paul usually cited Scripture according to the LXX, even when it diverged from the Hebrew text,[33] but Origen also acknowledged that Paul's citations sometimes departed even from the LXX.[34] Origen's commentaries and homilies also display his willingness to subject to exegesis and homiletical exposition not only passages under asterisk (thus added to the LXX in agreement with Hebrew) and passages under obelus (thus in the LXX but not in the Hebrew) but also passages that he had already critically judged to constitute scribal error.[35]

Origen usually considered the Septuagint to be a very faithful translation, which contributed to its high status in his estimation.[36] But unlike his Christian predecessors Justin and Irenaeus, Origen recognized that the Three accurately reflected the current Hebrew text. Origen did not hold to Philo's position that the LXX perfectly matched its Hebrew *Vorlage*; not only

---

[30] See Kamesar, *Jerome*, 14–15.

[31] Pantaenus also discussed some problems with the tenses of verbs in the LXX, but not quite in the same way as Origen, according to the testimony of Clement of Alexandria, *Eclogae Propheticae* 56; see Ronald E. Heine, *Origen: Scholarship in the Service of the Church* (Oxford: Oxford University Press, 2010), 55.

[32] For a further example from Ezekiel 7:27, see Gallagher, *Hebrew Scripture in Patristic Biblical Theory*, 184–85.

[33] See *Comm. Rom.* 8.6.2 on Romans 10:16; *Comm. Rom.* 8.6.12 on Romans 10:21.

[34] *Comm. Rom.* 8.8.4, at Romans 11:9–10; *Comm. Rom.* 8.12.5 on Romans 11:26–27; *Comm. Rom.* 10.8.5 on Romans 15:8–12.

[35] Gallagher, *Hebrew Scripture in Patristic Biblical Theory*, 178–89.

[36] Kamesar, *Jerome*, 15–16.

did he assert, as we have just seen, that the Seventy translators sometimes adjusted the wording of the biblical text (for good reason, Origen thought), but he also said on occasion that the Three translated more literally than the Seventy,[37] an impossible feat in Philo's estimation. As we saw in greater detail in the previous chapter, Origen made adjustments in the text of the LXX for three types of divergence from the Hebrew text: quantitative differences, spelling of proper names, and word order.[38] He also insisted that Providence had provided the church with the correct Bible. Such tensions in Origen's textual theory could not but provoke competing interpretations.[39]

AFTER ORIGEN

Origen's textual work made it difficult to accept unchanged the position of the second-century Fathers. Whereas Irenaeus and Justin assumed that the received form of the LXX corresponded with the received form of the Hebrew Bible, Origen showed that the received LXX diverged often from the Hebrew text current in his day. Many Christians after Origen continued to echo arguments for the LXX's inspiration that implied that it was the most accurate translation. The Fathers of this period argued that, on the one hand, the translation that preceded Christ would not exhibit bias for or against the Christian message, and on the other hand, the agreement of seventy(-two) translators trumped that of three, especially when those three

---

[37] Sébastien Morlet, "L'utilisation des révisions de la Septante dans la première littérature chrétienne. Philologie, exégèse et polémique," in *La Bible juive dans l'Antiquité*, ed. Rémi Gounelle and Jan Joosten (Prahins: Éditions du Zèbre, 2014), 117–40, at 119n10. Morlet cites *Comm. Matt.* 16.19, where Aquila renders τὸ ἀκριβὲς τῆς λέξεως, and *Frg. Ps.* (PG 12.1144a), where the "precise sense" corresponds to τὸ κύριον τοῦ Ἑβραϊκοῦ. On the meaning of κύριος here, Morlet points to *Comm. Gen.*, frg. (PG 12.89a), where κυριώτατα means "de la façon la plus propre"; see also Philo's use of κύριος in the context of the translation of the Seventy (*Mos.* 2.38), along with the explanation of this term by Adam Kamesar, "Biblical Interpretation in Philo," in *The Cambridge Companion to Philo*, ed. Adam Kamesar (Cambridge: Cambridge University Press, 2009), 65–91, at 69.

[38] Origen himself acknowledged only the first type of revision (*Comm. Matt.* 15.14; implied at *Ep. Afr.* 7, as noted by Morlet, "L'utilisation des révisions de la Septante," 123).

[39] On the competing interpretations of Origen's views in Jerome, Epiphanius, and Rufinus, see Kamesar, *Jerome*, 6.

did not always agree among themselves.[40] These two arguments, the early date of the translation and the agreement of the translators, were intended to demonstrate that the Seventy sages deserved more respect and trust as faithful and accurate translators than did the Three; that is, the LXX matched the Hebrew text more closely. The Fathers not infrequently charged the Three with distorting the Old Testament, which again implied that the Hebrew text would not correspond to the newer translations.[41] In the wake of Origen, Greek writers did not adopt his claim that the Seventy translators somewhat adjusted the wording of the biblical text to suit the Christian message. Indeed, this idea would have directly contradicted the two usual arguments for the authority of the LXX.

Christians after Origen continued to uphold the LXX's fidelity to the Hebrew text, but they also had to grapple with the evidence for textual divergence that Origen compiled. Below we will analyze the views of a few of the Greek Fathers who attempted to reconcile these notions. A brief examination will demonstrate that Eusebius of Caesarea (d. ca. 340), Gregory of Nyssa (d. ca. 395), and Theodoret of Cyrus (d. ca. 460) found a solution to this problem by assuming that either the LXX or the Hebrew had become corrupt. In the minds of these Fathers, the original LXX accurately reflected the original Hebrew text, and the current deviations between these texts should be explained as either intentional or unintentional alterations during the course of transmission. On the other hand, a detailed investigation of Epiphanius's views will show that he generally attempted to minimize the divergences between Greek and Hebrew, assessing these as mere stylistic variations, while also reaffirming the traditional argument that the LXX and Hebrew texts agreed against the newer translations.

Eusebius of Caesarea, as we saw in the previous chapter, involved himself in promulgating the Hexaplaric recension of the LXX. Without himself knowing Hebrew, Eusebius understood that the Hebrew text could be stylistically superior to the LXX, a view he perhaps adopted from Origen

---

[40] Both arguments appear in Chrysostom, *Hom. Matt.* 5.2; Theodoret, *Comm. Is.* 7:14. For the first argument, cf. also Hilary, *Tract. Ps.* 2.3; for the second, Epiphanius, *Mens.* 17; Augustine, *Ep.* 28.2.

[41] Cf. Chrysostom, *Hom. Matt.* 5.2; Theodoret, *Comm. Is.* 7:14; for references in Epiphanius, see the discussion below.

and that will come to fruition among patristic authors only in Jerome.[42] Apparently he considered Origen's work a restoration of the original LXX, cleansing it of scribal corruption. Eusebius seems to have viewed the original LXX as an inspired text; he quoted—no doubt, approvingly[43]—Irenaeus's account of the translation, complete with the separate cells that demonstrated the inspiration of the translators (*Hist. eccl.* 5.8.10–15; cf. Irenaeus, *Haer.* 3.21.1–2). In another work, Eusebius summarized the story from the Letter of Aristeas, but without the crucial passage about the translators' consulting with one another (*Praep. ev.* 8.2–5). Eusebius often thought the LXX less clear than other translations.[44] We might recall how he used the other translations to interpret the LXX's unusual use of κτίζω, "create," at Proverbs 8:22 (noted earlier). But he also thought that the Hebrew text itself was often ambiguous, susceptible to multiple interpretations.[45] Eusebius, in his *Chronicon*, argued against the idea that Christians should prefer the Hebrew text to the LXX, basing his chronological calculations on the numbers reported in the LXX rather than those in the Hebrew text. However, Eusebius's arguments did not serve to drive a wedge between the LXX and its *Vorlage*; rather, Eusebius suspected that the Hebrew text current in his day transmitted numbers at variance with the LXX due to falsification perpetrated by the Jews.[46] The original Hebrew corresponded to the text one now reads in the LXX, as confirmed occasionally by reference to the

---

[42] Origen, *Cels.* 7.59; Eusebius of Caesarea, *Praep. Ev.* 11.5.2. On Jerome's views of the stylistic superiority of the Hebrew text, see Kamesar, *Jerome*, 46–49.

[43] But see Kamesar, *Jerome*, 37–38n109.

[44] Kamesar, *Jerome*, 37–38; M. J. Hollerich, *Eusebius of Caesarea's Commentary on Isaiah* (Oxford: Clarendon, 1999), 77.

[45] See *Dem. ev.* 5, preface (at the end), discussed by Hollerich, *Eusebius*, 76–77, on which see also Adam Kamesar's review in *Journal of Theological Studies* 52 (2001): 892–96, at 894. See also Haar Romeny, *Syrian in Greek Dress*, 120–23.

[46] See page 40 (lines 13–20) of the edition by Josef Karst, *Eusebius Werke V: Die Chronik, aus dem Armenischen übersetzt*, GCS 20 (Leipzig: Hinrichs, 1911). The text of the *Chronicon* has been preserved in its entirety only in Armenian, which translation Karst has rendered into German. On the history of research into this Armenian translation, and the present state of its text, see Armenuhi Drost-Abgarjan, "Ein neuer Fund zur armenischen Version der Eusebios-Chronik," in *Julius Africanus und die christliche Weltchronistik*, ed. Martin Wallraff (Berlin: de Gruyter, 2006), 255–62. The relevant passages are preserved in Greek by George Syncellus; see Georgius Syncellus, *Ecloga Chronographica*, ed. A. A. Mosshammer (Leipzig: Teubner, 1984), 99–101.

Samaritan Pentateuch.[47] Eusebius concludes that the LXX should be followed because it was translated "from an old, as it seems, and uncorrupted writing of the Hebrews" (ἐκ παλαιᾶς, ὡς ἔοικε, καὶ ἀδιαστρόφου Ἑβραίων γραφῆς).[48]

The view of Gregory of Nyssa lines up well with that of Eusebius—it is not so much that the Three have distorted the Hebrew text as that the Hebrew text itself has become corrupt. The LXX testifies to an earlier and more authentic form of the Hebrew. Gregory reveals this position in his treatise *On the Inscriptions of the Psalms*, where he includes a section (2.8–9) on psalms lacking superscriptions. He lists twelve psalms for which the Hebrew lacks a superscription present in Gregory's copy of the LXX.[49] He gives the reason at the beginning of *Inscript. Psal.* 2.8. After mentioning that some psalms lack superscriptions in both Hebrew and Greek, he writes,

> In the rest, however, the inscriptions are ecclesiastical and mystical
> and indicative of the piety related to our mystery. But these do not
> exist for the Hebrews in accordance with that charge made against

---

[47] Karst, *Eusebius Werke V*, 44, lines 20–23.

[48] Syncellus, *Ecloga Chronographica*, ed. Mosshammer, 100 line 26–27. See also *Chron.*, ed. Karst, 45, lines 13–15, who translates the Armenian as "aus alten und fehlerlosen Vorlagen der Hebräer übersetzt worden ist." See C. P. Bammel, "Die Hexapla des Origenes: Die Hebraica Veritas im Streit der Meinungen," *Augustinianum* 28 (1988): 125–49, at 134. On the other hand, Veltri (over)interprets certain statements by Eusebius (similarly to Hollerich) so as to position him as a forerunner of Jerome with an emphasis on the Hebrew text even to the point of reducing the authority of the LXX; see Veltri, *Libraries, Translations, and "Canonic" Texts: The Septuagint, Aquila, and Ben Sira in the Jewish and Christian Traditions* (Leiden: Brill, 2006), 54–56. On the contrary, Eusebius makes plain in this passage of the *Chronicon* that the LXX retains its authority as the Church's Old Testament.

[49] The twelve psalms are, according to the LXX numbering, 32, 42, 70, 73, 90, 92–96, 98, 103. For this list, see McDonough's edition in Jacob McDonough and Paul Alexander, eds., *In inscriptiones Psalmorum, In sextum Psalmum, In ecclesiasten homiliae*, GNO 5 (Leiden: Brill, 1962), 93.15–24. (Page and line numbers for this treatise will be cited according to this edition.) Psalm 73 (Heb. 74) does have a superscription in Hebrew and Greek; Gregory includes it in his initial list, but he omits it from his later discussion of these individual psalms. There is some other confusion in his discussion, as in his treating the first verse of Psalm 32 (Heb. 33) as if it were the superscription (94.4ff.). Ronald E. Heine proposes that Gregory was working from a list of psalms without superscriptions in Hebrew and did not bother to verify his information; see Heine's translation of this work, *Gregory of Nyssa's Treatise on the Inscriptions of the Psalms: Introduction, Translation and Notes* (Oxford: Oxford University Press, 1995), 145n85.

them in the Gospel, that they established a precept that *if anyone should confess the Christ, "he should be put out of the synagogue"* [John 9:22]. They, therefore, have not accepted those inscriptions which they perceive to contain some indication of the mystery.[50]

Gregory then discusses the superscriptions present in the Greek Psalter without a corresponding superscription in the Hebrew text. Interpreting these Greek superscriptions messianically, he accuses the "Hebrews" of not accepting them because they also understand their messianic import. That he considers the Hebrew text corrupt in these passages is evident from the two times he charges the Jews with "silencing" (σιγάω) these superscriptions (95.23; 103.6). In other words, Gregory does not regard these superscriptions as the inspired invention of the Seventy translators, but rather he considers them faithful translations of the original Hebrew superscriptions, now absent from that text because of Jewish "unbelief" (ἀπιστία; 93.14) and "willful misunderstanding" (ἀγνωμοσύνη; 94.2).

In his *Commentary on the Psalms*, Theodoret of Cyrus observes the same differences in the Psalter's superscriptions between the Greek and Hebrew texts, but he usually concludes that the LXX itself has become corrupt through its transmission. The Seventy translators did not add superscriptions but were careful to transmit only what they found in their Hebrew *Vorlage*. This is clear from the very first psalm, where Theodoret finds in his local text the heading "without a superscription among the Hebrews" (ἀνεπίγραφος παρ' Ἑβραίοις), which he takes to be a note appended by the Seventy translators themselves to indicate their fidelity to their source text.[51] However, at LXX Psalm 70 he again finds this note, but here it follows a superscription that Theodoret considers irreconcilable with the Bible.

---

[50] Translation by Heine, *Gregory of Nyssa's Treatise*, 143. For the Greek text, see the edition by McDonough and Alexander, *In inscriptiones Psalmorum*, 91, line 27 through 92 line 4.

[51] PG 80.865b–c; cf. Psalm 32 [LXX], PG 80.1093b. Theodoret finds the note ἀνεπίγραφος παρ' Ἑβραίοις several times in his copy of the LXX; cf. his comments at Psalm 2; 32; 42; 70; 90; 92–96; 98; 99. Cf. also Alfred Rahlfs, ed., *Psalmi cum Odis*, Septuaginta 10 (Göttingen: Vandenhoeck & Ruprecht, 1931). Rahlfs does report that some Lucianic manuscripts and other sources contain the note as indicated by Theodoret; see the apparatus of Rahlfs's edition at Ps. 2 (p. 81); 32 (p. 127); 70 (p. 196); etc. Rahlfs gives no indication that any manuscript contains the note at Ps. 1 (p. 81).

Therefore, here the note "without a superscription among the Hebrews" must be an admission from a later interpolator that he has invented a superscription (PG 80.1417a–b). This is the explanation Theodoret continues to advocate as he dismisses the superscriptions at LXX Psalm 90 (PG 80.1608b) and following. He confirms at LXX Psalm 92 (PG 80.1624a) that the Hexapla lacks both the superscription and the note conveying the absence of a superscription in Hebrew.[52] That Theodoret conceived of the original Hebrew and LXX as equivalent is clear from his comment at LXX Psalm 93 (PG 80.1629b–c): "It is clear that some others have inserted the superscription, not the prophet or the original translators."[53] The text of the "prophet" (i.e., David)[54] and the original translators (the Seventy) would have agreed in omitting the spurious superscriptions. Theodoret's comment here agrees with his characterization of the LXX elsewhere as slavishly following the Hebrew text (τῇ γὰρ Ἑβραίων γλώττῃ δουλεύσαντες οἱ Ἑβδομήκοντα).[55]

---

[52] Theodoret's references to the Hexapla are collected by Jean-Noel Guinot, "La fortune des *Hexaples* d'Origène aux IVᵉ et Vᵉ siècles en milieu antiochien," in *Origeniana Sexta: Origène et la Bible/Origen and the Bible*, ed. Gilles Dorival and Alain Le Boulluec (Leuven: Peeters, 1995), 215–25, at 219n22. Guinot says of Theodoret's use of the Hexapla, "il ne semble pas non plus avoir consulté cet ouvrage à Césarée, et il n'en connaît peut-être guère plus que le nom. En tout cas, dans ses commentaires, 'l'Hexaple' paraît désigner le texte de la Septante hexaplaire plutôt que la synopse d'Origène" (219). Guinot notes (219n24) that Theodoret always uses the term *Hexapla* in the singular (τὸ Ἑξαπλοῦν), and he seems to access its readings through commentaries, such as those by Eusebius of Caesarea (220–225), as indicated even in our passage (LXX Ps. 92; PG 80.1624a): Τὸ Ἀνεπίγραφος παρ' Ἑβραίοις οὐκ ἔστιν ἐν τῷ ἑξαπλῷ, οὔτε παρ' Εὐσεβίῳ.

[53] Cf. also LXX Psalm 95, PG 80.1644c–d; LXX Psalm 96, PG 80.1652b. For another translation of this passage, see Robert C. Hill, *Theodoret of Cyrus: Commentary on the Psalms*, 2 vols., FOC 101–102 (Washington, DC: Catholic University of America Press, 2001), 2.117. Hill translates οἱ [. . .] ἐξ ἀρχῆς ἑρμηνεύσαντες as "those commenting on it [i.e., the psalm] from the beginning" (similarly at vol. 2.127 for Ps. 95). However, the context demands that the reference be to the Seventy translators, and so the rendering should be "the original translators."

[54] Theodoret cautiously sides with those who affirm Davidic authorship of all the psalms; cf. *Comm. Ps.* praef. (PG 80.861c–d) and at LXX Psalm 74 (PG 80.1441b–c).

[55] *Comm. in Cant.* 3:6 (PG 81.120a); see Jean-Noel Guinot, "Théodoret de Cyr: Une lecture critique de la Septante," in *Κατα τους ο'—Selon les Septante: Trente études sur la Bible grecque des Septante en hommage à Marguerite Harl*, ed. Gilles Dorival and Olivier Munnich (Paris: Cerf, 1995), 393–407, esp. 396.

Epiphanius of Salamis stands apart from the Greek Fathers we have just examined. In the first place, he is one of a handful of patristic authors who gained a reputation for linguistic competence in multiple languages, including Hebrew.[56] Second, Epiphanius pursues a different explanation to account for the divergences between the Hebrew text and the LXX. Nevertheless, in harmony with the majority of the Greek Fathers, Epiphanius strongly advocated the authority of the LXX within the church, and, like Eusebius, he attributed some differences between the church's Bible and that of the Jews to intentional corruption in the synagogue. However, this explanation constitutes a relatively minor component of his overall theory. A proper understanding of this theory requires a detailed discussion due to the length and nature of Epiphanius's treatment of the differences between the LXX and Hebrew text.

Epiphanius presents an extensive introduction to the Greek versions of the Old Testament in the opening part of his *On Weights and Measures*.[57] He first discusses the critical signs that appear in manuscripts of the Hexaplaric LXX, especially the asterisk (*Mens.* 2) and obelus (*Mens.* 3; 6). He informs his readers that Origen used these symbols to represent quantitative differences between the LXX and the Hebrew text, the latter being reflected in Aquila and Symmachus, and "occasionally" (σπανίως; *Mens.* 2, line 17) Theodotion, at least with regard to passages under asterisk. Epiphanius is clearly at pains in this discussion to acquit the Seventy of altering the biblical text. This he does by emphasizing several key points that we will examine in detail: (1) the asterisked passages, representing omissions in the LXX vis-à-vis the Hebrew, are superfluous; (2) the obelized passages, being additions

---

[56] Cf. Jerome, *Ruf.* 2.22; 3.6; but Jürgen Dummer is very skeptical of Epiphanius's knowledge of Hebrew and Aramaic; see "Die Sprachkenntnisse des Epiphanius," in *Philologia Sacra et Profana: Ausgewählte Beiträge zur Antike und zu ihrer Wirkungsgeschichte* (Stuttgart: Steiner, 2006), 29–72, esp. 35–47; repr. from *Die Araber in der alten Welt*, ed. Franz Altheim and Ruth Stiehl, vol. 5.1 (Berlin: de Gruyter, 1968), 392–435.

[57] This work is abbreviated as *Mens.* in accordance with its Latin title, *De mensuris et ponderibus*. I have used the edition by Elia D. Moutsoula, "Τὸ «Περὶ μέτρων καὶ σταθμῶν» ἔργον Ἐπιφανίου τοῦ Σαλαμῖνος," *Theologia* 44 (1973): 157–200; indications of lines numbers in the present context refer to this edition. I have also consulted the English translation of the Syriac text found in James E. Dean, *Epiphanius' Treatise on Weights and Measures: The Syriac Version* (Chicago: University of Chicago Press, 1935). For references to other editions of Epiphanius's work, see Veltri, *Libraries*, 59–60n116.

in the LXX vis-à-vis the Hebrew, are explanatory; (3) all such differences are too minor to affect the meaning of a passage; and (4) the agreement among the LXX translators, and between their work and the Hebrew text, was confirmed at Ptolemy's court.

With regard to the passages under asterisk, Epiphanius asserts repeatedly in *Mens.* 2 that the content omitted by the LXX is superfluous. For example, at *Mens.* 2 (lines 18–20), we read, "The Seventy-two translators omitted [παρῆκαν] it and did not translate it, because such expressions are repetitious [δισσολογουμένων] and superfluous [ἐκ περισσοῦ] to read." Indeed, the word περισσός (superfluous) appears five times (lines 19–20, 41, 45, 48, 51) in this context to describe these passages, while δισσολογία (repetition) and its cognates appear three times (lines 19, 28, 51) and δευτερολογία (repetition) once (line 38). To bear out this point, Epiphanius takes an example from Genesis 5:5, where he says that Adam's age is listed in the Hebrew text (and Aquila) as "thirty year and nine hundred year" (τριάκοντα ἔτος καὶ ἐννακόσια ἔτος; lines 23–24), while the LXX has "thirty and nine hundred years" (τριάκοντα καὶ ἐννακόσια ἔτη; line 31). In the opinion of Epiphanius, the LXX reading conforms to good Greek style—it displays "smoothness" (λειότης; line 30) and "clarity" (τρανότης; line 28)—while Aquila's more literal rendering exhibits "tiresome repetition" (βόμβησις; line 30)[58] and "harshness" (κακοφωνία; line 41). This does not mean that Epiphanius thinks that the Hebrew text itself is harsh and redundant, for he understands that Hebrew style is not the same as Greek style:

> And having made nothing defective (ἐλλιπές) in word, on the contrary they even established the reading with a view to clarity, although in Hebrew it cannot be said as concisely as the Seventy-two have done. (*Mens.* 2; lines 31–34)

Epiphanius regards this example from Genesis 5:5 to be representative of the asterisked material, for he introduces it with the assurance that readers

---

[58] Cf. G. W. H. Lampe, ed., *A Patristic Greek Lexicon* (Oxford: Oxford University Press, 1961), 301 s.v., where our passage is cited.

will understand similar passages from this one minor instance.[59] He is also careful to point out that none of the material omitted by the LXX is heretical (κατὰ τῆς πίστεως; line 50). Epiphanius thus characterizes the omissions in the LXX vis-à-vis the Hebrew as semantically irrelevant and intended only to conform the biblical text to Greek style. He effectively denies that the asterisked passages represent real omissions in the LXX.

For the obelized passages, Epiphanius follows a similar approach. The LXX added these words not to change the meaning of the biblical text, but to make it clearer:

> For the Seventy-two translators added these expressions from them-
> selves [ἀφ' ἑαυτῶν], not without purpose [οὐκ εἰς μάτην], but rather
> usefully [ἀλλὰ μᾶλλον εἰς ὠφέλειαν]. For having added to these
> defective expressions, they brought the reading to clarity, with the
> result that we suppose them to have been not lacking the Holy
> Spirit. For they avoided all unnecessary repetition. But where a word
> seemed to be lame when translated into the Greek language, there
> they made an addition. (*Mens.* 3; lines 68–74)

At this point, Epiphanius is concerned that his readers might find fault (μέμ-ψιν ἐπάγειν; line 75) with the LXX, so he provides a report of LXX origins designed to assure his readers of the translation's divine nature (*Mens.* 3–6). We will consider his account of the translation legend below. When Epiphanius returns to his discussion of the obelus (*Mens.* 6, line 157), he takes an example from Psalm 140:1 (LXX; 141:1 in Heb.). Epiphanius says that the Hebrew verse ends with the words "pay attention to the voice" (πρόσχες τῇ φωνῇ; line 164), which he describes as "lame" (χωλός; line 165).[60] The Seventy

---

[59] Cf. *Mens.* 2, lines 20–21: λεκτέον διὰ βραχείας λέξεως εἰς τὸ ἀπὸ τῆς μιᾶς λέξεως περὶ τῶν λοιπῶν σε γνῶναι.

[60] Epiphanius does not reveal how he is accessing the Hebrew text of this psalm; on this question, see Dummer, "Sprachkenntnisse," 40–41. The reading Epiphanius presents for the Hebrew text does not exactly conform to the MT, which has האזינה קולי. Aquila's text would presumably reflect the pronominal suffix on קולי, but no Hexaplaric evidence for this verse appears in Frederick Field, *Origenis Hexaplorum quae Supersunt: Veterum interpretum graecorum in totum Vetus Testamentum fragmenta*, 2 vols. (Oxford: Oxford University Press, 1875), 2.296.

added the words "of my supplication" (τῆς δεήσεώς μου), thus making the line "not lame" (ἀχώλωτος; line 166). In view of the solution offered by the LXX, the description of the Hebrew reading as "lame" probably means that the expression is somehow ambiguous because it does not clarify the nature of the "voice." Indeed, later Epiphanius will say that the purpose of the additions made by the Seventy was "for clarity of expression" (σαφηνείας ἕνεκα τοῦ λόγου; Mens. 17, lines 465–66). In light of his earlier discussion concerning the asterisked passages, where the redundancy of the literal Greek translation was not considered poor Hebrew style, it is likely that Epiphanius conceives of the ambiguity in Psalm 140:1 not as a component of the Hebrew text itself but only of its literal translation into Greek.[61] Such an understanding is also indicated in the above quotation from Mens. 3 where he says that a certain passage may be "lame" when it is translated into Greek (εἰς Ἑλληνικὴν διάλεκτον μεταφερόμενος; lines 73–74). Therefore, Epiphanius probably thinks that the Hebrew text is perfectly clear to Hebrew speakers but its translation into Greek requires some clarifying words. He concludes that all the additions made by the Seventy, all the passages under obelus, were intended "for literary style and for assistance" (εἰς φράσιν καὶ ὠφέλειαν; line 171). Again, Epiphanius intends this example from Psalm 140:1 to be understood as representative of all obelized passages.[62] In this way, for Epiphanius, the LXX represents an inspired interpretation of the Hebrew text for the church.

It will be clear from this presentation that Epiphanius does not think that the Seventy translators made any substantial changes to the biblical text. The changes he identifies were necessary either for Greek style as opposed to Hebrew style or to clarify Hebrew expressions that would be ambiguous in Greek. His account of the translation legend confirms that he deemed the LXX an accurate rendering of the Hebrew text. In Mens. 3–6, Epiphanius presents an elaborate version of this legend: seventy-two translators worked

---

[61] Alternatively, Hilary of Poitiers (Tract. Ps. 2.2) notes that ambiguity in the Hebrew text results from the lack of written vowels. See Adam Kamesar, "Hilary of Poitiers, Judeo-Christianity, and the Origins of the LXX: A Translation of Tractatus super Psalmos 2.2–3 with Introduction and Commentary," Vigiliae Christianae 59 (2005): 264–85, at 280.

[62] Cf. Mens. 6, lines 169–70: Ἐπίστηθι τοίνυν ἀπὸ τοῦ βραχυτάτου λόγου τοῖς ὁμοίοις αὐτῶν κατὰ τὴν προσθήκην πανταχοῦ ὑπὸ τῶν αὐτῶν ἑρμηνευτῶν κειμένοις.

in pairs separated into thirty-six rooms, each pair translating the twenty-two books of the Jewish scriptures. At the completion of their task, each pair of translators brought their translation to King Ptolemy. Comparison among the thirty-six translations revealed no disagreement. (Or, at least, not much disagreement. It is allowed that some pairs of translators used synonyms instead of exactly the same words. Epiphanius explains Origen's use of additional critical signs, the lemniscus and hypolemniscus, in his Hexaplaric text as marking such deviations among the original pairs of translators.)[63]

> And wherever they added a word, they all added it together, and wherever they omitted something, they all equally omitted it. And the things they omitted were unnecessary, but the things they added were necessary. (*Mens.* 6; lines 155–57)

Here, again, Epiphanius says that the Seventy translators made certain changes in the biblical text, and he says that these changes correspond to "necessity" (χρεία; cf. *Mens.* 17, lines 465, 468). As we have seen, Epiphanius conceives of this necessity as related to the transfer of the Hebrew idiom into the Greek language. These changes, consisting of only insignificant details as Epiphanius represents them, either clarified the sense of a Hebrew phrase or deleted what would be perceived by Greek speakers to be redundant. That Epiphanius does not envision any alterations regarding the message of the Bible is clear when in the same context he depicts the comparison of translations as including the Hebrew text without any disagreement being found (*Mens.* 6; lines 149–52).

From this analysis of Epiphanius's statements, we can conclude that he did not think that the Seventy translators were inspired to change the content of the biblical text. This conclusion challenges the views of some scholars. Half a century ago, Heinrich Karpp pitted Epiphanius's desire to minimize the differences between the texts, a desire we have noticed

---

[63] Cf. *Mens.* 8, lines 204–25; *Mens.* 17, lines 477–82. Contrast Augustine, *Civ.* 18.42: *in nullo verbo, quod idem significaret et tantumdem valeret, vel in verborum ordine, alter ab altero discreparet.*

repeatedly in our study, against the passage just quoted from *Mens*. 6 emphasizing the additions and subtractions made by the Seventy; Karpp saw here a contradiction.[64] More recently, Müller has claimed that Epiphanius "admitted to some discrepancies between the Greek translation and the Hebrew text which were not owing to later corrections."[65] Both Karpp and Müller have assumed that *Mens*. 6 refers to changes in the content of the Bible, but our study has made it clear that Epiphanius does not, in fact, admit "to some discrepancies between the Greek translation and the Hebrew text." On the contrary, he spends a good deal of time and effort absolving the Seventy of the charge of changing the biblical text. His discussion of the very minor changes we have examined only shows that he knows something about the business of translating, that no translation worth its salt can be absolutely literal (*contra* Philo, *Mos.* 2.40). Aquila's excessive literalness provides the prime example of what not to do, in Epiphanius's view (*Mens.* 2, lines 35–45). That he spends so much time downplaying the changes made by the Seventy, describing these changes as merely stylistic and explanatory and characterizing them as exceedingly minor details insignificant for meaning, shows that he and his readers could hardly tolerate any difference between the Hebrew and LXX. Epiphanius further emphasizes the close relationship between the two texts by including the Hebrew text among those compared at Ptolemy's court, where no disagreement was found. Epiphanius does not see the LXX and the Hebrew text as essentially different but as essentially the same.

---

[64] Heinrich Karpp, "'Prophet' oder 'Dolmetscher'? Die Geltung der Septuaginta in der Alten Kirche," in *Vom Umgang der Kirche mit der Heiligen Schrift: Gesammelte Aufsätze* (Cologne: Böhlau, 1983), 128–50; repr. from *Festschrift für Günther Dehn: Zum 75. Geburtstag am 18. April 1957 dargebracht von der Evangelisch-Theologischen Fakultät der Rheinischen Friedrich Wilhelms-Universität zu Bonn*, ed. Wilhelm Schneemelcher (Neukirchen: Kreis Moers, 1957), 103–17, at 138.

[65] Müller, *First Bible*, 78. Giuseppe Veltri also emphasizes the idea of "changes" in Epiphanius's account; see, e.g., "The Septuagint in Disgrace: Some Notes on the Stories on Ptolemy in Rabbinic and Medieval Judaism," in *Jewish Reception of Greek Bible Versions: Studies in Their Use in Late Antiquity and the Middle Ages*, ed. Nicholas de Lange, Julia G. Krivoruchko, and Cameron Boyd-Taylor (Tübingen: Mohr [Siebeck], 2009), 142–154, at 143. Veltri thinks that Epiphanius's version of the "changed LXX" influenced the rabbinic tradition of the changes made for "King Talmai" (cf. *b. Meg.* 9a–b).

Epiphanius does recognize that the disagreements between the LXX and the other Greek versions extend to more passages than he has so far discussed. These are cases in which the three Jewish versions have misrepresented the meaning of the Hebrew. He says that Aquila intended to distort messianic prophecies (*Mens.* 15, lines 414–18) and that Symmachus intended to distort the passages relevant to the Samaritans (*Mens.* 16, lines 445–47). He does not say that Theodotion had evil motives, but rather that Theodotion usually agreed with the LXX. Nevertheless, he may imply a criticism of Theodotion in saying that this translator worked alone (ἰδίως), unlike the Seventy (*Mens.* 17, line 454).[66] He does lump all three of these translators together, contrasting them with the Seventy. Whereas these three disagree among themselves, the miraculous agreement of the Seventy ensured the "truth" (ἡ ἀλήθεια) of their translation (*Mens.* 17, line 458). It is obvious that this type of disagreement between the LXX and the Three entails no disagreement between the LXX and Hebrew; like Justin and Irenaeus before him, Epiphanius thinks that the LXX and Hebrew agree against the Three, whose translations distort the original text. Epiphanius does not say whether he has confirmed this assumption by referring to the Hebrew text directly, although this seems altogether unlikely. Rather, he probably assumed the correctness of his hypothesis based on his characterizing the Three as distorters whereas the Seventy translators enjoyed the guidance of the Holy Spirit. Since both of these points were long-held Christian views, Epiphanius probably felt no need to confirm them. In any case, Epiphanius presents the view that the LXX translation represents most accurately the Hebrew text.

The post-Origen Greek Fathers whose views we have examined each judged the LXX translation to be a Providentially provided Greek rendering of the original Hebrew text. While Eusebius, Gregory, and Theodoret used the idea of textual corruption to reconcile their traditional belief in the accuracy of the LXX with Origen's demonstration of variation between the translation and the current Hebrew text, Epiphanius simply denied the

---

[66] This observation is made by Alison Salvesen, "A Convergence of the Ways? The Judaizing of Christian Scripture by Origen and Jerome," in *The Ways That Never Parted: Jews and Christians in Late Antiquity and the Early Middle Ages*, ed. Adam H. Becker and Annette Yoshiko Reed (Tübingen: Mohr Siebeck, 2003), 233–58, at 247.

existence of real variants between the Greek and Hebrew, echoing the old argument that the Three had distorted the Hebrew Bible. Despite these differences, all four of these Fathers did defend, sometimes vehemently, the position that the Seventy translators accurately rendered their source text. They do not serve as direct forerunners to Augustine's view of a double biblical text because they understood the content of the original LXX and of the original Hebrew text to be fundamentally identical.

9

Jerome

The Use and Abuse of the LXX according to Jerome

The truth should be taken from the Hebrew codices.

—Jerome, *Epistle* 20.2

The Christian reception of the Septuagint came to a turning point in the Latin-speaking world of the late fourth and early fifth centuries. The way it is often represented is that Jerome (ca. 346–420) opposed the LXX and Augustine (354–430) defended it, and that depiction is basically true—and somewhat misleading. We will see in the next chapter how Augustine came to value (Jerome's translation of) the Hebrew Bible while maintaining a firm commitment to the LXX as the traditional Bible of the church. In this chapter, we will see that Jerome maintained a concern for the Septuagint as the traditional Bible of the church while also promoting his new Latin translation from the Hebrew as providing a superior basis for Christian theology.

The Old Testament in Latin[1]

The origins of the Latin Bible are obscure, but the earliest Latin Old Testament translations were based on the traditional Greek versions and probably originated in second-century North Africa.[2] The Old Testament seems to have been translated by Christians (not Jews) from the Greek versions of the books.[3] The evidence suggests a single translation for each book.[4] These Latin translations were also called "Septuagint" by Latin writers,[5] but today scholars call them by the Latin term *Vetus Latina* or the equivalent English, *Old Latin*. By the late fourth century, the textual tradition of the Vetus Latina had suffered corruption to the extent that revision was necessary,[6] and Jerome stepped forward to perform the task. His various efforts to improve the Latin text of the Bible eventually resulted in the Vulgate (though it received this name only much later), a new biblical text that proved controversial at its creation.

In a radical move, Jerome ultimately based his translations of the Old Testament on the Hebrew text available in his day rather than on the Septuagint. Perhaps uniquely among Latin-speaking fourth-century Christians, Jerome learned Hebrew well and put this knowledge to use in his biblical scholarship.[7] He advertised himself as a *Vir trilinguis* (*Ruf.* 2.22; 3.6), a three-language man

---

[1] This section reproduces material originally written for my essay "The Septuagint in Patristic Sources," in *The T&T Clark Handbook of Septuagint Research*, ed. William A. Ross and W. Edward Glenny (London: T&T Clark, 2021), 255–67.

[2] Pierre-Maurice Bogaert, "The Latin Bible," in *The New Cambridge History of the Bible*, vol. 1: *From the Beginnings to 600*, ed. J. Carleton Paget and J. Schaper (Cambridge: Cambridge University Press, 2013), 505–26; H. A. G. Houghton, *The Latin New Testament: A Guide to Its Early History, Texts, and Manuscripts* (Oxford: Oxford University Press, 2016), 3–18.

[3] Matthew Kraus, "Hebraisms in the Old Latin Version of the Bible," *Vetus Testamentum* 53 (2003): 487–513.

[4] Houghton, *Latin New Testament*, 12.

[5] Cornelia Linde, *How to Correct the Sacra Scriptura? Textual Criticism and the Latin Bible between the Twelfth and Fifteenth Century* (Oxford: Society for the Study of Medieval Languages and Literature, 2011), 9–13, 126–7.

[6] On the poor state of the Latin manuscripts in the late fourth century, see Augustine, *Doctr. chr.* 2.16; Jerome, *Praef. Evang.* 12–13; *Praef. Jos.* 11–13.

[7] Michael Graves, *Jerome's Hebrew Philology: A Study Based on His Commentary on Jeremiah* (Leiden: Brill, 2007); Hillel Newman, "How Should We Measure Jerome's Hebrew Competence?," in *Jerome of Stridon: His Life, Writings and Legacy*, ed. Andrew Cain and Josef Lössl (Burlington, VT: Ashgate, 2009), 131–40.

(Latin, Greek, Hebrew), garnering authority as a premier biblical exegete. He promoted knowledge of the Hebrew Bible, the *Hebraica veritas* (Hebrew truth), as important and beneficial to Christians, and others seem to have thought similarly as they wrote him questions requesting his insight into biblical passages.[8] His commission from Pope Damasus in the early 380s to revise the Latin text of the Gospels (mentioned only in Jerome's *Preface to the Gospels*)[9] initiated his career of revising or translating the text of Scripture, which took up much of his time over the next two decades. Aside from the Gospels, Jerome worked on the biblical text of the Old Testament exclusively. (He did write commentaries on some other New Testament books, but he did not produce translations of the books of the New Testament outside of the Gospels.) At first, he revised the Latin translations of the Septuagint, basing his work on Origen's Hexaplaric Greek recension complete with asterisks and obeli, a project that elicited the commendation of Augustine (*Ep.* 28.2). However, Jerome perhaps did not finish this project.[10] From around 390, he devoted himself to an all-new project: translating the entire Hebrew Bible directly into Latin, which he completed around 405. He also produced translations of Tobit and Judith, from a "Chaldean" (Aramaic) *Vorlage*, according to his prefaces to these translations.[11] Jerome's version became well known during his own lifetime, and it would eventually dominate the Latin biblical tradition, especially from the ninth century.[12]

---

[8] On Jerome's correspondence, see Andrew Cain, *The Letters of Jerome: Asceticism, Biblical Exegesis, and the Construction of Christian Authority in Late Antiquity* (Oxford: Oxford University Press, 2009).

[9] For the Latin text of the preface, see Robert Weber and Roger Gryson, eds., *Biblia Sacra iuxta uulgatam uersionem*, 5th ed. (Stuttgart: Deutsche Bibelgesellschaft, 2007), 1515–16. For Latin text and French translation, see Aline Canellis, ed., *Jérôme, Préfaces aux livres de la Bible*, Sources Chrétiennes 592 (Paris: Cerf, 2017), 470–81. On Jerome's translation of the Gospels, see Cain, *Letters of Jerome*, 48–52.

[10] See below for the surviving material for this translation project, and see Adam Kamesar, "Jerome," in *The New Cambridge History of the Bible*, vol. 1, *From the Beginnings to 600*, ed. James Carleton Paget and Joachim Schaper (Cambridge: Cambridge University Press, 2013), 653–75, at 661. For an argument that Jerome may have finished his Latin translation of the LXX, see Adam Kamesar, *Jerome, Greek Scholarship, and the Hebrew Bible: A Study of the Quaestiones Hebraicae in Genesim* (Oxford: Clarendon, 1993), 53–54.

[11] Edmon L. Gallagher, "Why Did Jerome Translate Tobit and Judith?," *Harvard Theological Review* 108 (2015): 356–75.

[12] Linde, *How to Correct the Sacra Scriptura*, 34–38.

The Hebraica Veritas[13]

Jerome coined the term *Hebraica veritas* in about 391 at the conclusion of the prologue to his *Hebrew Questions on Genesis*. Describing Origen's handling of the scriptural text, Jerome reported that the great Greek theologian had used the LXX in his homilies but in his more scholarly commentaries he had resorted to the *Hebraica veritas*, the Hebrew truth. The term became a hallmark of Jerome's exegetical writings, appearing about a hundred times as a way of referring to the overriding authority of the Hebrew text of the Old Testament, especially in comparison to the LXX: the *veritas* resided in the Hebrew text and not in any translation. In a similar fashion, Jerome spoke of the *Graeca veritas* for the New Testament (*Praef. Evang.* 4)[14] and the *Chaldaica veritas* for the Aramaic (Chaldaic) portions of the Old Testament (*Comm. Dan.* 5:11).[15] Earlier patristic authors had generally recognized the importance of the Hebrew text of Scripture, but the way Jerome opposed the *Hebraica veritas* to the LXX, claiming authority for the former and attempting to diminish the authority of the latter, quickly generated controversy and forced his contemporaries to rethink the nature of the biblical text.

The term *Hebraica veritas* was not used before Jerome. We saw in the previous chapter that earlier Christians respected the Hebrew text of the Old Testament as authoritative and inspired—or, at least, the original Hebrew text; some Christians thought the contemporary Hebrew text may have suffered corruption from scribes, in which case the original text would have been attested in the LXX. (The Dead Sea Scrolls have provided renewed legitimacy to this patristic argument.) Of course, the LXX itself may have suffered corruption, and so Christian scholars produced recensions of the LXX, often aiming to adjust the wording of the LXX toward the Hebrew text. Jerome's comment on the *trifaria varietas* (threefold variety) of the LXX in

---

[13] Much of this section was originally written for my essay "The *Hebraica Veritas*," in *Language and Culture in Early Christianity: A Companion*, ed. T. Denecker, M. Lamberigts, G. Partoens, P. Swiggers, and T. Van Hal (Leuven: Peeters, forthcoming).

[14] I cite the line numbers of Jerome's Vulgate prefaces according to the edition of Weber and Gryson, *Biblia Sacra*. Already, Tertullian had used the phrase *in Graeco authentico* (*De monogamia* 11).

[15] On Jerome's use of the term *Chaldaic*, see Edmon L. Gallagher, *Hebrew Scripture in Patristic Biblical Theory: Canon, Language, Text* (Leiden: Brill, 2012), 126n72.

his day (see the epigraph to Chapter Seven) was intended to justify his own return to the *Hebraica veritas*: he was arguing that the LXX manuscripts were untrustworthy and the only remedy was to go behind them. Jerome also used other arguments for his return to the Hebrew text, arguments designed to reduce the Septuagint's authority in the church. We will look more closely at these arguments below. By translating directly from the Hebrew text, Jerome sought to bring stability to the Old Testament text in Latin.

In the late antique Christian world, Jerome was perhaps uniquely qualified to produce a Christian translation directly from the Hebrew Bible: few other Christians leave any trace of a knowledge of Hebrew.[16] According to his own report, Jerome began studying Hebrew during the mid-370s while he lived a monastic life in the desert of Chalcis, east of Syrian Antioch (*Ep.* 125.12). His initiation into the language came with the help of a Jewish convert to Christianity, and he continued to use teachers as they were available. He grew in his knowledge of Hebrew with the aid of the written resources available in Greek, including the later versions, especially Aquila.[17] Eventually he became the teacher of others who would submit to his instruction; his friends and supporters Paula and Eustochium learned to sing the Psalms in Hebrew under his guidance (*Ep.* 108.26). When he returned to Rome from the east (ca. 382), he started promoting Hebrew learning as a significant tool in biblical interpretation.[18] Though he did not yet use the phrase *Hebraica veritas*, he did argue that "the truth should be taken from the Hebrew codices" (*ex Hebraeis codicibus ueritas exprimenda est*; *Ep.* 20.2), showing that he already accepted the idea that the Hebrew Bible should serve as the authoritative text of the Christian Old Testament.[19] This was

---

[16] C. J. Elliott, "Hebrew Learning among the Fathers," *Dictionary of Christian Biography*, ed. W. Smith and H. Wace, 4 vols. (London: John Murray, 1877–1887), 2.851–72.

[17] See *Ep.* 32.1; and on the tools Jerome used to progress in his knowledge of Hebrew, see Graves, *Jerome's Hebrew Philology*, 84–97.

[18] The evidence comes from Jerome's letters written at this time. See Kamesar, *Jerome*, 41–49; and, for a less sympathetic account, Cain, *Letters of Jerome*, 53–67.

[19] A few years later, in 388, Jerome labeled the Hebrew text the *fons veritatis* (*Comm. Eccl.* prol.) and used the expression *iuxta sensus hebraici veritatem* (*Comm. Eccl.* 8:13). As mentioned earlier, the term *Hebraica veritas* first appears in the preface to his *Hebrew Questions on Genesis*. See Pierre Jay, *L'exégèse de Saint Jérôme d'après son "Commentaire sur Isaïe"* (Paris: Études Augustiniennes, 1985), 89–102, 142–47.

not a particularly radical opinion; as we have seen repeatedly, Christians generally considered the Hebrew Bible to be authoritative. Jerome's radical move was denying that the LXX was a good and accurate representation of the Hebrew Bible.

Corresponding to his emphasis on the Hebrew text of Scripture, Jerome promoted a particular view of the Old Testament canon that did not command universal consent. The most prominent explanation of his views on the Old Testament canon appears in his *Prologus Galeatus*, the "helmeted" preface he composed in ca. 393 and attached to his translation of Samuel and Kings.[20] Here he described the Old Testament in terms of its traditional Jewish threefold division of Law, Prophets, and Hagiographa, and he mentioned the books forming each division. The canon, according to this reckoning, comprised twenty-two or twenty-four books, depending on whether Ruth and Lamentations were considered individually or as part of Judges and Jeremiah, respectively. The makeup of the canon matches precisely that of the Jewish canon, which in itself was not very unusual; Christians had been producing canon lists of the Old Testament for centuries that basically corresponded to the Jewish canon.[21] But around the same time that Jerome was producing this list, some Christians, especially in North Africa, were issuing lists that included books outside the Jewish canon, books that would much later receive the label deuterocanonical.[22] Jerome explicitly rejected such a move, calling these other books "apocrypha" and insisting that they form no part of the biblical canon (*Prol. gal.* 52–57).[23] Even though there did exist disagreement about the canon of Scripture, Jerome's translation does not seem to have generated controversy on this issue.

---

[20] Edmon L. Gallagher and John D. Meade, *The Biblical Canon Lists from Early Christianity: Texts and Analysis* (Oxford: Oxford University Press, 2017), 198–203.

[21] See especially the Greek lists collected in Gallagher and Meade, ch. 3.

[22] See the list in Codex Claromontanus, the Mommsen Catalogue, the Breviarium Hipponense, and the lists of Augustine of Hippo and Pope Innocent I, in Gallagher and Meade, ch. 4.

[23] Edmon L. Gallagher, "The Old Testament 'Apocrypha' in Jerome's Canonical Theory," *Journal of Early Christian Studies* 20 (2012): 213–33; Gallagher, "Jerome's *Prologus Galeatus* and the OT Canon of North Africa," in *Studia Patristica* 69, ed. M. Vinzent (Leuven: Peeters, 2013), 99–106. As mentioned earlier, Jerome did translate two of these "apocryphal" books, Tobit and Judith. He also included the deuterocanonical additions of Esther and Daniel, under obelus, in his translations of these books.

But his version did generate controversy. Some Christians disapproved of his decision to translate directly from the Hebrew rather than the LXX, a decision that resulted sometimes in a Latin translation very different from the traditional one. For example, since some parts of the Greek Daniel (both LXX and Theodotion)—that is, the story of Susanna, the story of Bel and the Dragon, and Azariah's Prayer and the Song of the Three Jews—were absent from the Hebrew version of the book, Jerome's translation included them with a prefixed obelus to indicate their inauthentic nature. (Jerome adopted the obelus from Origen; see Chapter Seven.) Rufinus of Aquileia, Jerome's onetime friend, especially objected to this feature (*Apol. Hier.* 2.35). Rufinus also claimed that the Hebrew text employed by Jerome had been corrupted by the Jews, with the implication that the *Vorlagen* used by the Seventy would have been more trustworthy (*Apol. Hier.* 2.40). Augustine of Hippo wrote a letter to Jerome to ask him to stop translating from the Hebrew and return to the LXX (*Ep.* 71.3–6). Most commonly, Jerome's challengers doubted his competence in Hebrew, especially whether his proficiency in the language exceeded that of the Seventy translators.[24] The idea that the apostles had approved of the LXX continued to weigh heavily in the discussion.[25] Augustine feared that the new translation would create a division between the Greek and Latin churches if the LXX was no longer the common text (*Ep.* 71.4).[26] Jerome assumed that these opponents would accept the authority of the Hebrew text, and he responded to the charge against him of incompetence by challenging his readers to ask the Jews whether his translation was accurate.[27]

The prefaces that he issued with each portion of the Bible that he translated allowed him to present repeatedly his reasons for using the *Hebraica veritas* instead of the LXX. In these prefaces, and also in his letters, Jerome urged his readers to accept his translation, but he had different ways of representing its significance: sometimes he suggested that Christians may

---

[24] For examples from Rufinus, Augustine, and Theodore of Mopsuestia, see Gallagher, *Hebrew Scripture in Patristic Biblical Theory*, 204–7.

[25] Rufinus, *Apol. Hier.* 2.37–38; Augustine, *Ep.* 71.6; 82.35.

[26] Augustine (the subject of the next chapter) eventually came to value Jerome's translation, and he even used the term *Hebraica veritas* a few times (*Quaest. Hept.* 1.152, *bis*; *Civ.* 18.44).

[27] E.g., *Prologus Galeatus* 69–73; see Gallagher, *Hebrew Scripture in Patristic Biblical Theory*, 202–3.

use his translation as a complement to their study of the LXX; sometimes he emphasized its independent value as a possible replacement for and improvement upon the LXX.[28] At about the same time that he began translating the Bible from the Hebrew text, Jerome also inaugurated a series of commentaries on the prophetic books that would occupy the rest of his life. In these commentaries, he demonstrated the benefit of attention to Hebrew matters for biblical exegesis and theology.[29] While Jerome recognized his own innovation in Christian Hebrew scholarship and promoted his work in some cases as "new,"[30] he also tried to diffuse some of the criticism directed at him by contending that his work stood in harmony with Christian tradition, in that Christian biblical scholars had long sought to correct the LXX based on the Hebrew (or the newer translations) and that his predecessors had recognized the value of Hebrew knowledge for etymologies and exegesis, even if they were less adept at acquiring and employing that knowledge than Jerome himself.

Jerome against the Septuagint

In his *Epistle* 57 to Pammachius, written in 395 CE, Jerome asserted, "The edition of the Seventy has rightly prevailed in churches, whether because it is first and was made before the advent of Christ or because it was used by the apostles, in those passages, however, where it does not diverge from the Hebrew" (*in quibus tamen ab hebraico non discrepat; Ep.* 57.11).[31] This statement exhibits some of Jerome's paradoxical ideas about the LXX: on the one hand, he argued repeatedly and forcefully for the authenticity and authority of the *Hebraica veritas* as opposed to the Greek translation traditional in the churches; on the other hand, he routinely interpreted the LXX alongside

---

[28] For citations and discussion, see Kamesar, *Jerome*, 58–72.

[29] On Jerome's final commentary (Jeremiah) and his Hebrew philology in general, see Graves, *Jerome's Hebrew Philology*.

[30] See the description of his *Qu. Hebr. Gen.* as a "new work" (*opus novum*) in the work's prologue.

[31] Isidore Hilberg, ed., *S. Eusebii Hieronymi Epistularum Pars I*, Corpus Scriptorum Ecclesiasticorum Latinorum 54 (Leipzig: Freytag, 1910), 523, lines 10–13.

the Hebrew in his commentaries and he claimed to use the LXX version of Psalms in worship. Moreover, in his Vulgate translation, he sometimes followed the LXX even when it diverged from the Hebrew, and despite his statements to the contrary, he acknowledged that the apostles did as well, even if rarely. In this section, we explore Jerome's negative statements about the LXX. In the next section, we will look at his more positive evaluations of the traditional Greek version.

First, we should establish some of the basic facts regarding Jerome's relationship with the LXX. On more than one occasion Jerome claimed to have translated Origen's Hexaplaric LXX text into Latin, complete with asterisks and obeli.[32] The prefaces to these works actually do not mention Origen, and it seems that Jerome wanted to present the text-critical work as his own accomplishment—as Augustine assumed (*Ep.* 28.2)—though in the prefaces to his later translations from the Hebrew for the same books, he did acknowledge that Origen created the *Vorlage* for his earlier translations.[33] Jerome's LXX translation survives only for the Gallican Psalter (which became Vulgate)[34] and the books of Job and of Song of Songs, along with prefaces to Chronicles and the Solomonic books.[35] Scholars generally doubt

---

[32] See, e.g., *Ep.* 106.2.2. For the basic data, see J. N. D. Kelly, *Jerome: His Life, Writings, and Controversies* (New York: Harper & Row, 1975), 158–59; Kamesar, "Jerome," 660–61. Jerome also claims to have seen the Hexapla (*Comm. Tit.* 3.9; *Comm. Ps.* 1), a claim doubted by Pierre Nautin, *Origène: Sa vie et son œuvre* (Paris: Beuchesne, 1977), 329, but see Matthew A. Kraus, *Jewish, Christian, and Classical Exegetical Traditions in Jerome's Translation of the Book of Exodus: Translation Technique and the Vulgate* (Leiden: Brill, 2017), 107–8.

[33] See, e.g., *Praef. Iob Iuxta Hebraeos (IH)* 6; *Praef. Par. IH* 11; also *Praef. Pent.* 8–11. See also Megan Hale Williams, *The Monk and the Book: Jerome and the Making of Christian Scholarship* (Chicago: University of Chicago Press, 2006), 79–81.

[34] Jerome did translate the Psalter from the Hebrew text as well, but his earlier translation from the Hexaplaric Greek is what came to be accepted within manuscripts of his translation, especially since the time of Alcuin (eighth century). The edition of the Vulgate edited by Weber and Gryson, *Biblia Sacra*, presents both Psalter texts side-by-side.

[35] For the prefaces to all of Jerome's biblical translations, see Canellis, *Jérôme, Préfaces.* The Job translation has survived in three manuscripts (VL 132 160 161) and was printed from VL 161 in Pierre Sabatier, *Bibliorum sacrorum latinae versions antiquae seu vetus Italica*, 3 vols. (Reims: Florentain, 1743–1749), 1.826–910, taken over by Migne in PL 29.61–114; see Jean-Claude Haelewyck, "11.4.1 Job: Vetus Latina," in *Textual History of the Bible*, vol. 1, ed. Emanuel Tov and Armin Lange (Leiden: Brill 2016); Pierre-Maurice Bogaert, "Job latin chez les Pères et dans les Bibles: D'une version courte à des versions longues sur le grec et sur l'hébreu," *Revue Bénédictine* 122 (2012): 48–99, 366–93; Joseph Ziegler, ed., *Iob*, Sepuaginta

that he completed any more of this translation, though he may have done.[36] While scholars traditionally interpreted this translation as an early project for Jerome, before his awakening to the importance of the Hebrew text, Adam Kamesar has argued persuasively that Jerome had already long been awake to the importance of the *Hebraica veritas* before he began translating Origen's Greek text and that this translation of an LXX edition corrected against the Hebrew served within Jerome's wider agenda of promoting the authority of the Hebrew text within the church.[37]

Jerome did translate more of the LXX than what is preserved of his Hexaplaric translations. In his biblical commentaries, Jerome routinely translated the LXX alongside the Hebrew and interpreted both texts. Very often, in fact, Jerome provided two lemmas for a biblical passage, the Hebrew text and the LXX (both, of course, translated into Latin). He followed this practice all the way through his Minor Prophets commentaries. His presentation of the double lemma is less consistent in his commentaries on Isaiah, Ezekiel, and Jeremiah, but still the LXX features prominently in these works.[38]

11.4 (Göttingen: Vandenhoeck & Ruprecht, 1982), 37–40. On the translation of Song of Songs—preserved in VL 160 (available online at https://www.e-codices.unifr.ch/en/list/one/csg/0011) and in the biblical lemmas of the Latin translation (by Epiphanius Scholasticus, early sixth century) of the commentary by Philo of Carpasia (fourth century; Latin translation preserved in Vat. lat. 5704, available online at https://digi.vatlib.it/view/MSS_Vat.lat.5704)—see José Manuel Cañas Reíllo, "13–17.2.1.2 Canticles," in Tov and Lange, *Textual History of the Bible*, vol. 1; Eva Schulz-Flügel, ed., *Canticum Canticorum*, fasc. 1: *Einleitung*, Vetus Latina 10/3 (Freiburg: Herder, 1992); Reinhart Ceulemans, "The Latin Patristic Reception of the Book of Canticles in the *Hexapla*," *Vigiliae Christianae* 63 (2009): 369–89, esp. 370–75. The text is edited in A. Vaccari, ed., *Cantici Canticorum Vetus Latina Translatio a S. Hieronymo ad Graecum Textum Hexaplarem Emendata* (Rome: Edizioni di Storia e Letteratura, 1959).

[36] See Stefan Rebenich, *Jerome*, The Early Church Fathers (New York: Routledge, 2002), 53–54; Kelly, *Jerome*, 159. For an argument that Jerome may have completed the Latin translation of the Hexaplaric LXX, I cite again Kamesar, *Jerome*, 53–54.

[37] The seminal argument is in Kamesar, *Jerome*, ch. 2. Canellis, *Jérôme, Préfaces*, 92–93, represents the older view.

[38] On the double lemma, see Jay, *L'exégèse de Saint Jérôme*, 42–104; Williams, *Monk and the Book*, 119–23. Jay, *L'exégèse de Saint Jérôme*, 114–19, points out that Jerome essentially provided a translation of Hexaplaric Isaiah in his commentary on that book. Williams, *Monk and the Book*, 65n6, mentions the Minor Prophets commentaries similarly. Full Latin translation of the LXX lemma is also found often in the commentary on Ezekiel (particularly book 5), less often in his Jeremiah commentary. In the preface to his Ecclesiastes commentary, Jerome says that he follows the LXX only when it does not diverge from the Hebrew: *quod nullius auctoritatem secutus sum; sed de hebraeo transferens, magis me septuaginta interpretum*

Jerome often cited Origen's text-critical work and its reception in the churches as precedent for his own work on the biblical text (cf. *Praef. Paralip.* 12–19):

> But if, after the LXX edition, when Christ's gospel was already flash-ing, the Jew Aquila, and the Judaizing heretics Symmachus and Theodotion were received among the Greeks, they who hid many mysteries of the Savior by a treacherous translation and, neverthe-less, are found in the Hexapla in the churches and are explained by ecclesiastical men, how much more I—a Christian, from Christian parents and bearing on my forehead the banner of the cross, whose zeal was to restore things omitted, to correct things corrupted and to disclose by pure and faithful speech the sacraments of the church—I ought not to be reproved by fastidious or spiteful readers?[39]

The fact that the church received the Hexaplaric LXX, that Christian preachers based their homilies on its text, which had been filled out with additions from the later Jewish (or Judaizing) translators, should eliminate any criticism directed at Jerome for his translation project. In other words, the church had already made room for a Hebraized LXX, and Jerome was simply taking the next step. Moreover, the common Greek form of Daniel in the churches was actually not the form known as LXX but the form associated with Theodotion, a fact that Jerome exploited to further his

---

consuetudini coaptaui, in his dumtaxat, quae non multum ab hebraicis discrepabant. Interdum Aquilae quoque et Symmachi et Theodotionis recordatus sum, ut nec novitate nimia lectoris studium deterrerem, nec rursum contra conscientiam meam, fonte veritatis omisso, opinionum rivulos consectarer.

[39] *Praef. Iob IH* 41–45. He says at *Ep.* 106.2.2 that the Hexaplaric Psalter is sung in Jeru-salem and in the churches of the East. At *Ep.* 57.11, he mentions the asterisks and obeli in the church copies of the LXX. Jerome elsewhere (*Praef. Ios.* 21–23) implies that the obelized passages were omitted in church; on Origen's use of the obelus: *quo ostenditur iugulandum esse et confodiendum, quod in authenticis libris non invenitur* (*Ep.* 106.7). See Alison Salvesen, "A Convergence of the Ways? The Judaizing of Christian Scripture by Origen and Jerome," in *The Ways That Never Parted: Jews and Christians in Late Antiquity and the Early Middle Ages*, ed. Adam H. Becker and Annette Yoshiko Reed (Tübingen: Mohr Siebeck, 2004), 233–58, at 244. For different understandings of the asterisks and obeli, see Rufinus, *Apol. Hier.* 2.36; Augustine, *Civ.* 18.43.

own cause.[40] His argument about ecclesiastical use of material added from Aquila, Symmachus, and Theodotion implied that the traditional LXX was inadequate because it did not sufficiently correspond to the Hebrew text. The lack of correspondence between the LXX and the Hebrew text was well known in Jerome's day, having been established unequivocally by Origen's text-critical researches. In Chapter Seven, we saw that at least in one passage (*Comm. Matt.* 15.14), Origen represented his Hebraized LXX as an effort to "heal" the LXX. There are times that Jerome's statements tended toward the same idea, as if Origen's work had healed the LXX by restoring it to its pristine state. But probably Jerome was promoting Origen's Hexaplaric LXX not because he genuinely thought Origen had returned the LXX to its original form but because Origen had eliminated many of the faults of the LXX—the original LXX.[41] Jerome filled his commentaries with notes about passages omitted by the Seventy and added by Origen under asterisk, or added by the Seventy,[42] implying that in Jerome's thought the original translation diverged from its *Vorlage*.[43]

Jerome sometimes used literary arguments. He noted that the Latin rendering of the LXX—a translation of a translation—was like a liquid poured into a third jar (*Praef. lib. Sal.* 24–25), so that it was necessarily inferior to a translation directly from the Hebrew.[44] While Christians often found the translations of biblical writings to be of low literary quality,

---

[40] *Praef. Dan.* 1–3; *Ruf.* 2.33; see Kamesar, *Jerome*, 59.

[41] See Gallagher, *Hebrew Scripture in Patristic Biblical Theory*, 197–99.

[42] See Jay, *L'exégèse de Saint Jérôme*, 115, citing *Comm. Isa.* 3.10 on Isaiah 6:11–13; 4.5 on Isaiah 10:5–11; 8.7 on Isaiah 24:16; 17.4 on Isaiah 60:5. Cf. *Comm. Jer.* 5:27–29. He is very critical of the LXX in *Qu. Hebr. Gen.*, e.g., at 4:6–7; 5:4; 5:25–27 (on Methusaleh's lifespan); 13:1–4; 13:13 (they unnecessarily added "in the sight of God"); 14:5 (misread a Hebrew word); see C. T. R. Hayward, *Saint Jerome's Hebrew Questions on Genesis: Translated with an Introduction and Commentary* (Oxford: Oxford University Press, 1995), 94. Also at *Qu. Hebr. Gen.* 31:7–8; on the way other exegetes handled this verse (Eusebius of Emesa, Diodore of Tarsus, Origen), see Bas ter Haar Romeny, "Les Hexaples et la recension origénienne. Diffusion et influence sur l'exégèse chrétienne," in *La Bible juive dans l'Antiquité*, ed. Rémi Gounelle and Jan Joosten (Prahins: Éditions du Zèbre, 2014), 97–115, at 110–11. Sometimes Jerome gives the LXX a pass (Kamesar, *Jerome*, 53n46): *Qu. Hebr. Gen.* 14:5: the LXX conveyed "the general signification rather than the literal meaning" (translation by Hayward, *Saint Jerome's Hebrew Questions on Genesis*, 46).

[43] See also *Praef. Isa* 11–14; *Praef. Ezech* 9–11; *Praef. Pent.* 21–25.

[44] On all these arguments made by Jerome, see Kamesar, *Jerome*, 58–69.

Jerome promoted the original Hebrew text as high literature on the level of the Greek and Latin classics.[45] Such arguments suggested that the LXX manuscript tradition, along with the Latin manuscripts based on it, was hopelessly corrupt, and Origen already provided a precedent for a return to the Hebrew text.

Jerome also attacked the theological arguments traditionally used to establish the LXX's preeminent position in the church. While he made these arguments in various writings, he collected several of them in the preface to the Pentateuch, which he composed in ca. 405. Against the general assumption that the apostles used the LXX exclusively, Jerome contended that they did so only when the LXX agreed with the Hebrew and that a number of New Testament quotations agreed more closely with the Hebrew than with the LXX (*Praef. Pent.* 11–19).[46] The LXX translation legend that supposedly proved the Seventy's inspiration—that they independently produced identical translations—found no basis in the earliest sources, such as the Letter of Aristeas and Josephus (*Praef. Pent.* 25–29). Whereas Christians sometimes followed Philo in declaring the Seventy to be prophets more than translators, Jerome insisted that they were, in fact, merely translators (*Praef. Pent.* 29–34). For Irenaeus (*Haer.* 3.21.1) and others, the authority of the Seventy translators in part rested on their date: they lived before Christ and therefore could neither favor nor disparage Christianity. Jerome overturned this chronological argument, asserting that the Seventy were ignorant of the meaning of the prophecies because they had not witnessed their fulfillment (*Praef. Pent.* 35–39). With such justifications Jerome sought to dislodge the LXX from its revered position as the Christian Old Testament, advocating instead a return to the *Hebraica veritas*.

NEW TESTAMENT QUOTATIONS

Perhaps the most important argument had to do with the apostolic sanction of the Septuagint. Any attempt to diminish the authority of the LXX within

---

[45] See Graves, *Jerome's Hebrew Philology*, 86; Kamesar, "Jerome," 664–70.

[46] See Teppei Kato, "Jerome's Understanding of Old Testament Quotations in the New Testament," *Vigiliae Christianae* 67 (2013): 289–315; Gallagher, *Hebrew Scripture in Patristic Biblical Theory*, 199–202.

the church would have to devise an answer to this powerful argument, and Jerome repeated his answer many times: the apostles did not use the LXX, they used the Hebrew, and even if they did use the LXX, they used it only when it agreed with the Hebrew.[47] Jerome had some evidence: there are some New Testament quotations that agree more closely with the Hebrew than with the LXX, such as the quotation of Hosea 11:1 in Matthew 2:15: "Out of Egypt I have called my son." As we saw in Chapter Six, the LXX has in Hosea 11:1, "Out of Egypt I recalled his children" (NETS), which prevented some readers of the LXX from recognizing the source of Matthew's quotation. Priscillian of Avila, for instance, used the absence within the LXX of anything resembling Matthew's quotation as part of an argument for the apostolic use of noncanonical books.[48]

Priscillian was thinking along the same lines as Origen, who wrote at the end of the prologue to his *Commentary on the Song of Songs*,

> It is common knowledge that the apostles and evangelists borrowed and put into the New Testament many things that we read nowhere in the scriptures that we account canonical, but that are found none the less in the apocryphal writings, and are quite obviously taken from them.[49]

---

[47] Kato, "Jerome's Understanding of Old Testament Quotations." See also Kamesar, *Jerome*, 50–70; J. S. Cameron, "The *Vir Tricultus*: An Investigation of the Classical, Jewish and Christian Influences on Jerome's Translation of the Psalter *Iuxta Hebraeos*" (DPhil diss., University of Oxford, 2006), 203–42. See the passages cited in Otto Wermelinger, "Le canon des latins au temps de Jérôme et d'Augustin," in *Le Canon de l'Ancien Testament: Sa formation et son histoire*, edited by Jean-Daniel Kaestli and Otto Wermelinger (Geneva: Labor et Fides, 1984), 153–96, at 190n152. Note Pierre Benoit, "L'inspiration des Septante d'après les Pères," in *L'homme devant Dieu: Mélanges offerts au père Henri de Lubac*, vol. 1 (Paris: Aubier, 1963), 169–87, at 182–83, esp. nn. 86 and 89. Christoph Markschies emphasizes the importance for Jerome of the apostolic sanction of texts; "Hieronymus und die 'Hebraica Veritas': Ein Beitrag zur Archäologie des protestantischen Schriftverständnisses," in *Die Septuaginta zwischen Judentum und Christentum*, ed. Martin Hengel and Anna Maria Schwemer (Tübingen: Mohr Siebeck, 1994), 131–81.

[48] See Priscillian's *Tractate III: Liber de fide et de Apocryphis*, in Marco Conti, *Priscillian of Avila: The Complete Works* (Oxford: Oxford University Press, 2010), 82–99 (Latin text and English translation, with notes on 273–78). For his use of Matthew 2:15, see lines 80–83.

[49] Translation by R. P. Lawson, *Origen: The Song of Songs Commentary and Homilies*, Ancient Christian Writers 26 (Westminster, MD: Newman, 1957), 56. This commentary is preserved only in Rufinus's Latin translation.

An example of this is when Origen, in his *Commentary on Matthew* (ser. 117),[50] said that the apocrypha of Elijah was the source of Paul's obscure reference in 1 Corinthians 2:9: "As it is written, 'What no eye has seen, nor ear heard, nor the heart of man imagined, what God has prepared for those who love him.'"

This same quotation from Paul came up in Athanasius's *Festal Letter* 39.26–32, where he argued against those who "said that Paul took a testimony from the apocryphal books."[51] Instead, Athanasius pointed to Isaiah 29:18–19 as the source of the quotation: "The deaf will hear on that day the words of the book, and the eyes of the blind that are in darkness and fog will see, and those who have no hope among people will be filled with joy."[52] Athanasius certainly recognized that the wording was not very close, so he acknowledged that we do not find Paul's quotation "written in the Scripture just as it is," but any apocryphal work containing the words of 1 Corinthians 2:9 stole them out of Paul, Athanasius assured his readers, rather than the reverse.

Jerome also dealt with this particular quotation,[53] and like Athanasius, Jerome was convinced that Paul did not rely on an apocryphal source but rather that he reworked a passage from Isaiah. Jerome did not point readers to Isaiah 29 but instead to Isaiah 64:3 (or verse 4 in English): "From of old no one has heard or perceived by the ear, no eye has seen a God besides you, who acts for those who wait for him." Jerome recognized that this verse from Isaiah did not precisely match Paul's quotation, but he argued, "The Apostle did not speak word for word, but 'paraphrastically' indicated the same meaning by different wording" (*Ep.* 57.9).[54] We should note briefly here that the LXX of Isaiah 64:3 is not all that different from the Hebrew, and they both diverge somewhat from 1 Corinthians 2:9, but Jerome argued

---

[50] Erich Klostermann, ed., *Origenes Matthäuserklärung, II: Die lateinische Übersetzung der Commentariorum series*, Origenes Werke 11, Griechischen christlichen Schriftsteller 38 (Leipzig: Hinrichs, 1933), 250, lines 3–6.

[51] Translation by David Brakke, "A New Fragment of Athanasius's 39th *Festal Letter*: Heresy, Apocrypha, and the Canon," *Harvard Theological Review* 103 (2010): 47–66, at 64.

[52] This is Brakke's translation (previous note) of Athanasius's quotation of the passage, from a portion of Athanasius's letter preserved in Coptic.

[53] *Ep.* 57.9; *Praef. in Par. IH* 22; *Praef. in Pent.* 12–13, 18.

[54] Kato, "Jerome's Understanding of Old Testament Quotations," 303–4.

that only reference to the Hebrew text allowed one to locate the source of Paul's quotation.

Several times Jerome cited such verses as proof that the apostles preferred the Hebrew text. As he said to Rufinus, "wherever the Seventy do not disagree from the Hebrew, there the apostles have taken examples from their translation; but where they diverge, they put down in Greek what they had learned among the Hebrews" (*Ruf.* 2.34).[55] He then challenged Rufinus to find any Old Testament verse cited in the New Testament in agreement with the LXX and not the Hebrew. As we have already seen in the case of Isaiah 64:3, sometimes the New Testament quotation does not line up precisely with the Hebrew text, in which cases Jerome argued that the meaning was still the same; he more rarely made similar arguments in the case of the LXX.[56]

There are occasions when Jerome admitted that a New Testament quotation corresponds more closely to the LXX than to the Hebrew truth. For example, when the book of Acts portrays Paul as arriving in Rome and quoting against the obstinate Jews the words of Isaiah, "You shall hear but never understand, you shall see but never perceive" (Acts 28:26), this quotation of Isaiah 6:9 matches the LXX but not the Hebrew. Jerome explains that the historical Paul would have quoted the Hebrew text, but Luke recorded the LXX form, first, because he knew only Greek and, second, as an accommodation for his readers.[57] Jerome made a similar comment with regard to an earlier passage in Acts when Stephen cited the figure seventy-five as the number of Israelites that descended into Egypt (Acts 7:14), as opposed to the number seventy cited in the MT (Gen. 46:26).[58] It turns out that with regard to apostolic reliance on the Hebrew text rather than the LXX, the Gentile Luke does not count.

---

[55] Pierre Lardet, ed., *Saint Jérôme, Apologie contre Rufin*, Sources chrétiennes 303 (Paris: Cerf, 1983), 196, lines 31–34.

[56] Kato, "Jerome's Understanding of Old Testament Quotations," 304, etc., emphasizes Jerome's double standard; sometimes Jerome allows for the divergent LXX text to share a meaning with the Hebrew.

[57] See Jerome, *Comm. Isa.* 3.9 on Isaiah 6:9–10; Kato, "Jerome's Understanding of Old Testament Quotations," 312–13.

[58] *Qu. Hebr. Gen.* 46:26.

THE *HEBRAICA VERITAS* AS MORE
CHRISTIAN THAN THE LXX

Jerome often criticizes the LXX for omitting certain portions of Scripture,[59] sometimes portions that rendered the Hebrew more amenable to christological exegesis than the LXX.[60] For example, the MT of Isaiah 2:22 says, "Turn away from mortals who have only breath in their nostrils, for of what account are they?" (NRSV). This verse does not appear in the traditional LXX,[61] compelling Jerome to comment,

> Though I have privately examined this in detail with a quiet mind, I am not able to discover the reason why the Septuagint was unwilling to translate into Greek so clear a prophecy of Christ. As for the other translators, who translated to be sure, but who twisted the ambiguous words into an impious meaning, it is no wonder they translated badly, since they did not want to say anything glorious about Christ in whom they did not believe. That is to say, they translated it like Jews, or like half-Jews, that is, the Ebionites.[62]

Similarly, at Jeremiah 23:36, the Seventy have omitted a portion of the verse that Jerome interpreted as a reference to the Trinity. Sometimes the Seventy made improper additions to the text, as at Isaiah 66:23, where they added the

---

[59] See Jerome, *Comm. Ezech.* 33:23–33, where he points out that verses 25–26 of the MT are almost completely absent from the LXX. This passage is highlighted by Thomas P. Scheck, trans., *St. Jerome, Commentary on Ezekiel*, Ancient Christian Writers 71 (New York: Newman, 2017), 389; and see Scheck's discussion on 11–13.

[60] See Jay, *L'exégèse de Saint Jérôme*, 278.

[61] The verse does appear in the Hexaplaric LXX under asterisk; see Joseph Ziegler, ed., *Isaias*, 3rd ed., Septuaginta 14 (Göttingen: Vandenhoeck & Ruprecht, 1983), 131 (also 60–61). Several Greek commentators drew attention to the addition of this verse in Origen's text; see the commentaries by Eusebius of Caesarea, Basil of Caesarea, and Theodoret of Cyrus.

[62] Translation by Thomas P. Scheck, *St. Jerome: Commentary on Isaiah*, Ancient Christian Writers 68 (New York: Newman, 2015), 106. Sebastian Weigert, *Hebraica Veritas: Übersetzungsprinzipien und Quellen der Deuteronomiumübersetzung des Hieronymus* (Stuttgart: Kohlhammer, 2016), 216, also notes that Jerome is sometimes baffled by the differences between the LXX and Hebrew.

word *Jerusalem*; Jerome saw the absence of this place name in the Hebrew text as more suitable to the universalist Christian gospel.

Jerome also argued that he, as a Christian, could produce a more Christian-friendly translation of the Hebrew Bible than could the Seventy translators, who were necessarily ignorant of the fulfillment of the prophecies that they were translating.[63] There are examples in Jerome's translations and commentaries where he carried out this idea.[64] The Vulgate of Habakkuk 3:13 reads *egressus es in salutem populi tui in salutem cum christo tuo* (you went out for the salvation of your people, for salvation with your Christ). The MT has the word *mashiaḥ* (משיח), "anointed," but it is in a parallel relationship to the people of Israel; the LXX makes the reference explicit by rendering *mashiaḥ* with a plural, τοὺς χριστούς σου, "your anointed ones." Jerome's rendering is certainly more "Christian," in a manner of speaking, but also probably less faithful to the meaning of the Hebrew than is the LXX. A similar instance is at Daniel 9:25–26, where the Vulgate twice uses the Greek word *Christus*—and not a Latin word such as *unctus*, "anointed"—to represent the Hebrew *mashiaḥ*, whereas the LXX does not have χριστός, *christos*, either time (though Theodotion does have it in verse 25, not verse 26). Again, Jerome's version could be interpreted more straightforwardly as a reference to Jesus than could either the LXX or MT. Jerome's translations from the Hebrew actually include the name *Jesus* a few times, such as at Habakkuk 3:18, translating the Hebrew *yishi*, rendered in the LXX as *my savior*.[65] As Jerome's great English-language biographer commented, "He translated a large number of passages in such a way as to give them a much more pointedly

---

[63] Kamesar, *Jerome*, 67–68; Anne-Isabelle Bouton-Touboulic, "Autorité et tradition: La traduction latine de la Bible selon saint Jérôme et saint Augustin," *Augustinianum* 45 (2005): 185–229, esp. 188–209; Linde, *How to Correct the Sacra Scriptura*, 110.

[64] For examples in his translation of Exodus, see Kraus, *Jewish, Christian, and Classical Exegetical Traditions*, ch. 5. Examples in his commentaries abound.

[65] Jerome mentions—but does not really explain—this translation in his commentary on the verse. See also his Hebrew Psalter at 50:14 (English 51:12); 78:9 (English 79:9); 84:5 (English 85:4); 94:1 (English 95:1); 149:4. Each of these verses has the name *Jesus* in Jerome's Hebrew Psalter, and each is rendered in Jerome's Gallican Psalter (Vulgate) with the idea of "salvation" or "savior," thus corresponding to the LXX and the MT.

Messianic or otherwise Christian implication than the Hebrew permitted."[66] But he did it in the name of the *Hebraica veritas*.

Jerome for the Septuagint

Jerome did not completely abandon the LXX—far from it. For instance, notice how he handled a famous text-critical issue early in Genesis: after God accepted Abel's sacrifice and not that of his brother, Cain invited Abel to his murder with the words, "Let us go into the field." These words spoken by Cain are not found in the MT of Genesis 4:8, but they are in the Samaritan Pentateuch, and, more to the point, they are in the LXX,[67] from which they have found their way into some English versions, such as the New International Version (NIV) and the NRSV (but not the KJV or the English Standard Version [ESV]). What did Jerome think about these words? To no one's surprise, in his *Hebrew Questions on Genesis*, written about 391, Jerome labeled the words in the LXX "superfluous."[68] It is somewhat surprising, though, that about a decade later when he produced his Latin version of the Pentateuch *iuxta Hebraeos*, Jerome provided the words of Cain as *egrediamur foras*, or "let us go outside," very similar but not identical to how they read in the LXX.[69] Perhaps these words were not so superfluous after all.

What did Jerome think about the LXX? He criticized the LXX and Christian use of the LXX, but he also used the LXX extensively in his biblical scholarship: in the days before Bible software or much at all in the way of language learning resources (dictionaries, grammars, etc.), the LXX was a primary tool for Jerome's translation *iuxta Hebraeos*.[70] As mentioned earlier, Jerome often included interpretations of the LXX in his biblical

---

[66] Kelly, *Jerome*, 162.
[67] See the textual note in Abraham Tal, ed., *Genesis*, Biblia Hebraica Quinta 1 (Stuttgart: Deutsche Bibelgesellschaft, 2015), 88*.
[68] See the translation and commentary of Hayward, *Saint Jerome's Hebrew Questions on Genesis*, 34, 122; see also Kamesar, *Jerome*, 100–101.
[69] Cf. *Epist.* 36.6, where Jerome reports the words from the VL, *transeamus in campum*.
[70] See Kraus, *Jewish, Christian, and Classical Exegetical Traditions*, ch. 4.

224 • SECTION III: The Text of the Septuagint among the Fathers

commentaries, particularly where the LXX's text diverged from the Hebrew text. He admitted on occasion that the apostles sometimes used the LXX even when it diverged somewhat from the Hebrew text. And though he considered his own translation from the *Hebraica veritas* to be more "Christian" than the LXX, he regarded the LXX as frequently containing a helpful—and perfectly Christian—interpretation of a Hebrew text that itself could be difficult or not easily adaptable to his theology.

Jerome frequently defended himself against the charge that his work on the Hebrew aimed at denigrating the church's traditional Bible.[71] Several of his biblical prefaces contain such passages, and in his *Apology against Rufinus* he wrote,

> Have I said anything against the Seventy translators, whom many years earlier I diligently corrected and gave to the studious people of my language, whom every day in the gathering of the brothers I expound, whose psalms I sing in continual meditation? Was I so stupid that I would wish to forget as an old man what I learned in youth? All my treatises are woven with their testimonies. The commentaries on the Twelve Prophets expound my own edition and that of the Seventy. (*Ruf.* 2.24)[72]

Jerome made several points about his continued appreciation for the LXX. He preached from the LXX and used the LXX Psalter in worship.[73] He interpreted the LXX in his biblical commentaries.[74] We earlier mentioned Jerome's practice of the double lemma in his commentaries: he

---

[71] Kamesar, *Jerome*, 59.

[72] Lardet, ed., *Saint Jérôme, Apologie contre Rufin*, 170, lines 30–37.

[73] See Alfons Fürst, *Hieronymus: Askese und Wissenschaft in der Spätantike* (Freiburg: Herder, 2003), 114–16; Jay, *L'exégèse de Saint Jérôme*, 90n141; Kamesar, *Jerome*, 55; E. F. Sutcliffe, "Jerome," in *The Cambridge History of the Bible*, vol. 2, *The West from the Fathers to the Reformation*, ed. G. W. H. Lampe (Cambridge: Cambridge University Press, 1969), 80–101, at 95, citing *Praef. Par. IH* 35–37. See also Wermelinger, "Le canon des latins," 193; Bouton-Touboulic, "Autorité et Tradition," 208. Of course, Jerome knew that the Seventy translated only the Pentateuch, not the XII or the Psalter. See *Qu. Hebr. Gen.* prol.; Gallagher, *Hebrew Scripture in Patristic Biblical Theory*, 98.

[74] On the textual form of Jerome's LXX lemmas in his *Comm. Isa.*, see Jay, *L'exégèse de Saint Jérôme*, 113–18, who shows that Jerome translated Origen's text.

often translated and commented on both the Hebrew and the LXX. He followed this practice, not consistently, throughout his career. In the passage quoted above, Jerome mentioned the Minor Prophets commentaries that he was still engaged in writing at the time, and indeed it is in these commentaries that he most consistently presented the double lemma. Jerome often tied the LXX to a spiritual interpretation, whereas he interpreted the Hebrew text according to history.[75] In his *Commentary on Hosea*, he wrote, "The Hebrew and the version of the Septuagint translators differ greatly between themselves. Let us try, therefore, to weave together the history following the Hebrew, and the anagogy following the Septuagint" (*Comm. Hos.* 11:3–4).[76] But this schema was a matter of convenience, to save time and space. Theoretically, he could have interpreted both versions in both ways, as he asserted in the same commentary: "Let us pass to the spiritual understanding in accordance with the Septuagint translators, lest, should we wish to explain both versions according both to the historical and to the anagogical, we should increase the size of the book."[77]

In his preface to his Isaiah commentary, he mentioned the same motivation for omitting the LXX lemma,[78] though as the commentary progressed he interacted with the LXX more and more, even dedicating two whole books (6–7) to the spiritual interpretation of the LXX version of the

---

[75] See Jay, *L'exégèse de Saint Jérôme*, 276–79. Cf. *Comm. Isa.* 4.5 (Isa. 10:5–11); 9.3 (Isa. 28:5–8) (tropology); *Comm. Nah.* 3:13–17; *Comm. Isa.* 7.41 (Isa. 22:15–25); 9.22 (Isa. 30:15–17) (anagogy); *Comm. Isa.* 14.14 (Isa. 51:21–23) (spiritual sense: *ceterum ut veniamus iuxta Septuaginta ad intellegentiam spiritalem*). See also Aline Canellis, "Jerome's Hermeneutics: How to Exegete the Bible?," in *Patristic Theories of Biblical Interpretation: The Latin Fathers*, ed. Tarmo Toom (Cambridge: Cambridge University Press, 2016), 49–76, esp. 72–75.

[76] Translation by Maria Veritas Marks and Thomas P. Scheck in Jerome, *Commentaries on the Twelve Prophets*, ed. Thomas P. Scheck, 2 vols., Ancient Christian Texts (Downers Grove, IL: IVP, 2016–17), 2.235. This passage is quoted and discussed in Williams, *Monk and the Book*, 120.

[77] Translation by Marks and Scheck (previous note), 236. See Williams, *Monk and the Book*, 120, and her immediately following quotation from the Amos commentary. However, Jerome sometimes represents the LXX as opposed to the historical sense: *Comm. Nah.* 1:14; cf. *Comm. Isa.* 3.29 (Isa. 8:19–22); 13.16 (Isa. 48:12–16). Sometimes he reverses the procedure; Kraus, *Jewish, Christian, and Classical Exegetical Traditions*, 46.

[78] *Sicubi autem praetermissis LXX de hebraico disputaui, illud in causa est quod aut eadem aut similia sunt pleraque cum ceteris et duplici editione proposita nolui libros explanationis extendere, qui etiam in simplici expositione modum breuitatis excedunt*; Roger Gryson and P.-A. Deproost, eds., *Commentaires de Jérôme sur le prophète Isaïe. Livres I–IV* (Freiburg: Herder, 1993), 139 lines, 103–7.

Oracles against the Nations (Isa. 13–23).[79] His *Commentary on Jeremiah*, left incomplete at his death, rarely presented two complete lemmas, instead treating the LXX only where it differed from the Hebrew, which is fairly frequently in Jeremiah.[80]

In those frequent occasions when the LXX diverges from the Hebrew text, the divergence sometimes bewilders Jerome,[81] but he explains the source of the Seventy's error when he can figure it out.[82] For example, in the *Hebrew Questions on Genesis* at Genesis 14:5, in a context about the battle that would result in Lot's capture and need for rescue by Abram, Jerome explained that the LXX reading ἅμα αὐτοῖς, "with them," derives from a misreading of a Hebrew letter *ḥeth* (ח) as if it were a *he* (ה): the Hebrew does not say *bᵉhem*, "with them," but *bᵉḥom*, "in Ḥom." Jerome often made this sort of comment, helping his readers understand that the Seventy translators were mere men who made simple mistakes like every other translator and scribe. This particular case is, however, a little more complicated. The Masoretic Text does point the word as a place name, as Jerome insisted, but it actually spells the place with a *he* rather than a *ḥeth*, the opposite of what Jerome had reported from his Hebrew text. The MT reads "in Ham" rather than "in Ḥom." On the other hand, the Samaritan Pentateuch has the *ḥeth*. We have attestation of Hebrew texts (MT) with a *he*, in agreement with the LXX, and Hebrew texts (Samaritan Pentateuch) with a *ḥeth*, in agreement with Jerome. Whether or not the Greek translators misread their Hebrew text, some Hebrew scribe(s) clearly did (whether the original text had a *he* or *ḥeth*). Jerome's explanation for the source of the LXX's reading might not hold up, but the MT does support Jerome's larger point that the Hebrew

---

[79] From *Comm. Isa.* book 8 onward, Jerome often has the double lemma.

[80] See Michael Graves, trans., *Jerome: Commentary on Jeremiah*, Ancient Christian Texts (Downers Grove, IL: IVP, 2011), xxxiv, where Graves suggests that Jerome forgoes the double lemma for Jeremiah either because it would increase the size of the commentary or because the divergences between Greek and Hebrew were too severe.

[81] See *Comm. Isa.* 3.8 (Isa. 6:8); *Comm. Isa.* 5.34 (Isa. 14:20–21); *Comm. Isa.* 5.101 (Isa. 19:18); *Comm. Isa.* 5.113 (Isa. 21:8); *Comm. Isa.* 6.16 (Isa. 13:12).

[82] For Jerome's criticisms of the LXX in *Qu. Hebr. Gen.*, see Hayward, *Saint Jerome's Hebrew Questions on Genesis*, 120, in Hayward's commentary on *Qu. Hebr. Gen.* 4:6–7. An example of Jerome's explaining the error of the Seventy is at *Comm. Isa.* 5.43 on Isa. 14:32 (cf. *Comm. Isa.* 6.35).

text has a place name rather than the words "with them." Why, then, in his Vulgate translation of Genesis does Jerome reverse course by inserting "with them" (*cum eis*) instead of the place name, in agreement with the LXX and Targum Neofiti and a reading at Genesis Rabbah 41:6? Jerome seems to have decided that his criticism of the LXX was unwarranted. Perhaps he encountered a Hebrew text in agreement with the LXX. Perhaps he came to see in the LXX reading a useful interpretation of the Hebrew.[83]

Examples abound. Studies of the Vulgate translation have shown the significant influence of the LXX on Jerome's version, sometimes where it seems to have led him away from the Hebrew text, at least as interpreted by modern scholars.[84] Alison Salvesen has commented, "An examination of his translation reveals that he did not necessarily abandon distinctive readings of the Septuagint (such as Isa 7:14) but merely tried to justify them on Hebrew grounds."[85]

NEW TESTAMENT QUOTATIONS

We have seen that Jerome repeatedly insisted that the apostles did not cite the LXX but the Hebrew, though he was willing to acknowledge that they sometimes cited the LXX if it matched the Hebrew or if the writer happened not to know Hebrew (i.e., Luke). What about all the evidence we saw in Chapter Six, where the apostles did cite the LXX even in those passages where the LXX read differently from the MT? Jerome often provided interesting

---

[83] On this example, see Hayward, *Saint Jerome's Hebrew Questions on Genesis*, 152–53; Tal, ed., *Genesis*, 112*–113*.

[84] Weigert, *Hebraica Veritas*, 215 (in relation to Deuteronomy): next to those passages oriented toward the Hebrew, "there exist a not inconsiderable number of passages in which the LXX and MT deviate from one another and Jerome follows the LXX instead of the MT, sometimes also against the hexaplaric tradition." For influence of the LXX on the Vulgate of Exodus, see Kraus, *Jewish, Christian, and Classical Exegetical Traditions*, ch. 4, esp. 119–21; Kraus discusses translations in which Jerome follows the LXX's interpretation of the Hebrew and influence on Jerome from the Vetus Latina and the *recentiores*. See also the sources at Kraus 105n2. On the Psalter, see Cameron, "Vir Tricultus," 214–16 (Ps. 22:1, Vg 21:2), 216–18 (Ps. 22:18, Vg 21:19). Another example is Isaiah 21:13, "Arabia" or "evening"; cf. *Comm. Isa.* 5.115 (Isa. 21:13–17).

[85] Alison Salvesen, "A Well-Watered Garden (Isaiah 58:11): Investigating the Influence of the Septuagint," in *"Translation Is Required": The Septuagint in Retrospect and Prospect*, ed. R. J. V. Hiebert (Atlanta: SBL, 2010), 191–208, at 197.

interpretations for these examples; at least some of these instances were interpreted by Jerome—counterintuitively for us moderns—as cases in which the LXX and the Hebrew correspond, or even where the New Testament matches the Hebrew better than the LXX. A prominent case is Amos 9:11–12, the passage quoted by James in Acts 15:16–17 as a prooftext for the Gentile mission (in accordance with the LXX), in contrast with the MT, which has the (ostensibly) less welcoming phrase "they shall possess Edom." In his *Commentary on Amos*, Jerome is explicit that the New Testament governs his interpretation of the prophetic passage, not by leading him to accept the LXX reading but by guiding his understanding of the Hebrew passage:

> It says that he will raise up and restore all things at the resurrection of the Lord, so that what had fallen among the synagogues might rise among the churches, and believers might gain possession of the remnants of Idumea, namely, all nations. As a result, whatever remains from the bloody and earthly kingdom might be changed into the heavenly kingdoms, and all the nations who had forgotten the Lord might be converted and return to him.[86]

This is Jerome's interpretation of the Hebrew text, which he follows up immediately with an interpretation of the LXX. He interprets the place name *Idumea* (*Edom*) as equivalent to "all nations," in line with the LXX and, more to the point, the New Testament.

We also saw in Chapter Six that the Gospels sometimes represent Jesus quoting the LXX, sometimes making a point based on the distinctive wording of the LXX.[87] For one such passage, the quotation of Psalm 8:3 (verse 2 in English) at Matthew 21:16, Jerome's translation of the Hebrew agrees with the LXX in its reading "praise" (αἶνος, *laus*) against the MT's "strength" (עֹז).[88] But perhaps "praise" is a valid interpretation of the MT's word, as

---

[86] Jerome, *Comm. Amos* 9:11–12; Marks and Scheck trans., in Jerome, *Commentaries on the Twelve Prophets*, 2.395.

[87] Richard N. Longenecker, *Biblical Exegesis in the Apostolic Period*, 2nd ed. (Grand Rapids: Eerdmans, 1999), 45.

[88] Jerome mentions nothing of a textual issue in either his *Commentary on Matthew* or his *Commentarioli on the Psalms*.

suggested by the reading of Psalm 29:1.[89] Another example in which Jesus seemed to rely on the distinctive wording of the LXX is the quotation of Isaiah 29:13 at Matthew 15:8–9. According to Jerome, "Here we should take note of what we have warned about on many occasions, that the evangelists and apostles have not translated word for word, nor have they followed the authority of the Septuagint translators, whose version was being read at the time, but as Hebrews and as those instructed in the Law, they made use of their own words without loss of meaning."[90]

Jerome came to this conclusion on many occasions: the Old Testament quotations always agreed with the Hebrew, in sense if not in words, except, perhaps, for Luke: "And we have observed this in the Old Testament—apart from a few citations that Luke alone makes use of, who had more knowledge of the Greek language—wherever anything is expressed from the Old Testament, they record it not according to the Septuagint, but according to the Hebrew, following no one's translation, but rendering the sense of the Hebrew in their own words" (*Comm. Isa.* 9.4 on Isa. 28:9–13).[91] So also with the LXX: Jerome attributed to the LXX on many occasions the correct meaning of a passage even in the absence of a literal translation.[92] In these situations, the Seventy translators captured the intent of Scripture, and it was no wonder that the apostles capitalized on those expressions.

---

[89] See Dominique Barthélemy, *Critique textuelle de l'Ancien Testament*, vol. 4, *Psaumes* (Göttingen: Vandenhoeck & Ruprecht, 2005), 25. But Jerome's Hebrew Psalter at Psalm 29:1 renders עז as *imperium*.

[90] *Commentary on Isaiah* 9.11 (Isa. 29:13); Scheck, trans., *St. Jerome: Commentary on Isaiah*, 450.

[91] Translation by Scheck, *St. Jerome: Commentary on Isaiah*, 435. On the "sense," see Kraus, *Jewish, Christian, and Classical Exegetical Traditions*, 45–49, who examines *Ep.* 57. See the quotation earlier from *Ep.* 57.9, where Jerome also says that the apostles followed the sense of the Hebrew, and see the earlier discussion in this chapter on Jerome's view of the quotations in the New Testament. For another example, see *Comm. Isa.* 3.16 (Isa. 7:14), on "they will call": "One should pay very careful attention to the fact that in many testimonies that the evangelists or apostles have adopted from the old books, they did not follow the order of the words but the meaning" (trans. Scheck, 170).

[92] A few examples: *Comm. Isa.* 1.34 (Isa. 1:25); *Comm. Isa.* 2.35 (Isa. 5:1); *Comm. Isa.* 6.15 (Isa. 13:11); *Qu. Hebr. Gen.* 14:5, discussed earlier.

LXX HELPFULLY INTERPRETS THE HEBREW

Jerome's commentaries present us frequently with similar evaluations, *viz.*, that the LXX seemingly diverged from the Hebrew but in reality offered a helpful interpretation. In one of his first biblical commentaries, Jerome said about Ecclesiastes 2:15–16, "The Septuagint translators rendered the sense of the Hebrew more clearly in this place, although they did not keep close to the Hebrew wording."[93] This passage reads as follows in the ESV:

> Then I said in my heart, "What happens to the fool will happen to me also. Why then have I been so very wise?" And I said in my heart that this also is vanity. For of the wise as of the fool there is no enduring remembrance, seeing that in the days to come all will have been long forgotten. How the wise dies just like the fool!

That last phrase, rendered by the ESV as a despairing exclamation, is in the MT ואיך ימות החכם עם הכסיל and could be read as a question, "How will the wise die with the fool?" (cf. NRSV). That is the way it is translated in NETS, representing the LXX's καὶ πῶς ἀποθανεῖται ὁ σοφὸς μετὰ τοῦ ἄφρονος. The LXX has offered here a very close translation of the Hebrew (as commonly in Ecclesiastes), but the clause under discussion (in Hebrew or Greek) could be taken in two different ways—whether as affirming a common fate for the righteous and wicked or denying the same—but only one of those interpretations (the second) fits easily into traditional Christian theology. Jerome understood the passage in this traditional Christian manner, as pointing toward not the common fate for sage and fool but their distinct reward and punishment.[94] His commentary interpreted the Hebrew to mean that "the wise man and the fool will not

---

[93] Translation by Richard J. Goodrich and David J. D. Miller, trans., *Jerome: Commentary on Ecclesiastes*. Ancient Christian Writers 66 (New York: Newman, 2012); *apertius in hoc loco sensum hebraicum septuaginta interpretes transtulerunt, licet uerborum ordinem non secuti sint.*

[94] Jerome translates in his commentary *et quomodo morietur sapiens cum stulto.* His later Vulgate translation seems to offer a different interpretation: death comes to all (*moritur doctus similiter et indoctus*).

have similar memory in the future, when the consummation of all things will come; and it is by no means a comparable end that will hold them, because one will go to consolations, while the other will go to punishment."[95] He was able to achieve this interpretation of the Hebrew by taking "this too is vanity" at the end of verse 15 as a reference—not to the fact that a similar end befalls the sage and fool, but—to the Preacher's former judgment that a similar end befalls the sage and fool. Jerome thought that the Preacher had concluded that this was a vain judgment. He regarded the LXX "more clear" here, not because the translator overturned the sense of the Hebrew but because the Greek translator clarified the Hebrew by adding a clause in verse 15, "since the fool speaks from excess" (διότι ἄφρων ἐκ περισσεύματος λαλεῖ).[96] As Jerome said, "He [the Preacher] is clearly demonstrating that his earlier opinion was foolish and testifying that he spoke unwisely and was wrong to take that earlier view."[97] Jerome understood the Hebrew in the same sense, but the LXX was easier to interpret along these lines; it was "more clear." While modern commentators might say that the LXX disagrees with the Hebrew text in this passage,[98] Jerome's interpretation ascribes to both texts the same meaning, but the LXX text points toward that shared meaning in a much more obvious way and perhaps served as Jerome's initial guide toward the correct interpretation of the passage.

There are other examples in which the LXX became the basis for interpretation because it presented the clearer text, such as at Isaiah 22:1, where the LXX's "valley of Zion" made more sense than the Hebrew's "valley of vision."[99] Sometimes Jerome did not judge between the texts but offered an interpretation of both of them sequentially. His commentaries routinely

---

[95] *non enim similiter sapiens et insipiens habebunt in futuro memoriam quando consummatio veniet universitatis; et nequaquam pari exitu tenebuntur, quia hic ad refrigeria, ille perget ad poenam.*

[96] This clause is not Old Greek but is found in many manuscripts, including those of the Origenian recension; see Peter John Gentry, ed., *Ecclesiastes*, Septuaginta 11.2 (Göttingen: Vandenhoeck & Ruprecht, 2019), 145.

[97] *quod uidelicet priorem opinationem suam stultam esse convincens, insipienter se locutum esse testatus sit, et errasse, quia ante sic senserit.*

[98] Jerome's translators are an example: Goodrich and Miller, *Jerome: Commentary on Ecclesiastes*, 12–13.

[99] See *Comm. Isa.* 5.116 (historical interpretation) and 7.31 (spiritual interpretation).

presented a historical interpretation of the Hebrew text and a spiritual interpretation of the LXX, as we saw earlier. Sometimes he presented historical interpretations of both texts and allowed readers to choose, as if he might not have been sure which reading to prefer. The last clause of Isaiah 53:8 is difficult and attested in various forms.[100] According to the lemmas in Jerome's Isaiah commentary (*Comm. Isa.* 14.24 on Isa. 53:7b–10a), the Hebrew has "for the wickedness of my people he struck them" (*propter scelus populi mei percussit eos*), while the LXX has "because of the iniquities of my people he was led to death" (*ab iniquitatibus populi mei ductus est ad mortem*).[101] Jerome commented that "this has two meanings. For either by his death he struck the persecutors and wicked members of his people"— here Jerome is interpreting the Hebrew reading, and now he turns to the LXX—"or because of the greatness of the sins of the people whom he always regarded as special, he was led to death in order to call them back to life through his death."[102] This practice of offering two interpretations could be understood in at least two ways: perhaps Jerome wanted to provide his readers with an interpretation of whatever biblical text they might have in front of them, or maybe Jerome could not decide on the better understanding so he wanted to cover all his bases.[103]

Jerome presented a spiritual interpretation of the LXX very often even after he argued that the LXX text represented a mistranslation. At the beginning of the Song of the Vineyard in Isaiah 5, God says, "I waited for it to produce grapes and it produced wild grapes" (Isa. 5:2, *et expectavit ut faceret uvas et fecit labruscas*).[104] In place of "wild grapes," the various Greek translations have a few different options, with the LXX and Theodotion both

---

[100] See Dominique Barthélemy, *Critique textuelle de l'Ancien Testament*, vol. 2, *Isaïe, Jérémie, Lamentations* (Göttingen: Vandenhoeck & Ruprecht, 1986), 397–99; John Goldingay and David Payne, *Isaiah 40–55*, vol. 2, ICC (London: T&T Clark, 2006), 315.

[101] Edition: Gryson and Deproost, *Commentaires*, 1521–22; translation by Scheck, *St. Jerome: Commentary on Isaiah*, 669–70.

[102] Translation by Scheck, *St. Jerome: Commentary on Isaiah*, 672.

[103] Other examples: *Comm. Isa.* 6.29 (Isa. 14:19–20); *Comm. Isa.* 14.25 (Isa. 53:10–11).

[104] The Latin is the Vulgate, which matches the lemma in Jerome's commentary (*Comm. Isa.* 2.37 on Isa. 5:2c). Translation by Scheck, *St. Jerome: Commentary on Isaiah*, 130. For the attestation of Greek witnesses, see Ziegler, *Isaias*, 137. Aquila has σαπρίας, "rotten"; Symmachus ἀτελή, "incomplete."

offering "thorns" (ἀκάνθαι, *spinae*). Jerome did not think that this translation was correct.[105] But it will preach. He related the mistranslated thorns to the crown of thorns worn by Jesus, and to the thorns that choke out the gospel, as Jesus said in the Parable of the Sower (Matt. 13:22 and par.), and to the prickly blasphemies with which the Jews assailed Jesus. Along the same lines, Jerome sometimes mentioned words that were under obelus in his copy of the LXX, but then he proceeded to offer an interpretation of them,[106] a procedure reminiscent of Origen.

Jerome interpreted Isaiah 9:6 in a messianic way, as a prediction of the Christ who would be called Wonderful Counselor, Mighty God, Everlasting Father, Prince of Peace. But in place of these exalted titles, the LXX has merely Μεγάλης βουλῆς ἄγγελος, "Messenger of Great Counsel." Jerome commented,

> I imagine that the Seventy were terrified by the majesty of these names. They did not dare to say openly of a child that he should be called God, and the other things; but in place of these six names, it is recorded what is not found in the Hebrew: "messenger of great counsel" and "I will bring peace upon the princes and his health."[107]

But even this LXX rendering, the product of fear on the part of the translators, Jerome still interpreted messianically:

> To me this seems to have the following meaning: the "messenger of great counsel" is the one who announced to us that Israel must be set aside for a time and the Gentiles are to be saved, and who gave peace to their princes, to the apostles and apostolic men, and left behind the health of their doctrines to those who believe.[108]

In another example, Isaiah 49:5, Jerome commented, "And I am quite surprised at how the common translation undermines this very forceful

---

[105] *Comm. Isa.* 2.37 (Isa. 5:2); he brings up the translation issue again at 2.39 (Isa. 5:5–6) just to reiterate that "thorns" is the wrong translation.

[106] *Comm. Isa.* 6.9 (Isa. 13:4–5); *Comm. Isa.* 6.10 (Isa. 13:6–8).

[107] Translation by Scheck, *St. Jerome: Commentary on Isaiah*, 192.

[108] Scheck, 192. For this double interpretation, see already Irenaeus, *Epideixis* 54–56.

testimony."[109] He went on to say that Theodotion and Symmachus agreed with his own translation from the Hebrew, while Aquila had perverted the meaning not out of ignorance but rather malice. But a few lines later, Jerome returned to the LXX rendering: "Now as for what one reads in the Septuagint . . . it can be understood as follows."

In his *Commentary on Jeremiah*, interrupted by Jerome's death, the LXX still played a large role. For example, at Jeremiah 1:17, the LXX has the clause not found in the Hebrew: "For I am with you, to deliver you, says the Lord." Jerome acknowledged that the Hebrew omits the clause, and then he offered an interpretation of it, consistent with the themes of the chapter.[110] Or commenting on Jeremiah 2:23–24, Jerome began, "In this passage, the edition of the Seventy differs significantly from the Hebrew truth. Yet, each has its own sense."[111] This type of double exegesis appears frequently in the Jeremiah commentary, as indeed in all Jerome's commentaries. Jerome allowed the reader to follow whichever text and interpretation he prefers, or perhaps he implied that both texts should be accepted as revealing truth.[112]

Conclusion

It is difficult to summarize adequately Jerome's views of the LXX. Jerome never considered the LXX superior to the Hebrew in any way, except perhaps occasionally in clarity of expression. But clarity was not the exclusive purview of the LXX; sometimes the Greek could be quite obscure where the Hebrew was clear. Certainly Jerome did not entertain the idea that the LXX might preserve a more authentic form of the Old Testament than did the Hebrew.[113] Even at Genesis 4:8, Jerome perhaps inserted Cain's words, "let us go outside," not because he thought they had dropped out of the Hebrew text but because

---

[109] Scheck, *St. Jerome: Commentary on Isaiah*, 617.

[110] See Jerome's similar interpretation of 1:8.

[111] Translation by Graves, trans., *Jerome: Commentary on Jeremiah*, 15.

[112] Jerome regards the LXX of Genesis 49:27 as a clear prophecy of the apostle Paul (and he so uses it elsewhere, as do others), but the Hebrew reads differently; cf. *Qu. Hebr. Gen.*

[113] See his *Comm. Gal.* 3:10, where he does suggest a corruption in the Hebrew on the basis of the LXX, the NT quotation, and the SP.

he thought those words were already implied in the Hebrew text—that is, they offered a correct interpretation. Also, Jerome argued that the Seventy translators went out of their way to render certain passages in an obscure manner whereas the clear meaning of these passages in Hebrew supported Christian doctrine.[114] And the Hebrew text was in no way devoid of spiritual truth. Sometimes the Hebrew presented a text more easily adaptable to Christian theology than did the LXX.[115] And it was always the Hebrew text that had to be explained. On Isaiah 14:20 (*Comm. Isa.* 5.33), Jerome regarded the LXX as easy to understand but the Hebrew as difficult, so he enumerated three different possible meanings of the Hebrew. The very next verse, Isaiah 14:21, had an obscure LXX rendering and Jerome simply confessed himself confused and moved on without offering any possible interpretation of the LXX (*Comm. Isa.* 5.34 on Isa. 14:20–21). His discussion of Isaiah 6:9–10 (*Comm. Isa.* 3.9; discussed earlier) demonstrates that, even if the LXX was easier to understand, and even if the New Testament quoted the LXX form of the text, Jerome still felt compelled to explain the Hebrew.

But we have seen that the LXX was an important conversation partner for Jerome. He nearly always had his eye on the LXX, and he may have ascribed to it an important position in the divine economy. To be sure, the translation was sometimes misleading or wrong, but very often even these passages could yield an edifying meaning if handled with care. Frequently the LXX provided helpful renderings of a difficult Hebrew text, pointing in the right theological direction. Jerome recognized that the LXX had served as Christian Scripture, and despite his insistence that the Hebrew text was the standard against which any version ought to be judged, the LXX could still serve—in the hands of the right interpreter—to instruct the faithful in the ways of God.

The subsequent history of the Latin Bible attests to the growing dominance of Jerome's translations *iuxta Hebraeos*, not necessarily because the majority of readers found Jerome's textual arguments convincing but more

---

[114] *Praef. Pent.* The obscurity of the LXX was a common theme in patristic exegesis.

[115] See the earlier discussion on *Comm. Isa.* on Isaiah 2:22; *Comm. Isa.* on Isaiah 66:23; *Comm. Jer.* 23:36. See also *Qu. Hebr. Gen.* 25:8, where Jerome says that the LXX ("full of days") rendered the sense but the Hebrew ("full") provides a better *anagoge*. Jerome regards the Hebrew of Genesis 49:10 to be more applicable to the Christian (though even the LXX had been used so).

because of Jerome's elegant Latin. In the early seventh century, Isidore of Seville praised Jerome's translation as preferable to others due to its accuracy and clarity (*Etymologies* 6.4.5). In the early ninth century, two editors of the Latin Bible, Theodulf of Orléans and Alcuin of York, both chose to incorporate Jerome's translations into their editions, reflecting and effecting the increasing prominence of the translation from the Hebrew.[116] Whether or not Jerome intended to disparage the Seventy—a charge he frequently denied—his work led to the eclipse of the LXX in the West in favor of his own translation, which would eventually be acclaimed (like the LXX earlier) an inspired translation superior to all rivals.[117]

---

[116] Linde, *How to Correct the Sacra Scriptura*, 34–38.

[117] See Allan K. Jenkins and Patrick Preston, *Biblical Scholarship and the Church: A Sixteenth-Century Crisis of Authority* (New York: Routledge, 2007), 53–64.

10

Augustine

Augustine's Theory of Two Inspired Biblical Texts

> Hence even I, in my small measure, follow in the footsteps of the apostles; for they themselves quoted prophetic testimonies from both—that is, from both the Hebrew and the Septuagint; and I have deemed it right to make use of both as authorities, since both are one, and both divine.
>
> —Augustine, *City of God* 18.44[1]

"Yet forty days and Nineveh shall be overthrown" (Jon. 3:4). Or is that three days? Our extant textual witnesses diverge: the Masoretic Text has the prophet Jonah specifying a period of forty days, while the Septuagint (LXX) has the number "three."[2] Which is right, and how to explain the difference? Or do both numbers really point to the same reality? The Church Fathers who examined the available texts of the Old Testament encountered numerous such variants and developed a variety of ways for solving the

---

[1] This chapter represents a revised version of "Augustine on the Hebrew Bible," *Journal of Theological Studies* 67 (2016). Translation by Augustine, *The City of God against the Pagans*, trans. R. W. Dyson (Cambridge: Cambridge University Press, 1998), 659.

[2] No variants in the main LXX tradition are listed in Joseph Ziegler, ed., *Duodecim Prophetae* (Göttingen: Vandenhoeck & Ruprecht, 1984), 249. The Greek Minor Prophets Scroll from Naḥal Ḥever apparently attests the reading [τεσσερ]άκον[τα]; see Emanuel Tov, ed., *The Greek Minor Prophets Scroll from Naḥal Ḥever (8ḤevXIIgr)*, DJD 8 (Oxford: Clarendon, 1990), 30–31, frg. d, line 14(43), with plate iii.

difficulties these variants presented.[3] In accounts of the reception of the LXX in early Christianity, Augustine often appears as the most ardent defender of its scriptural status and special position within the divine economy.[4] As Anne-Marie la Bonnardière has said, "Until the end, Augustine maintained his fidelity to the LXX version of the Old Testament."[5] But the bishop of Hippo's unwavering support for the LXX did not prevent him from coming to see the value of Jerome's Latin translation of the Hebrew Bible, despite the dangers that this version also presented. An examination of texts spanning Augustine's ecclesial career reveals a developing attitude toward Jerome's translations, which he acquired only incrementally.[6] We will see that in his mature years Augustine came to appreciate the contribution of the Hebrew Bible to Christian theology.

Augustine encountered the Old Testament scriptures primarily in Latin versions translated from the LXX, but the textual situation had become very complex by his day. He accepted the inspiration of the LXX, but he knew that the Latin translations of the LXX were not always accurate. In the 390s, he came into possession of some of Jerome's translations, about which the bishop of Hippo harbored mixed feelings. Augustine expressed his concerns about Jerome's work in several writings throughout his career, not least in a series of letters to the translator.

Before turning to Augustine's correspondence with Jerome, we should note two ways that Augustine saw knowledge of Hebrew to be valuable to the

---

[3] See Chapter Eight.

[4] See Timothy Michael Law, *When God Spoke Greek: The Septuagint and the Making of the Christian Bible* (Oxford: Oxford University Press, 2013), 161–66; Josef Lössl, "A Shift in Patristic Exegesis: Hebrew Clarity and Historical Verity in Augustine, Jerome, Julian of Aeclanum and Theodore of Mopsuestia," *Augustinian Studies* 32 (2001): 157–75, esp. 159–63.

[5] "Jusqu'à la fin, Augustin a conservé sa fidélité à la version biblique des Septante de l'Ancien Testament." Anne-Marie la Bonnardière, "Augustin a-t-il utilisé la 'Vulgate' de Jérôme?," in *Saint Augustin et la Bible*, ed. Anne-Marie la Bonnardière, Bible de tous les Temps 3 (Paris: Beauchesne, 1986), 303–12, at 312.

[6] On how and when Augustine encountered Jerome's various biblical translations, see H. A. G. Houghton, *Augustine's Text of John: Patristic Citations and Latin Gospel Manuscripts* (Oxford: Oxford University Press, 2008), 10–15. On Augustine's appreciation for Jerome's translations, see Carol Harrison, "Augustine," in *The New Cambridge History of the Bible*, ed. James Carleton Paget and Jocahim Schaper, vol. 1 (Cambridge: Cambridge University Press, 2013), 676–96, at 677.

biblical critic that will, nevertheless, receive no attention in this chapter. First, already in the 390s he recommended knowledge of Hebrew to the budding exegete, or—barring actual expertise in the language—he advocated the use of literal translations based on the Hebrew text as helpful for interpretation (*Doctr. chr.* 2.11.16–13.19). Of course, it was this latter method that Augustine himself employed in order to access Hebrew learning; he himself knew no Hebrew, and his knowledge of even the Greek language progressed to a proficient level only in his later years.[7] Second, Augustine believed that the Hebrew text, or Jerome's Latin translation of it, provided a better example of eloquence than did the LXX version (*Doctr. chr.* 4.7.15).[8] These two points demonstrate respect for the original language of Scripture without diminishing Augustine's commitment to the traditional Christian Bible.

We will see that, throughout his career, Augustine recognized the authority of the Hebrew text, though at first he assumed—in common with most of his patristic predecessors—that the LXX accurately represented the Hebrew Bible. He initially responded to Jerome's divergent translation by doubting the latter's linguistic competence, which surely did not surpass that of the Seventy translators. Neither Jerome nor Augustine gave any thought to the possibility of multiple Hebrew textual forms, which the Dead Sea Scrolls have so dramatically demonstrated for the earlier period. Once Augustine became convinced of the accuracy of Jerome's translation, he confronted two divergent texts, one transmitting the original writing and the other accepted as authoritative by the church. His innovative response to this potentially disturbing situation exalted both texts, even in their differences, as inspired by God.

Augustine first wrote to Jerome in about the year 394, and at this time the future bishop mentioned having seen only Jerome's translation of Hexaplaric Job, which he praised exceedingly for the use of the critical signs indicating where this translation diverged from the traditional LXX (*Ep.* 82.2).[9] There

---

[7] See Houghton, *Augustine's Text of John*, 48–49n13.

[8] See Madeleine Moreau, "Sur un commentaire d'Amos 6, 1–6. De Doctrina christiana iv, vii, 15–21, sur Amos vi, 1–6," in la Bonnardière, *Saint Augustin et la Bible*, 313–22.

[9] Studies of the correspondence include Ralph Hennings, *Der Briefwechsel zwischen Augustinus und Hieronymus und Ihr Streit um den Kanon des Alten Testaments und die Auslegung von Gal. 2, 11–14* (Leiden: Brill, 1994); Alfons Fürst, *Augustins Briefwechsel mit Hieronymus*

appears to be some confusion on Augustine's part: he apparently thought that Jerome had translated the LXX and added certain passages directly from the Hebrew text, when in fact the monk had only translated into Latin Origen's Hexaplaric edition of the LXX, which already contained the critical signs.[10] Augustine further implied that any new translation from the Hebrew could not possibly compare with the LXX, for the Hebrew text was either clear, in which case the Seventy translators would have produced an accurate translation, or it was obscure, in which case they would have had as great a chance of offering the correct translation as anybody else. Or, rather, the Seventy translators would have had a better chance because they constituted "so many translators, expert in that language" (i.e., Hebrew). This letter gave no indication that Augustine held a view of the relationship between the LXX and Hebrew text any different from his patristic predecessors—namely, that the translators adhered closely to their *Vorlage* and any divergences in the manuscripts arose from textual corruption.[11]

A couple of years later in 396 in his *On Christian Teaching*, Augustine more boldly affirmed the authority and inspiration of the LXX: "The authority of the Seventy translators is preeminent" (*Septuaginta interpretum . . . excellit auctoritas; Doctr. chr.* 2.15.22).[12] Their inspiration was confirmed by the account of the translation that represented the Seventy translators individually producing identical translations, although Augustine was unwilling at this point to place complete confidence in this story. He

---

(Münster: Aschendorffsche Verlagsbuchhandlung, 1999). Hennings interprets the controversy between Jerome and Augustine as concerning the Old Testament canon (note the title of his book), a view that Fürst corrects (140–41n360): the discussion did not concern the canon of Scripture but its textual form. Carolinne White presents a study with a translation of the entire correspondence in *The Correspondence (394–419) between Jerome and Augustine of Hippo* (Lewiston, NY: Edwin Mellen, 1990).

[10] See the analysis of this letter in Alfons Fürst, "*Veritas Latina*. Augustins Haltung gegenüber Hieronymus' Bibelübersetzungen," *Revue des études augustiniennes* 40 (1994): 105–26, who advocates reading this letter separately from Augustine's later *Ep.* 71, against the typical harmonizing reading strategy assumed in much scholarship, for example, Annemaré Kotzé, "Augustine, Jerome and the Septuagint," in *Septuagint and Reception: Essays Prepared for the Association for the Study of the Septuagint in South Africa*, ed. Johann Cook (Leiden: Brill 2009), 245–60, at 254–59. See also Fürst, *Augustins Briefwechsel mit Hieronymus*, 141.

[11] See Chapter Eight.

[12] Cf. Augustine, *Ep.* 28.2: *gravissima auctoritas*.

said that, even if they compared notes, the great number of them and their expertise established their authority:[13]

> Therefore, even if we find in the Hebrew versions something that differs from what [the Seventy] wrote, I believe that we should defer to the divine dispensation which was made through them. . . . It may indeed be the case that they translated in a way that the Holy Spirit, who was leading them and creating unanimity, judged appropriate to the Gentiles.[14]

Augustine did not provide any examples here. His wording suggests that the Seventy translators may have altered their biblical text, but altered it in what way? Earlier he had commented on obscure and ambiguous passages and the translations that could result from them. He represented himself as generally quite happy with obscurity in the text because he saw it as the Holy Spirit's cure for boredom.[15] Comparison of different translations could often relieve the obscurity, as Augustine discussed with regard to Isaiah 58:7 and Isaiah 7:9, for which he cited both the LXX and Jerome's translation of Isaiah—without actually mentioning Jerome or acknowledging that it was a translation from Hebrew (*Doctr. chr.* 2.12.17).[16] In these cases, he resolved the difference by interpreting the translations together, declaring them mutually illuminating. He followed this up with citations of different translations of Romans 3:15 and Wisdom 4:3, where he said that ambiguity in the Greek text (*ex ambiguo linguae praecedentis*) misled some translators to give the wrong Latin word (2.12.18). These wrong

---

[13] He may hint at the idea that wide circulation in the churches also established the authority of the LXX. He did not yet emphasize the apostolic use of this version.

[14] Translation from *Saint Augustine, On Christian Teaching*, trans. R. P. H. Green (Oxford: Oxford University Press, 1997), 43.

[15] *Doctr. chr.* 2.6.8: *obscurioribus autem fastidia detergeret.* On this issue, see Tarmo Toom, "Augustine on Ambiguity," *Augustinian Studies* 38 (2007): 407–33, especially at 423–24 on our passage. There is perhaps an echo of Origen's view of the pedagogic value of obscurity in the biblical text, on which see Dominique Barthélemy, *Études d'histoire du texte de l'Ancien Testament* (Göttingen: Vandenhoeck & Ruprecht, 1978), 186–87.

[16] On this comparison of Isaiah texts, see Kotzé, "Augustine, Jerome and the Septuagint," 249; Houghton, *Augustine's Text of John*, 12.

translations were not illuminating at all; Augustine told his readers not to try to interpret them but to emend them (*non enim intellegendos, sed emendandos tales codices potius praecipiendum est*). Students of the Bible should seek out literal translations (*interpretationes eorum, qui se verbis nimis obstrinxerunt*) because they help "control the freedom or error of others who in their translations have chosen to follow the ideas [*sententias*] rather than the words" (2.13.19).[17]

In the passage on the LXX, coming just a few paragraphs later, Augustine seems still to have the issue of obscurity and ambiguity in mind. The divergent translations of Isaiah that he had cited earlier were mutually illuminating because they both gave the sense, though only one of them could represent the actual wording while the other was more free; so also the Seventy translators "translated in a way that the Holy Spirit, who was leading them and creating unanimity, judged appropriate to the Gentiles," even if they did not reproduce the Hebrew wording (2.15.22).[18] But it may be that an examination of the Hebrew wording would help reveal the sense that the Seventy tried to express, which is why Augustine went on to say,

> But, as I said above, the comparison of translations which have kept more closely to the words [*qui verbis tenacius inhaeserunt*] is often not without its value in explaining a passage.[19]

What the Seventy changed, then, was the wording and not the sense. This explanation for the differences between the Hebrew and the LXX is somewhat reminiscent of the explanation of Epiphanius of Salamis, who had tried to show that the differences were only the typical lack of precision

---

[17] The "freedom" (*libertas*) of translators relates to the examples from Isaiah that Augustine harmonized; the error refers to the examples from Romans and Wisdom. On recourse to the original languages of Scripture for biblical interpretation in Augustine, see Toom, "Augustine on Ambiguity," 428–29; Kotzé, "Augustine, Jerome and the Septuagint," 252–54.

[18] It was not uncommon for the Fathers to see the Seventy as having translated more obscurely and more spiritually; see *Doctr. chr.* 4.7.15, and on Eusebius, cf. Adam Kamesar, *Jerome, Greek Scholarship, and the Hebrew Bible: A Study of the Quaestiones Hebraicae in Genesim* (Oxford: Clarendon, 1993), 37–28, 65–66.

[19] *Doctr. chr.* 2.15.22; cf. 2.13.19.

inherent in the act of translating.[20] Augustine was probably not dependent on Epiphanius; in any case, he pressed the idea further. For Augustine, what the Seventy translators did was not typical of all translation activity but resulted from divine guidance in expressing the sense of their *Vorlage* and choosing words appropriate to a Gentile audience.

By 403, Augustine had not yet received Jerome's response to his *Ep.* 28 written nearly a decade earlier, so he sent the follow-up *Ep.* 71 to reiterate some of his concerns. Augustine had by now obtained some of Jerome's Hebrew translations, and he had learned about his translation of Job from Hebrew (*Ep.* 71.3). This new translation troubled Augustine because it did not demonstrate the *verborum fides*, or "verbal fidelity," that the previous one had; that is, the later translation did not contain the critical signs marking its divergences from the traditional LXX text. As Augustine presented his case in *Ep.* 71.4–6, his major objection to a translation from the Hebrew was the inability of most Christians to confirm that Jerome translated the Hebrew correctly. There were only two possible recourses when a reading was questioned: either ask the Jews or ask Jerome, and if these disagreed there was no arbiter (71.4). As an example of such a problem, Augustine cited the trouble that arose in Oea (modern Tripoli) after the local bishop read from Jerome's translation of Jonah (71.5). The congregants did not like the unfamiliar wording—Augustine said that the bishop nearly lost his congregation—and the Jews consulted by the bishop for confirmation of its accuracy said that the traditional LXX, and not Jerome's new translation, agreed with the Hebrew.[21] Augustine concluded that even Jerome could be wrong sometimes.

In this letter, Augustine advocates retaining the LXX as the church's Bible for two main reasons: first, in order to promote unity between the eastern and western parts of the church; second, because of the easy access to Greek manuscripts and Greek speakers who can confirm a Latin translation of the LXX (71.4). He does not mention the inspiration of the LXX,

---

[20] On Epiphanius, see Chapter Eight and Edmon L. Gallagher, *Hebrew Scripture in Patristic Biblical Theory: Canon, Language, Text* (Leiden: Brill, 2012), 192–94.

[21] Whether the story is true or not, one wonders how proficient at Hebrew early fifth-century North African Jews may have been; for a brief, negative portrait, see Law, *When God Spoke Greek*, 166. Jerome himself questions their ability in Hebrew (*Ep.* 112.22).

but he does emphasize its wide circulation among churches and its use by the apostles (71.6). As for the incident at Oea, Augustine magnifies the gravity of the situation by not specifying the particular text that caused the trouble, a point that Jerome's response also highlights (*Ep.* 112.22). It seems that if the Jews had sided with Jerome's translation on that occasion, Augustine would not have had grounds for criticizing Jerome. Conformity to the Hebrew text seems to have been an important factor in this case. One wonders how Augustine felt about the bishop who introduced Jerome's translation into the liturgy.

In these criticisms of Jerome's new translation, it seems that Augustine was still thinking about passages in the Hebrew that were obscure and availed themselves of no single translation. It was these passages that might prompt Jerome to offer a different rendering from the LXX and that might cause Jerome and the Jews to understand the text differently from each other. Augustine said that he could not understand how there can be so many discrepancies between the LXX and Hebrew, a statement probably designed to elicit from Jerome the concession that the Hebrew text is obscure (*Ep.* 71.6). The obscurity of the Hebrew allowed for multiple interpretations for which, in Augustine's mind, confirmation was impossible due to general Christian ignorance of Hebrew. It was much easier to confirm a translation from Greek, and the Seventy translators, with their excellent qualities (not to mention divine guidance), no doubt found the appropriate rendering for their Gentile audience. Augustine also acknowledged that the LXX itself could be obscure, but he attributed this obscurity to the commitment of the translators to the spiritual sense (*Doctr. chr.* 4.7.15).[22] Jerome attributed the LXX's obscurity, in part, to the translators not understanding their *Vorlage*.[23]

Jerome finally responded to Augustine in the year 404 (*Ep.* 112.19–22). He offered a point-by-point retort to Augustine's letters: He said that Augustine seemed not to understand the function of the Hexaplaric critical signs; he refuted Augustine's early argument that newer translations of the Hebrew

---

[22] Cf. Kamesar, *Jerome*, 65–66.

[23] Jerome, *Preface to the Pentateuch*, in *Biblia Sacra Vulgata*, ed. R. Weber and R. Gryson, 5th ed. (Stuttgart: Deutsche Bibelgesellschaft, 2007), 4, lines 35–39; cf. Kamesar, *Jerome*, 68. Jerome also thinks that the obscurity of the LXX resulted from the translators' desire to hide the mysteries of Christ, which Jerome interpreted negatively; cf. Kamesar, 66.

could not improve on the LXX; he adjured Augustine to assume his fidelity as a translator of the Old Testament based on his demonstrated fidelity as a translator of the New Testament; and he responded to the story about Oea with the concession that his translation did not quite capture the meaning of the Hebrew word, but neither did the LXX, and in any case, it was only a matter of the type of plant under which Jonah sat (ivy or gourd; Jonah 4:6), hardly the type of thing that should cause a congregation to revolt against its bishop.[24] He also said that he did not intend his new translations to supersede the LXX but merely to reveal what things the Jews have "omitted or corrupted" (112.20).

It was this last point that Augustine later said had convinced him of the utility of Jerome's translations. This came at the end of the next letter in the correspondence, *Ep.* 82, the last time the two Latin Fathers discussed together this particular issue (*Ep.* 82.34–35). Actually, Augustine did not seem quite convinced that Jews bore responsibility for changing Scripture.[25] He wondered which Jews had corrupted the Old Testament and which texts were corrupt; Jerome had failed to say. He spoke again about the obscurity of certain texts that might result in divergent interpretations that were still united in one common faith. If Jonah's plant was not really either an ivy or a gourd, Augustine would prefer to retain the LXX reading "gourd" because the Seventy translators probably had their reasons for choosing this word. After all, the apostles themselves used this version, and we do not want needlessly to upset Christians who know the traditional wording. But Augustine seemed to imply that if Jerome's version of Jonah 4:6 really did correspond more closely to the Hebrew text than did that of the LXX, at least it should be given a hearing. He did not explore whether both the gourd and the ivy might point toward spiritual realities.

Near the time he sent this letter to Jerome, Augustine wrote his *Harmony of the Gospels* (*De consensu Evangelistarum*). Here he compared the differences among the Gospels to the differences between the Hebrew text and the LXX (*Cons. Ev.* 2.66.128). This discussion was prompted by the varying quotations of Zechariah 9:9 found in Matthew 21:5 and John 12:15. Whereas

---

[24] On this last point, see Fürst, *Augustins Briefwechsel mit Hieronymus*, 143.

[25] *Contra* Fürst, "*Veritas Latina*," 118–19.

Matthew said that Christ entered Jerusalem riding on a donkey (ὄνος, *asina*) and mentioned also a colt (πῶλος, *pullus*), the other Gospels referred only to the colt.[26] Analogously, he said that the LXX "differs in several passages from that which is found in the Hebrew" and that one could ask "why the great authority of the Septuagint translation diverges in many passages from the truth which is found in the Hebrew codices." He answered that the Seventy translators were attempting to demonstrate the same type of freedom in words, the same "harmonious diversity" (*concors diversitas*), used by the various Gospels in communicating the truth. Augustine went on to explain that this "harmonious diversity" did not involve a departure from the intention of God (*ab eadem voluntate dei*) and was simply a variation of expression (*eloquium*). He did not seem to think that this "harmonious diversity" was standard translation procedure, because it was a product of the presence of the Holy Spirit within the translators. This position is very similar to the one he articulated in the early portion of *On Christian Teaching*. He did not broach it in his correspondence with Jerome.

In the passages we have examined so far, Augustine did not think that the Seventy translators diverged substantially from their Hebrew *Vorlage*. They offered an authoritative rendering of obscure passages, and their authority was based on their number, date, and learning, and perhaps their miraculous agreement, although Augustine was willing to bend on this last point. He indicated that a translation should correspond closely to the Hebrew, but that the Seventy translators had good reasons for diverging from the wording of the Hebrew, though they also retained the sense (*sententia*) or intention (*voluntas*) of the original.

His ideas seem to have developed over the next decade and a half. In his *Questions on the Heptateuch* (419/20), he considered difficult or curious statements in the first seven books of the Bible. The base text continued to be the traditional Latin translation of the LXX. A few times he acknowledged the helpfulness of Hebrew for biblical exegesis.[27] In eighteen passages, he compared the LXX to the *interpretatio quae ex hebraeo est* (the translation which is from the Hebrew), as he termed Jerome's translation (without

---

[26] Cf. also, without the Zechariah reference, Mark 11:1–7; Luke 19:29–35.

[27] *Quaest. Hept.* 1.97; 5.3.

ever naming its translator).[28] La Bonnardière rightly stressed that this low number indicates the dominance of the LXX within Augustine's thinking on the Bible.[29] Though these eighteen passages "do not succeed in disturbing Augustine's esteem for the LXX,"[30] they do demonstrate some concern on Augustine's part for the original text of Scripture, and they show how his thinking progressed over the years.

Most of the time when he compared the LXX with Jerome's translation, he found the latter to be very helpful either in clarifying the sense of the biblical text or in confirming the interpretation that he proposed on the basis of the more obscure LXX text.[31] A few times he did not express an opinion on which text was correct or how they might be reconciled.[32] The new development in this work involves Augustine's suggestion on several occasions that the Seventy translators themselves were responsible for changing the text of Scripture.[33] For instance, the LXX has the word "hands" in Deuteronomy 30:14, though the Hebrew text lacks this word. Augustine believed that the translators added the word to stress that even our actions, signified here by "hands," ought to be controlled by our heart (*Quaest. Hept.*

---

[28] La Bonnardière, "Augustin a-t-il utilisé la 'Vulgate' de Jérôme?," 305–7, studied these passages. The eighteen passages she lists at 305–6nn12–15 do not correspond precisely to the ones I include. (She derived her list, as she says at 305n11, from the index of *Quaestionum in Heptateuchum libri vii*, ed. Joseph Zycha, CSEL [Vienna: Tempsky, 1895], which references the *PL* volume containing the first part of Jerome's translation.) I do not include *Quaest. Hept.* 1.97 because it does not contain a discussion of textual variation but rather illustrates the importance of knowing Hebrew for understanding certain biblical words. Also, la Bonnardière counts *Quaest. Hept.* 6.19 twice because it discusses two different verses of Joshua. She miscopied the citation of *Quaest. Hept.* 1.152. (She has in her list *Quaest. Hept.* 1.192.) I add to her list *Quaest. Hept.* 1.2 and 1.169. The complete list I am working with includes *Quaest. Hept.* 1.2 (Gen. 5:25); 1.152 (Gen. 46:26–27); 1.162 (Gen. 47:31); 1.169 (Gen. 50:3); 5.20 (Deut. 14:28–29); 5.54 (Deut. 30:11–14); 6.7 (Josh. 5:13–15); 6.15 (Josh. 10:5–6); 6.19 (Josh. 16:10); 6.24 (Josh. 23:14); 6.25 (Josh. 24:3); 7.16 (Judg. 2:13); 7.21 (Judg. 3:17); 7.25 (Judg. 3:31); 7.37 (Judg. 7:6); 7.41 (Judg. 8:26–27); 7.47 (Judg. 10:1); 7.55 (Judg. 15:8).
[29] La Bonnardière, "Augustin a-t-il utilisé la 'Vulgate' de Jérôme?," 305.
[30] La Bonnardière, 306.
[31] Augustine, *Quaest. Hept.* 1.2; 5.20; 6.7; 6.15; 6.24 (?); 7.16; 7.21; 7.41; 7.47; 7.55. Cf. la Bonnardière, "Augustin a-t-il utilisé la 'Vulgate' de Jérôme?," 306n17, though her list is not everywhere equivalent to mine. A few times Augustine found helpful—and regarded as original Hebrew—the interpretive additions made by Jerome; cf. *Quaest. Hept.* 5.20; 6.7; 7.47.
[32] Augustine, *Quaest. Hept.* 1.152; 1.162; 7.25; 7.37.
[33] Augustine, *Quaest. Hept.* 1.169; 5.54; 6.19; 6.25. Cf. la Bonnardière, "Augustin a-t-il utilisé la 'Vulgate' de Jérôme?," 306n16, though her list is not everywhere equivalent to mine.

5.54). Or, at Joshua 16:10, the translators have added historical details to their text because they, coming much later in time than the original author of the biblical book, had more information at their disposal as to how events transpired (6.19). At Joshua 24:3, the LXX has "all the land" where Jerome's rendering has "the land of Canaan." Augustine thought the Seventy translators had broadened the significance of the statement in order to point toward the Christian inheritance rather than the ancient Israelite inheritance of Canaan (7.25).[34] Augustine also attributed to the Seventy translators the change from forty days to three days at Jonah 3:4 (1.169), an example that will occupy us later when we get to the relevant passage of the *City of God* where he considered it at length (18.44). In each of these cases of changes wrought by the translators, the Hebrew text retained its value, at least as a point of comparison, but also as an inspired text in its own right to which one must give its due weight. At no point does Augustine propose that the Hebrew text is irrelevant to the Christian.

He dealt with the issue of textual variation between LXX and Hebrew most extensively in the later books of the *City of God* (*De civitate dei*), especially books 15 and 18. He still emphasized the authority of the LXX, especially because of the reception of this version within the church but also because of the story of the miraculous agreement of the translators (which it now seems he trusted more than he did earlier)[35] and because the apostles quoted the LXX, though now he said that the apostles quoted both the Hebrew and the LXX, perhaps a result of Jerome's influence (*Civ.* 18.43–44).[36] The many divergences between the LXX and Hebrew text must still be explained, and Augustine now developed a sophisticated theory to account for these differences.

He first encountered a major difference in book 15 in his treatment of the genealogy of Genesis 5 (*Civ.* 15.11–15). Later in his discussion of the genealogy in Genesis 11, Augustine mentioned but did not offer any

---

[34] Jerome's translation does not precisely correspond to the Masoretic Text, which does have the word *all*.

[35] See Kotzé, "Augustine, Jerome and the Septuagint," 250–52.

[36] On the apostolic use of the Hebrew and the LXX, see also *Civ.* 15.14. On Jerome's argument that the apostles quoted the Hebrew text, see Teppei Kato, "Jerome's Understanding of Old Testament Quotations in the New Testament," *Vigiliae Christianae* 67 (2013): 289–315.

explanation for the chronological problems in that chapter.[37] He did have an explanation for the discrepancies in Genesis 5, where the LXX and the Hebrew text often diverge by a century in their reporting of the patriarchs' ages. Augustine argued strongly that the Hebrew text preserved the correct numbers here. As a general rule, he asserted,

> when some divergence is found as between the two versions such that they cannot both be a true record of established fact, we should believe the original language rather than versions made by translators into another tongue.[38]

He did not consider whether both versions might point to spiritual realities. Rather, he thought the Greek manuscript tradition was corrupted early on by a zealous scribe seeking to support the strange theory that patriarchal years amount to only a tenth of our modern years. He rejected as completely implausible the notion that the Jews altered the Hebrew text (15.13).[39] In this view, he contradicted some earlier Fathers, such as Eusebius of Caesarea.[40] Neither could the error belong to the Seventy translators, "men of revered memory." Augustine was able to imagine only a devious motive and not a spiritual one, so it was unbecoming of the Seventy translators: "Rather, it should be attributed to the errors of the scribe who first received the text from the library of King Ptolemy ... in order to transcribe it" (15.13). This error should be corrected to accord with the Hebrew text.[41] But Augustine went on to say,

---

[37] *Civ.* 16.10: *in Hebraeis autem codicibus longe pauciores annos perhibent inveniri, de quibus rationem aut nullam aut difficillimam reddunt.* On all these differences, see Ronald Hendel, "A Hasmonean Edition of MT Genesis? The Implications of the Editions of the Chronology in Genesis 5," *Hebrew Bible and Ancient Israel* 1 (2012): 1–17, who explains the chronological variants in our textual witnesses as all arising from the desire on the part of ancient scribes to solve certain chronological puzzles, such as Methuselah's living beyond the time of the Flood in the LXX.

[38] *Civ.* 15.13; Dyson, trans., *City of God against the Pagans*, 659.

[39] He clearly had in mind the Hebrew text as the one particularly belonging to the Jews because he spoke at 15.11 of "the language from which the Scriptures themselves were translated."

[40] See the discussion of Eusebius's *Chronicon* in Chapter Eight.

[41] Cf. Augustine, *Doctr. chr.* 2.12.18, on texts that should be emended instead of interpreted.

Where there has been no error on the part of a scribe, and where the sense that they give is consistent with the truth and proclaims the truth, we should believe that the LXX translators chose to say things differently not in their office of translating but in their liberty of prophesying. (*Civ.* 15.14)

"Where the sense . . . is consistent with the truth and proclaims the truth": this criterion seems to distinguish Jonah 3:4 from the corrupted genealogy of Genesis 5. For Jonah 3:4, and whether the prophet said that Nineveh would be overthrown in forty days or three days, Augustine was able to imagine a spiritual reason for the difference.[42] Augustine recognized that the historical prophet could not have uttered both numbers, and once again (as in the case of Genesis 5) he granted the Hebrew text greater historical veracity. The Seventy translators intentionally changed the number "to admonish the reader not to hold the authority of either version in low esteem, but to raise himself above mere history and to seek out the meanings which the historical narrative was intended to convey" (18.44).[43] Reflecting on the historical period of time until Nineveh's destruction will not spiritually nourish Christian readers, but they will be edified if they recognize that the LXX does not report mere history but that the number "three" signifies the period of the death and resurrection of Christ. But even the Hebrew text points toward spiritual realities with the number "forty," the number of days Christ taught the apostles after his resurrection (Acts 1:3):

It is as if the seventy translators were rousing from sleep the reader who wishes to adhere to the facts of history merely; and it is as if the prophets were also appealing to such a reader to search the depths of prophecy. It is as if they were saying, "Seek in the forty days Him in

---

[42] For a suggestion by a modern Old Testament theologian on how to understand the difference in wording between the Hebrew and Greek at Jonah 3:4, see R. W. L. Moberly, *Old Testament Theology: Reading the Hebrew Bible as Christian Scripture* (Grand Rapids: Baker, 2013), 186 with n. 13.

[43] *admoneretque lectorem utraque auctoritate non spreta ab historia sese adtollere ad ea requirenda, propter quae significanda historia ipsa conscripta est.*

Whom you will be able to find the three days also. You will find the former in His ascension, the latter in His resurrection." (*Civ.* 18.44)

Augustine further asserted that this example was one of many passages in which some readers think the LXX diverged from the Hebrew text, but rightly understood, they were actually in harmony (*concordes*; 18.44).

Before discussing the example from Jonah, Augustine had enumerated four types of changes that the Seventy translators made to their *Vorlage*. Two categories included additions and omissions, for which Augustine supplied no examples, though he mentioned the material under either asterisk or obelus in the Hexaplaric LXX. Another type of change involved those passages where the Holy Spirit communicated the same meaning (*sensus*) in different words, and finally there were those passages where the Spirit said something different, just as Jeremiah and Isaiah said different things by the same Spirit (*Civ.* 18.43).[44] Into which category does Jonah 3:4 fit? It is hard to see how it would not fit the last category, where the translators said something different from the prophet. But it seems that Augustine treated the verse as an example of the translators saying the same thing in different words; he said that both the three days and the forty days point toward the spiritual realities revealed in Christ, so that they "convey exactly the same sense, though with another kind of significance" (*et in unum eundemque sensum, quamvis sub altera significatione*; 18.44).

Throughout this work, the LXX remained Augustine's point of departure, but the Hebrew Bible had achieved a significant position within his thought, precisely because the Greek translators chose not to render it precisely. In the case of Jonah 3:4, the reader might not have recognized the spiritual meaning to which the LXX was pointing if he or she failed to observe the divergence between three days in the LXX and forty days in the Hebrew text. The Seventy translators' goal of "rousing the reader from sleep" could prove effective only if the reader expected to see "forty days" in the text. Augustine realized that perceiving such changes required comparing the Greek and Hebrew texts (18.43: *nisi utrisque codicibus inspectis*). For his theory to hold together, the Hebrew text becomes increasingly important, as exemplified in the case of

---

[44] I have altered the order of Augustine's categories for ease of discussion.

Jonah 3:4. Later in the *City of God*, he quoted Zechariah 12:10 according to the LXX and according to Jerome's Hebrew translation and advocated interpreting both texts because "we recognise the truth of the Lord's passion more fully when we do not follow the one interpretation only, but unite both" (20.30). Almost every time Augustine compared the two texts in *City of God*, he thought either that they both said the same thing or that they could both be interpreted spiritually.[45] Lössl offers a minimalist interpretation of Augustine's use of the Hebrew Bible when he characterizes it as merely "a source for variant readings" for Augustine.[46] La Bonnardière seems closer to the mark: "Augustine accepts the two variants without sacrificing that of the LXX (even defending it), but not without admiring that it would be complemented for the better by the variant of the Hebrew."[47]

What is the reader to do with these multiple text forms? Read them both, said Augustine. Both the LXX and the Hebrew text evinced the *altitudo prophetica*; they were both authoritative, "since both are one, and both divine."[48] The LXX was sanctified by apostolic use, by the story of the miraculous agreement, and particularly by its reception in the church. But the Hebrew text was an accurate record of the things spoken by the prophets of God, sometimes at least a more accurate record than the LXX, it was also used by the apostles, and it likewise directed the reader to higher meanings. Augustine never advocated the use of Jerome's translation within the liturgy, but this had nothing to do with the inspiration or authority of the Hebrew

---

[45] For passages where Augustine said both texts say the same thing, see *Civ.* 22.29 on 4 Kings 5:26; for both being interpreted spiritually, see 18.48 on Haggai 2:7; 20.30 on Zechariah 12:10; 18.44 on Jonah 3:4. But see also 20.30, where Augustine attributed to the Seventy translators a clarifying addition in Isaiah 62:1–4; and 20.21, where Augustine critiqued Jerome's translation of Isaiah 66:24.

[46] Lössl, "Shift in Patristic Exegesis," 161.

[47] "Augustin accepte les deux variantes sans sacrifier celle de la Septante (en la défendant même), mais non sans admirer qu'elle soit complétée au mieux par la variante de l'hébreu"; La Bonnardière, "Augustin a-t-il utilisé la 'Vulgate' de Jérôme?," 311–12; cf. Anne-Isabelle Bouton-Touboulic, "Autorité et tradition: La traduction latine de la Bible selon saint Jérôme et saint Augustin," *Augustinianum* 45 (2005): 185–229, at 224.

[48] Augustine, *Civ.* 18.44: *utraque auctoritate utendum putavi, quoniam utraque una atque divina est.* For the term *altitudo prophetica*, see 18.43; cf. 18.28 (Hosea); 18.44 (*altitudo prophetiae*); *Speculum* 8; *Doctr. chr.* 3.34.49 (in a different context). For the contrary view, see Lössl, "Shift in Patristic Exegesis," 160: the LXX, "not the Hebrew version, was the text with the prophetic dimension."

text; he feared that its unfamiliar wording would needlessly disturb congregations, and the adoption of a non-Septuagintal text form might engender division between the eastern and western parts of the church.

We can schematize Augustine's mature thinking regarding textual variation in the following way. Often, of course, the problem resided in the Latin manuscript tradition, which Augustine early on recognized as frequently corrupt (*Doctr. chr.* 2.11.16). When he could confirm that the LXX differed from the Hebrew, he could follow one of three options: (1) assume textual corruption in the Hebrew manuscripts, (2) assume textual corruption in the Greek manuscripts, or (3) assume that the Seventy translators intentionally changed their text. As for the first option, we have seen that Augustine at one time expressed to Jerome some willingness to allow for textual corruption in Hebrew manuscripts (*Ep.* 83.34–35), but later he regarded such a suggestion as preposterous (*Civ.* 15.13). His reasons for this later view include that the Seventy translators would have corrected any error that preceded them, and any error subsequent to their translation could not have affected the entire Hebrew manuscript tradition. The second option he considered most plausible in the case of the genealogies of Genesis 5, for which he posited that an early copyist of the Greek text intentionally altered the numbers (*Civ.* 15.11–15). Augustine promoted the third option—intentional alteration of the text by the Seventy translators—when he was able to discern a spiritual intention behind the Greek variant, such as in the case of Jonah's three days. Possibly Jerome himself provided the initial influence pushing Augustine in this direction, for the monk of Bethlehem argued that the Seventy translators intentionally altered their text in certain passages, a move that Jerome usually interpreted negatively and as a reason to return to the *Hebraica veritas*.[49] Augustine also acknowledged alterations by the Seventy translators, but he interpreted this phenomenon positively because of their spiritual motive. In such cases, the Hebrew text still proved valuable as a counterpoint that allowed the reader to recognize the LXX variant that should be spiritually discerned, but it also provided an accurate witness to the text originally written by the Spirit of God and one that bore spiritual meanings of its own.

---

[49] Jerome, *Preface to Isaiam*, in Weber and Gryson, *Biblia sacra*, 1096, lines 11–14.

As opposed to the majority of Church Fathers who preceded him, Augustine did not think that the Seventy translators accurately rendered their Hebrew *Vorlage* in every passage. Often they did, and in these cases if contemporary Greek and Hebrew manuscripts diverged, the reader should conclude that one was corrupt; such was the case for the genealogy in Genesis 5, where Augustine advocated emending the Greek manuscripts toward the Hebrew. But there were also many passages, Augustine said, where the Seventy translators made some sort of change to their Hebrew *Vorlage*, whether adding or subtracting something, or even changing the meaning. Most early Christian writers did not allow this, but by the time Augustine developed his mature views, Jerome had demonstrated through his translations the many divergences between Greek and Hebrew. Augustine found it more expedient, and more spiritually edifying, to avoid charging the Jews with textual corruption in all these cases and rather attribute to the translators the intention of changing these many passages for the benefit of the reader. Comparison of the Greek with the Hebrew—accessing both in Latin translation—allowed the serious student of God's word to perceive the deeper significance that was inaccessible to those who used only one text. The LXX retained its primary place in the church's worship, mostly as an expediency, but in private devotion, Augustine's theoretical formulation granted an equally lofty place to the Hebrew text.

Epilogue

The LXX for Modern Christians

[Ladies and] Gentlemen, have you a Septuagint? If not, sell all you have, and buy a Septuagint.

—Ferdinand Hitzig (1807–1875)[1]

If you want to understand the Bible and early Christianity, you need to get yourself a Septuagint. That is not the only thing you need, but if you have not paid much attention to the LXX before, it might be the most important thing you do not yet have. After all, early Christians used a Greek translation of the Old Testament called the Septuagint, as the first sentence of this book declared. The entire book has been an effort to explain how that first sentence is true: What do we mean by *the Septuagint*—or, better, what did early Christians mean by it—and who were these early Christians, and in what sense did they use the LXX? I hesitate to say that we have answered these questions, but perhaps I may make bold to claim that we have explored some of the difficulties involved in these questions and have reached some conclusions. One conclusion: Hitzig was right. You need an LXX, but it probably will not require your life savings.

---

[1] Aside from my gender-inclusive adjustment, this epigraph is the "canonical" English form of this oft-cited comment with which, it is reported, Hitzig was accustomed to open his lectures on biblical theology. The earliest record is *Dr. Ferdinand Hitzig's Vorlesungen über biblische Theologie und messianische Weissagungen des Alten Testaments*, ed. J. J. Kneucker (Karlsruhe: H. Reuther, 1880), 19n2, where the original German appears as "Meine Herren, haben Sie eine Septuaginta? wenn nicht, so verkaufen Sie Alles, was Sie haben, und kaufen sich eine Septuaginta!"

This book stands on its own, I think, as a historical investigation, but it could also be seen as preliminary to theological reflection on the identity of Scripture for the modern church. If early Christians used the Septuagint, should modern Christians do likewise? This epilogue collects some thoughts I have on this topic that deserves a much fuller treatment. The topic has received a much fuller treatment elsewhere. A lot of people are asking this question these days, whether the Septuagint should play a bigger role in modern Western Christianity in light of its enormous role in early Christianity.[2] Luke Timothy Johnson's exploration of the LXX in the book of Acts two decades ago led him to ask these questions:

> Given the facts that Scripture for Luke—and for all the New Testament writers—was not the Hebrew but rather the Greek LXX, how should we think about western Christianity's long estrangement from the LXX? The Eastern Church continues to use the LXX as its Old Testament, and all Christian theology through Augustine was based squarely on the Greek Old and New Testament. But since Jerome's Vulgate, the West has based its translations on the Hebrew. Yet the implications of this shift have never adequately been addressed theologically. The seamless intertexture of Luke-Acts and the rest of the New Testament no longer exists. Indeed, the patterns of New Testament citation, allusion, and argument from Scripture no longer appear evident or even credible. It is perhaps time to honestly face the question whether the LXX is really the Christian Old Testament.[3]

---

[2] Some examples from the current generation: Mogens Müller, *The First Bible of the Church: A Plea for the Septuagint* (Sheffield: Sheffield Academic, 1996); R. Timothy McLay, *The Use of the Septuagint in New Testament Research* (Grand Rapids: Eerdmans, 2003); J. Ross Wagner, "The Septuagint and the 'Search for the Christian Bible,'" in *Scripture's Doctrine and Theology's Bible*, ed. Markus Bockmuehl and Alan J. Torrance (Grand Rapids: Baker, 2008), 17–28. In a previous generation, see Pierre Benoit, "L'inspiration des Septante d'après les Pères," in *L'Homme devant Dieu: Mélanges offerts au Père Henri de Lubac: Exégèse et patristique* (Paris: Aubier, 1964), 1.169–87. And from a century earlier: E. W. Grinfield, *An Apology for the Septuagint: In Which Its Claims to Biblical and Canonical Authority Are Briefly Stated and Vindicated* (London: William Pickering, 1850).

[3] Luke Timothy Johnson, *Septuagintal Midrash in the Speeches of Acts* (Milwaukee: Marquette University Press, 2002), 51.

I myself do not see it quite the same way. The evidence of the New Testament is, to my mind, more ambiguous than scholars often allow. We saw in Chapter Six that it may be true to say that the apostles quoted the Septuagint, but it would be even more correct to add "usually" to that assessment. Sometimes the New Testament quotes an Old Testament passage in a form that diverges from the Old Greek. These are the passages emphasized by Jerome to make the case that the apostles sanctioned the *Hebraica veritas*. Just because Jerome pushed his argument too far does not mean that he had no argument to make. The quotation of Hosea 11:1 at Matthew 2:15 would not have worked so well if Matthew had quoted the Old Greek; the Greek translation that the Evangelist used, one corresponding more closely to the Masoretic Text, helped him connect the ancient prophecy to the life of Jesus. More often, the New Testament contains quotations of the Septuagint / Old Greek that would not have worked so well had the writer quoted a Greek text more in line with the MT. The fact that both situations arise in the New Testament makes it hard to use the New Testament as a definitive witness in favor of a particular textual tradition.

The New Testament itself contains no theoretical statements about the correct text of the Bible. Such theoretical statements appear in Christian writings beginning in the second century, often promoting the inspiration of the Septuagint. Several issues hinder me from affirming what these patristic authors advocated. First, they misanalyzed the evidence; the apostles did not cite the Septuagint exclusively. If the theological claim was that the apostolic citations demonstrate that the apostles passed down the Septuagint as the Christian Old Testament, we are left wondering about the quotations that do not align with the Septuagint. Second, as I have argued in this book, I am not convinced that there was a "Septuagint" as such in the first century. There were a variety of Greek translations and revisions available to readers of the Greek Bible. Some Jews in the first century (e.g., Philo) thought the Greek translation of the Pentateuch (the entirety of "the Septuagint" in the first century, as far as our evidence allows) was inspired, but others seem not to have shared his view. At any rate, the different text forms attested in the New Testament quotations and the limited extent of the LXX in Jewish stories of the translation make difficult the proposition that Paul or Matthew saw themselves as sanctioning the LXX for the church.

Third, the patristic theoretical statements assume that the Septuagint is an accurate translation of its Hebrew *Vorlage* and that this Hebrew *Vorlage* was the best form of the Hebrew scriptures in the time of the translators. It seems to me that such a patristic theory on the correct form of the Old Testament justifies an examination of the Hebrew texts themselves. Certainly Jerome assumed that his contemporaries would consider the Hebrew text authoritative. Augustine came to accept this point. Early Christian use of the LXX does make the LXX important for modern Christians, as well, but the claim that the LXX—and not the Hebrew—ought to be modern Christian Scripture misses something about that early Christian use. A theoretical statement about the nature of the Christian Bible today ought to interact with early Christian biblical theory and not only early Christian practice.

Fourth, the evidence of some of the New Testament quotations is often, I think, misconstrued by modern scholars—or, at least, is taken as obviously attesting to a particular view when other views also seem possible. For instance, the first quotation in (the present canonical arrangement of) the New Testament is perhaps the most famous: Matthew 1:23 quoting Isaiah 7:14. Christians traditionally, and scholars routinely, think of this quotation as Matthew's prooftext for the Virgin Birth. This quotation became a point of contention between Jews and Christians early on, already in the mid-second century (cf. Justin Martyr, *Dial.* 70–73; see Chapter Eight). If it is the case that only the Septuagint and not the Hebrew text of Isaiah 7 contains the idea of a virgin giving birth, then perhaps Christian theology is inextricably bound to the LXX. Maybe so, but I remain unconvinced—but not because I think the Hebrew text of Isaiah actually does contain a virgin birth. Rather, it seems to me that we may have misconstrued the reason that Matthew quoted Isaiah 7 or which element of Isaiah 7 Matthew thought the birth of Jesus fulfilled. Matthew does not really highlight Mary's virginity to any great extent, as others have noticed. But he does highlight the name of the child, Immanuel, explaining that it signifies "God with us." Since the presence of Christ among his disciples is a theme of Matthew's Gospel,[4] perhaps we could say that Matthew quoted Isaiah 7 not to tie Mary's virginity

---

[4] Richard B. Hays, *The Moral Vision of the New Testament: Community, Cross, New Creation; A Contemporary Introduction to New Testament Ethics* (New York: HarperCollins, 1996), 104–6.

to a prophecy but to explain the significance of her child, "God with us"—which would mean that Matthew's point was not connected exclusively with the Septuagint. Moreover, scholars have argued that the Greek word used in LXX Isaiah 7:14 and often translated "virgin" may not have carried such connotations (but rather something more like "young woman") for the Greek translator (or Matthew?).[5]

To take a second example, James's quotation of Amos 9:11–12 in Acts 15:16–17 relies on the LXX for both its wording and its theology: Amos attests the Gentile mission according to the LXX wording ("the remnant of people might seek me") more so than in the MT ("they might possess the remnant of Edom"). But could James have derived the same point from the MT? Denying such a possibility may be tempting to modern scholars—Johnson says that the meaning James derives from Amos is "impossible in the Hebrew"[6]—but might run the risk of underselling the power and creativity of apostolic interpretation. It might have appeared to us strange for James to cite a passage reading "they might possess the remnant of Edom" in relation to the Gentile mission, but it would have hardly been the strangest interpretation in the New Testament. Moreover, as we saw in Chapter Nine, we actually have an ancient—or late ancient—example of an interpreter doing this precise thing—that is, taking the Hebrew text of Amos 9:12 as prophesying the Gentile mission. In his *Commentary on Amos*, Jerome cited Acts 15 as guiding his interpretation of the Hebrew text of Amos 9. To be sure, the choice to use the LXX reading in Acts 15 was not necessarily conscious. Either way, conscious or not, the quotation does not necessarily stand opposed to the MT Amos 9:12, at least, not according to apostolic hermeneutics, and certainly not according to patristic hermeneutics. The Fathers routinely stressed that the apostles were more concerned with the sense of a passage than the words. The LXX of Amos

---

[5] On the use of παρθένος in the LXX here, see Andrew T. Lincoln, *Born of a Virgin? Reconceiving Jesus in the Bible, Tradition, and Theology* (Grand Rapids: Eerdmans, 2013), 74–77; H. G. M. Williamson, *Isaiah 6–12*, ICC (London: T&T Clark, 2018), 139. Presumably the word does not mean "virgin" at Genesis 34:2–3. Of course, the opposite position has also been argued, both in the modern period and even in Antiquity (see Chapter Eight), *viz.*, that *almah* actually does mean "virgin."

[6] Johnson, *Septuagintal Midrash in the Speeches of Acts*, 18.

9:12 might have been based on a Hebrew text slightly different from the MT, or it might have been an interpretation of the Hebrew text preserved in the MT. Again, either way, an interpreter may have related the two traditions, suggesting that though the words diverged, the sense did not.[7] (Jerome says as much about this text.) An interpreter may have thought that possessing Edom would accomplish God's goal of incorporating the nations within God's people, especially as the next phrase mentions "all the nations that have my name called upon them." Perhaps Luke had seen a revised Greek text of the Minor Prophets (something like the Naḥal Ḥever Scroll, which itself, unfortunately, is not extant for Amos) and rejected it because he thought its reading of Amos 9:12 was wrong. Perhaps he would have said its reading was fine, but the reading of the LXX more directly makes the point he wanted to make. These are unknowns, which is the point I am trying to make. The quotation of LXX Amos 9:12 in Acts 15 does not necessarily mean that Christian theology—or even this particular Christian theological principle—is based on the LXX in the sense that it could not have been based on another textual tradition. In my mind, the proposals I have made in this paragraph do not seem at all farfetched in the ancient context, meaning that this example of apostolic use of the LXX accomplishes less than is often perceived.

On a minimalist reading of the theological significance of the textual form of the quotation in Acts 15, the LXX provided a very helpful (perhaps not essential) interpretive bridge toward the use of Amos 9 in the New Testament. Scholars often describe the LXX as the first interpretation of the Hebrew Bible,[8] and this example demonstrates that its interpretation

---

[7] Daniel Timmer, "Possessing Edom and All the Nations over Whom Yhwh's Name Is Called: Understanding ירשׁ in Amos 9:12," *Bulletin for Biblical Research* 29 (2019): 468–87: "The semantic contribution of James's quotation to its context is consistent with the sense of the MT" (486).

[8] Kristin De Troyer deals with interpretation in the LXX in the section "Character of the Translation" in her essay "The Septuagint," in *The New Cambridge History of the Bible*, vol. 1, ed. James Carleton Paget and Joachim Schaper (Cambridge: Cambridge University Press, 2013), 267–88, at 272–80. As a general comment (tied to no specific verse): "It could be argued that the Old Greek translations, in very subtle and very different ways, and in many cases within the limits of what the Hebrew text could have suggested, interpreted the text of the Hebrew biblical books" (278).

proved helpful in expressing one aspect of early Christian theology. This approach might not work for every New Testament quotation, and some readers might still be unpersuaded that it works even for Amos 9 in Acts 15, but I think it provides a promising avenue for thinking through how ancient Christians thought about the significance of their own practice of quotation. Do these quotations sanction the LXX textual form, even in the absence of evidence that a unified LXX tradition existed in the first century? Or, rather, do these quotations sanction the interpretation provided in the LXX for the specific quoted verses without any necessary implication about the overall textual form for the Christian Bible?

The latter approach seems to me to stand in some harmony with the patristic views we have surveyed in Chapters Seven through Ten. Of course, different Fathers had different views, but I have tried to show that, for the most part, they regarded the LXX as valid for Christians but not in opposition to the Hebrew text; rather, the LXX was valid insomuch as it represented in Greek what was contained in the original Hebrew text. Origen is a partial exception here, but his view is complex, difficult to summarize. He does occasionally advocate the idea that the Seventy translators enjoyed a special dispensation from God to change the biblical text in some rather minor ways. But he also spent a good part of his time revising the Greek text toward the Hebrew. The real exception to my characterization of patristic views is Augustine, who strongly argued in his mature years that God had most definitely given special revelation to the Seventy translators so that they were free to alter the biblical text. This seemed to Augustine and others a new idea. At the same time, Augustine affirmed the inspiration, authority, and spiritual value of the Hebrew text. Whereas for the earlier Fathers, the LXX—as an accurate translation—replaced the Hebrew text, for Augustine the LXX could not replace the Hebrew but had to stand alongside it because the two were not identical.

Augustine's innovative position of a dual Bible has appealed to some modern scholars,[9] but Jerome's position seems to reflect Christian tradition more closely. For Christians had often presupposed the authority of

---

[9] E.g., Benoit, "L'inspiration des Septante," 185–86, describes Augustine's position as "une vue singulièrement profonde et vraie."

the Hebrew text and assumed that the LXX mirrored it; Origen showed the problems with such a view: the LXX diverged often from the Hebrew text. Jerome then pushed the traditional view of the authority of the Hebrew Bible to its logical conclusion in light of Origen's work, by leaving aside the LXX as the authoritative text for the Christian Old Testament and working directly from the Hebrew Bible. Jerome did not abandon the LXX; he recognized that neither the New Testament nor Christian tradition would allow such a move. He routinely interpreted the LXX in his commentaries, so that his exegetical practice, so to say, enacted Augustine's theoretical position beyond what Augustine himself ever attempted. In light of the fluid nature of the scriptural text during the Second Temple period, perhaps Jerome's variation of Christian tradition provides a helpful way for modern students to think about and work with the biblical texts available to us.

The LXX as a textual witness to the Old Testament is important for the modern Christian reader of Scripture (to say nothing of the Jewish reader, or the nonreligious reader, for that matter) because it either reflects an alternative Hebrew tradition (sometimes earlier than the MT) or offers an early interpretation of the Hebrew tradition preserved in the MT. The New Testament frequently quotes the LXX, sanctioning at least the interpretive trajectory attested in the LXX in those passages. We may be reluctant to affirm that the New Testament quotations of assorted passages in a textual form agreeing with the LXX confer canonical status on the whole of the LXX, but the use of the LXX in the New Testament and—much more extensively—in early Christianity of the patristic era (and later in the East) bestows on this Greek translation of the Old Testament an exalted status among the textual options available today. In various ways, early Christians used a Greek translation of the Old Testament called the Septuagint, and we should think about following their lead.

Author Index

Subject Index

Aaron ben Asher, 101

Acts, Septuagint regularly quoted, 140

Africanus, Julius, 158

Aldine edition (1518), 52, 54

Aleppo Codex, 100

Alexandria, Greek Pentateuch originated in, 34

Alexandrian Canon theory, 65–68

Alexandrinus manuscript. *See* Codex Alexandrinus

Amos, James's quotation of in Acts, 140–45, 228

anaginoskomena (books "to be read"), 49, 78–79, 83

ancient Christians, translation story among, 31–32

ancient Judaism: textual pluralism in, 97–123; translation story in, 30–31

ancients, used the term *Septuaginta*, 53

Antiochene school of biblical exegesis, 184

Antiochene text, representing the Old Greek, 173–74

"Apocrypha," 48

Apology for Origen (Eusebius and Pamphilus), 167

apostles: use of the Septuagint, 187–88, 227–28; use of the Septuagint and the Hebrew according to Augustine, 181; use of the Septuagint and the Hebrew according to Jerome, 217–18, 224; use of the Septuagint as Scripture, 60, 120, 257

Apostolic Canons, textual history of, 82

Apostolic Fathers, 75–76

Aquila: Epiphanius on, 203; excessive literalness (Hebraizing), 113, 119, 188, 202; Jerome on, 215; translation method, 153; translator of the Old Testament, 8

Aristobulus, 24–25

Artaxerxes, 63

asterisk, 157–58, 159, 160

Athanasius, 78, 82, 93, 183, 219

Augustine: on the authority and inspiration of the Septuagint, 186, 240–41; on the authority of the Hebrew text, 239; on comparing the Greek and Hebrew texts, 248–54; on Hebrew names, 183–84; on the Hebrew text, 249, 261; on Jerome's Latin translation, 211, 243; on the Jews and textual corruption, 245, 254; knew no Hebrew, 239; on the obscurity of the Septuagint, 244; on retaining the Septuagint as the church's Bible, 243–44; on the Septuagint differing from the Hebrew, 253; on the Septuagint translators, 180, 247–48, 261; theory of two inspired biblical texts, 237–54; unwavering support for the Septuagint, 238; on the use of Jerome's translation within the liturgy, 252–53; on the use of literal translations, 239

Babylonian Talmud. *See* Talmud

Baruch, combining with the Epistle of Jeremiah, 49

Bible d'Alexandrie, La, 15–16

244; Septuagint interpreted in light of the original, 184; valuable as a counterpoint, 253. *See also* Augustine; Hebrew Bible; Jerome
Hebrew textual tradition, codified in the Masoretic Text, 123
Hebrew *Vorlage*, defined, 258
Hellenistic forms, replacing with Attic forms, 172
Hesychius, Egyptian edition of the Septuagint, 175
Hexapla: exposed textual variations between the Septuagint and Hebrew text, 188; in extant sources, 161–63; fragmentary copies of not containing the critical signs, 158; fragmentary remains of, 120; immensity of discouraged copyists, 155; made Aquila, Symmachus, and Theodotion the standard set of Jewish alternatives, 115; palimpsest fragments of contained six columns, 156; Pamphilus copied from and corrected against, 167; produced by Origen, 154–55; purpose of, 165–66; scholars debating about, 163. *See also* Origen
Hexaplaric Greek recension, of Origen, 207
historical books, manuscripts preserving the Lucianic text for, 170–71
historical interpretation, by Jerome of the Hebrew text, 232
Holmes-Parsons edition (1798–1827), 54
Holy Spirit, communicating the same meaning (*sensus*), 251

Idumea (*Edom*), as equivalent to "all nations," 228
inspiration, of the Septuagint, 113–15
International Organization for Septuagint and Cognate Studies (IOSCS), 15
interpretations, Jerome offering two in his commentaries, 232
introductions, to the Septuagint, 13–14

Invitation to the Septuagint (Jobes and Silva), 13
Irenaeus of Lyons: account of the inspiration of the Septuagint, 193; on the apostles and the Septuagint, 126; on Jewish translations, 152, 178; on new translations, 187; on the Seventy translators working independently, 180; on the translation and inspiration of the Scriptures, 177; on the translation of Isaiah as a part of the Septuagint, 31
Isaiah: divergent translations of, 242; quotations of in Romans, 131–32

James, quotation of Amos, 140–45, 259
Jeremiah, book of, 41, 111, 116–17
Jerome: accessing the Hebrew text directly, 153; on "apocrypha," 83–84, 210, 219; on the apostles and the Hebrew Bible, 126–27, 146, 209; on the authority of the Septuagint, 211; on commentaries, 182, 214; on the Hebrew text as authoritative, 258; on knowledge of Hebrew language, 206; on the Letter of Aristeas, 31–32; on the New Testament, 208, 220; on New Testament quotation of the Septuagint, 181, 233; on opponents, 186, 217, 224; on Origen, 215; on the Samaritan Pentateuch, 154; on the Septuagint, 210–13, 216, 221, 244; on the Septuagint translators, 94, 179–80, 217, 226; on the Vulgate, 209, 211, 222–23, 236, 245, 247
Jesus, Old Testament quotations attributed to, 136. *See also* Christ, prophecies of
Jesus ben Sira, 37
Jewish accounts, of the translation of the Septuagint, 114–15
Jewish Bible, 61–65, 113
Jewish Law, the Pentateuch, translation of, 30

Psalm 151, discovered among the Dead Sea
Scrolls, 65
psalms, some lacking superscriptions,
194–95
Psalter, scrolls of varying widely, 108
"Pseudo-Aristeas" (or Ps-Aristeas), 22,
26, 31
Ptolemy II Philadelphus (Greek-speaking
ruler of Egypt), 6–7, 20, 33–34, 177
public reading, Antiochene text designed
for, 174
Pythagoras, 24

Qumran, 70, 104–5, 106, 108

Rahlfs-Hanhart edition of the Septuagint,
12, 52
Rahlfs number, 85
Reader's Edition of the Septuagint, 12
recensions: Hexaplaric Greek, 192–93,
207; proto-Lucianic, 173–74; of the
Septuagint, 149–51, 166, 208
revisions: of the Greek Old Testament,
41–42; of Greek Scripture, 115–20;
necessary according to Josephus, 28
Roman Catholic Bible, 49, 51
Roman Catholic Church, 9
Roman Catholic edition of the Septuagint
called the Sixtine, 52–53, 54
Rufinus of Aquileia, 80, 83, 95, 211, 220

Samareitikon, edition of the Septuagint, 153
Samaritan Pentateuch (SP), 102–4; and
Dead Sea Scrolls, 107–9
SBL Commentary on the Septuagint
commentary series, 15
scholar-scribes, Qumran as a library used
by, 108–9
scroll of the Minor Prophets in Greek, 115
Second Council of Constantinople,
condemned Origen, 155
Septuagint (LXX), 6–10; and Alexandria,
Egypt, 66; according to Augustine,

247, 251–52, 260–61; and canon
development, 94; as collected in
early printed editions, 54; as a
collection of Greek translations, 53;
deuterocanonical books in, 52–60;
fixed collection of today, 94; influence
on the size of the Bible, 47–96;
inspiration of, 113–15; according to
Jerome, 205–36; and Jerome, 207,
212–34; in Jewish tradition, 113–22;
Latin translations also called, 206;
and modern Christians, 255–62; as
more an idea than a thing, 53; patristic
textual criticism on, 149–76; reasons
for studying, 4–5; resources available
for the study of, 11–16; revisions, 41–
42; student introductions, 14; survey
of the time and place of origin, 42–44;
translation legend, 24–30, 179–85, 188,
198, 217. See also Augustine; Jerome
septuaginta, as Latin for "seventy," 7
"Septuagint canon," exerted pressure on
early Christians, 79
Septuagint Commentary Series, 15
Seventy translators: according to
Augustine, 241, 242–43, 246, 251, 253;
as deserving more respect than the
Three, 192; according to Epiphanius,
200; according to Jerome, 221, 226,
235, 253; mentioned by Josephus,
27; miraculous agreement of, 203;
according to Origen, 190; story of,
17–18, 179–85; translators of the
Greek Pentateuch, 114
Shemuel ben Yaaqov, scribe for the
Leningrad Codex, 101
Sinaiticus manuscript. See Codex Sinaiticus
Sirach (Ecclesiasticus), 36–37, 65
Sixtine edition (1587), 52–53, 54
Society of Biblical Literature (SBL), 15
SP. See Samaritan Pentateuch
spiritual interpretation, of the Septuagint,
232–33

Scripture and
Ancient Source Index

Tobit
4:10 77
12 86
12:9 77

Judith
15 86

Psalms
151 65, 107n40

Dead Sea Scrolls
40, 85, 105

ANCIENT JEWISH WRITERS

Aristobulus
Epist. Arist.
180 26
312–16 25n23

Josephus
Against Apion
1.37–43 63n34
1.37 63
1.39 63
1.41 63
Antiquities of the Jews
5.318–37 64
10.78 64
11.1–158 64n37
11.159–83 64n37
11.184–296 63n35, 64n38
12.100 27
12.107 27
12.108–9 28, 30
12.11–118 27
12.39, 49, 56 27
12.57, 86 27

Philo
Migr.
20 182

On the Life of Moses
2.25–44 25
2.35 26
2.37 26
2.38 191n37
2.40 26, 114, 202
2.41 26

RABBINIC WORKS

Genesis Rabbah
41:6 227

Talmud
b. Meg.
9a 114
Megillah
9a 29

NEW TESTAMENT

Matthew
1:23 126, 138, 139, 152, 181, 258
2:15 138, 181, 218, 218n48, 257
2:23 138
3:3 138
4:15–16 138
6:2–4 73n62
6:7 73n62
6:14–15 73n62
8:17 138
11:28–30 74
12:18–21 138
13:22 233
13:35 138
15:8–9 136n26, 229
19:16–22 159
21:5 138, 245
21:16 136, 136n26, 228
27:9–10 138
27:9 69, 69n54
27:46 38n11, 125

www.ingramcontent.com/pod-product-compliance
Lightning Source LLC
Chambersburg PA
CBHW031122231224
19434CB00006B/156

9 781684 261710